T0373405

SIGILLUM UNIVERSITATIS SCOLARIUM STUDII PRAGENSIS

JAN MRÁZEK

ON THIS MODERN HIGHWAY, LOST IN THE JUNGLE
TROPICS, TRAVEL, AND COLONIALISM IN CZECH POETRY

CHARLES UNIVERSITY
KAROLINUM PRESS 2022

KAROLINUM PRESS
Karolinum Press is a publishing department of Charles University
Ovocný trh 560/5, 116 36 Prague 1, Czech Republic
www.karolinum.cz

Set and printed in the Czech Republic by Karolinum Press
Layout by Jan Šerých
First edition

A catalogue record for this book is available from the National Library of the Czech Republic.

ISBN 978-80-246-5112-5
ISBN 978-80-246-5126-2 (pdf)

The original manuscript was reviewed by Michaela Tomanová (Faculty of Arts of Charles University) and Michaela Budiman (Faculty of Arts of Charles University).

For my father

Na druhé straně světa jsou
Řepčice Wassenaarseslag Myšice Madrid Blitar Naxos Ayutthaya
Merauke Jerusalem Ypsilanti Texel Sibolga

In the glow of the headlights we pass lengthening arabesques of escaping snakes, among whom some, the stronger and bigger ones, assume the fighting pose of titans and perish in an unequal battle, dying with the poison of hate on their tongues, dying like the brains of calmly sprawled frogs, bluntly crushed like gravel on the road by the ever rising car; and we drive . . . where? One cannot finish that thought on this modern highway, lost in the jungle . . . we ride into the mysteries of disturbing details, visionary clearings, which only the lightning can accomplish, the teacher of philosophers and poets. It shows the jungle in a forceful and unusual light. It shows only a part and you must imagine the whole, ever veiled in darkness.

—Konstantin Biebl, "Ing. Baer"

TABLE OF CONTENTS

LIST OF FIGURES

ACKNOWLEDGMENTS

I remember my father, sitting in the bed in our sumptuous bridal suite in a hotel in Merauke, the easternmost town of Indonesia, in the Papua province. The overwhelming pinks and purples of the cavernous room's hyper-rococo interior decoration were punctuated by dark stains (tea or coffee, one hopes). I recall thick decorative curtains, a plentitude of dusty plastic fruits and flowers and the stench of stale cigarette smoke. It was the only available room in the whole town, because of an ongoing Pan-Papuan congress of government administrators. My father was reading an early draft of this book, scribbling on it with the fierce determination of an attacking Gathotkaca (the powerful airborne warrior of the Javanese shadow puppet theater), crossing whole paragraphs with sweeping arm movements, under the bed's plasticky pink canopy. We would then talk and argue about my text, Biebl, Czech history, Papua and prison camps (his topic then) over deep-fried prawns, of which he became enamored in a small food stall on the main road, and in our bridal suite.

My mother's knowledge of Czech poetry and history might be mistakenly thought to be encyclopedic, but it is something else. I utter a name or try to share a confused, prematurely born thought—and she is already reciting this and that poem, this and that poet's life, with the passion and force of a late-Romantic symphonic orchestra, with the all-conquering joy of a massive chorus of peasants in Smetana's operas, sweeping me away and into her world, as poems and lives interweave in an unstoppable Amazon of consciousness that carries me the closest I would ever get to an erupting Javanese volcano, as we eat our breakfast of scrambled eggs and some ham (as her Moravian grandmother said, "you must eat lots of bread and just a little bit of meat"), somewhat homeless in a short-term rental flat in Pankrác, as at home as it gets.

With my brother, we watched cockfights in the backstreets of Semarang, had been endlessly interrogated by the ranking army officer before we were commanded to take a picture with him and then allowed to climb an old Dutch lighthouse in the Semarang harbor, almost froze to death on the Dieng Plateau, sailed from Singapore to Sumatra, travelled in search of our grandfather in Aceh, and told our stories and recited Konstantin Biebl's poems in Prague cafés.

Precious has been unquestioningly with me as we keep each other awake with our questions and stories, as we crisscross Southeast Asian archipelagoes on all manners of ferries, sailing boats, and kayaks, as we eat and work in hawker centers. Her unsettled, unexpected, derailing ways of thinking have been forever pushing me off, or to the edge of, any established, accepted route of thought I might settle on, any route that I have mistaken for being mine. And when I helplessly burst into laughter or tears or both at once while reading an untranslatable Czech poem, she is closer to me and understanding me more than ever, more directly and plainly than I can understand myself.

Such were the most precious moments of writing this book.

But there were others, moments and people, such as: In the grand baroque study hall of the National Library in Prague or in the little *badatelna* of the archive of the Museum of Czech Literature, I often felt grateful for, and somehow humbled by, the care of the librarians and archivists—what would scholars, those ego-centric, spoiled babies forever asking for new toys, do without them?

Not fully written is the fact that this book is a reflection on my own life as a Czech in Indonesia, Singapore, Thailand and the Philippines. I think back with gratitude to the many people I have met and got to know here, with whom I have lived, cycled, sailed, played music, worked together, learned from and taught, and talked over tea and all sorts of other liquids and foods. Without them, and without what they have given me, this book would have been entirely different, or more likely it would not be at all.

My daughter Helenka Kopi O and I have journeyed through life together even when separated by oceans, sharing glimpses of the different worlds each of us is discovering. She was often on my mind as I was writing this book about artists creatively making sense of strange worlds and strange homelands.

I have received kind support from many people and institutions. Michala Tomanová, who has been researching and presenting Biebl in refreshing ways, has generously shared with me her discoveries and materials, which have been of a major importance for this book. I also thank her and Michaela Budiman for their supportive reviews of the book. I thank Guan Xinyu, then at NUS Press, who read and sensitively commented on the book manuscript. I thank Thow Xin Wei in Singapore for his careful copy-editing of my Czechlish, and for the hundreds of definite articles that he added to my text, along with a few indefinite ones; for his thoughts on the resonances between Dutch colonialism, as experienced by Biebl, and contemporary Singapore, as seen by him; and for the many years of playing gamelan together. I thank Peter Schoppert, the Director of NUS Press, for his advice and crucial support in publishing matters. I thank Martin Janeček and Alena Jirsová at the Karolinum Press, for their support and care in taking this book through the production process. I gratefully acknowledge the institutional support of the National University of Singapore, and the Singapore Ministry of Education grants that supported my research (FY2013-FRC1-002 and FY2019-FRC3-004).

Singapore, 1st May 2021

PREAMBLE

Look the train of things is gaining speed
And from its windows it throws colors[1]

In 1926, in Czechoslovakia, the train was the most common means of transportation, and the Wilson Station was the busiest in Prague. In its corridors, waiting rooms, and restaurants, travelers to and from Hamburg, Paris, Bucharest, and Istanbul mingled with "winding and unwinding yarn balls"[2] of passengers to and from small Czech villages and provincial towns. In waiting rooms and on trains, people's thoughts wandered near and far. One such passenger (who, like most, would never travel outside Europe) wrote in the 1920s about a train ride in Bohemia:

> And suddenly, touched, we recollect Batavia, the most beautiful city of our childhood dreams. . . . Oh, what do they mean, all the petty and indifferent names of cities, the apparent destinations of our journeys? Wherever we ride, we always ride to Batavia.[3]

International train number 29 was scheduled to depart daily at 11:15 in the morning. This was a branching line—west, southwest, and south—and there were direct carriages to cities in several European countries. Passengers on train 29 travelled to Czech towns, including Pilsen, Domažlice, and Cheb; but also across Germany, to Paris and on to Boulogne, with an integrated ferry/train transfer to London; southwest to Basel, Zurich and Geneva; and via Munich, Florence, and Rome, all the way south to Naples on the coast of the Mediterranean Sea.

---

1 Konstantin Biebl, *Zrcadlo noci* (F. J. Müller: Prague, 1939), no page numbers. Also in Konstantin Biebl, *Dílo*, ed. Z. K. Slabý (Prague: Československý Spisovatel, 1951–1954), 3: 78.

2 Konstantin Biebl, *Cesta na Jávu*, ed. Jakub Sedláček (Prague: Labyrint, 2001), 11.

3 Miroslav Rutte, *Batavie* (Prague: Kvasnička a Hampl, 1924), 9–10. For more on Rutte, see the First Excursion. At least for some international passengers, Prague train stations already felt Oriental. "The Orient is already in evidence at the Masaryk railway station in Prague," wrote a Swedish rabbi in his travel book titled *The Soul of the East*, originally published in 1926. Like most travelers to any Orient, he complained about a loss of authenticity: it was "a crumbling Orient, a traitorous deserter from itself . . . an artificial, trumpery New Orient." Quoted in Maria Todorova, *Imagining the Balkans* (Oxford: Oxford University Press, 2009), 125.

Inside the station, several people and a few suitcases formed a circle around the neatly dressed, young man whom they were sending off. He was waiting for the 11:15 train.[4] His boyish face had a complexion a tinge darker than those around him. Among those gathered here as friends, almost like fellow performers, were poets and artists who would be known in later literary histories as the leading figures of the Czech interwar avant-garde. Now, they were mostly in their twenties and at the early stages of their careers. Vítězslav Nezval was on his way to become the most influential poet of the generation, "the Duke of Czech Poetry." In the 1930s, he led the Group of Surrealists in Czechoslovakia. After 1948, he took up high-ranking positions in the Communist government and was awarded a long range of awards, including the title of National Artist. Karel Teige, who worked closely with Nezval in the 1920s and most of the 1930s, was the avant-garde's theoretical spokesman and the author of their manifestos, which envisioned a future world of beauty and poetry for all, where "tourists are modern poets."[5] When Nezval became the official poet of the Communist government, Teige became the arch-enemy, decried as the agent of Trotskyism and "cosmopolitanism." In 1951, he was hunted down in a vicious campaign and died on a sidewalk, at night, alone. Jaroslav Seifert, another poet standing on the platform, lived longer than the others, and before his death he was awarded the Nobel Prize for Literature, which he accepted on behalf of his generation, with a nod to the exciting times of the 1920s. Seifert, along with Teige, was a founding member, in 1920, of the art association Devětsil, which was at the center of the Czech leftist avant-garde of the 1920s; Nezval was another of its most influential members. Also on the platform stood Karel Konrád, who would become known as one of the most important writers of fiction associated with Devětsil; Josef Hora, a slightly older man, an eminent poet, literary critic, translator and the editor-in-chief of the Communist Party's official newspaper *Rudé právo* (Red right); as well as, among others, the much admired theater and cabaret actress Xena Longenová. A year and half later, she would commit suicide—but now, she stood on the platform with eyes "matte, darkly colored, yet glowing like on stage."[6]

4 My account takes Konstantin Biebl's travelogue, *Cesta na Jávu*, as the starting point. Based on my examination of the 1926 train timetables, it is almost certain that he took the 11:15 train. *Jízdní řád železniční, paroplavební a automobilový republiky Československé: 1926–27* (Prague: Čedok [1926]), 96–8, 426, 428, 444–5.

5 Karel Teige, "Poetismus," in *Avantgarda známá a neznámá*, ed. Štěpán Vlašín et al. (Prague: Svoboda, 1971), 1: 558. Several manifestos by Teige are available in English translation in Eric Dluhosch and Rostislav Švácha, *Karel Teige: L'Enfant Terrible of the Czech Modernist Avant-Garde* (Cambridge: MIT Press, 1999).

6 This quotation, as well as those in the next two paragraphs, are from Biebl, *Cesta na Jávu*, 11–12.

The poet Konstantin Biebl, the man standing at the circle's center, is fond of theater and opera (many of the best-loved Czech operas are comic), and the first sentence of his travelogue brings travel and performance together: "Carriages and automobiles are parked in front of the Wilson Station, as if in front of a theater before the end of the opera."[7] Those who have become actors in the poetic comedy, those waiting for the train, are already transformed by a journey that has not even begun; they

> put on a face as if they have just become employed by the state railways . . . they intend to perform their duties conscientiously; each minute they check their watches, they are nervous and suspect in advance that the express train will be delayed. A soldier with a bandaged hand begins to swallow one cigarette after the other, obviously derailed.

Biebl, a spectator and an actor at once, is derailed as well, but that affords him another, more intense vision.

> Never, I think, do we observe our friends with such a sense of importance as at the moment of parting. . . . We are stunned: "You've never worn a hard hat before, have you?" He looks at me puzzled. "I have, always!" And Berta has grey-green eyes! I always thought they were black.

He boards the train, "confused" and "stunned" by these "discoveries," "as if intoxicated [*omámen*]." (*Omámen*: "intoxicated, dazed, stunned, carried away"; the adjectival form of the word is often used to qualify and intensify beauty and fragrance; in 1924, Teige—in the same manifesto where he wrote that "tourists are modern poets"—used it when he spoke of "intoxicating fragrance of life" in the "blossoms of new art"; Nezval used it when he spoke of "the intoxicating lyrical light" of Biebl's poetry.[8] When I write "intoxicated" or "dazed," I would like to evoke the intense, somewhat hallucinatory sensations of *omámen*.) As the train speeds through morning mist, the passenger struggles to remember how his friends look—yet the intoxicated images that emerge reveal each man and his work with a fresh incisiveness.

> Now I have before me the head of Jaroslav Seifert. The color of his eyes is not his. I try to give him blue, violet, red, green, even black eyes, and I still don't know on which

---

7 One of the problems of moving between English and Czech languages concerns tense. In Czech, not only is present tense more common in accounts of the past—including in the passages quoted here—but frequent changes of tense within paragraphs and sentences are an accepted stylistic device. In my text, I try to compromise, which contributes to the strangeness of this text's "English."

8 Teige, "Poetismus," 554; Vítězslav Nezval, speech at the 2nd Congress of Czechoslovak Writers, 1956. < https://legacy.blisty.cz/art/58303.html >.

> I should decide. I shave Karel Teige's face a few times and then let him grow a beard again.... I have tried twelve striped jockey jackets on Nezval, but none of them are his. Josef Hora resembles himself, but has someone else's hat. Beethoven's, I think.

The text from which I quote is the beginning of Biebl's (unfinished) account, poetic and satirical, of his journey from Bohemia to Java in the Dutch East Indies. His train has only just left the station, yet some of the underlying questions of my book already begin to emerge: How, in the case of the long journey and the poet's whole life's work, did physical travel and poetic imagination come together like "two mirrors looking at themselves in each other"?[9] How did they "intoxicate" and intensify each other? And, taking Biebl's case as our point of departure, how is travel, the faraway, internationalism and all manners of (anti-)colonialism variously entangled with Czech poetry, during the turbulent decades of Biebl's lifetime (1898–1951) as well as before?

In the years preceding Biebl's 1926 journey to Java, Czech avant-garde writers and painters had travelled in imagination around the globe (like and unlike their predecessors in the nineteenth century, but perhaps with greater, modern, speed and lightness). Their imagery twinkled with palms, parrots, ocean-liners, busy harbors and tropical seas—colorful adventures written against the dark grey of Europe after the Great War. They looked with desire beyond Czech borders; and already colonialism was for them a symbol of oppression and a failed, old world order. They aimed to create (in the sense of *poesis*) not just new art, but new life—to make life into poetry. (It is in this originative, overflowing, far-reaching sense that I speak of poetry in this book—a poetry ever expanding, beyond verses and poetic prose, beyond words too, even as it keeps coming back to them.) For the avant-garde artists, poetizing travel, travelling poetically, was also a fulfillment of these ambitions. They adored the circus, cinema, Charlie Chaplin and the Marx brothers. Biebl's journey was a consummation of the avant-garde's defining tendencies and fantasies, yet it was also unique, even outlandish; it shows the avant-garde works and dreams in a particular light, highlighting their contours, their shallows and depths; it lets us see Czech poetry afresh, like when he saw his friends anew at the moment of his departure. For Biebl and for Czech modern(ist)[10] poetry, the voyage was both an enactment and a new, transformative experience. The intoxicating, intensifying collision of physical travel and poetic imagination, in an interplay with other experiences, inspired a poetry not with more monkeys and parrots, but with a different kind of movement and reach.

---

9 Biebl, *Plancius* (Prague: Sfinx, 1931), 8.

10 In the texts by Biebl, as well as artists and art theorists of his generation, the distinction between modern (world) and modernist (art, poetry) is generally not made—poetry and the world were equally modern.

Derek Sayer, in *Prague, Capital of the Twentieth Century: A Surrealist History*, writes in the conclusion of the chapter on Devětsil artists:

> Who by the 1920s any longer expected art to confine itself to representing reality? On the contrary: it was the transformative power of the *imagination* that made Devětsil's art what it was. Had Prague's younger writers and artists not been marooned in the landlocked center of Europe, far from seas and skyscrapers alike, their work might well have been a good deal less adventurous than it was. . . . The kids at the intersection were ideally situated for dreaming.[11]

This is both illustrated and complicated by Biebl's case. His lone *actual* journey outside Europe, however brief and dream-like, destabilizes—like a disturbing detail seen in a flash from the train's window, or like "a door in the neighborhood of an ocean" —the reality-imagination logic as presented, perhaps not surrealistically enough, by Sayer.

Writes Nezval:

> *Skutečnost* ["actuality", related to *skutek*, "act, action"] is the dictionary for the creation of poetry. . . . It was necessary to lay a star on a table, a glass near an upright piano and angels, a door in the neighborhood of an ocean. It was a matter of revealing actuality, to give it its shining form like on the first day. . . . It was an extremely realist [*realistická*] effort. . . . [A poem] will evoke . . . old, indifferent actuality so that it will bewitch you.[12]

Much later, Nezval wrote in an open letter to Biebl, with reference to his poetry about Java: "This art of handling actuality so that it would become a poem, allowed you to intervene also in social actuality, without using old, worn-out didactic methods."[13]

The relationship between actuality/action and free imagination was crucial for Devětsil artists, as glimpsed in this book with a view intoxicated by Biebl's interplay of poetry and actual travel to colonial Asia; and by his surreal credo that poetry—dreams, travel-intoxicated visions, surprising metaphors and associations, comedy—is a mode of *poznání* (cognition, knowledge) of *skutečnost*. "I have tried twelve striped jockey jackets on Nezval, but none of them is his." What a revealing picture of Nezval; of the clownery, of the exciting horse races and lonely hobby-horse play that is Nezval's poetry in the 1920s!

---

11 Derek Sayer, *Prague, Capital of the Twentieth Century: A Surrealist History* (Princeton: Princeton University Press, 2013), 220.

12 Nezval, "Kapka inkoustu," *ReD* 1 (1927–28), 313.

13 Nezval's letter, for Biebl's fiftieth birthday, was republished in Biebl, *Dílo*, 5:7.

The chronology of the contact between travel and poetry is not simple: Biebl's journey to Java, however outlandish, grew from and into Biebl's whole life—his village childhood, his first long journey to the "Orient" (especially southeast Europe) as a teenage soldier in the Great War, his involvement with the avant-garde and its exoticisms in the interwar period, and with communism since the earliest 1920s until the end of his life, when it was the state ideology.

This book traces the manifold growth toward the Javanese voyage in Biebl's life and work, and follows how he continued to return to the journey, in ever new poetic, personal and political entanglements, in the tumultuous quarter century between his homecoming and his death. Coconut palms, jungles, and tropical seas appear in his poetry already before his trip, as do metaphors and dreams that bring the near and the distant together and allow them to blend or mirror each other, as does a concern with social reality and (perverted) "justice." His book of poems *S lodí jež dováží čaj a kávu* (With the ship that carries/imports tea and coffee), published a year after his return from Java, is a travelogue of sorts. It parallels his prose texts and collage-like photographic compositions published in a popular magazine. Tropical islands, jungles, steamers, oceans, Javanese, Chinese, Acehnese, and mestizos abound in his 1929 book-long poem *Nový Ikaros* (New Icarus), in his surrealist poetry written around 1930, in poems in which Bohemia under Nazi "protectorate" (1939–1945) mirrors the Dutch colonies, and, after the war, in poetry struggling uneasily for and with socialism and against imperialism, as well as

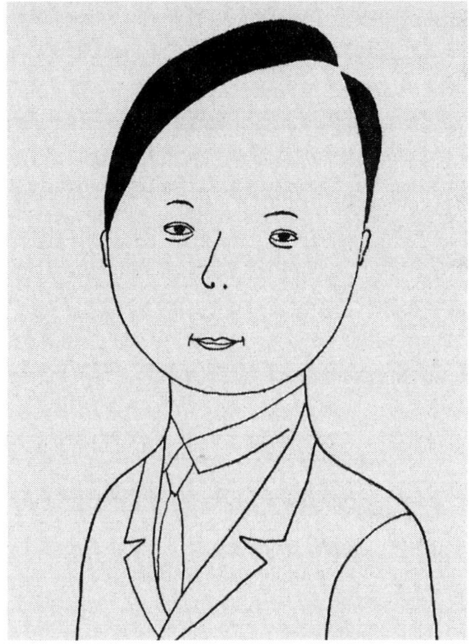

Figure 1. František Muzika, *Konstantin Biebl*, 1927.

in private verses that speak about and to Death, written before his suicide in 1951. Finally, just before and after his death, his journey to Java, mostly judged in line with Zhdanovist ideology of socialist culture, figures prominently in assessments of his work.

However outlandish, Biebl's poetic travel also grew from and into the history of Czech poetry. With a focus on the association between travel and poetry, images of faraway lands and peoples, representation of foreigners, and various kinds of exoticism, with a view intoxicated by Biebl's poetry, this book looks anew at the writings of prominent 19th century poets Karel Hynek Mácha and Josef Václav Sládek, as well as the work of Biebl's contemporaries, especially Seifert, Nezval, Teige and Karel Schulz. With the same focus, or in the same daze, the book also examines the broader visual culture of the 1920s, especially as manifested in the magazine where the photos from Biebl's trip were published.

Biebl's journey grew from and into Biebl's life; and from and into a broader history and a literature. I trace the poetic journey's roots and rhizomes, some of them hair-thin and nearly invisible, its branches, creepers and lianas in the jungles of his homeland, in order to richly hear the resonances and overtones of his images of the tropics, travel and colonialism. In turn, Biebl's poetry is an entry point into the Czech jungle. Like when "two mirrors look at themselves in each other," through Biebl's travels and poetry I hope to show something of his larger world and longer history, including a particular relation to tropics, travel and colonialism. Rather than presenting either a survey or a grand argument, I work with fragments and glimpses, and try to listen closely to the manifold resonances and overtones of each image or word.

This book revolves around Biebl's life and work, but it is neither his biography nor a comprehensive study of his work or personality; nor is it limited to his poetry. One might rather think of it as an account of my cosmic travels through a constellation of certain motifs, dreams, sensations, and poetic acts.

ON THE PARTICULAR: "OUR LITTLE CITIZEN" AND THE EMPIRE

This book reflects on particularly Czech and particularly modern reincarnations of age-old desires and displacements at the crossroads of travel and writing.

"So you are from Czechoslovakia? That's a good one! And how come you are so black? Forgive me, I thought that you were a mestizo."[14] Thus speaks a

14 Biebl, *Cesta na Jávu*, 47.

Dutchman to Biebl aboard a ship bound for Batavia. In his travelogue, Biebl tells about a series of his transgressions against colonial etiquette and racial and class distinctions. "We are not able to behave, as soon as we leave Europe," he writes. When he mentions his nationality, it is to articulate this position of an awkward stranger in the colonial society.[15] He is Švejk-like[16] in the way his comic "ignorance" and transgressions make particular sense of (colonial) propriety and correctness. He is a "*Pierot lunaire* . . . who fell from the moon and who feels somewhat unsure on this wildly spinning planet,"[17] in the words of a critic. Biebl writes:

> The ship in a storm is another land, quite another planet than our earth: it is Mars! It has different natural laws, before which our little citizen [*náš občánek*] lies prostrate, and foreign and salty water revives him. Inhabitants of Mars cackle, obviously amused by the miserable and disobedient earthling, who doesn't want to go to his cabin, where he, a little dove, should have long been. He wants to act as a Martian! Hahahaha![18]

The eminent American historian Paul Fussel writes in the preface of his seminal work *Abroad: British Literary Travelling Between the Wars*: "Because the most sophisticated travel books of the age are British, I focus largely on them, although now and then I have considered an American example as well."[19] "Rich Americans and Englishmen, for whom our Earth is becoming tiny" (in the words of a Czech writer who traveled to Java before Biebl),[20] may also have been particularly sophisticated travelers. It is the very weakness, strangeness, and lack of particular sophistication of "our little citizen" (experienced and performed) that, alongside the confusion and intoxication that he already felt at the Prague train station, help him to perceive in a particular way—sometimes with the vision of the child who does *not* see the Emperor's new clothes.

The comic light in which "our little citizen" shows himself illuminates also the Czech nation. After one of his transgressions—talking to an Indian passenger "camping" on the open deck, socially below the fourth class—Biebl describes the "awe" with which Englishmen from the first class look at him,

---

15 This is an experience that other Czech travelers at that time, too, have written about. Jan Mrázek, "Returns to the Wide World: Errant Bohemian Images of Race and Colonialism," *Studies in Travel Writing* 21, 2 (2017): 135–155; and Jan Mrázek, "Czechs on Ships: Liners, Containers and the Sea," *Journal of Tourism History* 13, 2 (August 2021): 111–137.

16 See Jaroslav Hašek, *Osudy dobrého vojáka Švejka* (Prague: Cesty, 2000). For an English translation, see Jaroslav Hašek, *The Good Soldier Švejk*, trans. Cecil Parrott (London: Penguin, 2005).

17 F. X. Šalda, *O poezii* (Prague: Klub přátel poezie, 1970), 160.

18 Biebl, *Cesta na Jávu*, 25.

19 Paul Fussel, *Abroad: British Literary Travelling Between the Wars* (Oxford: Oxford University Press, 1980), vii.

20 J. V. Daneš and Karel Domin, *Dvojím rájem*, 2nd ed. (Prague: J. Otto, 1925), 1:6.

and he addresses his nation, alongside the first ruler and the patron saint of the Czech state:

> Saint Wenceslas, what have I done again? They [the Englishmen] looked at each other, at me, at the Indian in rags, again at each other, and they burst into laughter entirely openly. They realized that I was a Czech. You nation around Vltava and Labe rivers, if only you saw how because of me you were lowered in the eyes of foreign lands. It's because we do not have the sea.[21]

The landlocked position of Bohemia has made the sea particularly seductive and the dreams and images of distant oceans particularly poignant and exhilarating. The small country—Czechs, at least, tend to think of it as small—lies in the geographic middle of Europe, yet never quite at the center: on the western periphery of the Slavic East, in the eastern margins of the imperial West. It is surrounded—north, west, and south—by German(ic) territories. Not only did the Czechs never have a colony in Asia, but throughout long periods of their history, they were in a position in some ways not unlike that of a colony. These historical and geographical circumstances—and the way they have been variously represented, poetized, and/or ideologized—have shaped Czech attitudes, although neither uniformly nor predictably.

For some three hundred years (symbolically, from 1620 to 1918), Bohemia was ruled by the Habsburgs from Vienna, and during the first centuries of this rule, German largely replaced Czech as the language of education, science, and politics.[22] During the "national rebirth" (beginning in late 18th century), whose central aim was the cultivation of Czech language and culture, German was ironically the initial medium, and works of German arts and scholarship continued to inform and inspire Czech "rebirth"—rather like in the case of the Javanese, Chinese and mestizos to whose land Biebl traveled, and for whom the language and concepts of European colonizers were key in decolonization.

The East was not only the distant Orient, but more immediately, the space of another exoticism, a fantasy of homeland—the origin of Slavs. Sometimes, as Czechs gazed toward the East, borders between the Pan-Slavic homeland and more distant Asia became indistinct. The Habsburg Empire itself was, from the German and Western European perspective, the "Eastern Empire" (*Österreich*, Austria in German), and consisted of multiple easts, sharing shifting, porous borders with the Ottoman and Russian empires. Seen from the distance of time, the Czech national awakening—which was also an emancipatory struggle—has something of the charm of voyage narratives. There

21 Biebl, *Cesta na Jávu*, 47.
22 For a Czech history in English, see Derek Sayer, *The Coast of Bohemia: A Czech History* (Princeton: Princeton University Press, 1998).

were campaigns propagating the use of ancient Indian poetic meters in the revival of Czech literature; claims that Czech was closely related to Sanskrit;[23] and expressions of the sense that the Czechs shared a common fate with other subjugated peoples, such as the Irish, the American "Indians" or, indeed, the Acehnese of Sumatra in their struggle against the Dutch colonial army.[24] Yet Czechs also felt or fantasized to be "Europeans," variously adapting/rejecting "Western" views of "the East." Travel—crisscrossing Bohemia on foot as well as journeys to other countries or continents—played an important role in the national awakening: in emancipatory efforts at a Czech vision of homeland and its place in the larger world, in navigating Czech, Slavic, and/or European identities, but also, as Wendy Bracewell writes, "not least, travel writing's range of registers allowed the Slav travel account to mock absurdities and overturn ideological orthodoxies."[25] Feelings of being a stranger in one's own land, as well as figures of wanderers, exiles, and peoples without a homeland, such as the Jews and the Gypsies (both were associated with the East), are at the origins of modern Czech literature, as I explore in this book in the cases of Mácha and Sládek. Biebl's poetry is *a* summation of this history.[26]

In the Great War, Czechs were sacrificing lives for the Austro-Hungarian Empire, which many saw as their own nation's oppressor. They were in a position to perceive particularly sharply the imperial war's absurdity. Few works in world literature expose it better than *Osudy dobrého vojáka Švejka za světové války* (The fortunes of the good soldier Švejk during the World War) by Jaroslav Hašek.[27] In Czech poetry, no other work shows the "darkness and emptiness" of the World War more powerfully than Biebl's *New Icarus*, a

---

23 Vladimír Macura, *Znamení rodu: České národní obrození jako kulturní typ*, 2nd ed. (Prague: H & H, 1995), 36–39, 48.

24 For Czech images of the "brave Acehnese," see Jan Mrázek, "Czech Tropics," *Archipel* 86 (2013): 179–88.

25 Wendy Bracewell, "Travels through the Slav World," in *Under Eastern Eyes: A Comparative Introduction to East European Travel Writing on Europe* (Budapest and New York: Central European University Press, 2008), 159.

26 A particular summation, which resonates with some and differs from other Czech writers. In another mirror, we might see a different mien. See my "Czech Tropics" and "Returns to the Wide World" for a sense of how Biebl's attitudes figure among those of other Czech traveler-writers to the Malay Archipelago. The case of the ethnologist Pavel Šebesta / Paul Schebesta, who traveled to Singapore, Malay peninsula and Sumatra just before Biebl (in 1924–1925), contrasts revealingly with Biebl. Compared with Šebesta, Biebl comes across as "Czech like a log of wood" (as one says in Czech). Šebesta's origin in a small borderland Moravian community, his broader Slavic allegiance, the fact that he spent most of his adult life in Austria and much of his writing is in German (his second language), and his complicated relationship to borders, states and empires—including Czechoslovakia—are mirrored in his representations of the nomadic "forest people" in Malaya, their homeland, and their difficult relationships with "invading" Malays, Chinese and Europeans. See Jan Mrázek, "Primeval Forest, Homeland, Catastrophe: Travels in Malaya and 'Modern Ethnology' with Pavel Šebesta / Paul Schebesta," 2 parts, *Anthropos* 116 (2021), no. 1: 29–54; no. 2: 345–365.

27 This is the original title, often variously abbreviated in different editions and translations.

poem permeated by images of tropical islands and seas, mestizos and colonial armies.

The youngest soldiers in the trenches belonged to Biebl's generation (Biebl was sixteen when the war began, eighteen when he enlisted). After a peaceful childhood in Bohemia, one of the most prosperous lands of Austro-Hungary, the World War was for them a powerful, different experience of the empire in which they grew up—an experience both of imperial violence, of an unprecedented darkness, and of the colorful wide world outside Bohemia, within and beyond the Eastern Empire's borders. During the Great War, hundreds of thousands of Czechs travelled as soldiers out of their land: many, Biebl among them, to the "Orient," as he and others saw southeastern Europe (the "Turkey in Europe," as it was known), and the Mediterranean Sea; and the differently exotic eastern fringes of the Austro-Hungary in Galicia, on the Russian front. They experienced various orients that were part of the same empire as Bohemia; the Eastern Empire that was, among European empires the most ethnically diverse—in this it was like European empires in Southeast Asia. Other Czechs, especially the Czechoslovak Legions, in the tens of thousands, travelled across Russia to northeastern Asia, sailing then home either across the Pacific or through Southeast Asia.

Czechoslovakia came into being as an independent state in 1918. Questions were asked with a renewed urgency about national identity, the nation's position in the international community, social justice, as well as national ethics and culture. Particular, multiple modernities were dreamed and lived with a fresh intensity in 1920s Prague. It was a busy time for travel and modern forms of fantasizing it, and perhaps the most exciting decade for Czech poetry. Poets and artists—each differently, and to different degrees—were enchanted as much by photographs of New York skyscrapers and gigantic ocean liners as by old buildings in Prague and Bohemian villages; as often by jazz and African music as by local folk songs and fairy tales.

The artists with whom Biebl associated looked for salvation to the East, to the rising star of communism and the recent revolution in Russia, which dreamed to unite the world—this was also the orientation (or *kiblat*, the direction toward Mecca, as one might say in Indonesian) of leftist anti-colonial writers, Javanese and others, who were influential in the Dutch East Indies at this time. Most of the leftist Czech artists were at one time or another linked with the artist collective Devětsil. Pervading their poetry was a certain constellation of attitudes to social reality, imperialism, and "people of all lands"; figuring in their art, well before Biebl's trip, were poverty, greed, "justice" as a weapon of power, violence, workers and capitalists, in Czechoslovakia but also in European colonies on other continents—and all this was also in and behind a poetry/*poesis*/production of new life, a life as poetry, full of "all the beauties of the world" (in the words of one of their mottos, taken from the most national of Czech operas, Bedřich Smetana's *Prodaná nevěsta* [*The bartered bride*]). Artistically they turned especially to Paris as the center of international avant-garde, although inspiration was also found in Soviet and German avant-garde art; their manifestos, even more than their poetry, had much in common with international interwar avant-gardes elsewhere in Europe. In terms of poetic imagery, they looked to the whole world—faraway lands, people of all continents and all skin colors, sailors, as well as ships, airplanes, and trains, appear frequently in their poetry and paintings.

However, so do Czech villages, grain fields, low hills or the streets and cafés of Prague; so do evocations of Czech fairy tales, folk art, and folk songs. "We were much more national than we thought or wished," reminisced Nezval, one of the poets we met at the platform at Biebl's departure.[28] In the extent and depth of linguistic abilities and international connections, each artist was different; visual artists and architects tended to travel and connect rather more easily than poets. Biebl's archives contain a notebook from his later years containing a large number of French poems that he copied, and it is telling that they are all in Czech translation. The avant-garde's infatuation with Paris and France was passionate and formative, but the sweet dream sometimes bordered on delusion when poetry slipped into theory (I am thinking of Teige), or a smiling, melancholy burlesque (as with Seifert). For poets, France was desirable but distant, even exotic, and an object of poetic tourism, just as streaks of Orientalist and touristic exoticisms are a feature of French poets' views of Prague.[29] Prague would never become Paris, despite some fantastic attempts to make it so,[30] just as Czech poetry and culture, the fantasies and tensions notwithstanding, would never quite become French—this was true for the Czech interwar avant-garde poets as much as for their predecessors.

Faraway seas and jungles, too, were painted with the shades and brushstrokes of Czech language and Czech imagery, sometimes with a poetic rhythm evoking Czech folk songs and nursery rhymes, even as tropical dreams—and, in some cases, actual travels (most often to France and Italy)—expanded the range of colors in which poets felt and painted homeland.

Recent English (and French) language scholarship has contributed to locating the Czech avant-garde, particularly Devětsil, in a larger picture of Europe, with an attention to both its links with other European avant-gardes

28 Vítězslav Nezval, *Z mého života* (Prague: Československý spisovatel 1959), 116.

29 Images of Prague in Apollinaire's "Zone" is the most famous example. On French modernist visits to and representations of Prague, see Sayer, *Prague* and Sophie Ireland, "Paris-Prague: regards surréalistes croisés; Naissance poétique d'une ville" (PhD Diss., L'Université Paris Ouest Nanterre La Défense, 2016).

30 The grand project to build a Paris-style boulevard, later named the Paris Street, and the dwarf version of Eiffel Tower, are emblematic of these efforts.

and its specificity.[31] Teige is a dominant figure in this discourse[32]—understandably, as he was the loudest voice defining and prescribing the ideological direction of Devětsil. "But I kept silent. I was afraid that Teige might send me to . . . ," Seifert writes in his memoirs about his emotions that did not conform to "things that Teige strictly decreed for us."[33] There was (mostly) more camaraderie than fear of Teige, and his enthusiastic theorizing, organizing, and visual art (mostly) contributed to, rather than stifled, diversity and individuality (despite the decreed collectivism). Teige plays an important role in my story, both as a theorist and as a visual artist: he was the graphic designer of several books by Biebl, including *With the Ship*, which the poet dedicated to him. Biebl's poetry is in conversation with the work of other writers and artists, and with programmatic manifestos and theories, rather than conforming to or exemplifying them. Listening to this conversation, we get a *particular* impression of the Czech avant-garde's many voices, harmonies and dissonances, contradictions and unlikely affinities, which are sometimes obfuscated in larger pictures today, just like in manifestos then. A case in point: recent works that locate the Prague avant-garde in an "international" context ("international" tends to mean European) nonetheless lack any discussion of Biebl and his journey to Asia.[34] A view intoxicated by Biebl's poetry, travels, and solitude lets us see his friends and the larger picture in a different light. "I shave Karel Teige's face a few times and then let him grow a beard again."

Biebl has been, variously at different times, considered one of the most important modern Czech poets. When Seifert was awarded the Nobel Prize in 1984, the novelist Milan Kundera wrote: "There were five of them: Vítězslav Nezval, Jaroslav Seifert, Konstantin Biebl, František Halas, and Vladimír Holan . . . the greatest constellation in the entire history of Czech poetry." Kundera "adored" Biebl.[35] Biebl is typically included in histories and textbooks of Czech literature as an important poet. Yet this book's perspective, intoxicated by his travel, also brings out that even among his own, in Prague

31 See especially: Sayer, *Prague*; Meghan Forbes, "In the Middle of It All: Prague, Brno, and the Avant-Garde Networks of Interwar Europe" (PhD Diss., University of Michigan, 2016); Ireland, "Paris–Prague."

32 This is true, for example, about Forbes, "In the Middle of It All," but also a number of English-language books have been specifically dedicated to him, including Dluhosch and Švácha, *Karel Teige*.

33 Jaroslav Seifert, *Všecky krásy světa* (Prague: Československý spisovatel, 1982), 419.

34 For example, Sayer's comprehensive *Prague, Capital of the Twentieth Century*, which presents a diversity of Czech modernisms and their European interconnections; and Meghan Forbes's dissertation "In the Middle of It All: Prague, Brno, and the Avant-Garde Networks of Interwar Europe," in which international travel is one of the main topics.

35 Originally published in *Le Nouvel Observateur* in 1984. Republished in English as "A Lesson in History" in Jaroslav Seifert, "A Tribute to Vladimír Holan," *Index on Censorship* 4 (1985): 5.

or in his village, he was like among Martians; or among "antipodes," which is how he sees Europeans from Java in a poem by that title.

Biebl's journey was just one of numerous literary voyages of 1920s Europe. Everywhere on the continent, the tropics were dreamt in the trenches of the Great War and in the euphoria or emptiness of peace-at-last. Images of ocean-liners and tropical islands did not appear just in Czech poetry.[36] Only when one reads closely does one realize the differences.

Some French, British, or Dutch also at times felt like being among Martians on ships or in the colonies, even among their own people, just like Biebl sometimes "walked around Prague like in a foreign land."[37] Yet, as one reads, for example, about the lives of the French avant-garde poets who travelled extensively to other continents, and with whom one would expect Biebl to have much in common, such as Blaise Cendrars, Philippe Soupault, Robert Desnos, and Paul Éluard, one realizes how their experiences must have been in some basic ways *also* different. While Biebl travelled the farthest among the Czech modern poets, his journey was brief compared to the far more extensive travels and sojourns of the French poets. Biebl set off from a place remote from the sea, from where Paris and, even more, the seashores of southern France, were distant and exotic with their palms and ships. The French, like the British and the Dutch, sailed from their own ports, often on their own ships or on vessels where they met their own people, and among the most frequent destinations were their own colonies. In the 1920s, many people on ocean liners and in the colonies were not even aware of the existence of the Czech language and Czechoslovakia, the newly created country.[38] Some of the Czech travelers—and certainly those of earlier generations—were comfortable in German, and often several other European languages. Not so Biebl, whose archives show him as essentially monolingual. He used mostly German to communicate, a language he probably didn't speak well. On the ship on his way to Java, as well as when he reached there, he was learning conversational Malay as well as some Javanese words—which must have come in handy (especially because he did not know Dutch), and which shaped the way he was making sense of what he saw, as his notebooks show. One can only imagine how he, as a traveler and as a poet, felt so much more like among Martians, or

---

36 This also applies to certain characteristics of Biebl's poetic travel, such a sense of intensified interpenetration between imagination and actuality, to links between travel and childhood, etc. On modernist travel and writing, see e.g. Kimberley Healey, *The Modernist Traveler: French Detours, 1900–1930* (Lincoln and London: University of Nebraska Press, 2003); Robert McNab, *Ghost Ships: A Surrealist Love Triangle* (New Haven and London: Yale University Press, 2004); and Fussel, *Abroad*.

37 Konstantin Biebl, *Nový Ikaros* (Prague: Aventinum,1929), 54.

38 See, for example, B. M. Eliášová, *Rok na jižní polokouli: Jáva, Australie, Afrika* (Prague: Českomoravské podniky tiskařské a vydavatelské, 1928), 24.

like a *Pierot lunaire*—perhaps like this book would feel on a bookshelf among publications on great French, British and American writers.

In Javanese jungles, Biebl hears the requiem for Arthur Rimbaud, he is touched by a matchbox deep in the jungle recalling Paul Gaugin's painting, and he repeatedly evokes Jules Verne. French avant-garde authors, too, kept returning to Rimbaud, Gaugin, and Verne. This suggests a connection between the French poets and Biebl, but also an asymmetry. French was not just one of the most widely spoken languages on ships and in hotels, but also the original language of the poets of travel closest to Biebl's heart. This displacement was the poetic ground on which he moved.

It is tempting to imagine what Biebl would talk about with Dutch, British, or French traveling writers, and how such conversations would have shaped his work, had he met them on his ship. I think of Dutch like E. du Perron or Jef Last, British like George Orwell, or French like Philippe Soupault or Paul

Figure 2. "Head of a Clown," a painting by František Tichý, on a postcard sent by Konstantin Biebl to Vítězslav Nezval as New Year's greetings in December 1948. Tichý also illustrated the first posthumous edition of Biebl's *Cesta na Jávu* (Journey to Java; see Figure 18). Archive of the Museum of Czech Literature, Prague.

Éluard . . . But he didn't.[39] One is compelled to look for connections and kinships. Yet, it may be equally important to respect the absence of encounters, to take seriously the fact that many of the connections, which are so tempting to make, remained unrealized, or almost-realized; to sense the shades of tenuousness of those links, and the particularity of each case. The other side of these chance non-encounters is that Biebl, even though he may sometimes appear to us as just one man in a crowd, also always travelled almost alone.

ON METHOD

> *Method:* ancient Greek < *meta+odos; meta-* trans-, change, transformation; *odos* way, path, travel < the same Indo-European base as Sanskrit *sāda* seat on a horse, Old Church Slavonic *xodŭ* going, walk, journey, *xoditi* to go, [and Czech *chodit*, to go, walk][40]

"I love actuality but also dreaming," the poet wrote, "and so I like to move on the border between the two worlds, where actuality overflows into dream and dream into actuality. . . . I am a traveler of all eras and of the most various dreams."[41]

It is an ancient state of being, lived afresh in a way particular to an age, (dis)location, and a life experience, with particular speed, manner of movement, and vision. To write about Biebl's poetic method is to write about his travels, and vice versa. Already in letters from his student years, he sees his poetry as fundamentally modern. With the eye moving swiftly between icy winters and the tropics, between Czechoslovakia and Asian colonies, his is a poetry of trains, steamships, asphalt roads and airplanes, of modern wars and dissection rooms; it invokes the powers of photography and cinema, and it struggles with colonialism and capitalism. This Czech encounter with Java is also an encounter with modernity.

Like in a photographic double exposure, or "as if someone projected two films simultaneously,"[42] Bohemia and Java are superimposed and seen through one another. A Czech landscape is disclosed through jungles and seas; Java is seen anew, in its nearness and its distance, never simply exotic, as it blends into Bohemia, and as colonial and Czech history mirror each other. Biebl's imagination reveals at once the immensity of the world and a nearness of faraway places.

39 Soupault and Éluard briefly visited Prague, but there is no evidence of Biebl interacting with them extensively. There is also no sign that he met on his trip (or even back home) any of the few Czech traveler writers of the 1920s who crisscrossed the world. See Mrázek, "Czech Tropics."

40 Compiled from the Oxford English Dictionary Online.

41 Biebl, *Cesta na Jávu*, 79–80.

42 Miroslav Rutte, *Doba a hlasy* (Turnov: Müller, 1929), 205.

Teige, in a manifesto of the "artists of life's unity," wrote that "no one comes up any more with proposals for modern art, but with plans of new life, a new organization of the world and its consecration."[43] *Skutečnost* (actuality), as the object of poetic, transformative creativity, and *poznání* (roughly "cognition," both the process and the resulting knowledge) were key words for contemporary theorists of modern poetry. Biebl wrote that "to poetize is a desire for *poznání*" and "poem is the poet's *poznání*."[44] His search for poetic words and images insists on being a search for knowledge of life, even as it is often through intoxicated fantasies that cognition operates. His politics and ethics, as this book tries to show, are indivisible from the inner workings and the silences of his poetry; his engagement with social actuality gains force and clarity from the freedom of his dreaming. The poetry of oceans and jungles reveals truths about homeland with a transformative force, while travel, distant lands, and colonialism are seen with a fresh clarity through his life experience at home: his childhood in a Bohemian village, the the World Wars, his own society and its "justice", his political convictions. Fantasy and actuality constantly overflow into each other; their liaisons are unveiled by the poet.

In Biebl's words, the poet's

> associations extend their hands toward each other across oceans. Poet, the promoter of polygamy, the promoter of polyandry, the implacable promoter of free love, unites the most distant and apparently the most unblendable images . . . because, in an instinctive mania to relate all things of this world, he had long ago intuited their liaisons.[45]

Not bound by conventional rationality, linear arguments, or any stable system, but through chains and clusters of free associations, sub- or half-conscious connections, metaphors, assonances, and surprising, often humorous, juxtapositions and displacements, Biebl's poetry gives glimpses of opposites only to destabilize their difference as they mirror each other and recognize themselves in each other—the sky and the ocean, dream and actuality, poetry and life, we and them. It topples conventional distinctions and conceptualizations, prejudices and stereotypes; it overcomes all sorts of distance and difference; it releases imagination into insecure heights and ventures into dark abysses of the unconscious.

The other side of this poetic "free love" and of these flights of imagination, or always underneath them, is silence—the poet's, of the dead, of the silenced "millions," in the Great War, in capitalist Czechoslovakia, or in Asian colonies.

43 Teige, Karel. "Obrazy a předobrazy," in *Avantgarda známá a neznámá*, ed. Štěpán Vlašín et al. (Prague: Svoboda, 1971) 1: 97.

44 Biebl, *Dílo*, 5:262.

45 Biebl, *Dílo*, 5:263.

A consciousness of the violence of words, flights away from them and falls into silence, are—like flights of imagination—indivisibly poetic, ethical and political; and the journeys away from words into various silences intersect (other) physical and imaginary travels.

To converse with such poetry, by Biebl and other poets, I believe, one needs to think in a way that is more poetic than argumentative; and that resists enframing (in Heidegger's sense) the particular Czech case or any specific image in any powerful master-narrative, general theory, or argument. I hope the book will tickle readers engaged in different debates and fields (post/decolonial studies, travel writing studies, scholarship on Central European avant-garde, and so on). Some of these were unavoidably on my mind while writing this book, and this is occasionally reflected in the text. But faced with powerful theories, arguments and approaches, I think, too, of Seifert's silent emotions in the face of "things decreed" by Teige's theories; and I think again of "our little citizen" in face of the empire, or among the chuckling "Martians."[46] Uncertainty, confusion, failure to be "proper," self-ridicule, intoxication, or seasickness—at least a tinge of these, like a constant doubt—as a ~~method~~? Or can we rediscover *meta-* and *odos*— transformation, travel, horse saddle, walking, journey—in method? This is a difficult task for a scholar: to let images resonate freely with multiple meanings and impressions, to let oneself be unsettled and disoriented by them, and gather them gently, uncertainly, unheroically, in ways that are evocative and associative rather than orderly and controlling.

Translations of poetry punctuate this text, not merely as examples or objects of analysis, but as poetic moments that may loosen, derail, intoxicate, sharpen feeling and thought, even at the risk of jarring clashes between the two apparently unblendable opposites, poetry and scholarship. Some parts of this book are like fragments from a logbook record of the stormy journey of seasick reading and translating across different imaginaries, memories, histories, and linguistic musicalities.

If Biebl's journey is the entry point to a broader view of Czech poetic travels, his poetry is an inspiration for the method—the transformative journeying—of this book. In English about Czech texts, by an academic about a poet, on a tropical island about a landlocked Central European country: this book dreams to cross oceans and to move between languages, places, and forms of knowledge. It struggles to translate and bring what is distant and apparently unblendable together. Translation and travel are not merely ways to get from one point to another. I write in (Cz)English, and risk traversing the seas in

46 For a brief Biebl/Czech-centered critique of the master narrative of postcolonial studies, and how its appeal and dangers haunt my own thinking, see Mrázek, "Czech Tropics," 156–60.

other ways, not out of practical necessity, but because crossing borders and oceans can be poetry. (Thus spoke the frog.)

In Singapore and in Java, I read and felt Czech poetry differently than in Prague. Actual palms under my office window, in their everyday familiarity, came alive in conversations with Czech palms. Like painted figures escaping from picture frames, like faces remembered from dreams and encountered in the waking world, images that in Prague had appeared like ethereal exotic fantasies, became uncannily real, at times hard and rough like bricks, as I recognized places and feelings that I knew from living in Java and in Singapore. The colonial world and the one in which I live today (in Singapore, Prague, Java, anywhere) mirror each other across time, and sometimes seem strikingly alike.[47] Remembrances of a childhood home (also: "I walked around Prague like in a foreign land") and the wanderer's sensations and realizations in the delightfully, painfully true poems cut to the quick (dictionary: the tender, sensitive flesh of the living body). Reading, travelling, translating, across oceans I follow in the footsteps of "our little citizen," a "miserable and disobedient earthling" choking on salt water, trying to understand him and myself, struck by our nearness and our distance.

THE PARTS

The book has two parts.

In Part One, "The Mirror of Time," I follow Biebl's life and work in a loosely chronological manner. The journey to Java was a brief moment in his life, a glimpse from a train window, but throughout his life, images—anticipations, reverberations—flare up and recede in the midst of the passing dreams, revolutions and nightmares of his time. "Mirror of Time" is simultaneously an exploration of the alchemy of the poetic image; an alchemy that is at the core of his *poznání* of *skutečnost*, including social actuality. The narrative is interrupted by two Excursions—journeys of sorts—away from Biebl's work, which allow his poetic travels to resonate with alchemic processes in the writing of his predecessors and contemporaries, and illuminate intersections of travel and Czech poetry in the 19th and 20th centuries, as well as certain attitudes to home and faraway, empires and colonies, and the exiled or the silenced.

In Part Two, "A hundred rose petals, on them no words," I contemplate silence and the poet's journeys beyond words: "the silence of the millions"; sounds, smells, tastes and the visuality of poetry (including typography, design, and illustrations, which were among the landmarks of Czech avant-

47 I explore such mirroring between the past and the present in my essays "Czechs on Ships" and "Primeval Forest, Homeland, Catastrophe."

garde visual poetry—another chance to catch a wider picture of interwar Czech art and literature); the poet's collage-like arrangements of photographs from Java (published in a popular magazine, and showing his travels and visual and verbal poetry as part of a broader landscape of modern Czech image-making and global fantasizing); his postcards; and the silent mirroring of poetry, travel, photography, and death.

PART ONE
THE MIRROR OF TIME

Ever so often you look at the clock
As if you were pacing the platform
And seconds pass
It's seven o'clock
It's beginning to rain
And all the windows on the first floor
Are suddenly transformed into an Oriental train
Yet nothing happens aside from speed
You feel how your face slowly becomes the mirror of time
Half past seven! your hair is starting to turn grey
The clock the theater of horrors
It has stopped raining
It is eight
Finally a little old woman enters[48]

48 Biebl, *Nebe peklo ráj* (Prague: Sfinx, 1931), 37.

PARROTS AND MONKEYS

Start running over fresh soil
in the footsteps of beings escaping into darkness[49]

"A forgotten poem is a silenced truth. . . . It is for our sake that we care for the paths he made for us by his steps."[50] I repeat these sentences after my father, who wrote them over forty years ago, in 1979, about Konstantin Biebl. Only a part of the essay was published; the full manuscript and several boxes of notes written on index cards were later lost. The published text ends by echoing Biebl's thoughts on loss and resurrection, which are like a reversed mirror image of the sentences with which I began:

> Wise Javanese shamans say that some people return to us even after their death, in the form of animals, birds and flowers, or a good word. When fifty years ago he dreamt under the Javanese sun, perhaps Biebl believed them. And perhaps, with a little bit of good will, there is a kernel of truth in what the old shamans claim.[51]

"Like in a hall of mirrors . . . you meet each other endlessly," wrote Biebl in a poem.[52] For me, returning to him meant also going back to one of my father's quests. Biebl, too, kept returning to his father's footsteps and dreams. The story I am telling is like that apparently endless series of repeated images produced by mirrors facing each other.

Biebl often remembered the tropical birds that his father (Petr Biebl, 1865–1916) brought to their village home:

> My need to breathe distances has its roots in my childhood. . . . When I was born, my crying was blending with the screams of the arara parrot; he sat on my cradle, curious what was happening. It was not a mirage, it was an actual parrot, philologist. . . . My mother could never forgive him that he deprived her of the most sacred right, as she herself put it; for it was he, the scamp, who was the first to address me, immedi-

49 Biebl, *Zrcadlo noci*, n.p. Also in Biebl, *Dílo*, 3:85.
50 Rudolf Mrázek, "Javánské motivy v životě a díle Konstantina Biebla," *Nový Orient* (1979), 175.
51 Mrázek, "Javánské motivy," 242.
52 Biebl, *Zrcadlo noci*, n.p. Also in Biebl, *Dílo*, 3:82.

> ately after my arrival in this world, with his *good evening*, although I was born in the morning.
>
> And even today I do not know who my father was more: whether that doctor who night after night trudged through the mud of his district, or the dreamer who grew palms, bought exotic birds, and loved above all his russet monkey from Java, sad and tame. She had absolute freedom; she climbed the trees in the garden, sometimes she wandered through the village, and whenever she felt like it, she entered into my father's surgery and put on a serious and learned face as if she were his assistant.[53]

I am sorry, parrot-philologist and monkey-doctor—if you make me smile, it is only because I recognize myself in you.

Biebl wrote: "my father's exotic desires, which I absorbed . . . are the oldest cause of my overseas journeys."[54] At the same time, the poet travelled to Java, in my father's words, "to test the border between literature and life . . . in the footsteps of the great pilgrims of poetry. . . . On behalf of the whole generation, he took up the challenge to go on such a journey."[55]

It was in the 1970s that my father wrote about Biebl's voyage—that is, before he was able to travel to Indonesia, at a time when he could do so only in his thoughts. He had already travelled around India, lecturing on Southeast Asia at universities. He recounted to me how he stood on the shit-covered beach in Madras, gazing and dreaming across the Indian Ocean in the direction of the Indonesian islands. Still earlier, in the 1960s, he and a few fellow students of Indonesian language in Prague were poring over maps, planning to make a raft on which they would sail from Europe to Indonesia—keeping always close to the coast, he would emphasize even when he was telling me about it decades later, perhaps so that I wouldn't worry about him too much, perhaps to remind me how real these dreams were.

He was neither the first nor the last for whom Biebl's poetry, and especially his journey to Java, would resonate in unforeseen ways. Four years after Biebl's death, in 1955, the writer Jiří Marek travelled to Java and Bali and published a book about his experiences. The playfully archaic paragraph-long chapter headings evoke old travel books. Such as: "THE FIRST CHAPTER, in which the kind reader will learn much that is of interest from the history of travelling, but still little about the goal of the trip. . . ." The chapter begins:

> We shall, kind reader, wander into a faraway land. In the poet's words (who wouldn't know that we are referring to Konstantin Biebl):

53 Biebl, *Dílo*, 5:269–70.
54 Biebl, *Dílo*, 5:68.
55 Mrázek, "Javánské motivy," 180.

With the ship that carries tea and coffee
I will one day sail to faraway Java. . . .[56]

"Who wouldn't know . . ."

In 1956, the Indonesian President Soekarno visited Prague. His interpreter was Dr. Miroslav Oplt. Soekarno invited Oplt to join him on his official travels around Indonesia. In Oplt's book about his Indonesian experiences, there is a chapter titled "In the footsteps of Konstantin Biebl," where he describes his search for Biebl's traces in the Javanese city of Semarang, where the poet was based.[57] Oplt brought Biebl's poetry back to Java in 1957 when he gave the lecture *Indonesia dalam kesusasteraan Tjeko* (Indonesia in Czech literature) at the Gadjah Mada University in Yogyakarta, Central Java, during which he also recited his translations of Biebl's poems.[58] Oplt also authored an Indonesian language textbook. It was given, as a birthday present, by my mother to my father, who would go on to become Oplt's student and later joined him as a researcher at the Oriental Institute in Prague and became a scholar of Indonesia. In the 1980s, in my early teens, I began to learn Indonesian in Prague using the same copy of Oplt's textbook, which I found on my father's bookshelf.

It must have been in part through my father's own snow-clad tropical dreams and travels through poetry that he could understand Biebl, and through growing up dreaming them in the same cold, sealess, beautiful country, with its changing seasons and its *úzkost* ("anxiety"; "narrowness"). It is through memories of my own childhood that I feel I can understand something about the roots of Biebl's dreams.

Understand—or parrot? Or could aping, parroting and mirroring, comic or anxious, lead to cognition and knowledge? Vítězslav Nezval, Biebl's longtime friend and one of the great poets of their generation—we met him at the platform in the Preamble—defined poetic image in 1924: "A form sharpened in a mirror. A fiery parrot . . ."[59]

Biebl's journey, too, was a repetition, a fiery parrot. "If we know Mácha, Baudelaire, Rimbaud, Neumann," wrote my father,

> then we already know much about the poetry and exoticism of Konstantin Biebl. But we certainly do not know everything about it, and also not what is fundamental. For poetry, like life, is unforeseeable and unrepeatable. Even Biebl himself once wrote that

56 Jiří Marek, *Země pod rovníkem* (Prague: Mladá fronta, 1956), 5.
57 Miroslav Oplt, *Hledání Indonesie* (Prague: Panorama, 1989), 110–121.
58 Miroslav Oplt, *Indonesia dalam kesusasteraan Tjeko* (Jogjakarta: Universitas Gadjah Mada, 1957).
59 Vítězslav Nezval, *Pantomima* (Prague: Ústřední nakladatelství, 1924), 31.

> the fundamental in his work had been determined in the first six or seven 'fatal years of life.' Hence, before he read his first poem.[60]

That is how old I was—six or seven years—when I was looking over my father's shoulder as he was checking the proofs of his essay on Biebl, where the drawing of the ship *Plancius* was placed improperly, with the ship's bow pointing to the sky—with a quick movement of his pen he saved the sinking ship. Perhaps a year or two later, I read my father's unfinished essay, and fragments of Biebl's poetry have been in my memory ever since.

I remember my father's simple mementos from India and Southeast Asia, among them two Balinese masks and a stubborn Javanese shadow puppet of an ogre who refused to let itself be hung on the wall of our Prague apartment, always bending or otherwise evading its destiny. A grinning demon, the fragrance of spices, and a menacing movement in the darkness of my memory: a Balinese *kris* (a dagger, usually treated with arsenic and fragrant oil), which my father was given by his father-in-law, my grandfather. The hilt was in the shape of a demon. My father impressed on me that the fragrant blade was poisoned.

Surrounded by such traces of faraway places in his small study, he was only one figure in the tropical world in which I grew up—I think only slightly more tropical than other Czech boys. Even before I could read, I vaguely remember, I had spent long afternoons in my grandmother's room. I don't know whether she was narrating or if we were both play-acting. I just remember I was a sailor on a white ship crossing an endless ocean through the thickening fog of cigarette smoke. I recollect no ports or islands—only the white ship, the vast sea and the cigarette smell.

In the next room, my grandfather, who had been at one time the Czechoslovak Ambassador to Sudan, had a few objects from Africa—in my mind I see the geometric ornaments on a basket, and whole *Afrika* in a spear of beautiful polished wood with a dark metal spearhead in the shape of an elongated leaf.

Recently I rediscovered a folder with watercolor paintings and verses which my grandfather made for me when I was six or seven years old (Figure 3). It contains playful and sometimes naughty poems about African jungle and animals, beautifully illustrated. The rhymes and Czech references are impossible to translate.

> When people are evil,
> I sit somewhere holed up
> and tell myself: By God!
> I'd rather live in jungle!

60 Mrázek, "Javánské motivy," 209.

Figure 3. An illustrated poem by Josef Pospíšil, author's grandfather, from the unpublished album "Afrika," 1970s. Collection of author.

Many books for children then, like in Biebl's time, were about faraway lands—from the Wild West to tropical seas swarming with pirates, from African desserts to the cities and rivers of China. The Dutch East Indies belonged to it as well. One of my favorite readings was a translation of the well-known children's book *Ship Boys of Captain Bontekoe* by Johan Fabricius, Dutch author of Biebl's generation; he was born in Java. With the other ship boys I sailed to the Indies, survived a shipwreck and walked for many days through the jungles of Sumatra. There were *verneovky*, Jules Verne's novels, with their sea storms, jungles and a fifteen-year old captain. Czech children had lived in the worlds of these books for many generations before me, and the poets of Biebl's era, too, loved them, evoked and quoted them in their poems and posed them as models in their theories of poetry. *Májovky*, books by Karl May set mostly in the American West, Africa and China, were among the best loved: the author, from a German town not far north of the Czech border, wrote most of them before he travelled outside Europe, and they show the Native Americans— "Indians"—fighting against the "pale faces" in a way that turned every boy into either a brave "red warrior" defending his ancestral prairies or a lonesome pale face fighting on the side of his "red brothers." I recognize my dream world in Biebl's when in his prose poem *Plancius* he daydreams on the deck of the ship in the midst of Dutch colonizers: "[O]n my body I feel all my old wounds which I had suffered in innumerable battles against pale faces."[61] *Indiánky*—thrillers about the "Indians"—were already popular since the first half of the nineteenth century, well before Karl May. Josef Václav Sládek (1845–1912), in his later years known as "the most national" of Czech

61 Biebl, *Plancius*, 12.

poets, travelled to America in 1868 and described his thoughts upon seeing "Indian" Mississippi for the first time:

> Mississippi! Who has not fantasized about that great American river, perhaps only as it is described a thousand times in stories about the Indians, whose gaudy pictures sparked our imagination when we were children to the point of sinful forgetting of the most sacred duties toward our homeland, family hearth, and our own health? Who would not then throw away the primer and, having picked up all our cash from a clay piggybank and if possible also the savings of our sisters, set out at three o'clock in the morning on a difficult journey beyond the oceans? There on the shore the kind trapper Rosewood would certainly be waiting for us with his bow, small straps for scalps, and with a pot of cinnamon porridge. Having put velvety moccasins on our feet, he would lead us to the tent of a black-eyed Indian princess, who would rear us as brave warriors against the white men[62] . . . Aye, how will that old teacher of ours plead for mercy—woe! a prosaic ear pull disturbed us from our delightful dreams.[63]

Long before Biebl, in Czech dreams of faraway lands there is already something of that parrot philologist who, with his "good evening" uttered in the morning, made the birth of the poet into a burlesque.

Teige, in his 1922 manifesto of "new proletarian art," mentions *indiánky* in one breath with fairy tales.[64] It was common to "play at Indians," in my time as in Biebl's and Sládek's. The popular traveler-writer A. V. Novák, who was in Malaya and Sumatra at the time of Biebl's voyage to Java, lost one of his eyes while playing as a child in a Czech village, when the arrow of another "red man" pierced it.[65] As a boy during summer vacations, I stayed in our cabin in the countryside, incidentally near the same river as Novák's village. I have memories—infused with the fragrances of the forest paths and the warm smell of cows and pigs from the small farm by the river—of dressing up as an "Indian," with big hunting knife in my belt and a headband which I cut out from a stolen placemat made of goat leather. Alone I walked through forests, in my canoe (from laminated plastic) I explored the river and, following in the footsteps of my red brothers, I was learning to genuinely experience the beauty and the peace of nature in my pale-face homeland. Not many other things evoke childhood, home and my cool, land-locked homeland as genuinely as images of high seas, "Indians," and trekking through the jungles of Sumatra.

---

62 I use lowercase initials for "white" and "black" to reflect Czech usage, since the words generally appear in quotations from Czech sources or my commentary on them.

63 Jos. Václav Sládek, *Americké obrázky a jiná prosa*, ed. Ferdinand Strejček (Prague: J. Otto, [1914?]), 2:130.

64 Teige, "Nové umění proletářské," 16.

65 Jan Šejbl, *Archibald Václav Novák: hříšná exotika* (Prague: Národní muzeum, 2020), 17.

Only flickering ghost-like fragments briefly appear from the darkness of the past, and, as I think of me and of Biebl, there is no reason to believe that what remains hidden has not guided one's steps and dreams—but who can say exactly in what ways and how much? I am now an "expert" on Javanese shadow puppets, I published on the *kris*, speaking of "the visible and the invisible in Southeast Asia," and I live on a Southeast Asian tropical island dreamed by others into a modern city. Is that the doing of that *kris* that my grandfather gave to my father, or the shadow puppet on the wall of my father's study? Most likely it is and it is not.

THE FIRST PALM

The literary historian František Kautman, in an article published a few years after Biebl's death, describes the small flat where the poet lived toward the end of his life:

> The attention of the visitor to Biebl's cozy flat was captured above all by trophies that the poet brought back from the Dutch Indies: ritual masks, native weapons, small effigies of deities decorated Biebl's bookcase and gave it a peculiar, exotic accent. But also the host's eyes began to shine with happiness when the visitor showed an interest in all those things. Child-like, unassuming, and trusting Konstantin Biebl prided himself on the fact that he visited the places of his most beautiful dreams, dreams that were not just his.[66]

Among the objects in Biebl's room, quite possibly there was also the Javanese shadow puppet visible on the wall of his earlier apartment in a photograph from 1932, or perhaps some of those souvenirs that are now stored in Prague museums, which include ten Javanese puppets and several paintings of puppet characters.[67]

I fancy Biebl's room might have felt somewhat like my father's study when I was little, the writer's room full of books and quiet memories of distant travels. For the aging "child-like" Biebl, who liked to travel in imagination across time and space, the same objects that evoked faraway lands must have also reminded him of the village home of his distant childhood, with his father's parrots and monkey. As in his poetry, home and distant lands, childhood and advanced age, memories and dreams, "like in a hall of mirrors . . . meet each other endlessly."[68]

Sunflower roots have the ability to penetrate even hard and dry soil and find moisture deep below. Nezval wrote in a letter to Biebl on his fiftieth birthday, three years before his death: "Fate gave you such a childhood that you carry it always with you like the roots of a sunflower."[69]

---

66 Z. Linkov [pseudonym], "Bieblova cesta na Jávu," *Kultura* 9 (1958). Clipping is in the Museum of Czech Literature, Prague.

67 A small number of Biebl's souvenirs, including Javanese shadow puppets, are kept in the Museum of Czech Literature and in the National Museum of Ethnography, both in Prague.

68 Biebl, *Zrcadlo noci*, n.p. Also in Biebl, *Dílo*, 3:82.

69 Nezval, "Drahý příteli," Nezval's letter to Biebl published as Preface in Biebl, *Dílo*, 5:5.

Let us listen to Biebl's own words about his childhood and his father's exotic animals:

> On the very threshold of my childhood, I formed many unusual friendships, which certainly influenced my sensibility. I began to hate winter because it harmed my overseas friends, especially by taking away their freedom. I will never forget those Decembers and Februaries when one parrot slept and the other would hang head down on his ring—perhaps he hoped that from that position the landscape outside of the window would appear more hospitable; and the black toucan, when he saw snow falling outside, was so lethargic that he was hardly able to support his huge beak; and the desperate monkey, whining and coughing, threw herself at flowery curtains to tear this false imitation of eternal spring. Thus I learned early about the suffering of people and animals.[70]

Biebl wrote this in 1941, in the middle of a world war and Nazi occupation of Bohemia, when he thought back to his father's suicide in the previous world war, and pondered following in his footsteps. This is how we catch glimpses of his childhood through his later writings, as fragmentary images blending and clashing with those of later years, "like in a hall of mirrors." Images of childhood become sharper, are felt more intensely, at a later age, just as the tropics are most intensely dreamt in winter, as we will repeatedly see in Biebl's writings.

December home and the tropics clash and blend, as do dream-like beauty and suffering—in Biebl's memories of his childhood as well as in his images of the colonies; and the child does not just watch an exotic spectacle, but forms "unusual friendships" with the "overseas friends."

> The physician's practice of my father was the practice of a child—future poet. Holding my breath, I was listening to the wailing that was sometimes audible from the surgery and that mixed with parrots' cries. It was the unusual weeping of children whom no one was punishing, who did not do anything wrong, and yet they suffered so much. Thus I learned early what cotton wool and blood were, what disease, death, and other adversities were. Terrified I breathed in the smell of iodine, carbolic acid, nothingness and the unknown—all that later became the building material of my [poetry]. Naturally also my father's exotic desires, which I absorbed, entered and are still passing through my work, and they are the oldest cause of my overseas journeys to Africa and the Dutch Indies.[71]

---

70 Biebl, *Dílo*, 5:70.

71 Biebl, *Dílo*, 5:267–8.

"Biebl is a medic," one reads in a review of his poetry.[72] Formative childhood experiences resonate with *poznání* of Java, where, in his words, he "was able to catch a glimpse of Chinese and Javanese life, especially at the moments of suffering that accompany sickness and death."[73]

As the son of a village doctor (even if it were not for those exotic animals in their house), Biebl must have been simultaneously an insider and something of a stranger among the children of farmers; at least somewhat, at least sometimes, like an exotic bird, or like a Czech poet among English and Dutch colonists, like a white man among the Javanese, like an earthling at sea, among cackling Martians. In the introduction to his 1940 film script, *Černá věž* (Black tower), Biebl writes about the main character, the village boy Jan:

> Each village has its oddball, its lunatic, its Jan. And this Jan is "god's human," as they sometimes call lunatics in villages. In fact he is a poet, even if he can't even sign his name well.[74]

In the (unrealized) film, he is bullied by village boys. He finds peace in solitude, and the person that understands him best is a stranger, a woman, Neznámá ("unknown, non-acquaintance"), who "arrived one day in a train with refugees" and "who does not utter a single word in the whole film."[75] She carries with her a golden cage with the arara parrot.

Biebl's father, as Karel Konrád remembered, was "an immensely conscientious physician, a true humanist and socialist. And he loved art, especially literature and the visual arts; he himself painted in aquarelles and oils."[76] Biebl's mother impressed visitors as a strong and cultured woman from a rather well-to-do family.

> The traces of my mother's guidance are evident. . . . It affected me, too, that she composed poetry. With her hairdo and eyebrows she resembled Japanese women, particularly when she held her pen high and wrote verses in a neat hand into a black notebook.[77]

Her brother, Biebl's uncle Arnošt Ráž, often visited. He was a lawyer—"an advocate of the periphery . . . mostly for free, so he always struggled with

72 Pavel Frankl, "Básnický projev Konstantina Biebla," *Host* 2 (1924–1925): 147.
73 Biebl, "Semarang," *Domov a svět* 1, no. 14: 7.
74 Biebl, *Dílo*, 5:287.
75 Biebl, *Dílo*, 5:89.
76 Karel Konrád, "O Konstantinu Bieblovi," in *Za Konstantinem Bieblem* (Prague: Československý spisovatel, 1952), 65.
77 Biebl, *Dílo*, 5:268.

poverty," Biebl would write.[78] He was also a visual artist and poet, not widely known but well respected. In his late teens, he published two collections of poems, and later his artworks and verses appeared in art periodicals. As a poet, he was a mentor for Biebl. In 1924, the uncle and the nephew published a collection of poems together—Ráž's last, Biebl's first.

According to the late-Cold-War verdict of a writer in the *Harvard Review*, Jaroslav Seifert's early "immature" poetry was "a bizarre mix of socialism and Catholicism."[79] Later representations of Biebl often pass over the fact that he came from a Catholic family. As was the case with a number of other poets of his generation committed to communism, allusions—in all shades, ironic and not—to biblical language, narratives, and imagery permeate his poetry. The magical 14th century narrative frescos depicting the lives of Jesus, Mary, and the saints in the Gothic church of St. Jacob the Greater near his house, at once surreal and homey like a child's drawing, must have been among the first images of the "Orient" that he saw. His grandfather and godfather Jan Nepomuk Ráž wrote fiction with a religious orientation and was close to other, better known writers associated with Catholic modernism. When J. N. Ráž writes of God's "spark of love that embraces and joins the whole world,"[80] for example, one senses that his world and times were different from his grandson's, yet, like between Catholicism and communism, there are resonances, common concerns, and "unusual friendships."

As people who visited Biebl in his village observed with a sense of wonder, the house where Biebl grew up was extraordinary and even "curious," and not only because of the exotic animals. Its interior, like its inhabitants, was not what one would expect in a village dwelling: it was "a kind of little museum of carefully selected artistic treasures, from diminutive angels from a baroque altar, to the painting, I suspect of Pope Innocent XI., a remarkable Italian work,"[81] wrote Zdeněk Kalista, who was friends with Biebl and A. Ráž in the early 1920s. Like others, Kalista felt a connection between the house and Biebl's character: "I found here the backdrop of [Biebl's] esoteric life: in that curious artistic richness . . . I realized that wandering in the midst of these collections . . . must have shaped or at least contributed to shaping his character, deeply sunk into realms of dreams."[82] "Full of antiquities, especially gilded angels and saints, about to blow the trumpets and beat the

78 Biebl, *Dílo*, 5:172.

79 Joel Brouwer, "The Early Poetry of Jaroslav Seifert by Dana Loewy" (book review), *Harvard Review* 14 (Spring, 1998): 115.

80 Quoted in Zdeněk K. Slabý, *Potkávání setkávání: listování v osudech* (Prague: Volvox Globator, 2015), 28.

81 Kalista, *Tváře ve stínu* (České Budějovice: Růže, 1969), 104.

82 Kalista, *Tváře ve stínu*, 229.

Figure 4. "Greetings from Slavětín." Postcard, mailed in 1900. Collection of author.

drums for the Last Judgement,"[83] the house seems to have been something of an enchanted space, yet homely and warm at the same time. According to Biebl's wife, the "angels from those mysterious and beautiful ancient hallways of the Slavětín house" were collected by Biebl's father,[84] like the exotic birds with which they shared the house. The angels would reappear in *New Icarus*, metamorphosing from "the last of all white elephants / deep in the burning jungles of Ceylon."[85] How, one may wonder, did the house and the family circumstances shape not only his sense of being at home with the exotic, dream-like and strange, but also his sensibility of home as a place at once homely, exotic, and mysterious?

On the other side of the world is Bohemia
a beautiful and exotic land
full of deep and mysterious rivers
which you cross with dry feet in the Name of Jesus[86]

83 Konrád, "O Konstantinu Bieblovi," 63–4.

84 Marie Bieblová, 1968 interview, in the recording archive of the Czech Radio.

85 Biebl, *Nový Ikaros*, 12.

86 Biebl, *S lodí jež dováží čaj a kávu*, 2nd edition (Prague: Odeon, 1928), 63. Like other scholars, I am using the "second edition" (1928), since the first edition (1927), reportedly identical to the second, does not seem to be extant.

No-one can say what all the roots of Biebl's tropical imagination and his travels were.

> Already in school he used to be a pirate on the deck
> of postage stamps.[87]

Adventure books about European men among "natives" in faraway lands, jungles full of wild animals, voyages in the age of sail, sailors and pirates, and (American) "Indians" evoke childhood in his later writing. *Brehm's Life of Animals* captivated his imagination, as did postage stamps (especially those from faraway countries), itinerant circuses with exotic animals, a container for sweets in the shape of a ship, even spices and fruits, like this banana:

> *Barbaric Love*
> I was a hunter of tigers, they walked around my little baby bed. Within reach my gun hung. How many of them I killed! So many tigers!
>
> How I loved Ceylon! And how I loved Celebes, Sumatra, Borneo, and all those islands down there. It was a great and barbaric love.
>
> Mummy bought one banana and the child ate whole Java.[88]

Leafing through textbooks from the time, one gets a sense how—especially in the midst of stupefying enumerations of geographic facts, technical terms, measurements (of the Earth, continents, oceans . . .), and classifications—the occasional picture or a sentence could be the opening onto a world into which a schoolboy could escape from the dreariness of school as well as from "those Decembers and Februaries." We have to imagine how a village boy might read the following sentences from a 1904 primary school geography textbook, living as he was among animals and plants, fields and streams, so different from the tropical lands near the sea. Try to feel the bitter cold outside—

> The eastern and southern parts of Asia near the ocean (China, Japanese islands, East Indian island-multitude,[89] and both Indies) belong to the most blessed lands on earth; there people grow rice, cotton and tea, in the tropical regions also coffee, spice, and sugar cane. In southern Asia there are vast tropical forests (tropical forests are luxuriant forests in the hot or tropical zone of the earth), the home of the tiger and the

87 Konstantin Biebl, *Zlatými řetězy* (Čin: Prague, 1926), 47.

88 Biebl, *Cesta na Jávu*, 8.

89 The textbook uses the unusual, evocative word *mnohoostroví*, which I translate awkwardly "island-multitude." "Polynesia" is close in meaning, but geographically misleading.

Figure 5. "Asia." Martin Kozák, *Zeměpis pro školy obecné* (Geography for public schools), 1904.

elephant. . . . In the highlands dwell the tiger and the lion. Important among domestic animals is the tamed Indian elephant.[90]

The Dutch East Indies often stand out, and especially on a winter day, the "humid and hot" tropical air and the smell of spice, tea and coffee are overwhelming:

Their climate is humid and hot, their plant-life exceedingly lush, diverse, and rich. In particular, coffee, rice, tobacco, sugar cane and spice thrive there. The natural riches are exploited by the Europeans. To the Dutch belong:

a) The Greater Sunda Islands: Sumatra, Java (the most fertile and most important island with the capital city *Batavia*), Celebes, a large part of Borneo, where diamonds and gold are found;
b) The Lesser Sunda Islands;
c) The Moluccas or the spice islands.[91]

In "Barbaric Love" as well as in *New Icarus*, Biebl speaks of the Indonesian islands as "all those islands down there." On this textbook map of Asia (which also includes much of Europe), Java, diagonally opposite to Central Europe,

90 Martin Kozák, *Zeměpis pro školy obecné* (Prague: Unie, 1904), 93.
91 Kozák, *Zeměpis*, 95.

Figure 6. "An approaching ship." Martin Kozák, *Zeměpis pro školy obecné* (Geography for public schools), 1904.

seems to be falling out of the frame, as if it were about to float out of the textbook page (Figure 5).

The engraving of "an approaching ship," in the same textbook, could easily be an illustration in one of Verne's novels, the *Voyages extraordinaires*, as they were called (Figure 6).

Biebl's childhood was forever interrupted by war, in which he fought as a teenager, and in which his father committed suicide. Forever unfinished, his childhood became a scintillating image perceived through and permeating his later experiences, clashing and blending with them, including the war and his Javanese journey.

The poetic prose "První palma" (The first palm) published in 1928, a year after Biebl returned from Java, begins with an image of the village cemetery in Slavětín. He remembers childhood by recalling the dead, perhaps in a desire to bring them to life: "Our graveyard is not large . . . in a few graves there lie many dead."[92]

Karel Hynek Mácha, who is to Czech poetry what Baudelaire is to French, wrote a century before Biebl:

> You, bright stars, you, stars in the heights!
> To you I desire to the realm of light,
> Oh, and only the earth is mine!

92 Biebl, *Cesta na Jávu*, 7.

I am a man, but a man will perish;
Into her womb again earth will embrace me.[93]

However, in "The First Palm," it is on a starless autumn night that the dead smile and, in stars' stead, light emanates from earth, from the smiling dead:

And one night in October, I don't know which one, I only know that the stars do not shine, all the farmers and goodwives in their graves smile and their gold tooth fillings glitter under the earth. All those tooth fillings were made by my father.[94]

The father's work glitters from the earth like a fairy-tale treasure. In the next sentence, but only through these images of the graveyard, as if passing through its moist soil and between corpses, we reach another, sunnier world and time, the daylight of the father's surgery, where the gold fillings were made: there and then the first palm stands.

While he was still alive, in the waiting room there was a palm. It had seven fans, one of them closed. Every morning, mother, grumbling, moved the palm into the light near the window, but as soon as she left I quickly returned it into the corner of the waiting room, into the greatest darkness, near the stove, so that one could not see that the palm was artificial. And in the winter after office hours, I, a pupil in the second grade of primary school, was hardly able to lug the heavy book with a golden lion sinking its claws into the cow leather, and there in the waiting room under that palm with pounding heart I leafed through *Brehm's Life of Animals*. Never did I feel fatigue in green jungle. . . . Never did I feel fatigue when I heard the cries of a peacock, an unmistakable sign that the tiger is near. And all the while my palm was becoming faint, bending its fan lower and lower, until it lightly touched my forehead. You poor palm! How many times did I straighten your waxed leaves, so fragile, so easily broken under the weight of villagers' gnarled sticks and umbrellas, hung there and forgotten by patients from across the fields.[95]

Again the tropics and the winter cold come together and clash: when once he took dates from the Christmas tree and hung them on the palm, his mother

took away the palm's first and last crop. — "Mummy, what are you doing?" I looked at her defiantly, as children are able to, yet with teary eyes. I could not believe that my mother, my dear mummy, couldn't grasp why it was inadmissible for the dates to hang

93 Karel Hynek Mácha, *Prosa* (Prague: Fr. Strnad, 1940), 143.
94 Biebl, *Cesta na Jávu*, 7.
95 Biebl, *Cesta na Jávu*, 7–8.

> on a fir tree, even a very beautiful one, when it could never be for them anything but a stepmother.[96]

An artificial palm with villagers' umbrellas and walking sticks hanging on it, seen through a boy's eyes—it has something of the cosmic loneliness that Mácha feels when he looks at the stars, and something of a cardboard prop in comic avant-garde theater. Czech tropical dreams, like childhood memories, are like the fragile, artificial palm.

The boy moves the first palm into darkness so that he would not fully see it in its artificial actuality. That the palm is artificial, and that the boy knows it, is at the heart of the narrative. It is not only the palm that is an imitation, an act—remember the parrot-philologist and the monkey-doctor; remember poetry and theater, one might add. A parrot's "good-evening," uttered in the morning, welcomed the poet into this circus of a world; but remember also how "the desperate monkey, whining and coughing, threw herself at flowery curtains to tear this false imitation of eternal spring." In those movements between artifice and actuality, between comedy and suffering, between flights of imagination and returns to the ground, Biebl's poetry and travel are (up)rooted.

The book-length poem *Zlom* (Break), first published a year before his journey to Java, is a poem of revolution, yet it is permeated by images and language from old Czech ballads and fairy tales. It begins:

> Poet, do not saddle a winged steed,
> we cannot follow you to the clouds,
> to earth binds us love, wrath, grief,
> let us remain on the ground![97]

The poet does and does not remain on the ground; he remains forever free and forever bound, forever charting the moment of the revolutionary "break," forever in-between flight and return, or flight and fall.

Biebl's love of dreaming is always coupled with a deep, painful awareness of the harm that dreaming and the desire for beauty may cause. There is a sense of responsibility to keep returning from dreams to the ground of actuality and action, and from oneself to others.

He remembers the beautiful, exotic animals brought home by his father, and, equally strongly, their suffering. Dying tigers and other images of colonialism in his poetry about Java strangely echo and reflect back on the happy shooting of tigers in his childhood memories.

---

96 Biebl, *Cesta na Jávu*, 8.
97 Biebl, *Zlom* (Prague: Hyperion, 1925), [5].

Similarly, he perceives the seeds of injustice in the dream world of fairy tales, and recognizes the need for a break with such dreaming—even as he struggles to hold on to something of their beauty, perhaps because it is by drawing on the power of dreams and imagination that he rebels and returns to actuality to transform it, perhaps with the dream of revolution. He rediscovers what fairy tales were for Czech writers in the nineteenth century: visions of a better world, not (only) escapes from ugly reality and from the oppression of the imagination, but real revolts against them. A critic speaks of another Biebl's poem, "Žebrák" (The beggar), as "a modern fairy tale, terribly sad and true."[98] Fairy tales keep appearing in *Break*:

One fairy tale I remember,
only a single one,
where there were no kings, princes
or princesses.

She did, didn't she, mother,
in the end survive after all,
Red Riding Hood?[99]

The "troubadour needs to be frugal with his heart, so that in time he will be able to love truly." He no longer desires palace ladies, but instead

her, who would rather love a bandit, a robber,

who at night secretly prowls around castles,
when in the land midnight calm is on the move,
only the moon and a dagger silently guide him,
and with him under ramparts they lay dynamite.[100]

98 Pavel Frankl, " Básnický projev," 148.
99 Biebl, *Zlom*, 43.
100 Biebl, *Zlom*, 45.

WHERE GRENADES FALL, THERE GREEN PALMS GROW[101]

With the eruption of the Great War, Biebl's childhood was cut short. A critic would later ask in a review of Biebl's *With the Ship that Carries Tea and Coffee*:

> At first sight one might say that the war accelerated the process of maturation and ripening of young people. But is it quite true? Was not this ripening violently rushed, maturity pathologically untimely? Has not something from that violently cut and wounded youth remained in the psyche of those who overnight became experienced and adult? And could this explain also Biebl's child-like imagination? And, moreover, hasn't the cruel experience of war lead in him, by way of a contrast, to a love of silence and intimacy?[102]

In 1916, at eighteen, Biebl went to war, first to Galicia in the easternmost borderlands of the Habsburg Empire, then to Bosnia-Herzegovina and Montenegro in southeast Europe. Already after a few months on the front, he wrote in a letter, in-between jokes:

> Nights are killing me—death—battle—bloodied skulls of classmates—all that—tortures my sick soul—and crushes the skull — —. . . But I have a good mask—and in time I will learn to laugh—just need to study my part![103]

One of his classmates later wrote:

> On a gloomy winter day Kosťa returned from the battlefield as an army runaway. In dirty army uniform, smelling of sweat and blood. Thickly overgrown. Eyes terrified by the horrors he experienced, feverish because of lack of sleep and bitter from pain. It was not the sunny, cheerful boy. Before us stood a destroyed, prematurely aged man . . . Kosťa returned home in heavy mental crisis. . . . In fever, he was vomiting blood.[104]

---

101 Biebl, *Nový Ikaros*, 20.
102 A. M. Píša, "Básník na Javě," *Host* 7 (1927): 202.
103 Letter published in Slabý, *Potkávání*, 38.
104 Quoted in Slabý, *Potkávání*, 35.

In 1916, Biebl's first year as a soldier, his father committed suicide elsewhere in the war.

From Biebl's experiences and memories, grew some quiet, intimate poems, as well as some of the most haunting images in the history of Czech poetry: images—more wounds and abysses than images—of war and death equally tactile and metaphysical, personal and anonymous; apocalyptic visions of pain and despair, at their most intimate in shuddering cosmic darkness and emptiness.

F.X. Šalda, the most influential Czech literary critic between the wars, wrote about *New Icarus*, Biebl's 1929 book-length poem which juxtaposes images of war and the tropics:

> I know little that is more shocking in Czech poetry than the conclusion of the first canto with the repeated refrain "into darkness and emptiness." . . . That has truly Mácha-esque claws. But between the vertigo of Mácha and the vertigo of *New Icarus* there lies the undefined terror of the World War. That is why *New Icarus* will remain one of a kind.[105]

"Undefined terror": for the whole of Europe, the war experience was darkness and emptiness beyond words, beyond comprehension. For many Czechs (although certainly attitudes varied), the idiocy of the war—and of greatness and imperial power—was especially dumbfounding since they went to their death not even for their own country, but for its oppressor (or at least a monarchy and a German-dominated alliance that they had few reasons to love). For a doctor's son from a Bohemian village who had liked to daydream under an artificial palm near the stove, it was an explosion that hit hard and deep, with much shrapnel. We should not expect a simple and logical picture—somehow I think of a broken mirror.

And yet, in all this, the war was a spring of poetry— "the war baptized us again." Images of war, killing, the silence of the dead, and his father's suicide, return again and again in Biebl's later work as the nuclei of his vision, his poetic cognition. The world would be seen in the shards of that broken mirror, as would the Asian colonies that he visited.

> We are different people the war baptized us again
> She gave you a new more illustrious name
> you are the poet of Death the launcher of splendid grenades[106]

Baptized again: but the reborn poet does not sing, he is

105 Quoted in Rudolf Mrázek, "Javánské motivy," 239–40.
106 Biebl, *Nový Ikaros*, 21.

a drummer gone suddenly mad who drums into darkness and emptiness
he wants to settle old scores with god who made a fool of him.[107]

The tone could not be more different, but this poet is on the same side as another "fool" living through the absurdity of the war, the good soldier Švejk.

"Splendid grenades": death and rebirth, suffering and beauty, folly and poetry, clash, blend, and mirror each other. Biebl's letters from the war give us only fragmentary glances, but in the midst of suffering, fear, desperation, disease, and killing, we can glimpse that the war was for him the first great journey into the wide world, as well as to Europe's south and to the East—a journey which prefigured his travel to Java. After a peaceful childhood in Bohemia, one of the most prosperous Habsburg lands, the World War was for Biebl a powerfully eye-opening, different experience of the Empire - an experience both of imperial violence, of an unprecedented darkness, and of the colorful wide world outside Bohemia, within and beyond the Eastern Empire's borders.

Postcards he sent from Bosnia and Montenegro show "Turkish women" in Muslim dress and with veiled faces, sometimes with palms in the background (Figure 7).[108] Years later at Port Said, on his way to Java, Biebl remembered how "during the war I viewed many mosques in Bosnia, Montenegro, and Albania."[109]

On his way to the war, to the Balkans, the "Turkey-in-Europe," as it was also known, he wrote to a friend that finally he is travelling to "the Orient of my dreams."[110] To a classmate he wrote, on a postcard with a picture of Budapest, from where he went south by train: "Accept warm greetings on way/journey to wondrous Orient."[111] (This view of southeastern Europe was not new: for example, the Czech Slavist Konstantin Jireček wrote from Belgrade some forty years before Biebl, "Here already begins the Orient.")[112] From Montenegro Biebl wrote in the first days of 1918 (after a first line in Turkish): "Pljevlja is a purely Turkish city—I have also adapted myself to Turkish lifestyle—I can say (to be honest) I have always had a predilection for 'it.'"[113] There is an alternation and mixture of cheerful exoticism and its

107 Biebl, *Nový Ikaros*, 26.

108 See letters to his mother Hermína Bieblová in the archive of the Museum of Czech Literature, Prague.

109 Biebl, *Cesta na Jávu*, 30.

110 Sent to Jiří Žantovský, who showed it to Rudolf Mrázek.

111 Published in Slabý, *Potkávání*, 42.

112 Wendy Bracewell, ed., *Orientations: An Anthology of East European Travel Writing, ca. 1550–2000* (Budapest and New York: Central European University Press, 2009), 225.

113 Slabý, *Potkávání*, 43.

Figure 7. "Greetings from Bosnia and Herzegovina, Turkish women conversing." A postcard sent home by K. Biebl from Pljevlja in Montenegro during the war, in November 1917. Archive of the Museum of Czech Literature, Prague.

satirical re-enactment, alternating with dark reports, about his experiences, fears and nightmares.

His mother wrote much later, after his suicide: "It's a pity that he never wrote his experiences from the war; it would have been another 'good soldier Švejk.'"[114] Like Švejk, Biebl found ways to undermine the pious seriousness and urgent efficiency of the "the great slaughterhouse of the world war."[115] When a friend visited him in the military hospital not far from his home village, he found "Biebl wonderfully feigned limping, and indeed he stayed there much longer than the nature of his diagnosis would suggest; when we entered a park, he no longer needed the ostentatious support of his crutches."[116] I have a wedding photo of my great-grandfather, with his hand bandaged—he shot himself in the hand to avoid going to war. Hašek dedicates a whole chapter, comical and horrific, to malingering.[117] Biebl's father was said to help soldiers on the warfront to feign sickness so that they could escape. Biebl's mother expresses gratitude and admires the "astonishing bravery" of a doctor who

114 Hermína Bieblová, *Můj syn Konstantin Biebl* (Prague: Československý spisovatel, 1955), 14.

115 Hašek, *Osudy dobrého vojáka Švejka*, 90.

116 Konrád, "O Konstantinu Bieblovi," 65; cf. Bieblová, *Můj syn*, 17.

117 Hašek, *Osudy dobrého vojáka Švejka*, 48–58.

helped her son to feign sickness.[118] Malingering was both comic and a matter of survival, just like comedy.

One of the most famous parts of *Švejk*, "Švejk's Budějovice Anabasis," is an account of a long march in a figure of 8 across the southern Bohemian countryside peopled with a population of deserters-vagabonds and deserter-friendly grandmothers and grandfathers, providing hot soup and intelligence and telling stories of desertion and malingering in this and previous wars. Yet Švejk is not deserting but dutifully searching for his regiment, although no one seems to believe it (although now even I am not sure). Biebl took enormous, ridiculous detours when he was escorting groups of Russian captives in Galicia across what should have been short distances, travelling on trains with them for days instead of hours so that he could briefly visit Prague or Slavětín.[119] When he was sent by train to the southeastern warfront, he got off in Sarajevo and walked for several weeks instead of continuing by train.[120] From Goražde, halfway between Sarajevo and Pljevlja (in Montenegro), he wrote to his classmate about his anabasis: "I am undertaking a fabulously hugely beautiful journey on foot from Sarajevo to Montenegro."[121]

Biebl wrote to his mother in 1916: "We have travelled for so many days and nights, climbing from train to train."[122] There is a close kinship between trains and Biebl's poetry. Associated with tourism, sightseeing and travel home, trains were also the movement of the war.

Into a misty landscape without horizon
lead the clasped hands of rails.
Faces sunk into helmets
of soldiers ferried away.

At a station of glass and silence
words are weighed in grams.
Rifles and bayonets ride to war.

Soldiers remained at the station.[123]

In *Švejk*, trains and train stations—and escapes from them—are part of hilarious misadventures, as thousands and thousands of soldiers are ferried to "the slaughterhouse like cattle, lead there by butchers-emperors, kings and

118 Bieblová, *Můj syn Konstantin Biebl*, 17.
119 Reported slightly differently in Konrád, "O Konstantinu Bieblovi," 65; and Bieblová, *Můj syn*, 17.
120 Bieblová, *Můj syn*, 15.
121 Postcard to Václav Kolátor, 2 Nov [1917], published in Slabý, *Potkávání*, 43.
122 Published in Slabý, *Potkávání*, 104.
123 Konstantin Biebl, *Věrný hlas* (Prague: Hyperion, 1924), 49.

other potentates and generals and by priests of all faiths"—as Hašek writes in a description of a "third-class eatery" full of soldiers at a train station.[124] There is something of Švejk in Biebl's anabasis, when he walked great distances on foot instead of staying on the train; and something of Švejk in how Biebl exploited and depicted trains during the Great War. In this, there is also something of later Biebl, "our little citizen" among the "Martians" on his way to Java. The following message from the war to his classmate, written after a three-day train ride eastward, foreshadows his later poem Globetrotters (an excerpt is translated in the last section of this book), except that there the list of places covers the whole world, connected also by steamships. The 1917 message prefigures later intersections of poetry, modern travel, and letters home—written and performed, like his exoticism, with a mix of amusement and a sense of the absurd. (The route traced by the city names starts in North Bohemia, passes through Louny—a town very near his village—then continues south to Prague, and from there far—three days on train—eastward across Moravia to the eastern front in Galicia, near today's border of Poland and Ukraine.)

Accept sincere greetings:
from Most on 5/10 at 3h 10 min
from Louny on 5/10 at 7h 3 min
from Prague on 6/10 at 6h 45min
from Olomouc on 6/10 at 11h 37 min
from Přerov on 7/10 at 4h 2 min
from Ordberk on 7/10 at 5h 47 min
from Krakow on 7/10 at 10h 1m
from Tarnov on 7/10 at 12h 52m
from Dembyc on 7/10 at 2h 6m
from Řešov on 7/10 at 5h 3m
from Přemyšl on 7/10 at 6h 58m
from Chyžóv on 8/10 at 3h 2m
from Zaguř on 8/10 at 11h 25m
from Sanok on 8/10 at 9h 35m in the evening
At Sanok on 9/10 1917.
Today I leave for a few days to Terst! I will send you a letter.
Greetings from Kosťa
Hello to Míla!
My respects to the ladies[125]

124 Hašek, *Osudy dobrého vojáka Švejka*, 90.
125 Letter to Václav Kolátor from Sanok, published in Slabý, *Potkávání*, 41–2. Except for cities with commonly used English names, I retain Biebl's Czech spelling.

Biebl's experience of the war, in its intersection with modern travel and literature, was not atypical. Karel Konrád, Biebl's schoolmate and life-long friend, went to fight on the Balkan front in 1917. His "factographic" novel *Rozchod!* (Dismiss!), about a group of eighteen-year old Czech boys, is based on his own experience. For the boys, the war meant also their first long train ride away from home, their first sight of the "gigantic beauty of the open sea,"[126] and a journey to the "south." Through the train window, "the Orient was looking inside."[127] Feelings of desperation and revulsion toward the crippling, "so deeply ridiculous"[128] war, blended with exhilaration at the sight of the peaceful, warm, "magically beautiful landscape"[129] of southeastern Europe and the Mediterranean Sea. "What a wondrous moon! Like from *The Arabian Nights*. We listened to the mysterious calling of the magically lighted space, unable to sleep in the cold of the trenches."[130] Screamed military orders were heard against the whisper of the surf, and the hated military discipline blended with the freedom of movement felt from the open sea and unfamiliar landscape—"Perhaps the most beautiful human condition is that of a wanderer."[131] One of the main characters (a real life person, an artist) "will always feel a compulsion to return to the south," in search of beauty. "Whoever but once saw palms, will always long for them, says an old Arab proverb. Anyone who has visited the south will feel the sad truthfulness of this wisdom," reflects one of the boys in the novel.[132]

At this time, over a million of Czechs—about one tenth of the population—traveled as soldiers out of their country, many of them much farther than Biebl and Konrád. Tens of thousands fought on the Russian side against their imperial "fatherland," the Austro-Hungarian Empire, and later, in the aftermath of the Soviet revolution, made their way east across Siberia to Vladivostok, from where they were evacuated across the world oceans: some further eastward, completing a journey around the world, while thousands returned by ships around Asia, stopping in Japanese and/or Chinese ports, as well as in cities that Biebl would visit a few years later: Singapore, Colombo, and Port Said. After the war, their memoirs and travelogues, some fictionalized, were widely published and read.

Sometimes one senses that the ugliness of war, even of their own actions, made the legionaries experience beauty and the greatness of the world even more intensely, with more thirst. Like other Czech travelers before and after

126 Karel Konrád, *Rozchod!* (Prague: Sfinx, 1934), 88.
127 Konrád, *Rozchod!* 159.
128 Konrád, *Rozchod!* 94.
129 Konrád, *Rozchod!* 112.
130 Konrád, *Rozchod!* 101.
131 Konrád, *Rozchod!* 148.
132 Konrád, *Rozchod!* 129–30.

them, the legionaries were awed by the sea and the great ships on which they travelled, and with undying enthusiasm marveled at the Asian port cities they visited—*all* are like from a fairy tale or *The Arabian Nights*—and tropical nature. Colonial cities overwhelmed them with unknown tastes, smells and fragrances, as well as with sights of poverty, exploitation, and colonial inequality.

War and tourism blended, also in the writing they inspired. The following passage comes from the preface to a representative collective volume by the legionaries:

> For the readers . . . views of unknown corners and tropical lands will open, hardly ever visited by Czechs before the war. They will read and follow images of the lands of the Far East, Kamchatka and magical Japan, they will learn about the beauty and the majesty of Pacific and Atlantic Oceans, they will travel in spirit with our legions across America and around Asia, they will ride into the interior of Ceylon, India and Egypt, to finally accompany them through Suez Canal and the Mediterranean Sea . . . They will participate in the most adventurous journey around the world that has ever happened.[133]

The contributions in the volume included, for example: "A Reminiscence of Java"; "Christmas in Tropical Seas"; "Quarantined in the Philippines"; "In the Hong Kong Bay"; "Impressions of Japan"; "In the Land of Chrysanthemums and Sakuras"; "On the Waves of the Pacific Ocean"; "The Sea"; as well as three chapters on Singapore and much more.

Experience was perceived through the prism of literary accounts of great journeys: titles and details of Xenophon's *Anabasis*, in connection with the overland movement eastward, and Homer's *Odyssey*, in reference to the sea journey home, were evoked especially often.[134] Adolf Zeman opens his 1920 book *Czechoslovak Odyssey*: "The Siberian anabasis of the Czechoslovak army in Russia already found enough of qualified and unqualified Xenophons, yet [our] Odyssey has not found its Homer. So I want to be its Homer . . ."[135] In Homer, Odysseus prays to see but the smoke rising from his homeland; Zeman writes that soon they, too, "will see the smoke of our Ithaca. Only, by God—may it not stink too much!"[136] The writing legionaries were conscious that they were travelers and travel-writers following in the footsteps of others: "The islands of Ceylon and Java have perhaps the most opulent tropical nature and so much has been written about them in our country

133 Adolf Zeman, ed., *Cestami Odboje* (Prague: Pokrok, 1926–1929), 5:[3].

134 The journey east across Russia was widely referred to as *anabáze* (anabasis), in reference to Xenophon's text about the march of Greek soldiers across Persia. *Anabáze* was also the title of perhaps the most famous fictionalized account, by Rudolf Medek.

135 Adolf Zeman, *Československá Odyssea* (Prague: J. Otto, 1920), 3.

136 Zeman, *Československá Odyssea*, 43.

that I wouldn't even think of repeating dithyrambs exalting Ceylon, written hundred-times before."[137] There was also a strong sense that the experience of war and travel—they were difficult to separate—lead to the "shaping of a new worldview"[138] and constituted a "great rebirth"; in Biebl's words, "the war baptized us again." Zeman writes:

> Our suffering and dangers in war, learning to know new lands and people, new nations and cultures, recognizing the infinite dimensions of the world and the seas, seeing new countries, entirely different from what we had known before, new races, old cultures—Japanese, Chinese, Indian, etc.—all those were massive shocks, which did not leave our spiritual constitution unaffected.[139]

There were times when the legionaries thought of extending the journey:

> In your mind you transport yourself into central Arabia, somewhere there, where behind the hills you guess sacred Mecca, you enter mysterious Egypt toward the valley of the life-giving Nile, and you would like so much to extend still the journey and delay the reunion with your loved ones and your native land, only to be able to see these age-blessed places.[140]

Quite a few of the legionaries, in fact, did just that. Professor Jaroslav Boháč, together with another legionary, stopped in Singapore, toured across Java, spent many months travelling through the jungles of Borneo and later around Ceylon, and recorded his experiences in a detailed travelogue, published four years before Biebl's departure.[141] His account of Java concludes: "What a pity it's not closer to our country!"[142]

Galicia, the eastern-most corner of the Austro-Hungarian Empire where Biebl was posted first, was geographically and socially far removed from Vienna. It related to the metropolis, more than some other parts of the Empire, somewhat like a distant colony. Its landscape, nature, and multi-ethnic Slavic and Jewish population were seductively exoticized and orientalized—as reflected, for example, in the title of a popular collection of stories set in the region, *Aus Halb-Asien* ("From Half-Asia), by Karl Emil Franzos. In the letters that Biebl, then a nineteen-year old soldier, was sending to his mother

137 Zeman, *Československá Odyssea*, 198.
138 Zeman, *Československá Odyssea*, 4.
139 Zeman, *Československá Odyssea*, 235.
140 Zeman, *Československá Odyssea*, 247.
141 Prof. Jaroslav Boháč, *V tropické Asii. Cesty legionáře po Singapore, Borneu a Ceylonu* (Prague: Památník Odboje, [1922]).
142 Jaroslav Boháč, "Vzpomínka na Jávu," in *Cestami odboje*, ed. Adolf Zeman (Prague: Pokrok, 1929), 5:348.

from Galicia in 1917, there are enthusiastic descriptions of long walks through "endless forests," "the sun shining in the cornflower sky," and beautiful, different nature. He sent the following letter from Sambor (in Polish) or Sambir (in Ukrainian), after which, according to some scholars, Joseph Conrad named Sambir on Borneo, the setting of his first novels:

> The weather here is truly fabulous. I am sunburned like that time long ago on Krk. Everything here is already beautifully green and exudes an intoxicating fragrance of spring. Thousands and thousands of anemones are in full bloom and one has the feeling that the ground is covered with fresh snow. Also the banks of streams in the forest are covered with thousands of flowers—marigolds, yellow buttercups, lungworts, violets, daisies, ferns and other flowers that do not grow in our country. I was thinking that it is a pity you are not here with me, where everything breathes freedom, so that you could see a spring unlike anything we have at home! In the mornings it rains almost daily, but in an hour there is not a trace of a cloud in the sky and not a trace of mud, and the sun is shining in the cornflower-colored sky almost like in Dalmatia.[143]

This letter from Sambor/Sambir on the eastern, Russian front already contains references to Krk and Dalmatia (in Croatia, on the coast of Adriatic/ Mediterranean Sea), even though it was written in May 2017, that is, *before* Biebl traveled south during the war (in October 1917). This suggests Biebl was previously on Krk at "that time long ago" (*kdysi*) perhaps on a childhood vacation. Krk was already a popular destination for Czechs before the Great War, with hiking routes marked by the Club of Czech Tourists and a large Czech-owned seaside resort for Czech vacationers in Baška (a village on Krk), a Czech tourist colony of sorts. Before the Great War, Croatia and Bohemia were parts of the Austro-Hungary, so in terms of imperial borders, this was "domestic" sea, and at that time the most accessible sunny "coast of Bohemia." Biebl went there again with his friends after the war, in 1922, and Baška, Dalmatia and the "Balkans" would figure prominently in his poetry. To my knowledge, such a childhood trip is not mentioned in any scholarly or other writings, but if it did happen, as it seems it did, it would have been the poet's first experience of a "southern sea." His "journey to the wondrous Orient" during the war in some ways evoked, the letter suggests, memories of a sunny childhood vacation —with "half-Asian" Galicia in the northeast, near the border with Russia, dissolving into the warm Mediterranean ("wherever we ride, we always ride to Batavia"). His images of the southern sea in his later poetry, connected to war and, later, to the death of his friends, might have this memory of childhood among their clashing overtones.

143 Biebl's letter to his mother, Hermína Bieblová, from Sambor, written on "first Sunday in May 1917." Archive of the Museum of Czech Literature; also published in Slabý, *Potkávání*, 107.

In "Smrt" (Death) one of many poems that return to the war in the 1920s, there are these lines:

In rose-colored rocks the crescent moon circles.
    The silver eagle
of the Balkan's clear nights.
    Let us forget all
    evil.

Yet all this—the beauty and warmth of a foreign land, the breath of freedom, the crescent moon of the *Arabian Nights*—in the midst of war and death. The poem continues:

    The blood on my bayonet will never dry.
    Darkness before me, darkness behind me.

I am able to load my gun.
I am able to saddle the horse well! To shoot!
    To kill!

But what would I do with your eyes?[144]

On this journey to the Orient in the fringes of the Austro-Hungarian Empire, beauty and suffering brutally collided—as they would a few years later in colonized Java. Empire, homeland, and the faraway intersect, somewhat like when Biebl wrote later about his home village that "our graveyard grew so much larger during the war," from Siberia to Italy.[145] Should one think back to Biebl's childhood memories of beautiful exotic birds suffering and dying of cold?

"The blood on my bayonet will never dry"—like later in the colonies, he was not a disinterested observer, but felt himself to be part of what he saw, in the same boat with murderers. From "Reservista" (Reservist):

Three years you were in Montenegro, my dove,
have not you and we killed anyone there?[146]

From "Vojenská" (Soldier's song):

144 Biebl, *Věrný hlas*, 50–51.
145 Biebl, *S lodí*, 20.
146 Biebl, *Zlom*, 19.

with uncertain eyes, holding our breath,
we stand silent like murderers.[147]

His poems often plead for the dead to be remembered, for the silenced to be heard.

The dead speak,
Only when you remember them.

After the world war
the dead crisscrossed the world,
but soon they lost their way
somewhere in the distance.
. . . .
Even if another was shooting
our deeds are in those wounds.
. . . .
Under the evening's shelter,
Let us remember the dead.
If we allowed the living to die,
Don't let the dead perish.[148]

The "poet of Death" pleads for the dead's silence to be heard. The silenced, the forgotten continue to haunt Biebl's poetry and insist on being remembered long after the war, such as in these verses from *New Icarus*, written a decade after the war's end:

The soldier blows the trumpet
but the dead do not listen
. . . .
all the dead look into emptiness
and all are silent

You the only witness of this immense tragedy
why did you not kill yourself
why did you not throw back into god's face his clay
. . . .

147 Biebl, *Věrný hlas*, 47. Biebl later revised and combined these lines from "Reservist" and "Soldier's Song" in one poem, in Biebl, *Dílo*, 1:47.

148 *Dílo*, 5:99.

Grave calm more terrible than when the war raged
the silence at night in November bombarded only by the beating of your desperate heart
You are a drummer gone suddenly mad who drums into darkness and emptiness
he wants to settle old scores with god who made a fool of him
drums the drummer drums to attack into darkness and emptiness
where all the dead gaze forward forward into darkness and emptiness[149]

149 Biebl, *Nový Ikaros*, 24, 26.

FIRST EXCURSION
PARROTS ON MOTORCYCLES: EXOTICISMS OF THE CZECH AVANT-GARDE IN THE 1920S

The word ***ŽIVOT*** (Life) is set in large bold type over a photomontage of an automobile wheel, an ancient Greek temple pillar, and the sea: a circle, parallel verticals, and a horizontal, a construction equally classical and modern. Below the blasphemous union of the temple and the automobile are the words *A Collection of New Beauty* (Figure 8).

Such was the cover of a volume published in 1922 by a group of young artists. Many of them were members of the Devětsil group, the most important organization of the emergent Czech interwar avant-garde. *Život: sborník nové krásy* (Life: a collection of new beauty) was one of two key publications. The other, *Revoluční sborník Devětsil* (Revolutionary collection Devětsil), was

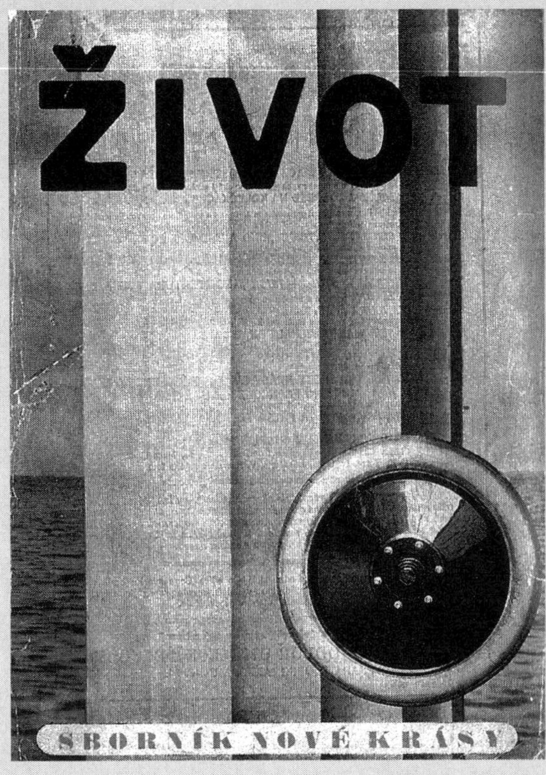

Figure 8. Cover of *Život* (Life), 1922.

published a few month before *Life*.[150] Against the backdrop of darkness and emptiness of the old world and the recent war, the volumes presented an exuberant vision of a radically new, modern world of beauty and laughter. It was inspired as much by the ideals of the Soviet communist revolution of 1917 as by the bright lights of Paris and New York; it strove to be international, yet it was also bound to, and sometimes immured in, the Czech world.[151]

Biebl's name appears in neither volume. I introduce *Life* as a point of departure for understanding the scene he was just entering and his position in it, with particular attention to the imagery and themes related to travel, internationalism, social reality, and exoticism (and, indivisibly, home and homeland) in the poetics of Devětsil and beyond. The action was already in full swing when he set foot on the stage. He would eventually become known as one of the most important poets associated with the group. At the same time, it would be limiting to see his poetry *only* through the lens of the group's collective program; his poetry is better understood as being in conversation with it, and with the diverse, individual works of Devětsil and other artists. Biebl's poetic journey was both a consummation of, and a departure from, Devětsil dreaming: *Life* was full of images of travel and "the world"—this *was* the new "life"—but whereas a few other Devětsil artists would travel in "Europe" (which, as far as their travels were concerned, meant primarily Paris and southern France), only Biebl, in a way the greatest dreamer of them all, would actually travel across oceans and to other continents.

As one leafs through *Life*, even before reading the texts, the illustrations transport one abroad, to the sea and to distant lands—starting with the Greek temple, the car wheel, and the sea on the cover. There are at least seventeen visual representations of ships, mostly photos, most of them modern ocean liners; as well as numerous pictures of cars, trains, and planes. There are New York skyscrapers, Paris (the Eiffel Tower alone is pictured several times), Tibetan monasteries, lighthouses, ports, sailors, American Indian totems, African masks, and cameras. There is America seen through stills from Hollywood movies. One finds many such images also in the poems, short stories, and articles in the volume, as well as in the Devětsil imagery generally. The manifestos in the volume celebrate the circus and especially the cinema (at that time, an entertainment inseparable from sights of faraway lands), as well as stories of sea adventure and thrillers from the American Wild West and other exotic places, in particular *verneovky*, *májovky* and *indiánky.*

---

150 J. Krejcar, ed., *Život: sborník nové krásy* (Prague: Umělecká beseda, 1922), also referred to as *Život* 2; J. Seifert and K. Teige, ed., *Revoluční sborník Devětsil* (Prague: Večernice, 1922).

151 In English, for a concise introduction to Devětsil, see Rostislav Švachá [sic], ed., *Devětsil: Czech Avant-Garde Art, Architecture and Design of the 1920s and 30s* (Oxford: Museum of Modern Art, 1990). For a more comprehensive picture of the interwar avant-garde, including Devětsil, see Sayer, *Prague.*

What the leading theoretical spokesman for the avant-garde, Karel Teige, wrote in *Life* about film, shows one side of their exoticism:

> it is not a decadent Baudelairian-Gauguinian exoticism, but a modern cosmopolitan exoticism: not the exoticism that is an escape from hyper-civilized countries to dreamed up paradises of Tahiti or the Orient, but the exoticism of transatlantic ocean liners, Pullman train cars, the Canadian Express Pacific, the exoticism of the travel diary, picture magazine, and globetrotter sensibility, which has always a fresh perception of the world.[152]

In *Life*, nonetheless, the latest wonders of modern engineering intermingle with fantasies of old-time adventure tales, which are sometimes self-consciously naïve and childlike, and childhood drawings and fairy tales are celebrated alongside *verneovky* and *indiánky*; with a certain imagination that in the same movement dreams far and returns to common, everyday things, life, and everyday modern actuality. In some ways, then, *Life* is like an ordinary picture magazine.

Josef Hora, an eminent poet and journalist (both he and Teige would come to the Wilson Station when Biebl was leaving to Java), pointed out the contradiction between the artists' "theoretical" alliance with Marxism and their orientation toward bourgeois achievements and entertainments. In their enthusiasm for the new, the modern and the technological, Hora argued, the artists forgot to question the capitalistic production process behind the new beauty. Moreover, while it is true that "*indiánky, bufalobilky*, film, and variety shows" are the life of the proletariat, "it is not the whole truth, because they are even more the life of the *petite bourgeoisie*."

> New collective beauty . . . is not in "materialistic" pleasures . . . which are for the people an alcohol that breeds mindlessness and powerlessness in the face of fate, just like the Church and the metaphysics of superstition did in the past. It is not a matter of what people laugh at and how they relax, but where their industriousness, will, and dreams of the future can gain ground. It is in the relation between a man and a woman, between two humans, between the worker and the work.[153]

Hora's criticism bears upon the artists' admiration of luxurious ocean liners or harbors vibrant with colonial trade—they too are the sites of a contradiction, in those moments when the artists seem to forget their war

---

152 [Karel] Teige, "Foto Kino Film," *Život: sborník nové krásy*, ed. J. Krejcar (Prague: Umělecká beseda, 1922), 161.

153 Josef Hora, "Mladí z Devětsilu," in *Avantgarda známá a neznámá*, ed. Štepán Vlašín et al. (Prague: Svoboda, 1971), 1:429.

Figure 9. Cover of Karel Schulz, *Sever Západ Východ Jih* (North West East South), 1923.

on capitalism, imperialism and colonialism. Except, perhaps, if one sees the ships and harbors, not just as what writers like Teige claimed them to be—models of new beauty for a better world—but as what they actually were for most of the artists—dreams of what they could afford to experience only in a Prague cinema or while reading a novel by Jules Verne; the most fantastic and most everyday experiences. Artificial palms, but also a beggar' vision of a pork roast. Modern engineering, communist ideals, and childhood dreams fused.

Teige, the author of manifestos, had to generalize; let us read the work of three Devětsil writers and listen to what their palms and ocean liners had in common and how they varied—keeping Biebl's journey in mind, of course.

"Sever-Západ-Východ-Jih" (North-West-East-South) by Karel Schulz (1899–1943) was one of the texts published in *Life.*[154] The short story's rapidly changing scenes read like a film script.

154 [Karel] Schulz, "Sever Západ Východ Jih," *Život: sborník nové krásy*, ed. J. Krejcar (Prague: Umělecká beseda, 1922), 65–73. The excerpts in the summary that follows are from these pages.

"The man who killed," walks through Prague and sees a policeman talking to a little girl lost in the city. The girl hugs the murderer, because he is nicer than the policeman. The murderer decides to take care of her.

One day, he sits at home. It is cold. The police are closing in on him. "Suddenly terror screams out of the walls of the room." He has an image of himself in a small dark cell, whose walls "strangle him earlier than the executioner's rope." Then "the murderer thinks of the world":

> He hears the rustling of palms. He tastes coconut juice and the sweetness of bananas. He walks through spacious avenues of great cities, through peripheries, and into his dreaming the sirens of Transatlantics sound. . . . The world is too beautiful not to be loved. Everywhere there are hiding places, and where there are many people, there is understanding for crime. It is possible to travel away to all continents and all the world's seas. The heart is the compass. The man who killed thinks of the world as salvation. . . . What hurts between four walls, hurts not between four horizons.

The passage from the stifling narrowness of home into the wide world is a beginning and a death: "The car of the freight train is his coffin, but also his tunnel through the world."

North. The man and the girl wander the streets of Stockholm and sleep at the train station. He finds work in the harbor, where ships from the whole world dock—from the south above all.

> The man who killed carries goods from cargo steamships in the Stockholm port, and later he works at the cranes. Large boxes of coffee (Guatemala brand) travel through the air from the ships to the shore. . . . The most precious colonial delicacies are imported into the cold city and flags on the mast ropes gaily flitter above air, song, sirens, and the little steamers and boats of ship owners. The world sings in the Stockholm harbor and the man who killed handles its song with his rough hands and daily work for 15 *ör*.

The prose is interrupted by a fictive advertisement for the "**OLYMPIC-LINE." Liverpool, Rio de Janeiro, New York, Suez, Bombay, Ceylon, Shanghai, Valparaiso, Hawaii! Safe transport, telegraphic connections with the whole world, excellent cuisine, salons, concerts, cinema!**

The man's boat capsizes in the harbor. He loses his job. He comes across a jewelry shop, and "the hungry Stockholm street pushes him into the glass" of the shop's display.

> He killed the jeweler only because he was hungry. And while blood flows across the threshold of the shop, he and the girl are already squeezing into the lower deck of a ship departing for New York.

West: New York's skyscrapers, the Brooklyn Bridge, bars on the periphery, ragtime and jazz "embrace the one who killed." An advertisement again: **GRAND THEATER VARIETY. ELECTRIC INTERNATIONAL COMPANY. WORLDWIDE IMAGINATION. EVENINGS OF JOY, ILLUSIONS AND MAGIC. Han Cho with his five Chinese. Acrobats. Jumbo! Negro** [*negerské*] **dances from Congo. Tiger man! —human head in tiger's mouth.** Like in a harbor, all the world comes together in the circus (one thinks of the "almost limitless" Nature Theater of Oklahoma in Franz Kafka's *America*). The girl joins as a dancer. The murderer tells her: "Give us more than reality can do. The world with the equator, coves, the poles, and seafarers—we do not expect it from the world, but from you."

They travel the world with the circus. One day they arrive in a small Czech town, which is "hiding behind its propriety." The poetry of the circus "opened a new world to the astonished citizens, who had been chewing on their lives," and "pale virgins in the stalls sweatily sighed during blacks' dances." The Mayor, a defender of "orderly life and morality," banned the variety after the first show. In the evening, the murderer and the dancer sit in the local cinema, more at home here, in fantasies of distant lands, than anywhere in Bohemia:

> Such moments you experienced in the evening before going to sleep, when you were very little, and your mother sat at your bed to tell you a new fairy tale. The lights go off and so does the real world. Projected on the screen is a wild and sweet tale of Klondike gold fever. Suddenly the screen is torn and in the hole appears the head of Sherlock Holmes with his pipe, pointing with his finger at the man who killed.

The murderer and the dancer barely escape the police and Holmes, who too is an agent of "orderly life and morality."

The account of the East is brief. They arrive in Moscow.

> PROLETARIANS OF ALL COUNTRIES UNITE! . . . "Old world, you taught me sins which you called laws. I believe in revolution. . . . I believe in a world and horizons without borders."

At the next moment, the murderer is in the "magical South," in Valparaiso, closest to the dream that he had at home before he left, farthest from the narrow cell that was home. He

> lies in a southern morning and his head rests among flowers. . . . Foreign port cities with magnificent names—uttering only one of them would be enough to make you happy on a rainy afternoon in your native city in the middle of Europe, exhausted by historicism like a whore by momentary love. Beautiful South, I needed you to make my world

> whole, and because of you I left Moscow, finding heart, shells, pictures, music, deeds, crabs and capsized ships on sandy beaches.

The story ends: "I love you, world, because you are exotic and because you turn."

Schulz's stories and poems recall classic adventure tales and movies. More so than the writings of other Devětsil authors, they resemble them in their atmosphere, in some of the characters, in the thrill of the narrative. Somewhat like Biebl's later poetry, they span the whole globe, moving from port to port and from continent to continent with the speed of dreams. Yet, like Biebl's later poetry about the tropics, they are also about the "small dark cell" that is home, its terrors and its fantasies; about dreaming at home. Unlike Biebl, however, Schulz never travelled to the lands he wrote about.

Dreaming at home—and dreaming in Prague cafés, as another story by Schulz reminds us. It begins, it seems to begin, in the Shanghai harbor, between temples, opium dens, and brothels.

> But woe! Indeed there was nothing true about my dreams except a small Prague café with an old waiter, a miserable band and gas lights. I always felt as a foreigner among familiar things, and in the everyday music of a café, my thoughts sailed following my desires. You too, I dreamed up, Shanghai harbor, when outside the windows the street roared like the sea and the waves almost reached the windows.[155]

The café, an institution so important for the avant-garde poets, merits a digression. Long after Biebl's death, his wife was recollecting the early days of the avant-garde: "In those days, people were meeting in the cafés.... everyone came together, debates were frank, sometimes there was even a quarrel... it connected people."[156] In one of Biebl's poems from his Javanese journey, the drowning poet has an image of heaven, where it is beautiful

> like in a café, where chandeliers glow and angels play billiard,
> there dead poets break bread buns and write poems on tables.[157]

The poem is part of the collection *With the Ship that Carries/Imports Tea and Coffee*—a direct link, for a daydreaming poet at least, between Prague cafés and Java. Just after Biebl had returned from Java, around the time he

155 Karel Schulz, *Sever Jih Západ Východ* (Prague: Vortel, 1923), 106–7.
156 Recording of interview with Marie Bieblová. Archive of the Czech Radio, Prague.
157 Biebl, *S lodí*, 43.

was preparing this collection of Javanese poems for publication, he wrote of sitting "for hours" in a café:

> Every regular café customer has his secrets, be it a student or a retiree. If you observe someone, even cautiously, he will feel it. Either he will leave, or he will scold you. You are invading his privacy, his religion. The café is a bit like the Chinese temple, Chinese *tengkleng*. The memory of the dead honored by smoking cigarettes and drinking black coffee, both of which are a part of the melancholy rituals when we remember Arnošt Ráž and Jiří Wolker.
>
> Smoking your cigarettes, sometimes you wander through faraway lands, which you hope to visit one day. If the red cigarette stub, your Bethlehem star, leads you to the north, your shoulders are weighed down by the image of a heavy fur coat.
>
> In the south it is the opposite: you can't find the matches, because they are in your pocket. You search for them around you, behind you, under the table. But who would think to look for them in a pocket when one is wearing a swimming suit?[158]

The writers, one senses, were often more at home at a café than at home. The café was a place to meet people and to be alone, to dream both with others and alone. It had something of the cinema, travel, a harbor. Dusty and ordinary, it had its own exoticism. It was a home that was also an escape from home.

The same could also be said about a boy's tropical daydreams under a paper palm at home. Indeed, these café reveries, in their willing abandonment of the here and now, in their passion for travel, are reminiscent of childhood daydreaming.

The dream of travel, the dream of home, and the dream of childhood, mirror and permeate each other, in Schulz as they do in Biebl. The "wild and sweet tale of Klondike gold fever," in the cinema, is likened to the fairy tales told by mother "when you were very little." Exotic women smoking cheap cigarettes in a harbor bar full of sailors "resemble women from fairy tales, the most beautiful ones, nymphs and princesses, from the dreams of our childhood."[159] Herman, one of Schulz's Czechs that wander the world, reminiscences as he travels across seas and through mountains in Peru and Ecuador: "This is how you saw it in your dreams, lying on your stomach in a little garden under an apple tree near the fence and with half-open mouth reading the beautiful books of Jules Verne."[160]

Schulz's dreams do not affirm home and staying at home. They reveal both the exotic beauty of this original place of fantasizing, and its claustrophobic

---

158 Biebl, *Dílo*, 5:256.
159 Schulz, *Sever*, 7.
160 Schulz, *Sever*, 8.

narrowness. Home is put into question when the dreamer in a Prague café feels like a stranger there, or when home dissolves into dreams of other lands, just like how the girl that Herman left at home dissolves into all the women he loved. Helena was her name: the archetype, the embodiment of light.

> Helena—Herman said to himself—Helena was her name. He met her one summer day in Prague, but where is Prague now? . . . perhaps it was you who I met under the scorching Javanese sun in Batavia's botanical garden, you who guided me through the low huts of Djokjokarta [i.e., Yogyakarta, in Java] and through the market in Benares, along the yellow marble of Peking temples and through Petrograd prison.[161]

Schulz does not idealize the world either. His wandering Czechs meet rough seamen, pirates, and sad women in seedy pubs in harbors. They meet poor and hungry people as well as American millionaires in great cities. We see the world through the eyes of "the man who killed." Hora, in his criticism of the avant-garde's enthusiasm for modern beauty, cited Schulz as an exception. Schulz's bustling harbors and cities are both magnificent and cruel. This, too, brings his vision, more so than that of some of their peers, closer to Biebl, despite the difference in tone. In Schulz, electrifying beauty and vitality, jazz bands, and cabarets are the other side of misery, hunger, fatigue, and emptiness. The love of life is the other side of the desire for death.

Schulz's sweeping vision of the world is reminiscent of some of Biebl's poetry, yet at their closest, I also sense a disparity: after reading Schulz's colorful, loud, so effortlessly, exuberantly free narratives, in Biebl's more melodious voice, even in his gentle satire, I sense more than ever an underlying darkness, emptiness, silence—I sense them in the shadows of the Great War and his Javanese journey, as the weight of actuality, of life.

Schulz's poem "Jazz nad mořem" (Jazz above the sea) was published in *Life* in the midst of photographs of ocean liners and an advertisement for the Holland-America Line, which all become part of the poem, itself a powerful poetic elaboration of two great motifs of Devětsil imagery, the ocean liner and jazz.[162] The poem is a whirl of images from the whole world, of sailors and gold-diggers from adventure novels and films, Longfellow and the "Indian" brand of motorcycle, dancing halls and hospitals, red flags and skyscrapers, the unemployed and miners on strike, murderers and suicides, colliding cars and tramways. A line in larger capital letters appears like a neon sign in the middle of the poem: FILL THE WORLD WITH NEW BEAUTY. All the world's beauties and suffering dance to the intense pulse of the new music above the ocean liner.

---

161 Schulz, *Sever*, 20–21.

162 K. Schulz, "Jazz nad mořem," in *Život: sborník nové krásy*, ed. J. Krejcar (Prague: Umělecká beseda, 1922), 35–38.

But here above the sea all musics are reflected from the whole world
and Transatlantic is their reception station
moved by the dancers of all dancing halls
by sighs of men buried in mines and shouts of pilots at airports
the music of concert halls collided above the ocean
and falls on us
and into the depth

In an image that—rather like some moments in Biebl's travelogue—not only evokes old narratives of adventure at sea and the circus, but also foreshadows avant-garde comic theater, a Czech poet appears above it all, as if the whole band of Czech avant-gardists were together sailing across the ocean, to Java perhaps:

on the masthead high near the sky linked by the line of the mast with the sea
and the world
Jaroslav Seifert sits
and calls
LAND

Seifert—we met him, too, at the Wilson Station—later a Nobel laureate, played a leading role in Devětsil in the early 1920s.[163] Together with Teige, he edited the *Revolutionary Collection Devětsil*. His poem "All the Beauties of the World" appears as the opening text in *Life*.

Poet, die with the stars, wither with the blossom,
Today no-one will yearn for you,
Your fame, your art will perish forever, for they are like flowers on the grave;
aeroplanes, which fiercely surge to the stars,
sing in your stead a song of iron tones
. . . .
Be silent, violin, and resound, automobile horns,
Let the man at the intersection suddenly fall into reverie,
Sing, aeroplanes, evening songs like nightingales[164]

163 For English translations of his poems from the 1920s, see Jaroslav Seifert, *The early poetry of Jaroslav Seifert*, trans. Dana Loewy (Evanston: Northwestern University Press, 1997).

164 [Jaroslav] Seifert, "Všecky krásy světa," *Život: sborník nové krásy*, ed. J Krejcar (Prague: Umělecká beseda, 1922), 5.

Modern life, actuality, here and now, is the new poetry. And yet, this orientation of Devětsil poetry, too, prefigures Biebl's actual journey to Java. The voyage—which was also a step from dreams towards the actuality of life, to life as poetry—grew as much from dreams of palms as from strolling through cities, riding on trains and admiring ocean liners and airplanes.

Even the strongly political manifestos of "proletarian art" from 1922 find the tropics at the heart of life. In the introduction to *Revolutionary Collection Devětsil*, Teige writes:

> Not stories from life in misery, not images of mines and steelworks, but of the tropics and faraway lands, poems of free and active life, which bring to the worker not the realities that crush, but realities and visions that electrify and strengthen! The writer of a communist moralizing nursery rhyme will have no success and does not bring excitement: only the passionate gesture of a speaker, an event on the movie screen, or a story from the unknown, great world, which one day will be our homeland, reaches the heart of the proletarian.[165]

Tropical fantasies and the love of actuality intersect. Both would grow even more prominent in *poetismus* ("poetism"), a movement proclaimed in 1924, with Seifert, Nezval and Biebl among its leading representatives. Poetism, in many ways continuous with the earlier "proletarian art," was also its critical re-evaluation, especially in moving even further away from "stories from the life of poverty" and "realities that crush." Teige wrote in his 1924 manifesto:

> Since [poetism] is the art of life, *the art of living and living it up*, it must eventually be as matter-of-fact, delightful and accessible like sports, love, wine and all delicacies. No individual life, if it is to be lived morally—that is: with a smile, happiness, love and dignity—can do without it.[166]
>
> The art brought by poetism is frivolous, mischievous, fantastic, playful, unheroic and erotic, with not even a pinch of romanticism. It was born in *a world that is laughing*; what of it that its eyes are teary? . . . Its emphasis moves to the delights and beauties of life, away from stuffy offices and ateliers, it is a pointer to a way that leads from nowhere to nowhere, it circles in a magnificent fragrant park, for it is the way of life.[167]

---

165 [Karel Teige], "Nové umění proletářské," *Revoluční sborník Devětsil*, 16.
166 Karel Teige, "Poetismus," 1:554–55.
167 Teige, "Poetismus," 1:556–57.

Like Seifert's "All the Beauties of the World," this already was an invitation for a walk, and perhaps a journey— "to the delights and beauties of life, away from stuffy offices and ateliers." Teige again:

> Leaving behind the concept of "art," we understand the word "poetry" [*poesie*] in its primary Greek sense: poesis, *supreme creativity*. Poetry today is not deposited in books, it is possible to make poetry with color, light, sound, movement, to make poetry with life. . . . It is poetry which shines even there, where there is not a trace of "art."[168]

As life becomes poetry, travel—in reality and in imagination, a walk in a park or a journey to the other side of the world—becomes part of the poetist *poznání* ("cognition, knowledge"), of the celebration of all the world's beauties, and of the revolutionary transformation of life in the image of, and through, poetry. Travel is part of poetism's internationalism—the dream of "the unknown, great world, which one day will be our homeland." For Teige, tourists and clowns—Biebl had a little bit of both—are among the poets of modern times: "Poetism is not literature. . . . Not philosophers and pedagogues, but clowns, dancing ladies, acrobats and tourists are the modern poets."[169] A journey to Java could now be performed, perceived, or experienced as poetry that turns to actuality and away from "philosophers and pedagogues," even at times away from writing; poetry that "wants to poetize its cosmos *[zbásniti svůj vesmír]* by all means made available by the present-day science and industry."[170] Of the Devětsil artists, only Biebl followed through —on behalf of the whole generation, as my father wrote, but perhaps also somewhat to their bewilderment—and actually travelled on ocean liners to the tropics. How he travelled and what he wrote resonated with Teige's visions, but it was also something of a break (one might recall, from *Break*: "to earth binds us love, wrath, grief / let us remain on the ground"). For example, Teige, despite his Marxist allegiance, ironically yet characteristically does not emphasize the entanglement of travel with class and colonialism—something that would weigh on Biebl's images of ocean liners and the colonies.

Let us return to Seifert. Back in 1922, in the *Revolutionary Collection Devětsil*, Seifert published his poem "Paříž" (Paris; he had not visited it yet when he wrote the poem).[171]

> I am no longer tempted to walk along the bank,
> When foggy darkness lies over Prague in the evening,

168 Karel Teige, "Manifest poetismu," *ReD* 1 (1927–28), 336.
169 Teige, "Poetismus," 1:557–58.
170 Teige, "Manifest poetismu," 334.
171 Jaroslav Seifert, "Paříž," *Revoluční sborník Devětsil*, 168–171.

. . . .
I no longer enjoy
forever walking along the same streets, where there is nothing new to see
. . . .
Am I not right, my love, here at home all things are inane,
There is no joy for us here.

And since it was not possible to be born
somewhere at the edge of dark jungle in Africa,
where the white glow of the sun sets everything on fire,
and in the branches red-haired monkeys jump,
since it was not possible in the waves of Nile
to bathe, looking into the eyes of a voracious crocodile,
to pick blooming lotus from the waves,
to escape with one leap from lion claws,
to have juicy coconuts for breakfast when hungry,
and to fall asleep in the storm of a waterfall,
since it was not possible for us to be dark and curly natives,
to warm ourselves in the rays of hot sun,
why, why is it our fate to live
in the streets of this city on the fiftieth parallel,
where fierce and passionate surge is foreign to everyone
and a good person breathes so heavily
where every feeling must wither before it's ablaze,
where on our necks we wear hard and starched collars
where instead of birds we prefer to listen to jazz bands,
and see lions only in a menagerie?
. . . .
There in the West by the Seine Paris lies.

An account of exotic Paris follows—"there are famous painters, poets, murderers, and Apaches"—and the poem ends:

At least Paris is one step closer to heaven,
come, my love, come with me to Paris.

To Paris, at least, since, even in the poem's world, the tropics can only be dreamed. In a 1923 article on poetism, the writer F. C. Weiskopf titled a section on Seifert "Africa in Žižkov." Žižkov then was the workers' quarter of Prague where Seifert grew up. Weiskopf writes: "Prague peripheries were small and Seifert set out into the far world . . . That is: he had not left, he actually remained here and only painted Žižkov with Oriental lacquers."[172] Seifert's tropics are ethereal, smiling, naïve, and mischievous: monkeys, giraffes, crocodiles and sailors drawn in colored pencils, with a large yellow sun on the top—one thinks of the greys of Žižkov, on a sunless slope facing north. It is not that these tropics are simply an escape from a dreary place; it may be, rather, that the most colorful tropical paradises thrive in cold and grey cities. My father, too, is from Žižkov.

The poet's palette has both the greys and the warm tropical colors.

I think it is sad to be only a European,
I cannot accept that fate,
God, if only I could sit in palms' shade,
or like those black women lie on the seashore.
. . . .
    a train departs,
    a ship sails,
    and an aeroplane flies above the sea
and I, sitting in a station restaurant,
weep over civilization's beauty,
what good are the aeroplanes to me, these metal birds,
if I can't fly in them,
and above me they disappear in the clouds in the distance.
O master John,
First we need to blow up Europe below the clouds,
for until that time all those charms and wonders
are triple-locked;
. . . .
perhaps, perhaps after that we will meet again
on the Ivory Coast.[173]

All Seifert's poems quoted so far were included in his 1923 collection *Samá láska* (All love). Tropical motifs here effortlessly mingle with verses about revolution ("we need to blow up Europe"), love and the city.

proscribed muse of the street,
you were there when on the banners of a circus
magnificent pictures were painted
on them a black man thwarts tiger's claws

---

172 F. C. Weiskopf, "100 Procent," in *Avantgarda známá a neznámá*, ed. Štepán Vlašín et al. (Prague: Svoboda, 1971), 1:80.

173 Jaroslav Seifert, *Samá láska* (Prague: Večernice, 1923), 53–54.

Figure 10. Otakar Mrkvička, frontispiece for Jaroslav Seifert, *Samá láska* (All love), 1923.

Figure 11. Otakar Mrkvička, illustration in Jaroslav Seifert, *Samá láska* (All love), 1923.

....
You, good muse, understand my confusion,
I want to sing everything that rocks a human being[174]

Seifert's *All Love* was illustrated by Otakar Mrkvička, a prominent member of Devětsil. The cover image shows Prague as a seaport: a large ocean-going vessel is visible floating on the sea behind Prague's Wenceslas Square. An aeroplane flies above and a red star crowns one of the buildings. The title image (Figure 10) combines a picture of the small Bohemian town Jičín (with which Seifert "fell in love ... it has a singular charm and the magic of strange plainness"),[175] Paris, New York, the sea with an ocean liner and a volcanic island. There are spruce trees in the foreground, in what appears to be Bohemian countryside, and palms in the background. A train speeds on a viaduct, a plane soars up into the sky, and, above all, the sun is shining. Other illustrations show Paris; lovers in the countryside; and a smiling sailor with a pipe in a fantasy land with palms, steamship, lighthouse, large-eyed fish, and the same glowing sun disc, the kind one sees in children's paintings (Figure 11).

174 Seifert, *Samá láska*, 8.
175 Seifert, *Všecky krásy světa*, 556–7.

The tropics, travel and the sea are even more prominent in Seifert's next, 1925 collection *Na vlnách TSF* (On the waves of TSF [Télégraphie Sans Fil, or radiotelegraphy]), one of the culminations of poetism. The poetry is more playful, free and sensual than ever, and there is little mention of "realities that crush." There are echoes of an actual journey: in 1924, the poet, together with Teige, travelled south to the seacoast, to Italy and France. Here, in the subtropics, "one step closer to heaven," the poet dreams of the tropics:

And above the terrace of the hotel "Cote d'Azur"
I fall asleep
    into a net of dreams
a red pineapple and yellow bananas
and waves like the backs of bitter fish
    by magic turned into art[176]

Seifert saw sailors and tropical fruits unloaded from ships. His images of harbors are permeated by distant tropics, which, however, "by magic turned into art," immediately acquire the character of Seifert's own exoticism, and have something of the homely intimacy and playfulness of children's poetry, or Žižkov painted into Africa. The following verses are from the poem "Přístav" (The harbor):

HELMSMAN in the evening to stroll in Marseille
mud from Singapore still on shoes

SHIP on the masts and spars among the lanterns
a parrot and a monkey thought they were at home
. . . .
CRANES and in long rows grotesque giraffes went to sleep
among the palms of an unknown continent[177]

Actuality sparks imagination, yet, especially here, the contact between the two is light and momentary, with no time for a conflict and no urge to keep returning to this, foreign actuality. In this, Seifert's poetry and his dreams are unlike Biebl's.

One part of *On the Waves of TSF* is titled "Zmrzlé ananasy a jiné lyrické anekdoty" (Frozen pineapples and other lyrical anecdotes). "I was remembering frozen pineapples," writes Seifert in the poem "Večer v kavárně" (Evening

---

176 Seifert, *Na vlnách TSF* (Prague: V. Petr, 1924), 19.
177 Jaroslav Seifert, *Na vlnách TSF*, 16.

in the café).[178] In his memoirs, there is a chapter in which the poet's granddaughter asks him for a fairy tale, and he tells her about shops selling sweets and cakes in Žižkov. As a little boy, he would stick his nose on the glass of the display case and admire the variety of candies and cakes he could not afford to taste, except for crumbs sold for a cent in a small cone made of newspaper sheets. Still, he could see the cakes and inhale the smell of baking, caramel, nuts, spices and preserved fruit—also pineapple.[179] Seifert's tropics, like his memories of childhood, have all the beauty, melancholy, and poetry of frozen pineapples and neighborhood bakeries.

It was Seifert who called Biebl's journey "an escapade." Seifert travelled only as far as France, and for most of his life he stayed in his native Prague, more a "native" there than most other poets of his generation. His parrots and monkeys, too, do not seem to have ever been torn by a desire to leave for actual tropics; their home is, with a poetic wholeness, in Žižkov.

For Vítězslav Nezval, too, travel to the tropics is a childhood memory. The following poem is titled "Na cestu" (For the road):

> I will ride away from people to Africa
> My wooden horsey will carry me there
> There will be oranges there will be figs
> and I will never be sad
>
> The horsey will neigh for you We will not cry
> if sometimes homesick we are
> rainbow-colored butterflies will entice us
> and fairy tales sky-blue fairy tales[180]

"For the Road" is in the future tense; it dreams childhood, fairy tales, and Africa into the future, like a traveler's longed-for destination, like a promised land. Elsewhere in Nezval, but also in Seifert, even the *poesis* of future revolutions, communist and anti-colonial—as a dream of happiness and life unburdened by concerns about livelihood— happens through returns to childhood imagination.

Nezval, and Šalda after him, say that childhood is significant as "a state particularly poetic"[181]—and Devětsil poetry suggests that so is travel. In Ne-

---

178 Seifert, *Na vlnách TSF*, 27.
179 Seifert, *Všecky krásy světa*, 46–50.
180 Nezval, *Pantomima*, 89.
181 F. X. Šalda, *O poezii* (Prague: Klub přátel poezie, 1970), 147.

zval's imagination, like in that of Biebl, Schulz, Seifert, or Mrkvička, trips to tropical lands overlap with returns home, to childhood dreams and fairy tales, that somewhat surreal, subconscious realm unfettered by narrow rationality.

But reflections on childhood also reveal the other side of happiness and the beauty of life—the passing of life. "Our graveyard is not large," begin Biebl's memories of childhood, which are inseparable from thoughts of his father's death. In Nezval's work, the rocking horse on which the boy will ride away to Africa appears in another poem:

Fiery roses perished
The violets' fragrance is gone
So quietly dreaming
Rides toward death
A little child on a horse[182]

Nezval's 1924 collection *Pantomima* (Pantomime), from which I quoted the poem "For the Road," was "a revolution and an inspiration" for early poetism, Teige would write a few years later.[183] According to Šalda, Nezval "most faithfully fulfilled Teige's poetist program, as an adventure of senses and ideas."[184] The often circus-like, magic-show-like, child-like playfulness and exuberant variety of colors and moods of Nezval's faraway lands in *Pantomime* is part of the variety show of styles, genres and typographies in the book, which includes poetry, plays, pantomime choreography, a film script ("photogenic poem"), a musical score, and more.

He is the true mestizo from Java
he mixes kisses and everything together[185]

Some images are closer to Seifert's mischievous monkeys and giraffes, others recall Schulz's sailors, criminals and tramps. *Pantomime* includes Nezval's poetically-theoretical manifesto "Papoušek na motocyklu" (A parrot on a motorcycle). "Behold! This is me! A collection of mental images, those parrots with magical names."[186] His definition of "poem" shows a child-like fascination with the circus of actuality: "a magical bird, a parrot on a motorcycle. Funny, cunning, and miraculous. A thing like soap, mother-of-pearl

182 "Zasnění." Nezval, *Dílo* (Prague: Československý spisovatel, 1950), 1:17. Originally published in *Most*.
183 Karel Teige, "Manifest poetismu," *ReD* 1 (1927–28), 319.
184 Šalda, *O poezii*, 146.
185 Nezval, *Pantomima*, 91.
186 Nezval, *Pantomima*, 31.

knife, or aeroplane."[187] What one might think to be the most child-friendly aspect of poetry, rhyming, for Nezval is the most magical of parrots, and one that flies across the whole globe—here Nezval comes close to Biebl's ambitions for poetry: "Rhyme: To bring close to each other remote wastelands, times, races and castes, through the consonance of a word. To invent remarkable friendships."[188]

Nezval's "Depeše na kolečkách" (Dispatch on wheels) was published in *Life* and then again in *Pantomime*.[189] It is "a vaudeville, which the author addresses to Karel Teige, Prague II, Černá 12a, Europe." It is a dispatch from tropical colonies, where the play also takes place. The prologue is sung by "buddies of all sorts, all races and both sexes, and anyone can sing with them." A police patrol arrives, locks down the pub where the scene was taking place, and puts the sign PRISON on the door, "in the name of the law . . . in the name of civilization." A policeman says:

> We are not in the mood to tolerate these masquerades! What's going on? This is supposed to be a colony! And where are the traders? The law protects them. Gentlemen, please! . . . Civilization watches over you, gentlemen!

A revolution against bourgeois art turns out to be part of a conflict between the "buddies of all kinds, all races and both sexes" on the one side, and civilization, law, and traders on the other.

A telegraphist is ordered by the police to dispatch messages "in the name of civilization." Unhappy about this, he speaks to himself:

> You are waking me from my dream!
> This is not how you imagined the colony as a child
> Oh Verne's great epics   when you sat
> under the table and the candle was burning out!

Voices from gramophones advertise "Best colonial merchandise of Mr. Walis!" "Fire powder, bullets, Brownings!" "Will supply a black man for the worst jobs!" Then the news of an uprising is heard from megaphones—workers are on strike, soldiers are deserting. The traders are alarmed: "Situation is bad. My private telephone just informed me that the so-called world revolution got out of hand and turned into a masquerade. . . . While blood flowed, we could use the army. . . . Merriment is a weapon against which we are helpless." But they swear to fight "to the last drop of their property." "Exotic

187 Nezval, *Pantomima*, 32.
188 Nezval, *Pantomima*, 31.
189 In Krejcar, *Život: sborník nové krásy*, 110–118; and Nezval, *Pantomima*, 35–49.

people" enter the scene, break into the prison/pub and free the people inside. Masks flood the stage. A sailor reports that in Europe, too, "the struggle for freedom is beginning." Music plays and a clown performs acrobatic feats. The Telegraphist is now happy: "This is how you imagined the colony as a child!" A black man shoots at the screaming gramophones and destroys them. The traders appear with guns. The clown is performing. The traders shoot each other, shouting: "Long live fighting! Long live free competition!" Everyone dances. At the end, a man runs across the stage, dressed like a circus clown with large letters on his outfit: ART.

In *Pantomime*, the text is followed by a quotation from Apollinaire: "Theater is no more life, which it interprets, than a wheel is a leg." "Dispatch on Wheels" is more like circus than an attempt at a realistic representation of a colony, and its "exotic people," colonists, and a sailor are like figures from a child's watercolor. And yet, more than in other Czech representations of the tropics at this time, the images of colonies and "exotic people" become part of a text that is explicitly political and anti-colonial. Moreover, Nezval's play, which Biebl certainly knew and most likely saw, is the kind of theater that might have been one of the inspirations behind the theatricality and style of comedy that we find in Biebl's work, especially his travelogue.

It is no coincidence that Nezval locates the action in the colonies, that capitalism, the target of revolution, is seen through images of colonial trade, that the text is a dispatch from these faraway lands, and that it is the "exotic people" who free everyone. Through the images of tropical colonies, the Czech poet shows *world* revolution for "buddies of all kinds, all races and both sexes." The mirth of vaudeville rebels in one stroke against the seriousness of bourgeois art and against colonial merchants. The future communist paradise achieved by world revolution is represented through, recognized in, circus merriment and the tropics of a child's imagination— "This is how you imagined the colony as a child!"

Among the members of the Czech avant-garde after the First World War, particularly those associated with Devětsil, there was a sense of collective effort. With their exotic imagery, they strove to address the time and place of their lives, their future, and the troubled question of where one is at home—Prague? the world? reality? dream? childhood? a better future? *Life* and the *Revolutionary Collection Devětsil* feature original and translated critical discussions of French Purism, Russian Constructivism, Primitivism, architects such as Le Corbusier (who wrote an article especially for *Life*), and more generally, international art, architecture, and cinema. Their imagery and desires were to an extent shared with revolutionary avant-gardes elsewhere in Europe, and they looked to Paris as the greatest center of new poetry—but it was their own, exotic Paris of "famous painters, poets, murderers, and Apaches," in Seifert's words.

Seifert narrates in his memoirs:

> Once on the way from a café I forced Teige to walk with me to [Queen Anne's] Summer Palace. . . . For a while he was reluctant. He was fully focused on the present moment and all museums were foreign to him. He did not allow history to charm him. . . . We sat with Teige on the balustrade, looking at the royal gardens. At the sight of the cathedral and the gloomy fortifications, my heart beat faster. But I kept silent. I was afraid that Teige might send me, with a friendly grimace, to write about it for *Národní listy* [National newspaper], which was a daily of intense nationalism and cultural reaction . . . I liked to look from here at the Prague Castle and I liked to forget all purism, constructivist functionalist architecture, helicopters landing on skyscrapers, and cold beauty of machines—things that Teige strictly decreed for us. And I fully succumbed to the magic of old places and old history.[190]

The "decrees" of avant-garde manifestos were not faithfully followed by the artists who rallied behind them. Despite a proclaimed antagonism toward art and culture that conflicted with the spirit of their manifestos, especially toward anything that could be labelled bourgeois, reactionary, or nationalist, the Devětsil artists' feelings and dreams were not entirely unlike those of their contemporaries with more or less different worldviews.

Their exotic imagery is a case in point. While it sparkled with new colors, significances and associations in avant-garde works, at the same time it had emerged from a greater sea of similar images and dreams in Czech literature and life.

For instance, the poetic prose text titled "Batavie" (Batavia), by the prominent literary and theater critic and essayist Miroslav Rutte (1889–1954), was published as the initial piece in a collection of the same title. From January 1923 till late 1930s, Rutte held an influential position as the permanent theater correspondent for the *National newspaper*, the very newspaper that for Seifert epitomizes "intense nationalism and cultural reaction." And yet, one finds that Rutte's imagery in some respects resembled that of the Devětsil avant-garde.

"Batavia" was written in 1922, the same year as when *Life* and the *Revolutionary Collection Devětsil* were published. It starts at the train station, the original point of the rift and clash between here and the faraway. Like the Devětsil poets, Rutte finds poetry in modern travel. Compare this to Biebl's departure with which I began the Preamble, the "intoxication" of the traveler

190 Seifert, *Všecky krásy světa*, 417–19.

which transforms his vision. Biebl's poetry, too, would be gripped by movement.

> [The air] reeks of titillatingly warm oil and smoke—a mysterious fragrance of the faraway—and the locomotive of strong shiny hips is beginning to move, with wise and cautious nobility. . . . It begins gently, as if someone were afraid that the faraway would penetrate too abruptly into the heart and capsize its balance. . . . But now we cross the viaduct and deep under us is the street . . . but to us it appears incredibly wretched and petty, as if everything was moved by a ridiculous mechanism, whose little wheels we cannot see. . . . So that is our life! . . . Movement has gripped us. . . . The wind that blows against our head, stuck out of the window, is not the wind of our street. It is the wind of the world. We feel in it the wide spaces of fields and the humid twilight of forests. We recognize that it descends from distant mountains, and that somewhere beyond them there are beautiful, unknown cities, whose names charmed us in childhood, when we travelled with a finger over the mysterious marks of maps, for the first time bewitched and wounded by the faraway.[191]

For Rutte, too, the journey away is a journey back into childhood, back to dreams sparked by maps, pictures, and strange names, exotic like fairy tales. ("Beyond the nine [or seven] mountains and the nine [or seven] seas" is the opening phrase of many Czech fairy tales, repeatedly evoked in the excerpt below.)

> And suddenly, touched, we recollect Batavia, the most beautiful city of our childhood dreams. Oh, we do not know anymore whether it was a picture or some label, or merely a magical foreign word, from which it was born deep in our heart. In Batavia everything was young and beautiful. In Batavia golden and red blossoms bloomed ceaselessly, the sun was shining and people smiled. And we, powerful and rich, rode through the streets and a dark-skinned girl next to us had many golden rings and a parrot on her shoulder. . . . In Batavia is our life. At home, whenever we smelled the fragrance of cinnamon and cloves, we saw our city and the wild, sad eyes of tigers. We remember cinnamon and cloves and we smile, because now we understand: it was since childhood that the faraway lived within us, a beautiful and great dream, which people created for their hearts, wounded and deserted. And suddenly we again believe that somewhere beyond the nine seas a land lies, where it is possible to begin again and where the heart can meet its hopes. Oh, what do all the petty and indifferent names of cities mean, which appear to be the destinations of our journeys? Wherever we ride, we always ride to Batavia. . . . What of it . . . that in the evening we lie down in an unfamiliar, unfriendly guesthouse like nomads, who come and go, driven by constant unrest? . . .

191 Rutte, *Batavie*, 5–6.

> What of it that the faraway will continually escape from us and that no ship will ever reach our Batavia? Boom, wheels! Run on, rails! Strike our head, wind of the world! Beyond the nine mountains and nine seas lies a beautiful land . . . We ride to Batavia![192]

Like Biebl's texts, "Batavia" is not only a reverie of exotic lands, but simultaneously a close description of the experience of modern travel, with the play of sensations, memories, and desires that is part of it. "Batavia" is the poetry of a train ride.

True, one feels—especially when one juxtaposes Rutte to Biebl—that Rutte's writing remains within the narrow dimensions of Bohemia across which the train rides, and its transformative power and span are less unsettling and more limited. It has the cozy charm of a Czech landscape seen from a train seat, not the vastness and the vertigo of the ocean flooding Prague, to evoke just one such image of Biebl. There is just enough shading to make the picture pretty with melancholy—no "darkness and emptiness." In Rutte, the realization that Batavia is merely a dream verges on reaffirming a settled reasonability, which celebrates dreaming provided it does not go too far. There is nothing revolutionary in Rutte, he is not disturbed by the "silence of the millions," at home or in the colonies, and in his Batavian fantasy he is "powerful and rich." Yet despite their differences, Rutte and Biebl use an overlapping vocabulary of experiences, sensations and dreams.

Rutte wrote about the childhood roots of his exoticism:

> My first literary attempt dates to the year 1896; then for the first time I was obsessed by the desire to write. It was aroused by an old, battered book with colorful pictures of tropical lands and animals. I pored over the book for long hours, I crawled through its bushes, I stood with black men on sugarcane plantations and climbed with monkeys up coconut palms. Those were my first journeys to Batavia. (Contribution to understanding the true genesis of my exoticism.)
>
> This book has a double serious significance in my life:
>
> 1. That for two years I desired to be the owner of a menagerie and that till now I am excited by ocean liners and cages with animals from faraway lands. (Practical consequences: I know very well the zoos in Berlin and Hamburg, and Hamburg harbor, but not a single museum in Berlin and Hamburg.)
> 2. I became a writer.
>
> . . . I loved above all *Brehm's Life of Animals*, but only mammals, then *Uncle Tom's Cabin* . . . and all *májovky* and *verneovky*.[193]

192 Rutte, *Batavie*, 9–10.

193 Rutte, "Jak jsem se stal spisovatelem a co z toho povstalo," *Rozpravy Aventina* 1, no. 3 (1925): 28.

Imagery and obsessions strongly characteristic of the Devětsil avant-garde, including imaginary trips to Java, were not theirs alone; and Biebl and his poetry are part of a larger landscape than that of Devětsil. By way of illustration: two of Biebl's books, published in 1925 and 1926, were delightfully illustrated and designed by Josef Čapek (Figure 13, page 111). He was older than, and not associated with, the Devětsil artists. However, his brightly colorful paintings—often evoking folk and popular art—of sailors, French ports, or the Black King, as well as Czech villages and especially children, his illustrations of translated French poetry and novels, and his writings in many ways resonated with (and to an extent anticipated) the imagery of Biebl and other Devětsil artists.

Beyond recognized writers like Rutte and visual artists like Čapek, in the 1920s all sorts of exoticisms flourished, from movies about faraway lands, to widely popular stories and novels written by Czech authors who actually travelled to the tropics, to the *tramp/tremp* movement: a widespread (anti-) social phenomenon, which began in the 1920s, and which was inspired in large part by adventure books by authors such as Jack London and Karl May, as well as films about the Wild West. "Tramps" were escaping the city, wandering through and camping in forests. "Tramp songs," sung at camp fires, were/are typically about the Wild West, sailors, exotic women (such as *Malajka*, "Malay woman"), and tropical islands. Richly illustrated popular travel magazines—one of which we will examine in some detail in the second part of this book—show in another way some of the same desires and dreams as the poetic writings of Biebl, Seifert, Schulz, and Nezval. In "A Parrot on a Motorcycle," Nezval writes that "the nervous health of 20th century is a precondition of modern poetry."[194] The particular "nervous health" of the time conditioned not just the avant-garde, but other literary, cultural, and social phenomena of the 1920s. Still, the Devětsil poets discussed here were closest to Biebl poetically and politically, and his journey to Java was to an extent a fruit of their shared, distinct imagination. It was with travel-intoxicated images of these friends—Seifert, Nezval, Teige, Hora, and Konrád (with his war novel *Dismiss!*)—that Biebl begins his travelogue to Java.

A shared imagination—and yet, each Czech writer's palms, ships, sailors and Paris were different. That is certainly true about Biebl and his relationship to the other poets of his generation.

He was writing poetry already during the war (as he reports in his letters), and started to publish soon after the war's end, in January 1919. At that

194 Nezval, *Pantomima*, 30.

time, his poems appeared in student periodicals in Louny, a town near his village, where he also attended middle school. His earliest development as a poet thus started outside the center, before he began to associate with other members of the avant-garde. In 1921 he moved more permanently to Prague. He began to meet and eventually develop close friendships with other young rising stars of poetry, such as Nezval, Kalista, and Jiří Wolker, and later to publish poems in their periodicals. However, even in late 1922, when the *Revolutionary Collection Devětsil* and *Life* were published, Biebl still neither contributed to these volumes, nor was he mentioned in the list of "active members and collaborators of Devětsil."[195] Although he had associated with the poets and artist much earlier, he officially became a member of Devětsil (which was founded in 1920) only in 1926. For comparison, Seifert and Teige were founding members, while Nezval joined in 1922.

Biebl was always both an insider and an outsider. He was sociable and well-liked, but even when he resided in Prague, he was often away, back in his village. In his memoirs, Nezval writes:

> He had several worlds and in each a different kind of people that attracted him. Among them were soldier friends, colleagues from the medical faculty, neighbors from Louny and Slavětín, women from the most diverse backgrounds, and literary people from various cafés. In their company he was escaping from some to the others and from himself.[196]

Šalda, writing about Biebl's poetry, called him a "wistful, timid, melancholy man. . . . *Pierot lunaire*, too, has his charm and poetry. Pierot lunaire, the little Peter who fell from the moon and who feels somewhat unsure on this wildly spinning planet."[197] The "little Peter"—yet in giving a feeling of his timidity, imagery turns both cosmic and comic, like Biebl's own "little citizen" on "Mars." Kalista, too, felt that Biebl travelled to and fro between this and another, distant realm:

> We approached Biebl's world—and yet we were not able to say that we penetrated it! . . . On first sight there was nothing conspicuous about him. . . . Still, when he began telling you about one of his dreams, at that moment you felt the current of his fantasy carrying you away to another, visionary world. No, he certainly did not dream it the way he told it. It is not possible that someone would remember a dream with all those details, on which he elaborated in his narration. It was as if he was just then dreaming and living the dream, with open eyes. . . . And it was not just with the stories of his

195 Seifert and Teige, *Revoluční sborník Devětsil*, [207].
196 Nezval, *Z mého života*, 218.
197 Šalda, *O poezii*, 160.

> dreams that you felt that he is dreaming while awake. . . . He would begin to tell about an experience from the time when he served as a soldier in Herzegovina. And soon you stood in a desolate night in the midst of steep rocks of Herzegovina, you heard an odd whistle and you inadvertently crouched your shoulders before what might at the next moment jump at you from the darkness.[198]

Fighting in the war, that first great journey, was for Biebl the single most pervasively unsettling experience, and one that set him (along with Konrád) apart from other leading poets of his generation, who were slightly younger. "Marks of what they saw, branded into them by the war, enriched—how grotesque this word is—their work. They were richer for this evil experience," wrote Seifert about Biebl and Konrád.[199] In 1921, Biebl began to study medicine, and although he did not finish, surreally cold encounters with death and the dissection of human bodies affected his poetry. "Biebl is a medic," a critic characterized his work.[200] In the summer of 1922, Biebl and Wolker, a close friend and a poet whose work Biebl immensely admired, traveled south to the sea. They spent a happy month in the seaside town Baška on the Krk Island in Croatia—a Czech resort of sorts, and the most easily accessible warm sea, one that Biebl probably visited during his childhood. There he met, among others, Jarmila Mikšovská, who fell in love with him, and they exchanged letters until her premature death. In 1924, Wolker died of tuberculosis at the age of 24, followed in 1925 by Mikšovská; four of the companions with whom Biebl spent that 1922 summer in Baška and who then "believed that Dalmatian sun is the best physician for ill lungs," all died by this time.[201] Biebl himself lived with the fear, or belief, that he had contracted tuberculosis. Also in 1925, another person very close to Biebl passed away prematurely: his uncle and mentor, the poet Arnošt Ráž, whom Biebl "terribly liked,"[202] and with whom he co-authored the 1923 collection of poems *Cesta k lidem* (Journey/way to people), Biebl's first book publication. The deaths of Wolker, Ráž, and Mikšovská, alongside with Biebl's war experiences and the images of corpses on dissecting table, are a constant presence in Biebl's poetry, not concepts, but lived darkness and emptiness.

One might trace Biebl's development (keeping in mind that there was a strong continuity across the art movements) from early lyrical poems and "proletarian poetry" to an involvement with poetism (in the mid-1920s) and surrealism (from the late 1920s and in the 1930s), to poetry more explicitly

---

198 Kalista, *Tváře ve stínu*, 224–5.
199 Seifert, *Všecky krásy světa*, 226.
200 Frankl, "Básnický projev,"147.
201 Biebl, *Dílo*, 5:167 and (for Biebl's memories of the 1922 summer in Baška) 5:159–68.
202 Interview with Marie Bieblová, Czech Radio, 1968.

engaged with communist and anti-imperialist ideologies (especially from 1945 till his death in 1951). Biebl was listening carefully and engaging with his contemporaries, in an atmosphere of "passionate love for perfect craftsmanship," which Šalda pointed out as a strength of the "youngest Czech poetry." However, on the whole, Biebl's poetry, often intensely personal, was always more than just an expression of any collective artistic program or political ideology, and even poems that strongly resonated with the work and ideas of his time were his own. And while, in the later part of the 1920s, tropical imagery begins to recede in the work of other writers, in Biebl's poetry it persists, in changing tonalities, until his death.

METAPHORS, DREAMS, TRAVEL

Biebl first saw a banana blossom in Port Said. He stopped there briefly on his way to Java in 1926. He was learning Malay during his voyage and perhaps he knew, or perhaps not, that in that language, the banana flower is called *jantung pisang*, "banana heart."

> Darkly black, almost violet! And the shape! God, where have I seen it? —I know now! It is the heart of the drowned prostitute, which I once extracted in the dissecting room. I don't know where that thought came from, to hold again the blossom in my hand, her banana heart.[203]

The experiences in the early 1920s—here it is the dissecting room in the medical school—continued to haunt Biebl's poetic vision, and they, like the prostitute's heart recollected at Port Said, persist in the images of his tropical travels. He wrote to his mother from Port Said: "We saw our first growing bananas, they are huge green grapes [*hrozny*], much bigger than what we usually see in delicatessen shops."[204] This seems to be a wide-eyed, open-mouthed child overwhelmed by sheer novelty. But first encounters would also be moments of recognition, the kind that gives birth to a metaphor.

"Oriental motifs" as well as images of the sea and faraway journeys appear even in Biebl's earliest poems, and become increasingly prominent in his poetry at the time of poetism. However, it would be misleading to focus too narrowly on this obvious "exoticism," which anticipates Biebl's journey to Java, or to see images of the East, the tropics, or the sea, merely as exotic. We get a richer picture if we reflect more broadly on Biebl's poetic vision—with its particular powers of association and paths of imagination—as it developed during the few years before his voyage; and on the liaisons linking poetic metaphors (juxtapositions, displacements), dreaming and travel. A continuity in his poetry—animated in transformative moments of recognition, like when he recognized the banana heart—is part of how Biebl saw the colonies: the beauty, displacement, perverted justice, and suffering there were and were not different from home.

---

203 Biebl, *Cesta na Jávu*, 29.

204 Letter published in Slabý, *Potkávání*, 116.

One of his very early poems, titled "Sníh" (Snow), was written in January 1919, immediately after his return from the World War:

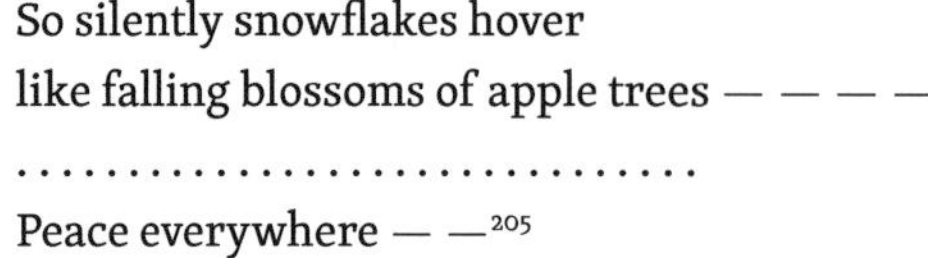

So silently snowflakes hover
like falling blossoms of apple trees — — — —
. . . .
Peace everywhere — —[205]

No exoticism here. Yet the first two lines already bring silently together two seemingly incompatible worlds, discovering the warmth and fragrance of late spring in "winter tenderness," like a soft foreshadowing of the coming together of home and the tropics. One may recall the more screechingly colorful and painful image, a memory of earlier years but written during Second World War: the exotic birds in the childhood home looking at the snow outside the window—which is and is not like a mirror—and "the desperate monkey, whining and coughing, [which] threw herself at flowery curtains to tear this false imitation of eternal spring."

The poem brings together other contraries: words and silence. It evokes silence through words ("So silently . . .") and punctuation (hyphen in Czech is *pomlčka*, from *mlčet*, "to keep silent"). It only hesitatingly, softly blends into silence, careful not to break it. "Peace everywhere— —" The war has just ended. But the silence of this poem is not the darkness and emptiness of nightmarish memories—although it may be their other face—but the silence of marveling at the wide world in each snowflake, in each flower.

Three minarets appear in another early poem, "Jeden den doma" (One day at home), from 1921:

All roads lead not to Rome, but under a young birch on the first clearing,
where (this much you can disclose) the softest moss will bloom in the evening.— —
And above you the great bellflowers Hoblík and Ranská mountains
and below them from a manor's yard poplars look to heavens like three minarets.[206]

Minarets are an "Oriental motif," but not simply an exotic Other. Tall, slim poplars are a familiar sight in Czech countryside. Mácha writes that they awaken "an unspeakably sorrowful feeling," for they reminded him of "the distant, unclearly marked pilgrimage of life."[207] The minarets that Biebl saw in southeastern Europe as a soldier, in which he then recognized the minarets of *The Arabian Nights* and other fairy images of Orient, are now recognized in

205 Biebl, *Dílo*, 5:13.
206 Biebl, *Dílo*, 5:52.
207 Karel Janský, *Karel Hynek Mácha: Život uchvatitele krásy* (Prague: Melantrich, 1953), 103–4.

poplars in North Bohemia, as they "look to heaven." In a letter written two decades later, in which he reports from South Bohemia, with amusement, on the "preaching" of a village priest about the local history of Turkish invasion, he mentions "Turks . . . enticing inexperienced Christian girls to their minarets."[208] One may suspect that in the poem, this near-silent evocation of "minaret," in intimate proximity to the "softest moss," was also a part of the tender image. Czech countryside, dreams of beauty in the warzone, and *The Arabian Nights* come lovingly together in a single landscape, which becomes more lusciously home—somewhat like the "door in the neighborhood of an ocean . . . a matter of revealing actuality, to give it its shining form like on the first day."

This momentary image of poplars-minarets mirrors others in the poem. The great world of imperial Rome is juxtaposed/displaced with a smile, to the familiar countryside, and the intimate "softest moss" displaces Rome as the center of the world. The mountains above are bellflowers—the great and the miniscule are again seen one in the other. In the fragment from "One Day at Home," in this gentle love-making of opposites, we already can see exoticism as well as how it is transcended—like when snowflakes become apple blossoms, but now, two years later, the poet's thoughts travel farther and his juxtapositions and displacements are more adventurous. On the other hand, "One Day at Home" both faintly foreshadows and differs from—like one day at home next to a journey to Java—the expansive vision of the mestiza Earth in *New Icarus*, which was composed after the poet's return from the East Indies.

I wonder if Biebl was remembering this poem (with what smile? with what image of hot Mexican desert or the Mediterranean Sea in Czech winter?) when a year later, in 1922, he sent a Christmas greeting to Jarmila Mikšovská, the young lady whom he met that summer on the island of Krk in Dalmatia. It is a postcard with a picture of his village. He wrote "our house" to indicate where he lives, and, next to poplars in the picture, he wrote: "these are not cacti, these are poplars."[209] Five years on, he wrote a caption for a photo from his sea voyage: "The ship *Yorck*. In the background, not mountains, but the waves of the Indian Ocean."[210]

"One Day at Home" is a long narrative poem about a journey, whose destination is home. It starts with a train ride from Prague to Slavětín, and most of the poem tells about time spent at home, as the narrator meets family and Typhoon—not a tropical cyclone, but their dog—eats a dinner cooked by his mother, and wanders about the village. Published in the summer holiday issue of a student periodical in nearby Louny, it is appropriately mischievous

208 Letter published in Slabý, *Potkávání*, 72.
209 Letter published in Slabý, *Potkávání*, 55.
210 Konstantin Biebl, "Ceylon," *Domov a svět* 1, no. 10 (1927): 3.

and mostly light-hearted, full of the tastes and smells of homely food, village gossip, memories of school, and an unromantic but exuberant enjoyment of free nature. Prague is evoked only by the image of a friend left behind in the city on a "creaky bed," "with cold salami in the stomach" (what a cruel juxtaposition with the warm dinner cooked by mother!). Slavětín is not romanticized, but for the student, the village home does appear like an exotic Island of the Blessed.

"One Day at Home" (along with Wolker's "Svatý kopeček" [Little holy hill], also from 1921) is one of the first Czech responses to Karel Čapek's 1919 translation of Guillaume Apollinaire's "Zone," which inspired a new poetic form in Czech poetry. Biebl's later *New Icarus* would become one of the greatest Czech poems written in that form. But the juxtaposition of "One Day at Home" and "Zone," and of Biebl's Slavětín with Apollinaire's Paris in their poems, is a bit like the juxtaposition of the "softest moss" and holy Rome in Biebl's poem. One suspects, also from the light tone of "One Day at Home," that if one can speak of inspiration, it was taken up with a smile, rather like when the poet depicted himself, "our little citizen," next to tougher travelers more at home at sea.

The following poem, published in 1923 in a periodical and then in 1924 in Biebl's first single-authored collection, is titled "Motýl" (The butterfly).

On the waves of flower stems and on the waves of grass
Into the distance a little boat drifts with white sails.
Propelled by the sun like by fair wind.
To red blossoms she sails, to coral islands.

Over vast seas to sail and sail,
in faraway lands silently to come to rest,
and to sail, farther to sail!

Above green waters a bird soars—
In a storm the little boat rocks.
I could still glimpse the sinking wreck.

The sea gives nothing back.[211]

Snowflakes are apple blossoms; poplars, minarets; and here, a homely meadow is the faraway sea, red flowers are coral islands, and the butterfly, a boat. They are and they are not. In the landlocked country, the sea (and

211 Biebl, *Věrný hlas*, 24.

Figure 12. Title page image by Cyril Bouda in K. Biebl, *Věrný hlas* (Faithful voice), 1924.

especially tropical sea, with coral reefs) epitomizes vast distances and open space, the otherest Other of Czech landscape. Biebl tests poetry's power to bring home and the faraway together. We see a Czech meadow more richly as the faraway sea, "like on the first day"; a little red flower more intensely as a coral island.

However, the sailboat is not simply a metaphor serving to elaborate an original image, the butterfly. In fact, a draft of this poem is titled "Plachetnice" (Sailboat), and it mentions no butterfly or meadow.[212] In the published version above, the title "Butterfly" does not establish the original image, but upsets origins, originality and hierarchy. The poem is less about a single place, but it instigates movement and mirroring between apparently distant worlds. The double poetic image of the butterfly | sailboat is, to use Nezval's term, "unanchored"[213]—precariously so, like the butterfly, like the sailboat. In this, and in the widening distances between the worlds juxtaposed in the poem—compared to snowflakes and apple blossoms—one senses an increasing freedom and spatial openness of poetic imagination, like a ship that leaves from the safety of the harbor "over vast seas to sail." (Figure 12)

Less than a year before his journey to Java, Biebl published a brief prose piece "Moře" (The sea), where he wrote:

> The sea, too, has its comrades and friends. They are sown fields, meadows and clouds. It is the cloth on a billiard table, uniforms of Italian legionaries and the emerald that our teacher wore on his tie.[214]

212 Archive of the Museum of Czech Literature.
213 Vítězslav Nezval, *Moderní básnické směry* (Prague: Dědictví Komenského, 1937), 9–25.
214 Biebl, *Dílo*, 5:189.

Here poetry begins to liberate, break down boundaries, and establish camaraderie and friendships across apparently disparate realms and vast distances.

The alchemy of poetic metaphors involves an intercourse between dreaming and actuality. Biebl writes:

> I love actuality but also dreaming, and thus I like to move on the border between the two worlds, where actuality overflows into dream and dream into actuality, where beauty is born from a beautiful sight and resonates for a long time behind closed eyes. I am a traveler of all eras and the most various dreams.[215]

One finds this movement of consciousness in Biebl's texts in many variations: the movement from seeing to (day)dreaming, in which memories, fantasies, desires, distant places and bygone times overflow into actuality, and actuality explodes into fantasy—such as when the boy sees an artificial palm and gets lost in the jungle, or when a butterfly fluttering above the grass awakens a desire to "sail, farther to sail" across vast seas.

> It was in primary school, in the first grade, that I first saw the sea. The old parish priest was unrolling something. One end slipped out of his hand, and the Holy Land unrolled down all the way to his shoes. He hung it on the blackboard. A map. . . .
>
> "This is the sea," said the vicar and sailed with his fat hand across the large green plane, and because the sea was then all dusty, he wiped his hand with a handkerchief.
>
> . . . when someone came in, he had to walk under the sea.
>
> Whole days I was looking at the map. Koudský was the worst reader in the whole class and he was breaking words apart with difficulty as if they were wagons. The teacher looked out of the window at the chestnut trees, blooming and fragrant. . . . The map began to overflow onto the green wall and soon the whole classroom was surrounded by sea. We were on an island, little Robinsons, and we hunted giraffes and elephants on postage stamps. The teacher had red eyes and from his cane we made an Indian bow.[216]

The text could be read as a comic phenomenology of the movement from seeing to dreaming, a description of daydreaming in its actuality. The sea, tropical islands, novels such as Robinson Crusoe, fantasies of being an Indian, images on postage stamps—all are drawn into a maelstrom of imagination by a dusty map, so much like the artificial palm. The travels in the imagination would not be the same, the achievement and futility of poetry so ecstatic, the

215 Biebl, *Cesta na Jávu*, 78–79.
216 Biebl, *Dílo*, 5:188–89.

comedy so poetic, without the dust and the vicar's "fat hand" sailing across the seas.

This kind of dreaming is the kernel of Biebl's poetic metaphors; dreaming that, like metaphor, is and is not travel. It is also a form of (re)cognition (*poznání*), like when the traveler in a strange land sees a banana blossom and thinks back to the prostitute's heart on dissection table, when he remembers suffering and death upon seeing beauty and life. It is dreaming that crosses the boundaries between apparently distant or incompatible realms and that frees—and doesn't free—from the constraints of space and time.

But also: dreaming ever anew inspired and forever cut short by actuality, forever returning from distant lands.

WORKERS . . . INDIANS!

In "Where we would like to be now," Biebl quotes Baudelaire: "Why should I go on faraway journeys, if my soul travels so easily, so quickly and lightly?" Biebl reflects:

> In Baudelaire's sense, we are all travelers. Each of us has, at one time or another, put down the book or pen in the office and looked somewhere indefinite. Through how many mysterious lands do lovers walk together, without stepping away from a window above an empty yard, and across how many burning prairies do children run barefoot.[217]

"I love actuality but also dreaming . . ."—yet, Biebl never travelled away from actuality for long. Dreaming is the source of revealing metaphors, but it is also a danger. In his poetry, flights of imagination mirror falls, and dreaming is ever interrupted by abrupt awakenings. He wrote about his first day on a tropical island: "dreaming takes revenge when it is realized."[218]

The journalist and writer Karel Nový wrote about Biebl's return from Java: "But he saw everywhere only the world of hard labor on plantations and white people's pursue of Mammon. With a joyless heart he returned back to his homeland—after a vain pilgrimage toward a mirage."[219] Biebl was indeed struck by the reality in the colonies, as Nový suggests, but it was a reality to which his poetry was open, even congenial. If it was an awakening, it was one that was always at the heart of his poetry, his cognition/knowledge (*poznání*) of actuality. The pilgrimage expanded Biebl's poetic actuality, and in this it was not in vain.

> *Primeval Forest*
> In the treetops monkeys and many-colored birds sleep
> under blue sky—

---

217 Biebl, *Cesta na Jávu*, 79.
218 Biebl, *Cesta na Jávu*, 53.
219 Editorial comment in *Domov a svět* 18 (1928): 7.

On the frozen window fall
  a flower,
  a leaf,
  a tree,
trees, jungles —

In my breath palms have disappeared,
in it a herd of elephants vanishes,
the flight of night moths,
even the gazelle's light steps.[220]

Not actions, not even words: just the poet's *breath* has this destructive power. Responsibility and guilt again; colorful exotic birds dying in the poet's house as they, too, look at the snow outside: it is not simply for the sake of beauty that the poet treads gently, weighs words carefully, and often prefers silence.

"Primeval Forest" was published two years before the poet's actual journey to Java. In *New Icarus*, which appeared two years after his return, there are these lines—the poetic voice now speaks from the Dutch East Indies:

how long ago was it in winter I stood by the window afraid to breathe on these palm leaves
their feverish shadows fall far into my dreams
again I am afraid to breathe that they may not vanish anew
it is enough that the Dutch are breathing deeply on everything[221]

The pane of glass between two worlds, the window-mirror-film with images forming and disappearing on it, embodies something of Biebl's poetic cognition, a fragile mirroring of looking out and mirroring. Not just that, and not just the particular images, but also his self-consciousness (another side of mirroring) of the later anticolonial sentiments, was already foreshadowed in the earlier poem— "in my breath palms have disappeared." (Something of the image—and the clash of opposites, the tropics and the home in winter—appears even earlier, in Biebl's letter from 1916, from the World War: "It is the Frost that creates tropical flowers on windows as they get colder.")[222] The actual pilgrimage was not in vain: it *further* expanded and sharpened the poet's vision, and gave a new intensity to the encounter between dreams and actuality. Now the tone is darker, harsher, and feverish, with an explicit mention of "the Dutch," as well as an anxiety about his complicity.

220 "Prales," in Biebl, *Věrný hlas*, 24; published as "U okna" (At the window) in Biebl, *Dílo*, 1:93.
221 Biebl, *Nový Ikaros*, 53.
222 Letter published in Slabý, *Potkávání*, 39.

In the following lines from the poem "Žebrák" (The beggar) published in 1924—the poem that a critic called "a modern fairy tale, terribly sad and true"[223]—an uprising starts from a dream; a dream for some, a nightmare for others.

A hand, pale and severed,
like a translucent dream it appears,
from steaming dishes it sails out,
for the gold of the rich it reaches.[224]

Images of (American) Indians, the "red men," we have seen, figure prominently in Czech imagination of faraway lands. The following poem, published in the same collection and on pages immediately preceding "The Beggar," foreshadows the poet's later images of colonialism and crossed out race, and helps one to sense their Leninist inspirations. Titled "Indián" (Indian [i.e., Native American]), it begins from a figure (wooden and painted, I imagine) of an "Indian" in front of a cinema that would no doubt show Westerns:

Outside the "Louvre" cinema, when dusk falls,
leaning against the wall an Indian stands.
In his hair feathers, in his hands a tomahawk he holds.

Beyond the sea there's a beautiful land. Who remembers still, whose
are those plantations, prairies, and woods?

Columbus discovered America
and capitalists the power of red warriors.
From native soil, taken away from them,
only labor in the fields remains,
from forests only the saw and the ax.
Gold they panned from their hands.

What is the view into the distance like, from under a shielding hand,
where herds of buffalos graze, at a lost land?

On the main promenade in Prague at six o'clock,
in their faces wrinkles and soot, workers are walking back from work,
garb ingrained with poverty, yet underneath you sense power,
each carries his tool on his shoulder.

223 Pavel Frankl, " Básnický projev," 148.
224 Biebl, *Věrný hlas*, 44.

Workers walk, son next to father,
past silk and gold and a movie theater.

In a curious half-circle the Indian stands.

He has a bitter smile. His eyes he might not even raise.
Quietly he might tell them: Indians![225]

From the wooden figure of the exotic, stereotyped "Indian," like from the artificial first palm, poetic dreaming begins, in which a recognition takes place: distances and racial differences are bridged, the silenced from different continents recognize their common destiny, and the "Indian" may feel that he shares a common lot with Czech workers, his "red brothers." Freedom of association(s)—such as the double connotation of "red" (with "Indians" and communism)—partakes in the "free love" of associations that "extend their hands toward each other across oceans."

Biebl's poetic metaphors and interplay between dreaming and actuality that annihilate boundaries and distances, are interwoven with communist internationalism. Biebl was at this time (since 1922) already a member of the Communist Party of Czechoslovakia. Communism was a new, hopeful dream, shared by many in Biebl's time; it was dreamt in particular ways in 1920s Prague, and it was dreamt in a particularly personal way by Biebl. For him, the communist inspiration was all the more profound because certain communist ideas resonated with his own, and had become part of his poetic vision, of the workings of his poetry. "Social reality/actuality [*společenská skutečnost*]"—a term used by a critic in a review of Biebl's first book,[226] as well as by others later—is part of actuality [*skutečnost*], to whose *poznání* (cognition) Biebl's poetry aspires. Its focus on all beings who suffer and are silenced—people dying of sickness, the individuals and the millions killed in war created by "butchers-emperors," people suffering any kind of injustice—grew early from personal experiences, and later blended with, but never quite disappeared in, a communist awareness of social actuality and dreams of better world. Concern with Czech workers would expand into a concern with people on all continents, especially in the colonies; the poem charts this potentiality of poetic cognition.

On Wenceslas Square, where the "Indian" from the previous poem stands, there is a monumental bronze statue of St. Wenceslas (c. 907–935), the Duke of Bohemia, who became the patron saint and a symbol of the Czech state.

225 Biebl, *Věrný hlas*, 42–45.
226 Frankl, "Básnický projev," 149.

The title of another Biebl's poem, "Svatý Václave" (Saint Wenceslas), is in the vocative case, as when he is addressed in prayer.

Saint Wenceslas
You are ours no more.
We are not your kin!

On an iron horse
leading the police,
armed from head to toe,
Saint Wenceslas,
you commanded to fire
at defenseless workers.

You are ours no more.
We are not your race!

We pray under the vast sky:

"Lenin,
lord of the earth!"[227]

The last word of the poem, *země*, which I translate as "the earth," can mean soil, ground, land, country, the Earth. St. Wenceslas, in a phrase that every Czech schoolchild knows, is *vévoda země české*, the Lord of Czech Land—here *země* translates as "land" in the sense of country and, for Czechs, the homeland. Biebl, at the end of this poem, evokes this phrase, but substitutes Lenin for Wenceslas, and omits the word *české*, Czech, so that the meaning now tends toward *země* in the sense of the Earth, while still retaining its ambiguity and especially a tension with—an uneasy departure from—the original phrase ingrained in Czech national self-imagination. Lenin takes the place of Wenceslas as the leader and saint, and the Earth replaces the Czech Land. Lost in translation are the connections within Czech language, which support the semantic movement from a nation-state to the Earth. It is the same earth as in *"Již vzhůru psanci této země!"* (Arise now, outcasts of this earth/land!), the Czech version of *"Debout, les damnés de la terre,"* the first line of The International (*L'Internationale*), the communist anthem.

The poem was published on 22nd February 1925 in the communist newspaper *Red Right*, less than two weeks after the police opened fire at demonstra-

227 Biebl, *Dílo*, 5:117.

tors against rising prices, who were marching across the Wenceslas Square. This was neither the first nor the last such shooting in Czechoslovakia under Tomáš Garrigue Masaryk, a philosopher and the country's revered first president, who often appeared in public and on photographs riding his horse. Readers of Biebl's "Saint Wenceslas" no doubt recognized Masaryk in the poet's image of the saint.

What does this poem reveal about Biebl's vision of homeland and the world? Bourgeois nationalism and the nation-state fire at the workers and can be "ours no more." Lenin and the Leninist dream of stateless communism, of the communist International—"Proletarians of all countries, unite!"—is evoked more explicitly here, yet in the reproach directed at St. Wenceslas—depicted in histories as a peace-loving, just, and charitable king who protected and cared for the poor, prisoners, and slaves—and the philosopher-president Masaryk, there is also a bitter disappointment, somewhat like when the poet had to dynamite the castles of his childhood fairy tales, or saw exotic birds die in his home in winter. When one reads Biebl in Czech, one feels his love, profound and sensual, for Czech language, poetry, and *země*, yet in this poem he cannot but give up his allegiance to the nation, the Czech "kin/race" (*plémě*) in favor of the allegiance, not to any particular nation or "kin/race," but to the "defenseless," the "outcasts of this earth," and in favor of a vision of borderless and race-less world that is like "the vast sky"—under which one is free, but also without shelter. The attitudes of this poem—they are Leninist, and equally deeply the poet's own—were among those that Biebl would later bring to his perception of the colonies, and among those with which he was and was not at home in Czechoslovakia.

In Biebl's 1925 collections of poems *Break* and *Zloděj z Bagdádu* (The thief from Baghdad)—the title follows that of the 1924 American movie *The Thief of Baghdad*, which represents the world of the *Arabian Nights* (more on this in Part Two)—exotic imagery, which is not simply exotic, continues to blend with other themes, from meditations on the death of his loved ones to revolution. For instance, in *Break*, images of tigers and lions appear in a poem about struggle for a better world:

Circus Konrado has fifty blond lions,
more the fragrance of blood,
than the fragrance of honey—

belittled and humiliated ones,
with eyes like oases
without water
                    stay with us!

Tigers with indelible shadows
of iron bars
on the whole body
stay with us![228]

The circus, which Teige liked to use as an example of proletarian entertainment, is seen in a different light. Biebl evokes, but also brings down to earth in a new way, a whole tradition of caged lions in Czech poetry—the lion being the heraldic symbol of Bohemia—such as in a famous poem by the nineteenth-century poet Jan Neruda:

Like lions we pound against bars,
like lions captured in a cage,
we desire to rise to the stars,
yet we are bound to Earth.[229]

One may again recall the exotic animals suffering in winter, the "unusual friends" of Biebl's childhood. Biebl's tigers and lions, less symbolic and more surrealistically real than Neruda's, are not simply exotic.

In January 1925, Biebl wrote a letter to the mother of Wolker, his close friend and the most important representative of "proletarian poetry," who had died a year earlier. By this time, proletarian poetry as a movement metamorphosed into poetism, which was more playful, lighter, and more sensual, although still programmatically Marxist. Biebl, with his "exotic motifs," is considered a leading exponent of poetism, yet, as the letter suggests, and as his work from this and later times demonstrate, he remained committed, in the spirit of Wolker, to what he calls here "social poetry"; or a poetry that is many things, but whose workings, emotions, dreams and flights are also indivisibly "social"—in a quiet deviation from the developing programmatic ideals of his peers (as articulated especially by Teige; recall Seifert admiring historical buildings in Prague, quietly afraid what Teige might think). By the way, observe, just like workers on Wenceslas Square are "Indians," the Czech literary scene is a seascape:

> Jirka [Wolker] (how different the literary situation looks today!) will be probably the last and the first poet of social poetry of this young generation—which increasingly gravitates toward light French poetism—so that his work will stand like a rock, heavy and sad, surrounded and washed by light waves, which will never hurt it, on the contrary they will be wrecked on it.[230]

---

228 Biebl, *Zlom*, 57.
229 Jan Neruda, *Básně* (Prague: Státní nakladatelství krásné literatury, hudby a umění, 1954), 2:38.
230 Biebl's letter published in Slabý, *Potkávání*, 57.

THROUGH THE TRAIN WINDOW—DON'T WORRY, I AM NOT GOING TO PARIS

When did Biebl depart for Java? It happened many times—ever since his childhood, in his imagination, words, and actions. One such departure was Biebl's trip to France in the autumn of 1925. The French trip can be seen as part of poetist tourism—Teige and Seifert, for example, travelled together to Italy and France a year earlier. At the same time, there is a continuity with later writings based on the longer Javanese journey in the following year.

Biebl's collection *Zlatými řetězy* (With golden chains) contains a poetic record of the trip. It was published in 1926, the same year that the poet left for Java. Here he comes closest to poetism, even as the poetry foreshadows his later turn to surrealism. Sensuality and play—of meanings, associations, colors, sounds, smells, all sensations—predominates on the warm, glittering surface of this poetry. Yet one is again reminded of Teige's statement, that poetism "was born in a world that is laughing; what of it that its eyes are teary."

In the first, titular poem of the collection, exotic tropical images are abundant: a black man, tropical fruits, the ocean, a Malay man. The poem progresses—rather like a sunset above sea—from a golden color (golden chains, yellow banana) to orange, to the dusky color of the skin of the dying Malay man and woman at the end, in a counterpoint with dark shadows and storms. Just like the sun and the orange, the images of the poet, the pilot, the black man, and the Malay mirror each other and blend—like when a Czech boy becomes an "Indian" warrior; but there is also a certain restlessness, unbearable lightness, anxiety. This flow of associations and sensations is freer, quicker, less anchored than ever—"poet / then pilot / God knows what in the end." "With golden chains bound to a lamp"—both chained and already far away.

With golden chains bound to a lamp
my shadow, like a mourning black man,
today the poet gives away his heart for a banana,
a yellow banana. A tropical puppet.

He possesses not his laughter. He has stranger's tears
  and melancholy hands.

Peel, fingers, the glowing peel. Peel the orange.
An orange cradle of the sun
the ocean used to rock.

Poet
then pilot—
God knows what in the end.

Perhaps scorched by the sky, perhaps tattooed by lightning
in a harbor pub a Malay man dies.

On his chest a warship.
On his hands a dusky woman.[231]

The poems in the collection are arranged into three parts: "Škály" (Scales), "Vlny" (Waves) and "Barvy" (Colors). The waves evoked by the title of the middle part, as a shape and kind of movement, are part of the scheme of the book that emphasizes sensations, shapes, and colors, but they also evoke the sea, travel, and distances. Already foreshadowed by the sea of the poem quoted above, "Waves" is a poetic travelogue, dreamy and disorienting, of Biebl's journey to France. The title page, designed by Josef Čapek, shows sea waves and a steamer on the horizon (Figure 13). This was a journey, in large part, toward the sea, a port, and steamships—one such ship would carry him to Java a year later. Teige wrote in a letter about his trip to Paris: "Paris is an absolutely beautiful city, there is real life there, and where there is life, there is everything, beauty, industriousness, intensity, everything, everything." That Biebl doesn't sing odes to Paris (there is not a single poem about the city), makes him an utter stranger among his peers. One of the several prose texts based on this trip, "Expres do Paříže" (Express to Paris) is about train travel rather than Paris. It begins: "Don't worry—I am not going to Paris to see the exhibition of decorative arts. My way leads to the Mediterranean Sea, to water and to sun."[232]

Biebl did visit the 1925 international exhibition of decorative arts in Paris, a world fair, and wrote a sarcastic, mostly appalled report about the "district of kitsch-makers from the whole world" and "tacky uselessness in which the bourgeoisie invests its money." The French pavilion "looks like a fancy spa toilet." The image of "the Englishman" photographing black sellers of jewelry in the "colonial pavilion" foreshadows images from his Javanese trip. "Everyone is taking pictures of them." A black boy eating ice-cream "stuck out his

231 Biebl, *Zlatými řetězy*, 11.

232 Biebl, *Dílo*, 5:179. Originally published 7th October 1925.

Figure 13. Josef Čapek, "Vlny" (Waves), illustration in K. Biebl, *Zlatými řetězy* (With golden chains), 1926.

tongue just as the Englishman pressed the shutter." Biebl's encounter with Asia here is "sad to death":

> Every quarter of an hour the performance is repeated. Today perhaps for the thirtieth time an Indian magician swallows a chicken egg, for the thirtieth time he tramples on a little boy inside a small woven basket.[233]

"Na cestu" (For the road), the first poem in "Waves," frames the trip with clusters of quickly moving images in which home merges with faraway seas and distant continents from adventure books. It is on the banks of the Vltava river in Prague, "in gulls' pinions," that "the Pacific Ocean begins." (Petřín is a wooded hill above Prague, with a view of the river and the city—from above, they appear almost like a map.)

> Above the map a young captain,
>   the shadow on the wall finished the drink,
> and beyond the seas the last of the Mohicans
>   smears clay paint on his face.

233 "Výstava dekorativního umění v Paříži," clipping is in the Museum of Czech Literature, Prague.

A pocket scarf fluttered on Petřín.
In one corner of the sea there was an embroidered star.

See, a butterfly, the red admiral,[234]
surveys the ships as they depart to the sound of music.

In gulls' pinions the Pacific Ocean begins.
Hair fluttering in the wind
smoothly I comb it to the back
under an English cap.

The ship sails through darkness, the night is stormy,
the captain lights up his pipe.

A match flared up in the darkness
unfolds the red flag.[235]

The sea, a map (recall the map on the wall of Biebl's classroom), "Indians" (from the 1826 novel *Last of the Mohicans* by J.F. Cooper), ships—all evoke distances and adventure. Again, actual sights and object spark fantasy—but then imaginary journeys may lead to physical travel. Just as the handkerchief becomes the sea, the flame of a match becomes a red flag—communism, too, dreamt of a new world, beyond this place and this nation.

Biebl published several prose texts after returning from this trip—"The Sea" was one of them. In another one, "Express to Paris," Biebl writes:

> Through the train window you can see to the heart of a landscape. Of course, it all flies by insanely, so that you are not able to swallow rivers, ponds, alder groves, and even quieter pictures in Bohemia, or wide screens such as the harvest or meadows in the evening. You catch only details, but they suffice for understanding the whole land [*země*]. After all, it is a film.[236]

Follows a series of fragments, indeed "snapshots," of the journey. (The last of them returns to the sea: "Here, just before Paris, [the insulators on telegraphic posts] are green and translucent like a bottle of wine. Or like the depth of the sea.")[237]

234 A species of butterfly: *Vanessa atalanta* in Latin, *babočka admirál* in Czech.
235 Biebl, *Zlatými řetězy*, 23.
236 Biebl, *Dílo*, 5:179.
237 Biebl, *Dílo*, 5:182.

The second poem in Waves is titled "V expresu" (In the express). Aside from the specific sights glanced from the express, the poem, alongside the prose "Express to Paris," and like "The Sea," disclose the method of the travelogue. More than that, these texts show travelling as a metaphor—the kind that "unites," that reveals a "liaison"—of Biebl's poetic vision; the capturing of fragments, fleeting images, that nonetheless reveal what is ordinarily hidden. It is specifically modern travelling—the views from the window of a speeding train. One recalls other windows and mirrors in Biebl's poems, but he also makes the connection with another powerful form of modern poetry —"after all, it is a film."

Even in Biebl's early work, travel and poetry mirror each other. After the trip to France, and not long before his journey to Java, the close relationship between travel and poetry is re-animated and infused with the new experience of actual travel and explicit references to the actual trip.

Trains, we recall, were a part of Biebl's experience of the Great War, his first great journey. In "Waves" as well as in "Express to Paris," Biebl is repeatedly reminded of the War. The next poem after "In the Express," is about a childhood friend who died as a soldier in the war. It concludes with a childhood memory of playing "at Indians" near his village.

Through the bushes he crept, a silent and flexible marten,
    he was the hunter of guinea fowls and woodcocks.
    Above his grave at night the moon became a vault.

An Indian bow.[238]

The poem is titled "Ludvík" (Louis) in the book, but an earlier version was titled "Versailles"[239]—one can imagine the poet walking in the royal gardens ("Louis, I step on orphaned grass"), and, instead of the eighteen French Louises, thinking back to his friend, a victim of "butcher-emperors." In his prose text "Paříž" (Paris), first published just after his trip, Biebl wrote:

Versailles. . . . I had a friend, whose name was Louis. He fell during the war at Piave. I don't know why I must think of him constantly here. All Louises are dead. Except one. But he is in a madhouse. He would often come to the palace and when the servant was not looking, in a flash he undressed and got into the bed of Louis XV. He ruled over everything, like a true ruler, except for his mind, so they put him into a madhouse.[240]

---

238 Biebl, *Zlatými řetězy*, 26.
239 In the magazine *M20* 1, no. 2 (1925): 1. Clipping in the archive of the Museum of Czech Literature.
240 Biebl, Dílo, 5:185.

Intoxicated images of sea waves, ships, palms, as well as birds of paradise and "the white blaze of white Algiers," and the atmosphere of the south, pervade other poems in "Waves." Biebl's poetry is still woven from actuality and dreams, but now actuality is a newly discovered, strange land; displaced not merely through poetic words, but through travel. In the play of colors, sounds and shape, unfamiliar images, intense yet fleeting—like views seen from a speeding train—express as if unmediated sensations, fragmentary memories and puzzlement. The rushing speed is rather different from his later poetry inspired by the longer, slower Javanese journey.

Colonialism and racism in France captured Biebl's attention, and not only at the colonial pavilion in Paris. Let us look at his prose piece "Marseille," which was published in a periodical in late February 1926, eight months before he departed for the British and Dutch colonies.

"The streets are empty" in Marseille, he writes, because there are no blacks or Chinese, because they are not part of the white society in the cafés and on the promenades.

> The first black: porter in the hotel. The second black: porter in a café. The third black: he walks on the street, people step aside puzzled and angrily glance at him: what is he doing here among us, on the promenade, and finally they smile. You know how they smile? You know how a Frenchman smiles? Rather than such a smile, directed at the back of the black who was carrying an advertisement, I would prefer a slap in the face.
>
> The black in France, just like in America, is considered inferior. The black is a scarecrow for little children. It is a slur, like idiot; he is the ass that pulls the ploughs in the colonies. A strong man, but he can be kicked and beaten because he is black.[241]

Biebl describes the parts of Marseille where blacks and Chinese live in poverty, where "a white rarely enters, except for curious foreigners," as well as the red-light district, which is quiet and empty until "a ship with the colonial army" lands. Marseille, France, the Mediterranean: another fairy tale is blown up. The final sentence of the text is vastly sad: "From here one cannot see the sea."[242]

"There are so many masts, I can't see the sea."[243] This is the first sentence of the text "Marseilles" by the Austrian-Jewish journalist and writer Joseph Roth, who visited the city at the same time as Biebl—in the autumn of 1925. That sentence already introduces the disappointment that is part of Roth's essay:

---

241 Biebl, *Dílo*, 5:192–3.

242 Biebl, *Dílo*, 5:195.

243 Joseph Roth, *Report from a Parisian Paradise: Essays from France, 1925–1929*, trans. Michael Hofmann (New York and London: Norton, 2005), 54.

> Is this the boundless gateway to the world of boundless seas? If anything, it's the boundless supply of goods for the European market. . . . I was looking for the boundless horizon here, the bluest blue of sea and salt and sun. But the water in the harbor is dishwater with vast grey-green fatty eyes. . . . [I] hope to catch a whiff of the distant shores that the ship has come from. But it smells like Easter did at home: of dust and aired mattresses . . . of insecticide, of naphthalene, of floor wax, of preserved fruit.[244]

The disillusionment of a Central European man traveling south to the sea recalls Biebl's impressions of Marseille. But Roth is overwhelmed by the "intoxicating cosmopolitan smell"[245] of the harbor, and the

> continuous mixing of races and peoples is palpable, visible, physical, and immediate. Royal palms stand next to the proud chestnuts. . . . This isn't France anymore. It's Europe, Asia, Africa, America. It's white, black, red, yellow. Everyone carries his homeland underfoot, and the soles of his feet carry it with him to Marseille. But all countries are blessed by the same near, hot, bright sun, and the one blue porcelain sky arcs over all nations. All have been brought here on the broad swaying back of the sea; all had a different fatherland, now they all share the one fathersea.[246]

Roth's northern disillusionment yields to an unjudging openness to the greatness of the city and the fullness of its life. He, too, sees that here "misery is as deep as the sea; vice as free as a cloud."[247] Yet for him, misery and vice, like the dishwater in the harbor and the masts that block the view of the sea, are part of the human comedy that is Marseille—"what I take a thousand words to describe is a tiny drop in the sea of everything that goes on."[248]

Compared to Roth's rich, sensual evocation, Biebl's account is less nuanced, and its emotions and protestations are deeply felt, but rather black and white, with something like an ideology constricting poetry in parts of the text. The livelier moments of the text are reminiscent of a political satire on a vaudeville stage, like Nezval's *Dispatch on Wheels*.

Roth opens himself to all the city's richness and lets the city touch him, and then composes an elegant picture, where emotions and thoughts are handled with the steady hand of an experienced master. "With the timidity of a villager you cross busy boulevards leading to the Old Port," wrote another Czech passing through Marseille on his way to Asia a few years after Biebl.[249] Biebl has something of "a frightened villager, taking half an hour to evade the

244 Roth, *Report*, 54–55.
245 Roth, *Report*, 54.
246 Roth, *Report*, 132.
247 Roth, *Report*, 131.
248 Roth, *Report*, 136.
249 Jaroslav Přikryl, *Putování po Cejlonu a v nejjižnější Indii* (Prague: Al. Srdce, 1934), 10.

tramway"[250] (as he described himself in Prague), who has dreamt about the metropolis since childhood, but when he now finally comes to the city, finds himself unprepared for the unfamiliar reality and overwhelmed by strong impressions, and must shut his eyes. "The little Peter who fell from the moon and who feels somewhat unsure on this wildly spinning planet": Biebl is a vulnerable, inexperienced traveler, and he will remain that throughout his Javanese voyage, just as he will retain a critical attitude. But in the future, the weakness, wonder and disorientation of an outsider— "our little citizen" among "Martians"— will be poetized and dramatized in layered, complex texts, pervaded by dreams, memories, sensual impressions, and humor.

250 Jiří Wolker and Konstantin Biebl, *Listy dvou básníků* (Prague: Československý spisovatel, 1953), 25.

SECOND EXCURSION
HIS HEAD THAT WATCHES US OVER THE CENTURY'S EDGE: POETIC TRAVELS IN THE NINETEENTH CENTURY

Poetry and travel were interwoven in the history of modern Czech literature long before Biebl. This is not the place for a survey—let us just take a brief stroll through the harbor before the departure of Biebl's ship to Java.

The interwar avant-garde had an uneasy relation to the older Czech literary tradition. When in 1928 Teige reflected on poetism, he claimed that the only contribution of earlier generations of Czech poets relevant to the present was that they "opened windows to Europe."

> The historical inheritance of home values offered us nothing that would be valid in the current European moment. (Except perhaps . . . the image of white towns drowned in the waters' womb . . . that magnificent passage of the pre-March poem, a free and cadenced sequence of images, embodying what we looked for in poetry.) We enjoined the rhythm of a collective European creativity, the rhythm whose metronome was . . . Paris as a hotspot, not of French, but of international production.[251]

French modern poetry was a formative inspiration for many Czech poets, of Biebl's time and several generations before; an inspiration in the realm of modern poetics generally, but also in relation to poetry's liaisons with travel. Biebl grew as a poet among the images of travel, ships, oceans, and the tropics that pervade French modern poetry. Unlike Teige, Biebl does not claim to have cut ties with Czech poetry. His intimate knowledge of earlier Czech poetry is playfully demonstrated in a love letter that he wrote in 1928 to his future wife, "divine Maria," in which he composed 12 stanzas "about her little finger," each in the style of a different poet of an earlier generation—one of them French (Mallarmé), eleven Czech, with an effortless mastery of each poet's style and language.[252] But Biebl certainly wrote admiringly of Baudelaire, Rimbaud and Apollinaire as the pioneers of modern poetry, and he was walking in their footsteps, too, even as he lived and wrote in a different world; even as for him and the avant-garde, part of the allure of French poetry was the appeal of travelling beyond Czech borders.

---

251 Teige, "Manifest Poetismu," 320.

252 Letter published in Slabý, *Potkávání*, 143–45.

In the passage quoted above, Teige renounces Czech poetry of the past with a sweeping gesture, yet even he halts at one exception, like a lighthouse in the darkness of the night. He does not need to mention the poet's name or the poem's title, but merely one line from the middle of a poem published more than two decades before Baudelaire's *Les Fleurs du Mal*, yet "embodying what we looked for in poetry."

The author of that line— "the image of white towns drowned in the waters' womb"—was Karel Hynek Mácha (1810–1836). Teige's admiration for Mácha was not exceptional. When Nezval set out to demonstrate the workings of modern avant-garde poetics and to contrast them to older poetry, he used, not an avant-garde poem as one might expect, but Mácha as a model of modernity, posing the first modern Czech poet as a measure of the latest developments.[253] Despite the avant-garde's desire to be international, they adored Mácha just like several generations of poets before them did. Mácha was the object of veneration for people and parties of incompatible ideologies, as was demonstrated (yet again) in 1936 during the centenary of his death, when a group of artists and intellectuals allied with surrealism—including Teige, Nezval, and Biebl—published a book protesting the official celebrations and images of Mácha as a national symbol. The book about Mácha became a manifesto of the Czech Surrealists.[254]

Biebl's poetic travel has deep roots in the history of Czech poetry. In Mácha's writings we find, perhaps more persistently than in the case of any other poet, poetry and travel fatally intertwined, like and unlike in Biebl's case.

The two poets are worlds apart, yet Biebl had an intimate connection with Mácha. Šalda sensed the kinship when he compared "the vertigo of Mácha" and "the vertigo of *New Icarus*." When Nezval asked Biebl to contribute a study on Mácha to the 1936 surrealist publication mentioned above, the poet first refused, because Mácha's "head that watches us over the century's edge does not deserve an article written in a hurry."[255] Later, Biebl contributed a poem instead, which paid homage to "Him", and in which Mácha the wanderer is invoked:

And the heel of decline turns always elsewhere
His moon-whipped strides[256]

---

253 Nezval, *Moderní básnické směry*, 9–25.

254 Vítězslav Nezval, ed., *Ani labuť ani lůna: sborník k stému výročí smrti Karla Hynka Máchy* (Prague: Otto Jirsák, 1936).

255 Letter from Biebl to Nezval, dated 5 May 1936. Archive of the Museum of Czech Literature.

256 Konstantin Biebl, "Hrob K. H. Máchy," in Vítězslav Nezval, ed., *Ani labuť ani lůna: sborník k stému výročí smrti Karla Hynka Máchy* (Prague: Otto Jirsák, 1936), 9.

The wanderer is omnipresent in Mácha's work, also as a (mirror-)image of a poetics—like the views from a speeding train or car would be for Biebl. Landscape and people are seen through the wanderer's eyes. He is infatuated with the beauty of the land which passes by him like the years of one's life. The wanderer's experience and perspective have philosophical resonances, yet pervading the whole body of Mácha's poetry and philosophy, we sense, like in Biebl, the actual physical experience of wandering through the landscape, the freshness of nature in spring, the physical sensations of decay and death, the actual emotions of the wanderer's joy and his "immense sadness."

As Nezval shows, in Mácha's writing, a simile or a metaphor is not a secondary image ("ice" in ice-cold) that would serve to clarify or enrich a primary image or idea (cold). Rather, images of equal poetic force merge and clash in sequences and aggregations in which the initial image does not have a strong anchoring function but is decentered by other images.[257] Biebl's images, such as the butterfly flying over a meadow that is equally a sailboat at sea, work in a similar way. Like with Biebl, the nature of Mácha's poetic images is indivisible from his (world)views.

Mácha's prose, too, is characterized by metaphorical but also descriptive and narrative aggregations of images, like in the following passage, where the intercourse between time and soil/land/earth/Earth (*země*), the beauty and impermanence of life, the wanderer's joy and grief, the sweetness and bitterness of love, and "my" heart echoing "her" (*země*'s) sorrow, all mirror each other—they are at once emotions, metaphysical thoughts, erotic desires, and physical sensations.

> May! —O May! —In your embrace the living earth [*země*] rejoices! But woe, no feeling is so pure that it would not blend with the feeling opposite to it!—Like when the wayfarer on his journey first sights a delightful landscape, and into that joy blends the grief of soon having to part with it; as into the sweetness of the first kiss immediately the bitterness of the last flows: so, for all the happiness and joy of your arrival, O beautiful May, her face shows sorrow and pain of near separation, and my heart like an echo deeply responds to her![258]

This torn and passionate relationship between a being and *země* is central to Mácha's poetic knowledge of life and death, being at home and wandering the world, patriotism and attitude to other peoples—all of which will resonate with Biebl's poetry and views of home and the world.

I was first compelled to discuss *země* as a key word in a poem by Biebl, which ends "Lenin, / lord of the earth [*země*]!" There too, *země* exceeds its

---

257 Nezval, *Moderní*, 9–25.
258 Mácha, *Prosa*, 139.

meaning as (Czech) Land to encompass the whole Earth. The narrator in Mácha's brief text "Návrat" (Return) is a man from a village who "made a pilgrimage" to the capital, his "homeland's stone heart." He addresses Prague as mother, yet he is a stranger in the heart of his homeland—rather like Biebl, who "walked around Prague like in a foreign land." The man has been "forever condemned to eternal solitary prison" in his homeland's heart.

> The moon shone brightly on the black floor through a tall window, and the image of its light was cut by the shadows of narrow and dense bars. Sorrowfully I gazed at the illuminated floor and it seemed as if I saw the land of my father in the moonshine, like in a miniscule picture, fluttering in pale light, with all her mountains, fir groves and streams. . . . But everything was so tiny, so slight, and it was becoming smaller and smaller, until after a while it was as if I saw the whole earth as a little ball rolling across the immense sky in the midst of an immense multitude of stars. 'Unhappy earth! . . . flying through space with all your graves . . . vast darkness makes you tremble and the vast sky is only a great grave for you, only what this prison is for me. . . . Unhappy earth, unhappy mother!'[259]

The Earth is again the "unhappy mother," so much like Prague. In a cosmic vision full of empathy, the man recognizes homeland in the whole Earth "with all [her] graves," like him a homeless wayfarer and a prisoner at once. Like in Biebl's poetry, the narrow and the immense are recognized in each other. There is no escape from the cell, the grave, that is the universe, yet "an immense desire" embraces the globe. The infinite longing for homeland grows from homelessness, and this love of the native soil (*země*) overflows into love of the Earth (*země*). In Mácha's vision, no simple exoticism or nationalism are possible.

Mácha's writing, like Biebl's, is pervaded with a desire to travel and a yearning for the faraway, but always already at the origin of that longing there is the realization of the impossibility of reaching any promised land or exotic paradise—just "as into the sweetness of the first kiss immediately the bitterness of the last flows," just like when, in Biebl's imagery, the jungle disappears in one's breath on a frozen window. The wanderer turns out to be a prisoner. The same is true about home(land) in Mácha and, as we will see, Biebl: it is a dream that can never be fulfilled, and so a human being is always a foreigner, a homeless wayfarer, in one's homeland.

There is no escape from the narrow prison of the universe, yet boundless love embraces the whole globe. At the end of Biebl's *New Icarus*, at the mo-

259 Mácha, *Prosa*, 276–77.

ment of the poet-Icarus's "terrible fall into eternity," the poet-Icarus sings: "how great is love . . . I sail all the seas."[260]

Mácha's "imagined community," like Biebl's, is a gathering of not just all human beings, but animals and flowers, even God. Mácha wrote in his notebook:

> I love the flower, for it will wither, the animal—for it will die; the human—for he will expire and shall not be; for he feels that he will perish forever; I love—more than love—I surrender to God, for he is not.—Every human being would love the other, if he understood, if he could glance inside the other, yet— — —[261]

In the tale "Marinka," Mácha's wanderer walks in Petřín—the park above Prague we have already encountered as the starting point of Biebl's poetic travelogue to Paris—and observes

> exotic [*cizokrajné*, lit., foreign-land] flowers, which, transplanted from their own climate to a strange land, friendlily cuddle up to the womb of the mother who is unknown to them, to the cold grave on a foreign soil; because the earth that is not suitable for them does not nurture the sad blossoms.[262]

Mácha's ideas are never purely contemplative: they are intense, conflicting emotions and physical sensations. The understanding that homeland is but a dream, and that man is but a foreigner in his land / on the earth, is manifested through an overwhelming compassion with the foreigner wandering or dying in a foreign land, with "the Other," and through a sense of common fate with all beings.

As in Biebl's case, there is a political side to Mácha's images of homeland, homelessness, and wandering. The motto of "Return" comes from the Old Testament Lamentations over the exile of the Jews: "The crown has fallen from our head . . ." This image relates "Return," not only to the oppression of the Jews, but also to the political situation of Bohemia, with which Mácha's poetic thought is interwoven. By Mácha's time, when ideas of "national rebirth" were gaining strength, nationalist historical representations of recent centuries focused on the humiliation of the Czech people "under the yoke" of the Austrian, German-speaking, Catholic Habsburgs ruling from Vienna—the burning of tens of thousands of Czech books by the Jesuits, reforms that took away rights and freedoms from Czechs, a massive wave of emigration.

260 Biebl, *Nový Ikaros*, 71.
261 In the Czech original, no masculine pronouns are used, except for God—"human" refers to both genders, unlike in the translation.
262 Mácha, *Prosa*, 140.

Mácha's images of homelessness in one's own land grew from a particular historical situation and from a passionate concern with his *země*, his native soil. Yet, his images uncontrollably exceed, poetically and philosophically, the historical moment and the narrow nationalist perspective, rather like in Biebl's "Lenin, / lord of the earth." That is in part why Mácha was denounced by many of his contemporaries as being detrimental to the cause of national rebirth, as being "so un-Czech" and "too cosmopolitan"[263]— like Biebl, who just before his death was accused by socialist critics of "cosmopolitanism" (then, in 1951, the "way of the enemy"), of which his Javanese journey became the emblem. In Mácha's writing, every image or experience can spark a chain of associations, moments of recognition, and unanchored metaphors. Many images in Mácha's poetry evoke the fate of the nation, but Czech national history freely mirrors that of other nations whose situation resonates with that of the Czechs. The national experience exceeds and challenges national borders and historical particularity. Moreover, Mácha does not think only in terms of the nation: the poet is moved by a wilting "foreign-land" flower as well as the earth with all her graves—no doubt he too, like Biebl, would identify with exotic birds suffering in Czech winter. The word *země* exceeds homeland and embraces the Earth; the poet's feelings for his own people overflow into empathy with all beings; homelessness becomes not merely a specific historical circumstance, but an existential condition.

Poetic cognition of *země*, being at home, and being foreign in Mácha's poetry resonate with Biebl's poetic travels to the colonies. Even the brief excerpts from Mácha's writing above—such as his empathy with a flower from foreign lands—are evocative in this respect. However, in his most extensive prose text, *Cikáni* (Gypsies), composed in 1835, Mácha writes explicitly about "Eastern nations" in Europe—the Gypsies and the Jews.[264] The work was banned by the Censor in Mácha's lifetime, and the complete work was published only in 1857, two decades after the author's death.

263 Janský, *Karel Hynek Mácha*, 175, 267.

264 In some languages, the same word refers to both peoples, the Bohemians and the Gypsies (*bohemien* in French—dictionaries tell us that it is because the Gypsies were thought to come to France from or through Bohemia); and even in English dictionaries the extended meanings of gypsy and bohemian overlap and sometimes merge; for example, one of the definitions of Bohemian in *Webster's* is "living a wandering or vagabond life, as a Gypsy." I am not sure whether these liquid connections were known to Mácha, but the sense of kinship between wandering strangers, or between those who are not members of the Club, was also brought out by him in his work.

This is not the place to discuss the whole tale; let a few images suffice. The narrative is set in a region of Bohemia, not far from Prague, where Mácha liked to wander:

> [The valley] is similar to a deserted Eastern city. . . . Thick bushes swayed in deserted streets as if in a light breeze, whispering like muezzin's dying voice from a minaret, calling the deceased faithful to prayer, and slim rocks, rising like little towers above the ruins of an eastern city, gleamed like silver domes in pale lighting.[265]

Like Biebl's minarets-poplars, like his meadow-sea, Eastern yet Czech, fantastic yet actual, resembling a ruined homeland of an Eastern people, the mestizo landscape—*země* as a mestiza will be important in Biebl—forms the setting of a story in which Jews, Gypsies, and an uprooted Czech (a tragicomic character constantly day-dreaming about foreign lands) find common ground in homelessness.

"A seventy-year old elder, the loyal son of the Israeli tribe" and his daughter Lea—wearing "a Turkish scarf, in the manner of the women of her nation who live in the Eastern lands"—hear "sad singing" from a distance. A Gypsy is singing about being an unwelcome foreigner in the beautiful land. After the words "my nation is scattered," Lea rejoins, singing about her own "scattered nation"—her faraway "unknown homeland," "desolate Jerusalem," "palms by the Jordan."[266] They recognize that their plight exceeds any one "nation," and they fall in love, a love that grows from their shared foreignness: "Stay with us; we too are foreigners in this land," she pleads with the Gypsy.[267] The old Jew tells the Gypsy:

> "Nobody can weigh her pain except one who wanders like us, remote from the homeland. . . . Who will protect a child of desolate Jerusalem from disgrace? Like wolves in desolate mountains they are on the prowl, waiting to divide the lamb's fleece among themselves," he whispered, looking around. . . . "You too are orphaned, your scattered nation does not know its son."[268]

Despite this recognition of common destiny, the Jews and the Gypsies remain lonesome wanderers among "wolves in desolate mountains." Lea is killed and her father dies of sorrow. The Gypsy—actually, but never quite, a

265 Mácha, *Prosa*, 10, 15.
266 Mácha, *Prosa*, 19–20.
267 Mácha, *Prosa*, 54.
268 Mácha, *Prosa*, 56.

native there—finds it "impossible to remain in this land" and he "returns to the wide world,"[269] to wandering endlessly.

> He did not look back at his native land; farther—farther away he goes— Around him blooming meadows, fertile fields, blue forests, his homeland, his heritage. . . . He sees nothing—farther—farther away he goes.[270]

The old veteran soldier Bárta contrasts sharply with the other characters in the tale. Instead of the deep existential woe that pervades the others' every word, he is permanently drunk and his words are loud and rough. He is "famous as the best storyteller in those parts." As Lea sings in response to the Gypsy's song and expresses her own sorrow— "across deep sea I sailed, / deeper than the sea is the sorrow I bear"—and as the old Jew stands silently weeping,

> the old veteran, as if awakened from slumber, torn from it, by the last words of the song, began to narrate again: "I was there too, on the sea—yes—on the sea—we were there three days. Oh, what a sight it is on that sea—You see nothing, nothing but water and the sky—upon my faith! And the boom of the cannon shots on the sea! Yes, a hundred times louder! No, no, that would be a lie, but five times— — yes five times for sure!"[271]

Bárta's incoherent stories drunkenly interrupt the lives of the other characters, yet strangely they echo them in a play of contrast and misunderstanding, like free, irrational juxtapositions of images in a surrealist poem; or a bit like Švejk in the World War; or, not exactly but somewhat, in the existential humor (moistness, as in Latin) of the character, Biebl's "little citizen" among "Martians." After all, Biebl, too was a veteran, who first saw distant lands as a soldier of an imperial army, and who too came back marked by the experience.

A brief digression: Karel Janský, a life-long researcher and biographer of Mácha, also ran the Hyperion publishing house and published most of Biebl's books in the 1920s (as well as a number of other important publications by Devětsil and other writers); he and Biebl then became friends, frequently corresponding since at least 1924 until the poet's death. From his 1925 trip to France, Biebl sent a postcard to Janský with a picture of palms and a short message: "Greetings from palms, sea and sun." In August 1926, just two months before his departure to Java, Biebl mentioned to Janský: "In the evenings I read Mácha and Baudelaire and I like them both more and more." Biebl also sent him a postcard from Java, and upon his return he wrote to

---

269 Mácha, *Prosa*, 128.
270 Mácha, *Prosa*, 130.
271 Mácha, *Prosa*, 20.

him: "I sit the whole day in my room, reading or writing. No one can stand it in here, because I keep feeding the fire in the stove. I am creating an artificial tropical climate here, so that I can better write about Java."[272]

Back to Bárta: like the Jews and the Gypsies, he spent much time wandering, and he returned home where he became a stranger (which on some level is also true about Biebl, I am tempted to add). Mácha's uncle, Václav Bárta, on whom the Bárta in the *Gypsies* was in part modeled, was a veteran and war invalid. Janský writes:

> According to local records, Bárta was hardly a pleasant tenant. In the village he moved from one place to another, and no one could stand him for long. Old eyewitnesses described him as an incorrigible drinker and a peculiar figure, always boasting about his war adventures.[273]

In Czech fairy tales, the veteran is a familiar type: a carefree single man, without a permanent home, who enjoys cards and drinking. Mácha's Bárta, especially at first, has something of this figure, with his comical, half-invented travels in faraway lands—exotic adventures, alcohol-drenched irrational fantasies. And yet, there is an underlying sadness and loneliness about the man, who has nothing left in life but alcohol and half-lied memories of distant travels. "Because no one listened to him here, he alone was narrating to himself the whole French war, and he did that, as usual, very loudly and in such a way that after every few words a cruel lie followed, which everyone must have recognized as a lie."

The drama of *Gypsies* culminates on a dark and stormy night. Bárta mumbles from his sleep, "repeating single words about the Rhine." When he awakens, he stands up and begins to grope around him in the dark, trying to remember where he is.

> Having found the table, he moved his hand across its stone top, and feeling a glass in his hand, he began to clink it against the table. No one was coming; long desolate silence, deep night. He reeled to the side and— "by the Rhine, by the Rhine, life was better there," he nourished himself with recollections. "As soon as I clinked, they'd come right away!"—At that moment there was a faint flash of lightning. In its light he saw Lea's white dress at her usual place near the cottage, and he staggered toward her to chat. He carried his glass with him, no doubt he wanted to ask her to fill it. Having reached her, reeling, he began to pull at her, asking for brandy. She was not moving or answering. "Will you get up or not? —Lea! . . .—on my faith, when I was at the Rhine—"[274]

---

272 From correspondence published in Slabý, *Potkávání*, 244–5.
273 Janský, *Karel Hynek Mácha*, 254.
274 Mácha, *Prosa*, 76.

As the events turn tragic, the comic figure of the drunken veteran creates an increasingly ghastly contrast with the other characters, but it is precisely as the chasm between them grows that one begins to glimpse that their fates are not unlike. The soldier's hilarious fantasies of the sea and the Rhine, in which he tries to drown his lonely homelessness, begin to feel, in their growing difference, strangely like the Jews' and the Gypsies' lamentation for homeland never seen; or like Mácha's own lament for the beauty of bygone childhood, "the image of white towns drowned in the waters' womb." Like the prisoner's vision in "Return," the "immense sorrow" and homelessness of each lone traveler, be it a man or a flower, is as insurmountably individual as it is cosmic.

A notable detail of the *Gypsies* are the epigraphs at the beginning of the book and every chapter, all, curiously, in Polish. Most are citations from Polish authors, but some are by English writers, in Polish translation. Mácha learned Polish after the crushed 1930 Polish rebellion against Russian rule, when he met Polish political refugees passing through Prague. Like many others, he sympathized with the rebels against oppression, whose plight resonated with the Czech situation under Austria. The language of the Polish epigraphs encourages the reader to relate the lost homelands in the *Gypsies* to the historical situation of the Polish nation—whose country did not exist on the map and most of the authors cited by Mácha lived in emigration—and to think in terms of multiple, unanchored analogies or metaphors—Czechs, Poles, Jews, Gypsies . . . —rather than a single nation alone.

The cosmopolitanism that Mácha was accused of was not unlike the internationalism of Biebl's generation. Among Mácha's favorite readings and models were, aside from the Polish authors, Lord Byron, Johann Wolfgang von Goethe, Walter Scott, and more generally the literature of European romanticism. Soon after Mácha's death, one author wrote approvingly about an attack on Mácha that it was "a dose of quinine against the romantic fever."[275] *Gypsies* is in many ways a typical romantic tale: a thrilling narrative with a few mysteries, a few murders, an execution, and a tragic love story set in mysterious rocky landscape, an old castle, and night storms—Mácha's beloved Walter Scott comes to mind. The exotic is part of this—Lea in her "eastern dress" sings of palms, Jordan and Jerusalem, and the Gypsies roam the landscape.

Bárta's stories of travels in distant lands and seas border on a parody of exoticism and travel accounts, such as when he tells how he sailed on the sea— "what a sight it is on that sea—You see nothing"—or when he remembers how once he was very hungry:

275 Janský, *Karel Hynek Mácha*, 323.

> So hungry that I could have eaten an elephant! Yes, yes— — and you think that I never ate an elephant? On my faith, excellent meat and even better soup from it! Yes yes— — you doubt this? Who would dare?[276]

Mácha here smiles at travel stories and dreams of faraway lands—as Biebl often does, especially at his own—yet Mácha was not immune to their charm, nor was he satisfied by fantasies alone. As in Biebl's case, dreams and actuality overflowed into each other. Mácha crisscrossed Bohemia on foot, sometimes wandering apparently aimlessly, sometimes going on well-planned trips, more like a modern tourist, at a time when tourism was becoming a part of modern life throughout Europe, as well as a patriotic, even nationalistic activity and also a growing commercial enterprise. What Mácha depicts as desolate spots were in some cases really nascent tourist centers. Just before he wrote *Gypsies*, Mácha went on foot to Italy, where for the first and last time he saw the sea. He sailed from Venice to Trieste and was seasick during the whole brief trip. A part of *Gypsies* is essentially a fictionalized account of the journey. Mácha's diaries contain notes about his travels as well as about what he read. His "affection for travelling manifested itself also in his reading," Janský wrote.[277] Aside from romantic works (Byron, Scott) that abound in travel narratives and descriptions of landscapes of distant countries, his diaries show that he was an avid reader of geographical literature about foreign lands, among which prominently figured Asia, from the Middle East to East and Southeast Asia. Among the many places that he read about—and excerpted some of the articles—are India, Ceylon, Sumatra, Malaya ("Pulopinang," that is, Pulau Penang), and the Philippines. One scholar has argued that Mácha might have been planning a trip to Asia, as was suggested by his notes on transport possibilities for travel to Constantinople.[278] Who knows, perhaps if Mácha had lived longer, he would have travelled to Sumatra and tasted the elephant soup, just like I did?

Biebl was born into a literature inundated with the sea. These are the first sentences of his text "The Sea":

> We are afraid to speak of it, let alone to write about it. We are afraid to love the sea; one day, out of embarrassment, we might not be even able to look at it, so much has the sea been spoiled for us by poets and especially painters.[279]

276 Mácha, *Prosa*, 22.
277 Janský, *Karel Hynek Mácha*, 208.
278 Antonín Ederer, "Máchův zájem o orient," *Nový Orient* 1, no. 6, (1945–46): 18.
279 Biebl, *Dílo*, 5:188.

One of Mácha's earliest poems, written long before Mácha saw the sea, "Kolumbus" (Columbus) presents elaborate and intense visions of sailing across the vast ocean. Columbus is an exile who is running away from his homeland, "which like a stepmother cast [him] out." After staying in Spain, where "the foreigner is hunted and cursed," Columbus sails across the ocean in search of new land. The ship's crew threatens to throw him overboard if he does not turn the ship back to their "beloved homeland." Columbus stays the course towards the "land yet unseen" and at the last moment is saved by the word "land!" heard from the mast, when land finally appears on the horizon.[280] In a few years, this ending might be too happy for Mácha, but the fantasy of sea travel foreshadows the visions of *země* in his later poetry.

In *Gypsies*, Mácha wrote that "in ancient times the whole Czech land [*země*] was just one great lake."[281] Biebl wrote about his native village that it "lies on the bottom of ancient seas."[282] The image of Bohemia as the sea haunted Mácha: in one text, a traveler stands on a hill and in the distance, in the evening dusk, above the mists veiling the low lands, on another hill he sees a ruined castle which appears "like a sea ship."[283] In another text, a Czech king points at a castle—"nothing was visible except a single, tall, slim tower rising above thick fog like a lonely rock above the waves of the sea."[284] Elsewhere, the poet stands on Blaník, the sacred mountain of Czech legends, and surveys his homeland: "below me plains like the green sea, / and above this sea I a madman stood."[285]

While Czech land is the sea, life is a voyage across it. In *Gypsies*, the young Gypsy visits Lea's grave for the last time, before setting out on a journey and forever leaves his country:

> . . . grave calm settled in his heart. He was bidding farewell to the first and last lover of his life, and his sorrow was peaceful. He envied her endless rest after the woes of a life tossed about in a storm; for he, too, was washed ashore by a terrible storm;—which had destroyed the ship that was to bring him to the promised land—he too was washed ashore on an island of deep stillness; he was lifted, elevated above all the passions and fervors of human days.[286]

In *Gypsies*, there is the sea also in songs:

---

280 Karel Hynek Mácha, *Dílo* (Prague: Československý spisovatel, 1986), 1:78–87.
281 Mácha, *Prosa*, 11.
282 Biebl, *Dílo*, 5:282–3.
283 Mácha, *Prosa*, 135.
284 Mácha, *Prosa*, 177.
285 Mácha, *Dílo*, 303.
286 Mácha, *Prosa*, 127.

Behold, a little boat on the waters,
That is my beloved;
He will sail here and kiss his love,
That is my beloved!

Oh, far—far away has he sailed,
That is my beloved;
He perished there in the deep sea,
Oh, my beloved![287]

The old Gypsy recounts his life in Venice. This is where Mácha actually saw the sea, and the distinction between fiction and travelogue is blurred here.

I sat on the Lido Island alone and gazed eastward, as the full moon was rising from the dark sea.[288]

Like for Biebl a hundred years later, the sea in Mácha had an ominous attraction:

. . . the sea mountains stretched to the distance. Deep mists rolled over the sea surface, in which the sun had long drowned. I felt I must leap into the quiet waters.[289]

Returning home from the sea, the old Gypsy—like Mácha?—feels like leaving one's homeland forever:

Once more I looked below—and for the last time I saw the sea;—never again have I seen the sea since those days! I hurried farther and farther in the wide world, without a goal, without an end!—[290]

Nothing separates the actual, poetic and existential seas.

My little boat! Do you still sway in the waves near Ponte Rialto, or have you been destroyed and your boards are floating out—out—toward the distant sea?[291]

Mácha is only one among many Czech writers whose work is saturated with representations of the sea and images of distant lands, including the

287 Mácha, *Prosa*, 46.
288 Mácha, *Prosa*, 122.
289 Mácha, *Prosa*, 124.
290 Mácha, *Prosa*, 125.
291 Mácha, *Prosa*, 125.

farthest, the tropics. Although Bohemia is a cold, landlocked country, its imagination has been flooded, long before Biebl, since "the ancient times," with images of the sea, just as it is dotted with tropical islands, overgrown with palms, and crisscrossed by ships—and it has been populated with people from distant lands or those of other "nations," such as Mácha's Gypsies and Jews.

Among these exotic peoples, the American "Indians" have been especially prominent in Czech (and Central European) imagination, and they also figure in Biebl's poetry and prose—we have seen how the poem "Indian," translated earlier, prefigures his poetry about the colonies. Among the many "Indians" that precede Biebl's, are those of the poet Josef Václav Sládek (1845–1912). We met Sládek earlier, as he was remembering his childhood daydreams about American Indians—before "a prosaic ear-pull disturbed us from our delightful dreams." Unlike most other Czech writers and painters who fantasized the Indians, Sládek, somewhat like Biebl, actually travelled to the distant land of his childhood dreams.

In Sládek's life, poetry and travel met as intimately as in the cases of Mácha and Biebl. He, too, loved the sea and wrote many poems about it. In a letter home, written on board a ship sailing in the Gulf of Mexico in 1869, he wrote as if the sea were his homeland: "How I missed that open/free [*volné*], blue eye, how I missed those foamy waves!"[292]

In 1868, Sládek, then twenty-three, left for America, where he stayed for two years. At a time when he and other patriots organized against foreign oppression, Sládek, for the sake of his homeland's future, wanted to learn about "unquestionably the freest and happiest land of our age."[293] Indivisible from his desire for political freedom for his country was a longing for travelling itself, for open spaces, free movement, and fresh air. He wrote to his parents before his departure:

> I finished my studies. What can books give to a man, even if he were constantly preoccupied with them? . . . I want to be content at last, and that will happen only through travelling. . . . Is it not better [than becoming a professor, as planned], to breathe free and open [*volný*] sea air? To wander through forests, across meadows—to be one year alive without cares? . . . I can never be happy, if I am not given what I thirst for—travelling.[294]

292 Sládek, *Americké obrázky*, 2:322.
293 Sládek, *Americké obrázky*, 2:29.
294 Quoted in Josef Polák, *Americká cesta Josefa Václava Sládka* (Prague: Státní Pedagogické Nakladatelství, 1966), 32.

The young man was not disappointed with travelling. His letters are full of excitement about everything from the beauty of nature to political freedom. However, that something is wrong even in the dreamland becomes clear from Sládek's writings on the blacks and Chinese in America, and in his images of the "Indians."

In his famous 1874 poem *Na hrobech indiánských* (On Indian graves), Sládek describes the beauty and freedom of America only to show the injustice and destruction caused by what today would be called development and globalization:

in the forests the firm axe
multiplies daily your work of devastation,
and fences cut forests and prairies
and across lakes steam engines fly
and distribute the loot of your robbery.
. . . .
each of you calls this or that mile your own,
where does the soil's [*země*] poor son has his share?
Where is enlightenment, "granted to the darkness of the slave"?
Like a deer from here you hounded him away,
he has no place where his fatigued head he'd lay,
with a "kind hand" you lead him to the grave.[295]

"All this," Sládek writes, "for the sake of the dollar." At the poem's end, he returns to the fundamental contradiction: building freedom and happiness on the foundation of injustice and cruelty.

For yourself you've built freedom here,
of which the European slave can't even dream,
but everywhere I see it stained with blood
today, in the past—and the future is mute.

And be free, unmatched in the world,
so from the dust slaves will look up to you
and let your enlightenment shine for you
like a new sun into a dark night,
and build thrones for everything that's human,
and reason will say: "You've saved us,"
but will not human heart

295 J. V. Sládek, *Na hrobech indiánských* (Prague: Československý spisovatel, 1951), 11.

once ask you: "Where are those fallen millions?
Cain, murderer, where have you left Abel?"
Who will answer for you in your prosperity,
who will rid your head's bright halo
of the red ray of shame?[296]

Elsewhere, too, Sládek found horror in the midst of dreamlike beauty: "I was leaving New Orleans. That old-French city, with its streets thousand times washed with the blood of the blacks, was, despite its palms and orange parks, rather suffocating for me."[297] Biebl, too would find injustice and unhappiness in a land of his dreams, and see how prosperity and "enlightenment" are built on the foundations of injustice and greed.

The Indian graves evoke a prominent motif in Czech poetry of national awakening: the dusty graves of Czech kings, a symbol of past glory and present humiliation. The plight of the Indians is analogical to that of the Czechs.

However, Czech settlers in America do not fit the analogy easily. Thousands left their country because of oppressive poverty and lack of freedom. The Czech-Americans should presumably empathize with the Indians; yet, they, too, were settlers, like other Americans.

Sládek's 1871 story "Válečná výprava" (War expedition)[298] comments on this issue, on the sense of being "in the same boat" with the oppressors, which also underlies Biebl's images of suffering and injustice, at home and in the colonies. Mikeš, a Czech farmer in Texas, found his beloved horse Ryzka dead, shot by an arrow. "Till this day I did not want to believe that one may spill Indian blood as lightly as deer's blood, but today we will go together—they killed my Ryzka!" Six Czech farmers gathered for the expedition. Sládek's comic vision—not unlike Mácha's cosmic vision—puts the actions of the Czech farmers into a larger perspective, in which their hatred and the Americans' efficiency appear preposterous.

The Americans went ahead; they said . . . Europeans are too inexperienced, overly sensitive, and not as suitable for chasing Indians as Americans. We were supposed to ride nearby, while they would go farther.

The parting began, as if we were about to ride to our deaths. The farmer's wife baked corn bread. A bit of bacon and ground coffee, a little bit of corn roasted with cinnamon—and off we rode to hunt the Indians.

Poor Comanches! What a terrifying regiment of enemies set out on a war expedition against you! Former Czech farmers, who at home covered their ears when women

296 Sládek, *Na hrobech*, 12.
297 Sládek, *Americké obrázky*, 1:136.
298 Sládek, *Americké obrázky*, 1:68–74.

> cut the ducks' throats, with guns and knives and all the war arms, were ready to spill human blood with their faces as cool as when they had used to go to the church back at home.[299]

They debated whether they should forgive the Indians. "Don't you think that the Indian is a brother, too?" said one of them. "Brother Slav," answers the narrator, including the Indians in a Pan-Slavic brotherhood. Finally, they encountered a few destitute, hungry Indian families. "The army unsaddled the horses, made fire, prepared coffee, and with the Indians merrily we ate lunch." (In the meantime, the American farmers captured a gang of Frenchmen and Mexicans who had used arrows so that their crimes would be blamed on Indians.)

The narrative's serious humor foreshadows both Švejk and Biebl. Sládek's farce conveys the frightening idea that Czech farmers are ready to join in the hunt on the Indians. One wonders at whom his accusations—also in the poem *On Indian Graves*—are aimed. Sometimes, he accuses explicitly the "European," and, through the pronoun "we," includes himself and Czechs in the group. The Czech position is uneasy and unresolved. In Sládek, too, there is a sense that, in Biebl's words, "even if another was shooting / our deeds are in those wounds."

———

When one reads Mácha, one can understand that for the poets of Biebl's generation, he was both the origin and the future ideal of modern Czech poetry. Mácha's desires, disillusionments, and poetic realizations, his dreams of home and faraway lands, are alive in Biebl's poetry. One suspects that some of Sládek's concerns and ideals—including his kind of nationalism—were quite foreign to Biebl. And yet, there are similarities between Sládek's and Biebl's writings and travels: their decision to go beyond dreaming about foreign lands to actually travelling there, their attention to injustice at the foundations of beauty and prosperity, their attacks on hypocritical misrepresentations that silence truth, their concern with the silenced, their propensity to recognize oneself in the other, their willingness to dynamite fairy-tale castles, and their shared sense that "our deeds are in those wounds." This does not mean that Biebl was directly inspired by Sládek; it does suggest that Biebl walked along a path of many footprints, including the footprints of those who might have been in some respects quite unlike him. Mácha and Sládek, two poets different from each other and from Biebl, are but two figures in the procession.

299 Sládek, *Americké obrázky*, 1:71.

Many footprints: and yet, the wandering poet is always treading an unknown path, alone, a stranger to others, always a tropical flower transplanted to Bohemia. Seifert's poem "Tři hořká jadérka" (Three bitter seeds), dedicated to Biebl, recalls a souvenir from southern France that Biebl brought for Seifert and Biebl's letter from Java, and at the same time evokes Mácha— "the earth unsuitable for them does not nurture the sad blossoms." It is about orange seeds and about Biebl's own foreignness at home.

Three bitter seeds
I received as a souvenir
. . . .
Who weeps, whose weeping is it?
From the seeds that you gave me
my orange
grew but has not ripened.

It is not at home in our land,
that precious blossom,
everything is foreign to it here
like ice.

The sun is cold
the soil is other,
the dew falls
and step-mother winter arrives

and foreign spring.

A letter arrived from faraway.
Where does that Java actually lie?
I remember your seeds
and here it snows.

What can one write about what one does not know?
On the sea a burning island floats.
Like monkeys gentle words jump
into verses on paper.[300]

300 Seifert, *Dílo Jaroslava Seiferta*, ed. Filip Tomáš (Prague: Akropolis, 2002), 2:116–7.

THE NOTEBOOK THAT HE LOST SOMEWHERE ON THE SHIP

As I write about Biebl's poetry, from which I hope to learn how to see and write, at times I succumb to the temptation to translate, order, explain. An academic anxiety about keeping silent and looking into darkness? Or a sense that there is enough fire in the poet's words?

In an open letter to a publisher, Biebl wrote that the modern novel "already has its safe path: Poe, Baudelaire, Rimbaud, Apollinaire. . . . It all depends on the courage and power of the young talent whether, as he walks through the fire of these damned poets, he will burn his own wings."[301]

In the same text, the poet wrote about the danger of travel writing—as if again wary that the sun's fire may burn the poet's wings in the tropics, where he "lives somewhat more lazily, because the most ordinary actuality is fantastic enough."

> [B]ooks from foreign lands, written then and there, bear a great amount of description; and if it is not the poet's task to present a precise list of all rivers that he crossed, all volcanoes that he climbed, what he drank and ate in different places, how much the train ticket from Batavia to Semarang was—then he would rather approach the writing of a book, provided he wants to do that, much later, at a time when he is lucky enough not to be able to find the notebook that he lost somewhere on the ship on his way back, when he cannot remember anymore the name of a rich Chinese merchant, although never till his death could the amazing carnival of a mad Chinese funeral disappear from his memory, or the river emitting violet light because of all the fireflies, or the expression of contempt on the face of a proud Malay in the post office in Dieng when he glanced at a European woman, who cut the queue by the insolent right of the ruling race.
>
> I approach the writing of the book for your publishing house from the distance of almost two years, with the aim to capture the air of Java rather than her firm land, the fragrance of flowers rather than her botanics.[302]

Biebl never completed the promised volume.

301 Biebl, *Dílo*, 5:249. Originally published in 1929.
302 Biebl, *Dílo*, 5:250–1.

When I began to research Biebl, I wanted to learn all the details about his journey to Java, his precise route, the names of all the places he visited, the books he read. Unlike Rimbaud, who stopped writing poetry just before he travelled to Java, Biebl wrote a good number of poems and prose texts about his trip. The relative scarcity of factual details was the more tantalizing. I was trying to find more, but sometimes, when I did—for example, in Dutch newspapers I discovered his name among passengers on a ship, and thus the date and route of his journey back from Java, previously unknown to scholars—I would feel that these details did not mean much. Once, I was reading a text by Josef Kořenský, a school teacher who a few decades before Biebl's journey travelled around the world and wrote books full of facts, names, dates, numbers, prices . . . —and it made me think about Biebl and about the passage quoted above; it made me think that the "lack" of this kind of information, a kind of silence, is part of Biebl's poetic journey. He consciously and carefully weighed how much to say, and he fashioned the journey and its representation rather like he wrote his poems, always careful not to say too much or too loudly. His words were like silently hovering snowflakes, his images like fragmentary glimpses from a train. These thoughts made me doubt my desire to uncover all the facts about Biebl's journey and life, and taught me to respect silence, "the air" (of Java, of his times), and the pure and fragile *poetry* of places, things, and people—even as such poetry often reveals itself in plainly naming and describing. Not easy. Especially for a "trained" academic.

Less than a year after Biebl returned from Java, a brief announcement appeared in a leading literary magazine:

> In the nearest future, Konstantin Biebl will publish a collection of poems titled *With the Ship that Carries Tea and Coffee*. He has ready for print: *Nunek*, a novel; *Journey to Java*, proses and causeries; *Suri*, an exotic novel; *Wajang*, lyric-epic poem; and a *play for theater*, so far untitled.[303]

Only the collection of poems was published in book form, and while a few texts from an early version of *Cesta na Jávu* (Journey to Java) appeared in newspapers and magazines, the planned book was never finished by Biebl. None of the other planned publications materialized, and it is not clear whether they were even begun. Against the backdrop of this absence, this inability or unwillingness to speak, Biebl's texts inspired by his Javanese

303 *Rozpravy Aventina*, 4 November 1927.

journey, those that were published, now appear as fragments, as flashes of light, in a darkness haunted by unwritten works.

One cannot but wonder what it was that remained unsaid. Biebl's notebooks from his Javanese journey[304] tell us nothing explicit about the planned texts, but they afford us a different glimpse of Biebl's experience than we get from his published works. Biebl's texts are usually meticulously crafted, but reading the notebooks, one is faced with scribbles—individual words, phrases, crude brief sentences, simple drawings. To go through the notes does not feel like reading a book; it is more like encountering scattered traces of Biebl's movements. The scribbles are part of travelling—finding one's way around a city, finding out what is this and that, learning how to name what one sees or what is happening. At the same time, one feels that these traces are the ground of poetry, although not yet poems. From them one senses something of what was behind the poet's writing and behind his silence.

The initial pages of what appears to be the first notebook are taken up by Malay words and phrases with Czech translations. The Malay is often written in Czech spelling (for example, *džalan* instead of *djalan*, *bava* instead of *bawa*), suggesting that Biebl noted down the words as he heard them. Especially in the beginning, the vocabulary is practical—asking for directions, bargaining in the market, hiring a horse cart, learning numbers, ordering food and drink, asking a person's name, finding out where someone's house is, and so on. Apparently Biebl was trying to move around independently using Malay, explore the towns and cities, shop (especially for fruits and vegetables), and meet people. At the same time, he seems to have had an interest in language, not just for the sake of communication, but in its sound and workings. His Czech translations often follow the word order and literal meaning of Malay, resulting in an incorrect or awkward Czech—or, a Czech modelled on Malay.

This glossary is interrupted by lists of Javanese and Chinese personal names. These lists have little practical value—one suspects, rather, that Biebl was learning to understand the sound and feel of names, and that he was collecting them for his poetry and prose. Most of the names that appear in his later writings are included here—Arsiti, Sina, Urip, Paviro, Reso, Liat, and others.

Follows a list of fruits. Here, and this increasingly happens in the pages that follow, translations and basic descriptions gradually grow into notes on what struck Biebl as remarkable. For example, for *kepel*, Biebl noted, "brown like *sawoh*, eaten by sultan's dancers, because after it, skin is fragrant."

The glosses also begin to be connected to Biebl's experiences. Next to one of the Chinese names, there is the note "a millionaire from Semarang, at

304 The notebooks—the stationary—were produced in Semarang. Apparently they contain Biebl's notes taken during his stay in Java.

whose grave we were." Or, elsewhere: "*kemoening* white blossoms on bushes, strongly fragrant, saw in graveyard." *Lombok rawet* is translated as "tiny chili terribly strong"; while *sambal asem*'s gloss develops into a recipe— "into cut chilies, two spoons of onion, a piece of *asam*, a bit of salt." "Serimpih" is a "Javanese dance at Sultan's court, old women wriggle among [the dancers] and straighten their dresses" (as indeed happens at the court dances). Biebl was tasting food, smelling flowers, exploring places, noticing details, and not just studying language from a textbook.

Some of these notes capture images that could be part of poems, yet they are not divided or clearly distinct from what one would think of as prosaic information and glossaries:

in the Javanese cemetery many white butterflies
lankse [is] *klambu* [mosquito net] for the dead
kapok [fiber from the silk-cotton tree] into mattresses, chairs . . .
white birds of paradise near rice fields

Some parts of the glossary, with their short lines, almost begin to resemble rough sketches of poems.

In Semarang
Three Chinese gods
The largest in the picture is an old man
Tjay == he is very rich, whoever gives offerings to him will become wealthy
Tjoe on his left
has many children
who gives offerings to him
will have many children
Sioe = on the right side
Has a long beard
will be very old
Tjay Tjoe Sioe

The glossing of Malay and Javanese words continues throughout the notebooks, but increasingly language learning notes develop into longer descriptions, narratives, or thematic constellations. Impressions and information that would serve as the basis of later texts were put on paper here for the first time: an account of the Javanese *slametan* ceremony, observations on Chinese and Javanese graveyards, diseases, cures, and magic, cooking, travel to Dieng Plateau, impressions from Javanese and Chinese puppet theater, and surrealist encounters with toads.

While Biebl's notes border on the ethnographic, they are not best described as objective descriptions of a culture. Biebl strives to capture in words his observations and sensations in the most immediate way, at their rawest—from nature, food, or markets to Javanese and Chinese ways of thinking and seeing. Yet even on the level of first sensations and quick observations, and perhaps especially here, his poetic vision is always already at work, as an opening onto the world, and as a search for moments, words, smells, or sights, for images and language, through which his poetry would evoke this world.

The style of the notebooks reflects these desires. Much of the writing consists of single words or short phrases—not so much ideas, but rather names and descriptions. When Biebl writes in sentences, they are mostly brief, plain, sometimes crude or incomplete. The notes are as if taken in a rush to capture fleeting sensations and quick glimpses in the raw, with words and phrases that first come to mind, without stopping to think, even at the cost of the poet's expressions being awkward or disjointed; in a rush, too, because there seems to be so much to take in. It is a frenetic endeavor to sense and to know, in a crushing avalanche of new things, tastes, smells, sights, sounds, names, and ways of thinking. "*Banjak pikiran* too much thinking, like the beginning of tuberculosis," he recorded in his notes on "Chinese diseases."

These are notes on a Chinese funeral:

Mrčon[305] boxes full of *mrčon* |
dragons dance rockets are fired
green, blue
head over the whole body and trail
champagne *Ut-čong-ham*

figures, gods

long sticks | in a crib | died previously
like pig, like devil, like monkey several
several

cartload of food | hundreds of roasted chickens
whole roasted pig

around the house of the dead
a sack from red fabric, in which

305 Firecracker in Malay/Javanese (*mercon*), in Czech spelling.

there is money | dragon (people who are trained especially
for this—the dragon's mouth opens and closes) lady of the house stands in front
of the house—three times she bows lady of the house to the dragon and dragon to her
| from a distance
as soon as the dragon approaches the house they start shooting
against him and they go there with beaters of the particular club (each club
has a dragon, its own dancers, there are as many clubs as there are dragons in the
parade)
dragon swallows sack | that is repeated)
then again the dragon is chased away with more shooting
[drawing of the dragon with notes]
at the crossroads they bow in all directions
and they shoot | evil spirits are chased away
[another annotated drawing of dragon]
music, mostly drums . . .

The Czech painter Otakar Nejedlý, who travelled to Ceylon in 1909, described his struggle to paint the tropics, his attempt to "submit like a child to new, powerful impressions", and the unexpected difficulty of "this rebirth"—a conflict between the "culture of European painting" and the different world.

> To the European painter, it seems as if his perspective on art were violated. . . . We, too wanted to submit to this force, but it was not quite possible, because we felt, we have a different foundation. That is part of the painful struggle which inevitably we had to experience in the tropics.[306]

Nejedlý's struggle concerned the foundations of painting. He described how he was trying to "adapt his pallete," to use colors differently, and to relearn how to paint forms. Biebl seems to be going through a similar struggle in Java. How to write poetry with these different flowers, fruits, trees, streets, and mountains? With these particular experiences of life, sickness and death? With these sights of beauty, violence, and injustice?

Biebl wrote in his unpublished text "Den na Jávě" (A day in Java): "Oh, the magic of new things! I know nothing about this blossom, about which the *babu* [nanny] tells the child. I never knew about it, never saw it, never heard about it before." He wishes he too could be helped out by a nanny:

> Can you smell that fragrance? she would ask me. That is the durian. My Czech nose would sense only a smell, even a horrible smell, which could never uncover all that,

306 Otakar Nejedlý, *Malířovy vzpomínky z Ceylonu a Indie* (Prague: Fr. Borový, 1923), 92–93.

which [in uttering the word durian] dripped from her mouth with cuddling indolence.[307]

Nezval said that "actuality is the dictionary for the creation of poetry,"[308] and Biebl's poetry in particular, in the words of a contemporary critic, "grew from that nearing to the essence of all things."[309] Biebl himself wrote that the poet "becomes an alchemist, and he is able to transform into gold each thing that he takes into his hand, if he has enough courage and understanding of the reactions of the complex chemistry."[310] However, one feels from his notebooks that in Java, he was faced with a world of new things and words, whose magic he felt but whose "complex chemistry"—sensations, emotions, memories— his "Czech nose" found difficult to understand.

If Biebl's published texts leave one sometimes wondering how much he saw of the colonies, the notebooks give one a sense of the intensity of the experience, and of how seriously Biebl, as a poet, was working; how he almost desperately tried to take in and learn as much as possible, and what an overabundance of poetic material he encountered. Like in the case of the painter Nejedlý, this was a "painful struggle," as if Biebl were drowning in new words, sights, smells, flowers, fruits, in different attitudes to death, in too much noise. Language begins to break down under the onslaught of new things. One wonders whether it was this very overabundance that reduced him to near silence. The notebooks evoke a loud, bright, colorful world, full of strong sensations—like "the amazing carnival of a mad Chinese funeral." His published poetry, in particular, only hesitantly emerges from silence.

307 Biebl, *Cesta na Jávu*, 55–6.
308 Nezval, "Kapka inkoustu," *ReD* 1 (1927–28): 313.
309 Pavel Frankl, "Básnický projev," 148.
310 *Dílo*, 5:263.

WITH THE SHIP THAT CARRIES TEA AND COFFEE

In late October 1926, Biebl set out by train from Prague to the Italian port city Genoa. He travelled together with Olga Trnečková, who was on her way to visit her brother-in-law Alois Kselík in the Dutch East Indies.[311] In Genoa Biebl boarded the German ocean liner *Yorck*, sailing to Singapore (Figure 14). He travelled second class. The *Yorck* called at Port Said, Biebl's first encounter with the "Orient" on this journey, and Colombo on Ceylon, the first tropical island. He had some time to walk around the port cities, and from Colombo, he went on a daytrip to the hill town of Kandy. There, he saw for the first time rice fields, coconut palm plantations, jungles, and the world of British colonialism. From Singapore, Biebl sailed on the Dutch ship the *Plancius* to Batavia, reaching there on 28th November.

However special and dream-like this voyage from Europe to Southeast Asia might have been for Biebl, this was a regular, busy route, along which thousands of people travelled every year. "It seems to me that the schedule Marseille—Colombo is more profuse than the schedules of some tramway lines in Prague," a Czech traveler wrote about a segment of Biebl's route in late 1920s; and Marseille, like Genoa, was only one of a number of busy European ports linked to Asia.[312] As the title *With the Ship that Carries/Imports [dováží] Tea and Coffee* suggests, Biebl was also conscious that he was following in the heavy footsteps of colonialism, "in the same boat"—Suez Canal being "the shortest way to the wealth of the Indies; the mouse hole leading to the larder."[313]

After a short time in Batavia, the capital on the north coast of West Java, Biebl took the train east, to Semarang. He based himself there, at the home of the Czech physician Alois Kselík, with whom he already corresponded before his trip. Surakarta (Solo) and Yogyakarta in Java's interior, with their royal courts, were and are more celebrated as tourist destinations and centers of

311 Her signature appears on a few postcards from the outward voyage and from Semarang, but she is otherwise absent from Biebl's own writings, except for a brief comic scene probably inspired by her: a teenage, German-speaking "Ema," who was supposed to travel under Biebl's guardianship to Sumatra to visit her uncle, sails off by mistake to America on the ocean liner *Julius Cesar*. See Biebl, *Cesta na Jávu*, 19.

312 Přikryl, *Putování*, 10.

313 Biebl, *Cesta na Jávu*, 33.

traditional Javanese culture and arts. Semarang, in contrast, was/is a large, modern city on the north coast of Java, a major port and a busy center of commerce and industry, with a strong ethnic Chinese presence. Having had some medical training, Biebl assisted Dr. Kselík in his practice (just like how he had at times assisted his mother in her practice at home), and was "able to catch a glimpse of Chinese and Javanese life, especially at moments of suffering that accompany sickness and death."[314] Kselík's surgery seems to mirror the practice of his father in his childhood home, "the wailing that was sometimes audible from the surgery and that mixed with parrots' cries," "the practice of child—future poet." "Biebl is a medic," and this too, must have helped him feel "unusual friendships" across oceans. He took many photographs—a large number were published in the magazine *Domov a svět* (Home and the world); they are discussed in the second part of this book. Biebl funded his trip in part using advance payments for his pictures and texts. He wandered the streets and markets of the city and saw its Chinese temples and cemeteries. From Semarang, he explored parts of the island: he visited the mountain town Wonosobo and the nearby Dieng plateau with its small Hindu temples and mountainous sacred landscape dotted with lakes, volcanic craters, and caves; Borobudur, the monumental Buddhist temple-stupa, and Prambanan, a large Hindu temple complex; the court city of Solo; among other places. He saw performances of Javanese and Chinese dance, puppet theater, and various celebrations and ceremonies. Many of the sites he visited were (and still are) on most standard tourist itineraries. At the same time, judging from his writings, diaries, and photographs, Biebl enjoyed walking around villages, towns, and countryside, and saw something of Java beyond its monuments—people, markets, cemeteries, small towns, plantations. He left from Batavia on 29th December 1926 on the Dutch ship *Grotius*, which called at Belawan (Sumatra), Colombo, Port Said, and Genoa, on its way to Amsterdam. On 22nd January 1927, Biebl was in Genoa again, and probably took the train from there back to winter Prague (or, less likely, sailed on to Amsterdam, which the ship was scheduled to reach on the 30th of January).[315] The whole journey took about three months, about two of which were spent on ships and in port cities.

With the Ship appeared one year after the poet's return. Reception was mixed. Šalda, the most influential among literary critics, warns readers not to expect "Faustesque, Karamazovesque, or Nietzschean discharges in this wistful, shy, melancholy human," but also speaks of "delightful humor,"

---

314 Biebl, "Semarang," 7.

315 The information about the return journey, previously unpublished, was compiled from lists of passengers in Dutch newspapers, available at < http://kranten.delpher.nl>. The lists disagree on whether he disembarked in Genoa or in Amsterdam.

"pure poetry," and "pure, glowing crystal-likeness" of the verses.[316] According to the young critic and poet Antonín Matěj Píša, in Biebl's poetry, "the nerves vibrate with music that is delicate, yet sometimes very painfully penetrating." However—if Šalda was somewhat disappointed that Biebl is not Goethe, Dostoyevsky and Nietsche—Píša would prefer him to be more like Gaugin or Baudelaire, and to show "a fundamental romantic desire for the exotic world":

> His tragic is illuminated by the tenderness of a lullaby . . . There is the sadness from life, from actuality, but not despair and hatred of the surrounding world. Therefore: Biebl does not flee to the exotic like Gaugin or Baudelaire. He does not have in him the fundamental romantic desire for the exotic world. . . . The Biebl of Slavětín is too similar to Biebl in Java. . . . Now the distant homeland is transformed into an exotic corner, which becomes more beautiful and darkens like a fairy tale in his vision, while Biebl experiences true exotic actuality with the same intimate, diminutive, warm and playful imagination like before he did in the environs of Slavětín. . . . He is in no way similar to the hero of Chadourne's "Vasco" [a sordid 1927 French novel set in Tahiti, with the main character modeled on Gaugin]. . . . He lets two worlds permeate each other. . . . It is exoticism almost privately familiar, in which there are no fatal depths, fiery excitement, or dramatic action.[317]

In their disappointment, the critics, in many ways perceptive, reveal their own expectations—travel outside Europe equates with heavy-weight German, French and Russian romantic or existential "discharges" and "fiery excitement"—and they put their finger on how Biebl's poetic travel was particular and different.

When *With the Ship* appeared, it was seen as *the* literary fruit of Biebl's journey, whereas the prose texts and photographs, which he published in periodicals, some soon after the trip and others years later, received no critical attention. *With the Ship* would become one of Biebl's most popular books, which may partly explain why the voyage to Java has become so much part of Biebl's image. At the same time, from the perspective of later years, *With the Ship* appears, not as the final poetic response to the Javanese voyage, but as the first, cautious step on a long journey.

Thinking of this tropical collection, I think again of quietly hovering snowflakes. As if with every word the poet more than ever hesitated to break the spell, to break the silence. As if the actual voyage—and even the expectation of the impending travel, for several of the poems were written before departure—had momentarily calmed down the faster, more easily moving

316 Šalda, *O poezii*, 160–1.
317 Píša, "Básník na Javě," 200–03.

imagery and striking juxtapositions of some of his previous work, especially *With Golden Chains*. The hesitation was not simply poetic: it was also a hesitation to speak about what others spoke too easily.

> again I am afraid to breathe that they may not vanish anew
> it is enough that the Dutch are breathing deeply on everything

The emphasis in his poetry is somewhat different from his prose writings. In the collection of poems, one motif emerges as a persistent concern: home and homeland as felt by a traveler—the desire to leave and the desire to return, the joy and anxiety of being at home and of travelling. One gets a sense that Biebl did not travel easily. Yet, the book's underlying emotion is not a sentimental "home sweet home" (or in the words of the Czech equivalent, "everywhere well, at home the best"), but more like Mácha's unsettling poetic knowledge of *země* in the prison cell of the universe, although in Biebl a dark, cosmic consciousness blends with a playfulness and a comic sense for the absurd.

Two Czech university professors, who in 1909 spent half a year in Java before travelling on to Australia, contrasted "us," the Czechs, with "rich Americans and Englishmen" in their description of ocean liners:

> On the floating colossi, there is a concentration of perhaps more comfort than any metropolis with luxurious hotels has on offer. Of course, a poor man cannot afford all this luxury, but rich Americans and Englishmen, for whom our Earth is becoming tiny, travel around the world rather like when we, people from Prague, leave to a summer house in a godforsaken little village. . . . For one, it is a momentous event when he leaves his solitude for a neighboring little village; another wanders the whole world, feels equally happy and "at home" everywhere, and his only regret is that there are not more continents.[318]

It is not only that our country is small; we live on an infinitely smaller scale, we are in the world differently than the lightly-travelling "rich Americans and Englishmen." Theirs is a greatness which dwarfs the Earth, while we are snails for whom the lawn is a jungle. Still, compared to Biebl, the two professors travelled light and far, and feelings about home hardly appear in their travelogues.

For at least sixty years before Biebl, quite a few Czechs—military doctors, sailors, musicians, adventurers, scientists, and "well-known travelers"—sailed to the Indies (some settled and died there) and a small number

318 Daneš and Domin, *Dvojím rájem*, 1:6.

wrote about their travels. In the 1920s alone, Jan Havlasa and A. V. Novák, for instance, writers popular with readers but not taken seriously by literary critics and historians, and the traveler, writer and teacher Barbora Markéta Eliášová (said to be the first Czech woman to travel around the world), stopped over in the Dutch East Indies as they crisscrossed the globe and wrote about the places they visited in their travelogues and fiction. The Moravian ethnologist Pavel Šebesta / Paul Schebesta spent two years in Malayan and Sumatran jungles living and nomadizing with the "Orang-Utan," the forest people, and he did extensive fieldwork in the Philippines and Africa.[319] Havlasa, Eliášová and Šebesta were each fluent in several foreign languages, unlike Biebl. Czech musicians spent their lives and built their careers in Batavia and other places. Hundreds of Czech and Moravian farmers migrated to Tahiti in the 1920s in search of better life. In comparison to their travels—not to speak about the superlight "rich Americans and Englishmen"—Biebl's brief trip seems like a brief stroll in a "magnificent fragrant park." Yet, in Czech literary history, as well as in the reactions of the poets and critics of his generation, Biebl's journey looms large, and the halo of a great traveler has been painted over the poet's head—literary historians commonly blow up the myth of Biebl's travel by misleadingly adding Borneo and the Pacific to the places he visited.

While people like Havlasa, Novák, Eliášová, Šebesta, and others globetrotted or lived and worked abroad, the Czech avant-garde poets and artists were daydreaming in Prague cafés about faraway seas, tropical islands, palms, a world connected by steamships, telegraph lines, and international art. Taking the actual train to actual Italy or France was a great journey for them. From reviews of Biebl's work at the time, one gets the sense that the Czech avant-gardists viewed his journey with a mixture of fascination and suspicion, a sense that for some of them, he might have just "gone too far." Biebl was and was not one of them—he travelled farther, and yet he always half-remained a villager, for whom Prague was a great city—at times too great. Reading Biebl's critics and admirers makes me think of the Czech word *zápecnictví* (from *za pecí*, "behind the baking oven"): the life experience and worldview of one who happily stays in the warm, cozy and protected place behind the baking oven, the antinomy of the cold, rain, or snow outside. Seifert's poem "Three Bitter Seeds," dedicated to Biebl and quoted earlier, gently captures some of the incomprehensibility of Biebl's journey— "It is not at home in our land . . . What can one write about what one does not know?"

---

319 Mrázek, "Primeval Forest, Homeland, Catastrophe."

The collection *With the Ship that Carries Tea and Coffee* has three parts. A reader might expect the book to open with an exotic theme; instead, the first and longest part is a set of poems more narrowly focused on home and Slavětín than one finds anywhere in Biebl's other collections.[320] The title of this part of the book is "Začarovaná studánka" (The little charmed spring). Píša wrote in his review: "There is much in just these two words. Childhood with its dreams, fairy tales, memories . . . image-transparency in the intertwining of two worlds. . . . Nerves vibrate with music that is delicate, yet sometimes very painfully penetrating."[321] The intimate, diminutive space of "The Little Charmed Spring" illuminates the ships, oceans and faraway lands evoked by the title of the book and poems in the latter sections, and in turn, as with the sailboat and the butterfly, faraway oceans are mirrored in the water of the little spring, the source, from which it is destined to journey toward the sea.

The sparrow is no albatross. The sparrow is not your typical poetic bird, that image of free flight and release from earthly bonds. The sparrow is a bird that is through and through common, ever-present in flocks in every Bohemian village or town park. It is as un-exotic as a bird can be. In Czech, "you have a sparrow's nest on your head" means your hair is a mess. The first verses of the book start in the middle of the poet's village—the saint's statue is still there today:

Near the chapel a sandstone statue stands
one crowned by a sparrow's nest
it remembers many loves[322]

Reminiscences of "many loves" recur throughout the first part: not Love with a deep pathos, but fleeting reminiscences of dates and playful lovemaking, its softness and its warmth, homely like the sparrow's nest crowning the saint's head, or like the "softest moss" in Biebl's earlier poetry.

Later in the first part, the mood changes. In the stumbling, broken verses of "Žně" (Harvest), the poet is snubbed by a proud farmer woman. He is a lonely stranger aimlessly wandering among the village folk with their straightforwardly meaningful lives, content with their fields' and their own fertility.

320 Six poems from the first part of the book appeared already in December 1926 in a private printing, under the title *Blue shadows*. Konstantin Biebl, *Modré stíny* (Královské Vinohrady: Kamill Resler, 1926).

321 Píša, "Básník na Javě," 200.

322 Biebl, *S lodí*, 11.

The moment has come no one is here
    I tear
    and throw into the wind the leaves of a black notebook covered with writing

They were poems probably not worth much
    like the love when I kissed doleful Soňa
Fly away husks when ears of grain crumble
    I can do without you Without her
    Without lorgnon

It is so difficult to walk by a full load of grain[323]

In the next poem, "V noci" (At night), sparrows reappear, now in a different key:

Fever, anxiety torture the sick one
    and heavy dreams.

I would like to ask you, sparrows,
whether you also feel anxious
when suddenly at night you dream about a malicious boy
    throwing stones at you.[324]

The words *úzkost* and *úzko*, "anxiety, angst" and "anxious," which appear in the last two poems, mean also "narrowness" in Czech. These are words that Mácha often used, also in reference to his home.[325] Biebl's feeling of anxiety in his native village, at home, is a claustrophobic sensation of being in a space that is increasingly constricting. That is the other side of the intimate cuteness of "Little Charmed Spring" and "softest moss"; it is also the other side of dreams of faraway lands. (Recall, in Schulz's "North-West-East-South," the small cell, whose walls "strangled him earlier than the executioner's rope," where the murderer begins to first dream of palms; or Seifert's "Am I not right, my love, here at home all things are inane, / There is no joy for us here.")

An undated letter written by Biebl from Slavětín expresses similar feelings about being at home:

Here in Slavětín it is terribly dreary [*hrozná votrava*, informal expression, literally "a terrible poisoning"]. With a friend, I go fishing, for sardines, his mother still has ten

323 Biebl, *S lodí*, 23.
324 Biebl, *S lodí*, 26.
325 See Janský, *Karel Hynek Mácha*, 247.

> cans in the pantry. Often it rains and I've bought motorcycle glasses, that's about all. . . . I would like to tell you many beautiful words, but whenever I come to the countryside, too quickly I become a peasant with all his cloddiness, consistently so unto the smallest part, so that even sadness and melancholy go somehow deep down. Everything sticks to me, just like the mud when one strides across the plowed field after rain, evenings are drawn out as if out of spite, so that darkness would last as long as possible, so that it would take as long as possible to get to midnight—relief comes always only in the morning.[326]

This may have been his feelings before he left for Java, but also after he came back and when he was revising, writing and compiling *With the Ship.* It was then, in March 1927, that he wrote, in another letter (to the Mácha scholar Janský): "We can't go out because of the amount of mud, which reaches up to our shoulders. One moves with difficulty, perhaps like a fish pickled in aspic." [327] Also sometime around this time, he wrote to Xena Longenová, who was among his friends at the train station when he was departing for Java (she herself committed suicide in 1928): "I am sad here. A man at home does not feel he is among his own."[328] This, too, is part of home and the world in his "Javanese" poetry.

With the final poem in this part, "Orient," the mood changes again:

> I always envied cooks
> anise, nutmeg, vanilla.
>
> I love Christmas,
> that Muslim holiday.
>
> On the Christmas Eve
> mother will divide an orange
> into twelve Turkish sabers.
>
> She gives us one each.[329]

After the angst of the preceding, feverishly claustrophobic poems, there is relief and release, not entirely unlike the momentary warmth of the home that Mácha's prisoner feels in his cell, in "Return." It is through a return to a warm image of childhood home, a fairy tale of sorts, that the poet escapes

326 Konstantin Biebl, archive of the Museum of Czech Literature, Prague.
327 Letter published in Slabý, *Potkávání*, 245.
328 Letter published in Slabý, *Potkávání*, 64.
329 Biebl, *S lodí*, 27.

from the presently-felt anxiety of home's narrowness. It is a return home, but a home in the past, a home that is gone. The return is already a departure. In this, the final poem of "The Little Charmed Spring" looks forwards to the journey to the East, the latter part of the book. It *already* senses the Orient at the heart of home, in winter: the most cherished homeliness of home smells of Eastern spices and tastes of faraway lands. The journey to Java was at the same time an impossible return home, a flight in search of "white towns drowned in the waters' womb . . . my childhood time."

Only prejudiced admirers and critics could (and did) see "home sweet home" as a conclusion reached by Biebl. Home is a Little Charmed Spring, wondrous, torturous, and pervaded by anxiety and contradictions, at once the stuff of fairy tales and suffocating, narrow normalcy.

Part of this home are memories of the World War and the death of the poet's father. Biebl's war experience was also his first trip to the Orient, and in *With the Ship*, the Great War and the journey to Java form a painfully dissonant chord, but a chord nonetheless. The great world is mirrored in the little charmed spring that is the village. The World War blows up home:

> Our graveyard grew so much larger during the war
> one tip reaches Siberia
> there blue-grey snow falls
> . . . .
> One tip reaches Piave
> on the grave oranges drum[330]

(In Siberia, the Czech legionaries fought against the Bolsheviks, and many died there. Piave is a river in Italy, and another battlefront in the Great War.)

The second part of the book is titled, like the book itself, "With the Ship that Carries Tea and Coffee." Its first poem, "Na procházce" (On a stroll), is still not about the journey to Java, but about a walk through a forest near Slavětín, and its fleeting impressions—as if the overseas journey were merely an extension of a walk near one's home, and at once an escape from such homely strolling. The last line of the poem speaks of departure: "There are so many abandoned nests in the forest."[331]

The rest of the second part of the book is a poetic travelogue of the journey across the sea—a collage of fragmentary sights, sensations, thoughts and daydreams. I recall the fleeting fragments of landscape seen through the window of a train—"you can see to the heart of a landscape." Yet, just like the more relaxed, expansive rhythm of ship travel is different from that of a

330 Biebl, *S lodí*, 20.
331 Biebl, *S lodí*, 33.

Figure 14. The *Yorck*, the ship on which Biebl sailed from Genoa to Singapore. Postcard, no date. Author's collection.

speeding train, so this poetry moves at a more relaxed speed, with more time for daydreaming, than the poems in *With Golden Chains*, where "it all flies by insanely," as Biebl says about the view from a train window.

The actual journey only gradually emerges from dreams of travel, in one of Biebl's most famous poems, whose song-like, warm mellifluousness, dactylic pulse and rhymes I utterly fail to translate. It begins:

With the ship that carries tea and coffee
I will one day sail to faraway Java[332]

The borders between actuality and imagination, seeing and daydreaming, remain blurred, as do those between the sea and the land. The bottom of the sea, magically revealed as the ship sails along biblical shores and times, is reminiscent of an ordinary Czech meadow, with fish resembling birds.

We will sail past the pyramids
the ship will wait till Moses and his people cross

332 Biebl, *S lodí*, 34.

With a tall staff and dusty sandals
he walks first over sea grass and blooming anemones

A flock of fish on dry land lift their wings like birds
fly over water and disappear in the waves[333]

If at home some years before the journey a butterfly flying over a meadow evoked a boat sailing across the ocean, now the sea evokes home:

On the vast sea November is beginning.
    On the vast sea
    just like at home in a tree-lined alley.[334]

There are moments when the great world is seen through the eyes of a carefree wanderer, an echo of "over vast sea to sail and sail"; and there are moments of anxiety and guilt.

Tramp's Song [Tuláckà]

The tramp with a cigarette wanders the world
and everywhere he feels happy
Yesterday he walked over the mountains in Tibet
today he sings and sails on the sea

How beautiful how blue God's world is
and the tramp hurries on
Christ Buddha and Mohammed
that was a holy trinity of tramps

On the sky the Southern Cross burns
what is my mother doing at home?
My son you are not returning
and the night is so long so long

She lights a candle then puts it out
the wick smolders with a red glow
You only stroked your little son's hair

For that now you have to suffer and keep vigil[335]

333 Biebl, *S lodí*, 34.
334 Biebl, *S lodí*, 36.
335 Biebl, *S lodí*, 37.

The Southern Cross joins a eulogy to tramping with an elegy on home; it joins careless freedom with anxiety, the tropics with the home, where his mother bears the cross. One may recall Mácha reaching to the stars— "and only the earth [*země*] is mine!"; his "Unhappy earth [*země*], unhappy mother!" There are religious, Catholic overtones in Biebl's poem, yet I have to think of the statue of a saint "crowned by a sparrow's nest," in the first lines of the collection: the next poem, "V Africe" (In Africa), quickly reassures us: "I am no saint."

An earlier, unpublished version of the "Tramp's Song," incidentally, lacks the whole second part as well as any feeling of homesickness. Instead, it ends:

Finally content finally free
Aching for distances the wanderer looks
How to the promised land his ship is drawn
By angelic quires of laughing gulls[336]

At some moments at least, the travelling poet felt an untainted exhilaration and home was blissfully forgotten. One might even wonder, at what point, how much later, and for whom, the evocation of anxiety and pious guilt was added.

Religious imagery becomes increasingly nightmarish in the concluding poem of this (second) part of the book about the sea voyage, "S očima k nebi" (With eyes heavenward), a fantasy where the ship sinks and the passengers drown; a grotesque, sarcastic Last Judgement, at once terrifying and irreverently humorous, foreshadowing Biebl's later poetry, especially the flight and fall of *New Icarus*, and even the poet's suicide.

On the sea the dance hall rocks
    where have the resplendent ladies disappeared?
Only now does the carnival begin
    in the embrace of waves and green lightning.

The drowning poet laughs at his "brother," a missionary:

I thought heaven, oh, heaven, was up there,
    and yet we are falling down!

I thought in heaven, oh, in heaven, it is beautiful there
    like in a café, where chandeliers glow and angels play billiard,

336 Konstantin Biebl, archive of the Museum of Czech Literature, Prague.

there dead poets break bread and write poems on tables.
For each female saint one madrigal.

I thought in heaven, oh, in heaven, they dance,
they dance modern dances,
Lord God is watching one angelic couple:
What elegance! What elegance!
Pity I am so old.

I thought in heaven, oh, in heaven, it's all music and glow
and here there is silence and not an iota of light.
At sea, brother, you prayed the breviary,
at least there the stars and a lighthouse shone.

Perhaps we aren't in paradise yet,
brrr! so cold, I tell you,
my hands are numb and legs feel weary.
We must go elsewhere. But where?

Perhaps we're standing at heaven's gate,
we know nothing, we aren't in luck.
And then: how can one even wish to knock,
when our bodies are already stiff?

I can't even pull out the mirror from my pocket.
Pity! You look like hell!
Your hair is full of green seaweed,
and your belly, brother, so horribly bloated.
See, on earth you had better times.

We must not despair. It is not the end.
We must go farther, we must go deeper,
just like every proper drowned man,
with our eyes heavenwards, with our eyes up![337]

A jazzy *danse macabre*—"drums the drummer drums to attack into darkness and emptiness"[338]—yet somehow a moment filled with deep silence from Mácha comes to mind again—the thoughts of a man sentenced to death:

337 Biebl, *S lodí*, 41–44.
338 Biebl, *Nový Ikaros*, 26.

There mere emptiness—above me
and around me and under me
mere emptiness there yawns.—
Without end silence—no voice—
without end place—night—even time— —
That is the mortal dream of mind,
that is what "nothing" is called.[339]

The sky and the water mirror each other; opposites, above and below, life and death, I and the other, are entangled in vertigo, like when tropical jungle appears in the ice-patterns on a frozen window. But if Biebl's own statements show a belief in poetry's powers—the poet's "fantasy moves with mile-long strides and his associations extend their hands toward each other across oceans"—in his poetry one also senses an abyss, a darkness, emptiness, silence, below the poet's "instinctive mania to relate all things of this world."

This intoxicating fear and alluring danger of drowning in the ocean is the concluding glimpse of the poet's sea journey. Death, end—and yet: "It is not the end, we must go farther, we must go deeper." As if this collapse of heaven were necessary to go farther, to go deeper, to see Java. Not that naked truth would now be suddenly manifest—we sink deeper still "with our eyes heavenwards," but deeper nevertheless.

The final, third part of the book, "Protinožci" (Antipodes), finally shows Java. Fragmentary views again. Through the poet's eyes, one sees and dreams nature (monkeys, fruits, palms, birds, the jungle, a tiger, and plantations), people (Javanese men and women, a Chinese coolie, a policeman), and social reality under colonialism and the "silence of the millions."

The first poem of "Antipodes" is untitled:

First I raise my hands to reach fruits
as high as I am able in this world.
Oh, tropical sun! Oh equatorial sun,
the oldest of Malay gods!

Palms, a naughty little boy sadly bows his head before you,
better than anyone else in the whole village he could climb the trees.
He'd like to move up there to room and board among you,
among coconuts and monkeys.

339 Karel Hynek Mácha, *Máj* (Prague: Academia, 2003), 32.

He'd like to climb high among colorful birds.
Oh, the color of wings so bright!
So easily they soar up above the clouds
    and alive to heaven they fly.[340]

The traveler has reached Java, and, "a naughty little boy again," he speaks to palms about childhood at home. Still he cannot reach the colorful birds of his dreams. This is a recurring dream: beauty overcoming time and death—but only birds fly to heaven alive.

I recall his childhood memories, the artificial palm, his father's colorful birds, beautiful and desperate. Not just dreaming of beauty, but poetic revelations of reality—the blending of beauty and suffering, dreaming and violence—seem to be, for Biebl, already prefigured in his childhood. "To earth binds us love, wrath, grief": this may be one achievement that remained underestimated by his contemporaries in Prague cafés—that his writings about Java poetically reveal the reality of the Indies, also through his own displacement, powerlessness, and disillusionment, equally at the sight of colorful exotic birds and sparrows. It was said that his journey was "a vain pilgrimage toward a mirage," but this failure, the poetic performance of disillusionment, the disturbing awakening from beautiful dreams, was part of the poetic truth-seeking.

At the same time, the case of this poem gives clues about how actuality is recomposed as it is poetically revealed. In the published book, the untitled poem opens the last section, about Java. However, an earlier, unpublished version of the poem is titled "Pozdrav Cejlonu" (Greeting to Ceylon) and instead of "the oldest of Malay gods" in the published version ("Malay" at the time was commonly used loosely to include also "Javanese" and other ethnic groups), it refers to "ancient Indian gods."[341] Thus, the poem was apparently originally written about Ceylon—the first tropical island where Biebl stopped on his way to Java—and the book's poetic image of Java is in part based on impressions of Ceylon. (This is just one example of such poetic reordering of the experience of reality. Another instance: a night encounter with a toad in his prose piece "First Night in Java," set in Batavia, actually took place in Wonosobo much later, according to Biebl's notebook.)

I traveled to "Ceylon"—Sri Lanka—in 2013. Unlike Biebl, I had known Java for many years before I visited Sri Lanka, but already while looking from

340 Biebl, *S lodí*, 49.

341 In the manuscript version of collection of poems, there is another version, apparently an intermediate one, on which one can see further how Biebl was transforming his poem: there is no more reference to Ceylon, and Indian gods are already replaced by Malay ones, while in other places this intermediate version is close to the earlier "Greetings to Ceylon."

the airport taxi, and throughout my trip, I was struck by the multitude of colorful birds in the trees, here and elsewhere in the country, which was unlike anything I had seen in Java. In the Colombo city center, there are lakes that are home to water birds, as are the deltas of large rivers, canals, and the many lakes in the lowlands around Colombo. There are coconut palms everywhere, more prevalent than in Java. Czechs who travelled to Ceylon before Biebl have been especially impressed by these. In Biebl's photographic reportages, coconuts first appear in his images of Ceylon (see Figure 33). He wrote: "You do not see Ceylon before you see its trees. Already the first strip of land, when it appears, is thickly green, from the innumerable forests of coconut palms." Biebl also travelled to Kandy—"you see first plantations, tea, coffee, pineapples."[342] The road leads through rice fields, coconut plantations, and later mountain jungles. For a European arriving in the tropics for the first time, Ceylon has much in common with Java, but there are also differences. First impressions are always strong, and one may wonder how Biebl's "Javanese" poetic motifs, some more than others, might have been first shaped by his experience of Ceylon. The history of "Greeting to Ceylon," the poem that would become the opening poem about Java, certainly suggests that.

"Na hoře Merbabu" (On Mount Merbabu), the second poem in this section of the book, begins with a description of the troubled beauty of Javanese jungle— "in the ferns . . . the royal tiger is dying . . . the blood flowing down his body will add neither color nor fame." The second half of the poem, a child-like fantasy is sparked by exotic names such as the "breadfruit tree":

God, this is the Java of my dreams
Land forested with the waterfall's murmur
    one needs only to pluck bread
    a tree gives fresh milk

One tree here is the gingerbread baker
    one needs only to collect the gingerbread
    and load it on a cart

One needs only to shake the treetop of a nutmeg tree
    and into the lap
    golden ducats rain

    But never ask
    to whose?[343]

---

342 Konstantin Biebl, "Ceylon," *Domov a svět* 1, no. 10 (1927): 3.
343 Biebl, *S lodí*, 51.

The fairy-tale-like yet homely paradise is abruptly upset in the last line, which shows everything in a sinister light: the people who profit from what appeared like a fairy land, are the colonizers; what first felt like playfulness with a touch of smiling irony, turns into bitter sarcasm. (One might recall Biebl's letter to Wolker's mother, where he speaks of "light waves" of "light French poetism" "wrecked" on the "rock, heavy and sad," of Wolker's proletarian poetry.) This is more than an anti-colonial commentary. It is an almost bodily sensation of disillusionment, a fall from beautiful dreams to painful reality. The poem is not simply a criticism of *them*, the colonizers. *Our* childhood dreams, the stuff of *our* fairy tales, are upset—shown first in their tender beauty, then in their ugliness and violence. Java is no longer an exotic land, but yet another place where certain questions are silenced.

Biebl dynamites dreams of Java like other fairy castles, and documents that destruction in his poems—even as he clings to beauty and dreams, like when, in his early poetry, he holds onto at least one fairy tale, "where there were neither kings / nor princesses // 'She did, didn't she, mother, / in the end survive after all, / the Red Riding Hood?'"

Already in the 1924 poem "Indians," Biebl wrote: "Beyond the sea there's a beautiful land. Who remembers still, whose / are those plantations, prairies, and woods?" In that poem, the fate of Czech workers mirrors the plight of the "Indians." Biebl saw exploitation in the colonies with the same eyes, the same emotion, as he saw exploited people in his own country—through the mirroring of his poetry, in which metaphors and imagination "form unusual friendships" across oceans. Five years after he returned from Java, in 1932, he wrote in a report on the conditions of workers and miners in North Bohemia: "I recognized immediately that I am in the colonies . . . somewhere far across the sea, where I am squeezing myself through the slums of Javanese and Chinese coolies."[344]

"Soudní referát" (Court report) describes the arrest of a "small Javanese woman" by a military patrol— "a flock of crows circle round and round." The Court questions her "in God's presence . . . a hundred times" whether she saw how a Chinese coolie shot and killed a policeman. The Javanese woman answers, "slowly, voice faltering, with every word a kiss," that she did not.

She did not see at all what happened,
for she was just pondering,
why it is, that all white orchids

one day will burst into bloom all over Java.[345]

344 Biebl, *Dílo*, 5:276.
345 Biebl, *S lodí*, 57.

Figure 15. "Cotton." Photo by K. Biebl. Archive of the Museum of Czech Literature, Prague; published in *Domov a svět*, 1927.

In "On Mount Merbabu" a dream is harshly interrupted by colonial reality; in "Court Report," the logic of power and "justice" is shattered by a (day) dream of beauty. The soft voice and the poetic image do not directly attack "justice," but seem to see through their impermanence and look toward a different future. The white orchids bloom as if out of nothing, out of silence and invisibility. Dreams, beauty, and poetry undermine, in a soft, faltering voice, the robust actuality of power-backed and power-backing "justice" in colonial Java.

Intertwined with images of familiar "justice" in the distant colonies, is tropical nature, strange yet strangely familiar. The *cicak* lizard sounds like a little dove from back home, and in the depths of the jungle the poet hears a rabbi's funerary psalms and Moravian Teachers' Choir. The strange is not simply reduced into familiarity, but rather the mysterious and the familiar are perceived afresh in their strange juxtapositions, displacements and blending—again like the "door in the neighborhood of an ocean . . . a matter of revealing actuality, to give it its shining form like on the first day." The poet also hears "sacred gamelan" in the jungle (Biebl does not explain that the gamelan is a Javanese orchestra consisting mostly of gongs and other bronze instruments), and hears how "there in the depths of the primeval forest plays the organ / a frog huge lazy and sad." Only if one has heard the otherworldly concert of Javanese frogs after rain can one fully sense the connection between those frogs and the organ (I think of the gothic church in Slavětín), or understand why one of the most sacred and majestic kinds of Javanese gamelan is called *Kodok Ngorek*, "Croaking Frogs." Biebl here makes poetry with Javanese worlds; a Czech reader is unlikely to fully understand. But Biebl, too, is conscious that he only half-understands what he sees and hears. The familiar, rather than being contrasted to the otherness of the tropics, is shown in its own strangeness and mystery. The "mad *toke* lizard" (*toke* is a small lizard commonly roaming on the walls of Southeast Asian houses, whose name imitates the sound it produces: to—keee) has the voice of Viktorka—a character and a haunting image from a classic of nineteenth-century Czech literature, *Babička* (Granny) by Božena Němcová. In the original story, Viktorka, a beautiful village girl, has become insane, perhaps because—neither the villagers nor the readers can be sure—of a "secret evil force," or perhaps because of her tragic love for a vagrant soldier. She lives without a home in the forest, singing lullabies above a stream where, some of the villagers believe, she drowned her baby.

Like Czech forests, tropical nature in Java is inhabited by supernatural beings and animals with human souls. Biebl was particularly interested in local beliefs about death. Thoughts of death, the dead as a living presence, and rebirth permeate his work and life. The dead reappear in the beauty and freshness of trees and flowers, like echoes of Mácha's "Return": "the grave will reunite me with you [*země*], and again, in new transformed form, new life will bring me out onto you."[346] At the same time, Biebl's interest in local ideas of death and rebirth was part of a curiosity about life and thought in Java generally—alongside Javanese cuisine, tropical fruits, and so on. His images of spirits and reincarnation appear to be based on a mix of information about, and direct observation of Javanese, Chinese, Buddhist, and Hindu beliefs and practices, which all coexist or blend in Java. Especially in his poetry (as opposed to his prose), they are not always "correct" as ethnographic representations. However, the general feelings of the presence of spirits and the supernatural in the Javanese world as captured by Biebl is not far from the

346 Mácha, *Prosa*, 276.

Figure 16. A photo taken by K. Biebl in Java, 1926. Archive of the Museum of Czech Literature, Prague.

reality of the "air" of Java, or from Javanese ways of being in the world, as one quickly learns when one speaks and lives with people in Java.

In a text he read on the radio, "Javští démoni" (Javanese demons), Biebl tells about Paviro, a Javanese man who "wrote poems and lovingly painted the gods of his land"—shadow puppets (*wayang*)—and who accompanied Biebl "everywhere." Biebl represents himself as an outsider who is afforded fragmentary glimpses into Paviro's reality—another reality, another imagination, yet resonating with and infusing Biebl's own. From their interaction and conversations, from their (sometimes awkwardly) being together, Biebl only gradually, and never fully, begins to feel how Paviro lives with a multitude of spirits inhabiting trees, old houses, statues, mountains, and other places. The spirits, whose forms and behavior must have had for Biebl a certain surrealist poetry about them, are also described in his Javanese notebook, and they would keep haunting his poems and prose texts. They are only glanced briefly from Paviro's actions, words, and silences, yet they come to inhabit Biebl's own vision of Java, just like how one's own experience is influenced by that of a fellow traveler.[347]

The poet's representations of the supernatural have neither the depersonalized objectivity of conventional ethnography nor the othering effect of some exoticizing accounts of "the Orient." What enlivens his poetry, rather, are personal perspectives, experiences, and feelings, of the poet and of the Javanese people he encountered. The jungle is described as evoking multiple feelings and associations, some of which are unabashedly his own, often conjuring specifically Czech memories. In the poem Amin, what might be otherwise described as the exotic and mysterious actions of a Javanese, becomes strangely comprehensible, and affects the reader more by evoking human feelings of love, sadness, and the lasting presence of a loved one who passed away. A frog comes to the doorstep, "you recognize the sacred eyes of Buddha"; "Riso, an old Javanese," comes out and feeds the frog "like one feeds a sick chicken."

When he takes it into his hand, he feels the coldness of the grave,
    tears shining in his eyes,
and no one in the world can swear,
    that it is not his dead child,

that this old and ugly frog,
    gasping for breath like an old hag,
would not one day sweetly whisper into his ear:
    Daddy, I am Amin,

    your nice and happy frog![348]

A record in Biebl's Javanese notebook suggests that this poem was based on observation of an actual "giant frog" he saw in Wonosobo. "The skin under its throat was moving up and down as if it were panting." It was fed by a Javanese man "like a chicken . . . every evening it was in its place."

The final poem in *With the Ship* is titled the "The Antipodes." Here is an abbreviated translation (the blank spaces between some paragraphs or lines are in the original; ellipses are mine):

347 "Jávští démoni," typescript with hand-written amendments. Archives of Czech Radio.
348 Biebl, *S lodí*, 55.

The eternal fatigue the horror under the palms

As if it were not Christmas
On the trees green leaves hang
and so much fruit

and forever forever bugs sing

. . . .
The sweet fatigue the horror under the palms
I walk as if on the ceiling
With my head below

Deep under me the heavenly abyss glows
I walk like Christ Southern Cross on my shoulders

On the other side of the world
people walk with their feet above them

I have to think of their worn soles

Of their little steps
in curious parks which change hues
and shed blood-colored leaves

On the other side of the world is Bohemia
a beautiful and exotic land
full of deep and mysterious rivers
which you cross with dry feet in the Name of Jesus

We have spring summer autumn winter

We wear winter coats ties
and sticks

Perhaps it snows
or the cherry trees bloom

At home strawberries grow

At home there is cold drinking water[349]

The last part of the poem has been (ab)used as a laudatory evidence of a simplistic home-sweet-home patriotism. Jiří Taufer, for example, wrote on the occasion of Biebl's death, at the height of Zhdanov social-realist era, that this poem showed how Biebl "overcame" "barren experimentation" and "romantic desire for the exotic."[350] But is it all there is to the poem—as the Czech, behind-the-baking-oven saying goes, "everywhere well, at home the best"?

Mirroring the exotic Christmas at childhood home in the poem "Orient," now cool Bohemia, seen from across the Earth, becomes an exotic, mysterious, miraculous land of antipodes. As home and dreamed distances become reversible on this tropical Christmas day, any final realization of a dream is put in doubt; if something is discovered, it is rather a degree of magical interchangeability and commonality between two sides of the world, and between the strange and the ordinary.

Space is increasingly disoriented and disjointed. Everyone in the world, on this side and the other, is upside down. One feels the cosmic vertigo when "deep under me the heavenly abyss glows," vertigo reminiscent of the last poem of the second part, where the ship capsizes and the poet sinks ever deeper into the bottomless sea "with eyes heavenward."

If the final part of the poem is calm and uncomplicated, it may be that the thought of home indeed provides a moment of respite from the vast world, like a glass of plain water, like the "Little Charmed Spring." But it could be, too, that it is the calm of acceptance that grows from the realization of interchangeability of spaces and the impossibility to leave; the prisoner's res-

349 Biebl, *S lodí*, 61–64.
350 Jiří Taufer, "Zemřel Konstantin Biebl—zemřel český básník," *Za Konstantinem Bieblem: Vzpomínky a projevy jeho přátel* (Prague: Československý spisovatel, 1952), 10.

ignation. Mácha already felt the claustrophobia or anxiety (*úzkost*), not just in one's village, but in the whole narrow (*úzký*) universe, the earth's prison cell. The homeland evoked in "The Antipodes" is a land fantasized from a great distance, as an "exotic land," a fairy tale, a distant memory, childhood time. The love of that home is that of a traveler who is far away from home's "mud, which reaches up to our shoulders"; far from home where "a man does not feel among his own"; far from home's anxieties/narrowness (*úzkost*), its "heavy dreams", poetized in the first part of the book. They and the cosmic narrowness/claustrophobia with which the book ends, mirror each other. Into the final confession of a love for home, the cosmic vertigo and the vast emptiness of the "heavenly abyss" flow; in the beauty of home, there is something quietly melancholy, like the blank spaces between the stanzas, spaces of white and silent emptiness. I think of Mácha's young Gypsy, forever leaving "far—far" from his native land: "grave calm settled in his heart . . . his sorrow was peaceful."

HALF-BLACK, YOU UNDERSTAND? HERE YOU HAVE TO BE CAREFUL!

With the Ship shows Biebl as a particularly vulnerable traveler. He neither dwelled nor travelled lightly, yet he felt the unbearable lightness of both being at home and of travelling. His constant self-doubt and anxiety, a sense of being out of place at home and in the world—which from the point of view of strong and rational men could appear as an appalling weakness—might have been the same self-doubt and insecurity that helped him to view colonialism with a particular sensitivity.

Among the seven poems of the third part of *With the Ship*, two deal with "justice" under colonialism. Java, one senses from them, is as far as Bohemia from paradise. Biebl's prose texts about his journey give him more space to unfold his impressions and reflections, and representations of colonialism and racism figure prominently here. The subtle humor of *With the Ship* takes on a more caricaturist tone, in its images of power often reminiscent of *Švejk*.

Some of the texts were published in weekly installments in the major Czech daily newspaper *Lidové noviny* (People's news) starting about a month after his return home (the series began on the 6th of March 1927 with his departure from Prague and three months later ended unfinished with his arrival in Ceylon), others appeared in magazines or were read on radio over the following decades. A number remained unpublished in Biebl's lifetime. While two different selections of these texts were published under the title *Journey to Java* after his death (in 1958 and 2001), it seems that his own unrealized plan for the book involved, not just a compilation and addition to existing texts, but a substantial rewriting. In a letter to Janský some months after his return from Java, he wrote: "I threw away all the feuilletons from Java and I am beginning to write them a bit more properly; I can't bear to do it so sloppily and frivolously and I am beginning to write a real book."[351] *Plancius* is the longest of the texts; it appeared in a private edition, a thin booklet, in 1931.

Colonialism and imperialism begin in Europe. The first foreign land that Biebl passed through on his way to Java was Germany, the Czechs' most intimate

351 Biebl's letter published in Slabý, *Potkávání*, 247.

Other. "I travel through the Empire," he writes, and he describes an "Imperial German" train passenger: "With the greatest calm and seriousness he unpacked a tropical helmet from his suitcase and put it on even before we passed Munich."[352] The German travelling to Egypt, wearing a light tropical outfit in cool autumn weather, was looking at the warmly dressed and coughing Slav with disgust, but when he saw the sticker

SINGAPORE

on Biebl's suitcase, "now, finally, he did not understand." For the imperial traveler, venturing into the otherness outside Europe required a colonial uniform, like when an astronaut leaves the Earth. For him, the Czech was first improper, uncivilized, and later incomprehensible; for the Czech, the "Imperial German" was the first of comically detestable characters epitomizing Empire.

Italy: on the one hand, a magical land of palms, olives, sunflowers, wine, Mediterranean *joie de vivre*, the splendid chaos of the harbor, and above all, like a silence overpowering all noise, the sea, which "like a sophisticated woman . . . only at the last moment revealing its nakedness."[353] On the other hand, Biebl saw the poverty that accompanies wealth, and, already, Mussolini's fascism. As in France a year earlier, here at the port of Genoa he felt, even before leaving Europe, the presence of colonialism and its global dimension: "On the pier, an Englishman threw away a banana peel and an Indian slipped on it."[354] World history is acted out on the tight stage of an avant-garde burlesque.

Prefigured by the "calm and serious German," Biebl's "Englishman" is a stock character of sorts. Shading and blending are crucial in Biebl's thought, but the "Englishman" is pure whiteness, the opposite of mixing, a poetic abbreviation of "the colonizer" bordering on caricature, not unlike how Pantalone represents money and greed in the *comedia del'arte*.

And yet, in the Englishman, comedy blends with horror—such as in the account of "the saddest place in the Red Sea, the saddest of all the world's seas . . . the English coal station Perim."[355] It is a succinct image of colonialism, which one can read almost like an allegory. A boat approaches the *Yorck*. It carries coal and "almost naked" Arab workers, "so much [like] animals, so little [like] people," who

> try to catch the attention of the passengers from the first class who have just come out on the deck. An Englishman stands on the deck as if nothing was happening. . . .

---

352 Biebl, *Cesta na Jávu*, 14.
353 Biebl, *Cesta na Jávu*, 15.
354 Biebl, *Cesta na Jávu*, 17.
355 Biebl, *Cesta na Jávu*, 40.

> A hundred throats scream at the ship: Ho-ho! Ho-ho! The Englishman does not hear, the Englishman enjoys himself, he has his calm and time aplenty. He aims his binoculars at a bird sitting on the shore. . . . A hundred throats are stretched to the point of exploding, trying to sound like a thousand throats; and if that's not enough, like ten thousand, so that the one up there would hear. But the one up there does not hear. In that consists his calm and enjoyment. He, an Englishman from the colonies, is fully convinced that he is not an evil person, God forbid, he will throw them a penny, to the colored ones, but first the devils have to deserve it. Faces disfigured, as if crucified, rise to him. It almost, almost appears that they will be noticed; but his light-colored head only tilts to look at his own hand, and he examines his fingernails so thoroughly and with such attention that it is impossible that something else could interest him.

When, after rereading an old letter and drinking his beef bouillon, the Englishman finally appeared to notice them—

> He lifted a copper coin high above his head for everyone to see. Below a brawl ensued. . . . The Englishman swung his arm. With one strike all the hands clasped empty air. For in their frenzy only they saw the falling coin, which remained in the Englishman's palm.[356]

Later the Englishman actually throws a penny, but intentionally so that it can't be caught. As the pandemonium below increases, he "looks for another penny but suddenly he remembers that it is time to change for lunch." "Ho-Ho!" shout the people below, and Biebl writes: "Suddenly I had only one wish: God, if only the Arabs finished the half-uttered word in Czech!"[357] *Hovno* means "shit."

The description of the Arabs evokes colonial stereotypes of Oriental poverty, dark skins, and uncivilized chaos. Yet soon one realizes that these images serve to describe the true despair of what is happening, which lies in the colonial Englishman's calm, civilized, pokerfaced self-confidence, his capability not to hear, to travel lightly.

When the poet imagines the Arabs shouting "shit" in Czech at the Englishman, his heart is more on their side than the Englishman's. Yet, while Biebl was not in the same class, he was in the same boat, looking down on the workers, who are "as if crucified." Again communist and Catholic visions blend; wrath and guilt, perhaps. The title of his book, *With the Ship that Carries/Imports Tea and Coffee*, suggests the poet's position: he must travel on the

356 Biebl, *Cesta na Jávu*, 40–2.
357 Biebl, *Cesta na Jávu*, 42.

same ship that carries the spoils of colonialism from Java to Europe.[358] "Even if another was shooting / our deeds are in those wounds."

Nation and class are intertwined in an asymmetrical and fuzzy manner here. Biebl's anti-colonialism is indivisible from his protest against exploitation that he saw also in Czechoslovakia of the 1920s—injustice and inequality independent of nationality. At the same time, he feels the political and economic inequality between different nations, and in this scheme of things, the rich Englishman represents the rich, the first class, the upper class. Biebl emphasizes the importance of class for the colonists in his description of the *Yorck*: "The second class is not very different from the first, it is almost the same, but it is *called 'second,'* which means much, very much, especially if one is an Englishman or a Dutchman."[359]

The same actions and attitudes that appear in Biebl's damning images of colonialism—such as the practice of throwing coins from ocean liners—were often advertised and enjoyed by Dutch passengers as the highlights of sea travel. The ship was a "colonial classroom," and the voyage "a crash course on proper imperial behavior and attitudes."[360] Biebl made a good use of the opportunity to learn; not to become a "proper European," but to see and represent colonialism with more clarity.

As their ship approaches Ceylon, Biebl fails to avoid a group of Indians who are returning from an extended stay in Germany, "camping" on the open deck, status-wise below the fourth class. Biebl's Englishmen, now in the plural, form a group whose colonial condescension is directed both against the Indians and the Czech, an outsider among Europeans, neither this nor that, embarrassingly improper, almost savage.

> It is horrible, how we [Czechs] have such bad upbringing. Forgive me, O Lord, because I don't know what I'm doing when I smile, perhaps at the sun, perhaps even at the Indians. One of them saw that I was smiling, walked over to me, smiled back, and asked me in German: "What time is it?" "Five," I said, looking at my watch. The Englishmen were petrified. I will never forget their licked hair and heads numb with awe. Saint Wen-

358 The dependence of travel writers on colonial power is of course a more general phenomenon, as has been discussed, for example, by Helen Carr in reference to British context. Helen Carr, "Modernism and Travel (1880–1940)," in Peter Hulme and Tim Youngs, *The Cambridge Companion to Travel Writing* (Cambridge: Cambridge University Press, 2002), 70–1. In Biebl's case, however—and no doubt in the case of some British and other writers—colonial power not only enabled writers to travel, but also made any critique of colonialism problematic.

359 Biebl, *Cesta na Jávu*, 21. Emphasis in original.

360 Kris Alexanderson, *Subversive Seas: Anticolonial Networks Across the Twentieth-century Dutch Empire* (Cambridge: Cambridge University Press, 2019), 103. An account and an illustration of the throwing of coins ares on pages 114–115. Alexanderson's book, which is based on Dutch sources, and especially the chapter on the ship as a "colonial classroom" (99–133), provides a rich counterpoint to Biebl's account of his voyage. For more on Czech experiences of ocean liners, see Mrázek, "Czechs on Ships."

> ceslas, what have I done again? Then they looked at each other, at me, at the Indians in rags, and again at each other, and broke into laughter. They knew that I was Czech. . . . At the dinner I caught a few sidelong and compassionate gazes. Half of the dining room was looking to see if I would start eating with a knife.[361]

Especially in some of Biebl's prose texts, images of the colonizers have, at times, something of the simplification and exaggeration of a caricature or a comic mask. At these moments, they do not represent the shades and complexity of colonial complicity of individuals and groups who are often "European," "local," or "Asian" in ways too complicated and fluid to be captured by a colonizer-colonized dichotomy. This kind of simplification could be related to his foreignness to colonialism and the way he experienced it briefly as a traveler. However, the caricaturist streak in his writing can be also seen as complementing and interacting with the mirroring, blending, and confusing reversals, which pervade his poems and emerge in the prose texts.

I have likened Biebl's Englishman to Pantalone, while Šalda likened Biebl to another character originally from the *comedia dell'arte*, the Pierot, or his later reincarnation, *Pierot lunaire*. Biebl's self-representation in his travel writing does have something of that naïve clown, in Šalda's words "the little Peter who fell from the moon and who feels somewhat unsure on this wildly spinning planet," and perhaps especially unsure on the ocean liners among self-confident English colonizers. It has something of both: the masks of a comic theater and the poetry of *Pierot lunaire*'s cosmic disorientation.

This is true also about "Noc ve Wonosobo" (A night in Wonosobo), an account of the poet's encounter with colonial authority in the small Javanese mountain town of Wonosobo, "the first night of an unexpected interrogation, which began in the evening and extended till dawn."[362] In this and other texts by Biebl, images of colonialism are entangled with tropical nature in a variety of ways. The interrogation was "the most entertaining and the most tragic thing I have experienced on the island of porcupines, monkeys and iguanas." These animals are exotic, surreal and funny to Czech eyes and ears—they make me think more of colorfully illustrated children's books than being in a jungle. The interrogation is set in this dreamlike world, but in its psychedelic bizarreness the colonial authority trumps the most exotic animals. The official, writes Biebl,

> offered me an armchair, whose seat was an Atacus Atlas, the largest living butterfly in Java; the backrest was a screaming peacock. He himself took a seat on a nest of hum-

361 Biebl, *Cesta na Jávu*, 47.
362 Biebl, *Cesta na Jávu*, 62–63. The quotation from the text that follow are from these pages.

mingbirds suspended between lilies, and rested his back against a chameleon embroidered in green silk.

Nature is reduced to ornamental colonial furniture, into extreme kitsch. At the same time, like when two films are projected simultaneously, it reveals itself through disorienting glimpse as a wild reality, in which live animals colonize the colonial office, having broken out of the cage of decorative representation: the seat *was* an Atacus Atlas . . . As if nature itself had rebelled and joined in the insurrection, to which this interrogation was a fearful response: "At that time, an uprising had just erupted in Java, and [the official] was under orders to deeply interrogate [lit., "examine the loin of"] every foreigner."

(Also, for example, in *Plancius*, the poetic account of the final leg of Biebl's voyage to Batavia, colonialism and an uprising are permeated by images of plants and animals. The Dutch passengers extol the beauty of Java in terms of manicured nature and gentle natives. They speak of hotels and their "parks with sand paths in the midst of roses." In Batavia, there is "the head of the Dutch queen with a diamond-studded crown; the crown alone is ten meters high. I tell you, it is a wonderful creation of the gardeners, made entirely from white orchids." The most stunning thing in the jungle are "beautiful asphalt roads." In Solo, one must visit "the zoological garden where you can see all the animals living in Java." And the Javanese—"Oh, the Javanese . . . so nice and gentle." Then suddenly, in the final paragraphs of the text, the colonial dream collapses when the news reaches the ship that "on plantations an uprising is ripening.")[363]

In "Night in Wonosobo," the jungle décor is an extension of the official, as the lair is of the witch, but behind this facade, the European is surreally, ridiculously out of place, like a massive spotted Dutch milking cow deep in Javanese forest. It does not help that his "strange name was Jetel," which means "clover" in Czech—in folk songs and in reality known as good feed for horses and cattle. "We were separated by a desk, an ocean, mistrust and many other things, such as his monocle, behind which the dandy was hiding his true mission, sowing a casualness with both hands, as if this was a god knows how pleasant visit." The whole meeting—in the setting of the decorative "jungle" on the verge of becoming actual, uncontrolled jungle—is a contest in pretense, suspicion and evasion, ultimately motivated by a fear caused or intensified by the ongoing uprising.

The second half of the text lists the questions swarming in Mr. Jetel's head about who this visitor might be, with his "suspicious photographs," and whether or not he might be dangerous. "But how to solve an equation that

363 Biebl, *Plancius*, 24–27.

is not given, an equation with an unknown number of unknowns?" Biebl struggles "to keep the circuit breakers of inner laughter from exploding." The whole experience is deeply, Dadaistically nonsensical ("it was not my fault that I was finally forced to provide Dadaist responses to Dadaist questions"), yet one also senses—perhaps like from the Dadaist laughter first emerging from the Great War—why the interrogation was simultaneously "the most entertaining and the most tragic thing." Something of the oppressiveness of colonial surveillance, which this story Dadaistically communicates, can be sensed from a letter Biebl wrote from Java:

> You cannot imagine the situation here. I went through crossfire of all offices, where I was interrogated to the point of exhaustion; I am not allowed to write anything, to send anything. I think a year would pass before you would receive it, censored and covered by stamps [of different government offices]. . . . With great difficulty, I obtained a permission to stay for six weeks, but I always see the same faces following me.[364]

One could understand why Biebl, with his poetic-political imagination, might want to fabulate that he witnessed an anti-colonial communist uprising in the Indies. In this world of surrealist coincidences, it so happened that a series of such revolts, the most significant in decades, were indeed taking place in Java and Sumatra between November 1926 and January 1927, just when he was there. They put the colonial machinery of surveillance, interrogation, censorship and repression into high gear. The "unrest" (as Biebl refers to it in one of his postcards from Java) and the communist purge, as perceived by the communist poet with senses and emotions intensified by travel and the tropics (think the interrogator's interior decoration), are poetically reflected in Biebl's narratives.

The following story should be read with double caution: it was not written by Biebl, but reimagined by the fiction writer Karel Konrád, Biebl's friend. It is perhaps best read as a dramatic reenactment of a moment of the "unrests," with Biebl as a character.

> What a shame that Konstantin Biebl did not at least write about how a native servant guided him through the jungle. The servant walked behind him in silent deference, the noble and gentle person that he was, just like the Javanese are in general (compared to that, what perfect slobs were the Dutch settlers!). Kosťa wanted to somehow bridge the native's estrangement. Cigarettes did not help: he thanked with a deferential bow of his head, crossing his arms (Kosťa claimed: with a fluid melodiousness, like a temple dancer, he crossed them over his chest). Unspeakingly. Nor were money able to change

364 Slabý, *Potkávání*, 62.

> the Malay's remoteness, his inaccessibility. And then, when they were alone in a *damar* forest, Kosťa gripped his arm and holding onto it, he shouted: "Lenin!" And the guide's face, until then stone-like, as if it had been unable to move, suddenly began to glow—and his fingers powerfully clasped the white man's right hand.[365]

Konrád retells this anecdote when he speaks about the stories Biebl used to tell his friends but never wrote down. He speaks of Biebl's "lyrical merriment," his "restless fantasy and his inclination to invent remarkable tales and add to them further fabulation (behind which, however, there was something approximating actuality or observed on reality)."[366] When he says, in the Javanese anecdote, that "Kosťa claimed," he seems to remind the reader that Biebl was moving in the borderlands between reality and imagination. One may sense that Konrád, Biebl's kindred spirit, is creatively restaging what he remembers from Biebl's own poetic play—here, too, writing feels like avant-garde theater, a pantomime abruptly, hilariously interrupted by "Lenin!" Some of the details seem to evoke, rather less subtly than Biebl usually does, the *Arabian Nights*, or perhaps the Hollywood film *The Thief of Baghdad*, which clashes with the puppet-like image of the type "Dutch settler." The fragments of a fairy-tale Orient clash with the cigarettes and tips offered to the "Malay," before the orientalism disappears as he bursts out from the picture of an "Oriental" and the distance between the two men is bridged, all by the magic of Lenin's name. (Against my own warning, I think of how the dreams of Leninism and dreams of Java, blending and clashing, somehow touch reality, ever so lightly yet deeply. Before their voices were silenced in the aftermath of the 1926 uprising, before some left Java for Moscow, communist writers in the Indies criticized the colonial world in their journalism and fiction, in "a style that was alternately intimate, witty, ironic and sarcastic";[367] they were reading Marx and Lenin while dreaming of a better world, like and unlike Biebl and others in Prague. Perhaps that powerful hand-shake in a Javanese *damar* forest did take place? Stranger things have happened; and there is a force to the image, exactly because it is strange and double-distilled—a force, and perhaps a truth, poet's *poznání*?)

Comically, nightmarishly a stranger in the English and Dutch colonial worlds, Biebl is equally but differently unsure and foreign among the Javanese. Nature is again prominent, but the unknown animals, fruits and flower are in some ways homely, perhaps like the anise, nutmeg, vanilla that evoke

365 Konrád, "O Konstantinu Bieblovi," 81.
366 Konrád, "O Konstantinu Bieblovi," 72.
367 Hilmar Farid & Razif, "Batjaan liar in the Dutch East Indies: a colonial antipode," *Postcolonial Studies* 11, no. 3 (2008): 284.

childhood home in the poem "Orient." On his first day in Java, he saw Javanese nannies, *babu*, caring for little children:

> Oh the magic of new things! . . . Here one knows less about the world than a Chinese child. Indeed, such a nanny would be good for me, such a dark babu, who would lead me by the hand from animal to animal, from flower to flower, from tree to tree, and she would talk to me: This is a rambutan! Wait, I'll pluck one fruit for you, you would not know which one is ripe. . . . And see the tall tree, with the top flat like a table? It's kapok. And I would repeat after her with wonder: It's kapok![368]

Images of Europeans educating and civilizing the "natives" were widespread in colonial representations professing a civilizational and racial superiority and justifying colonialism. Biebl, in contrast, feels like a little child in need of education. One feels again Pierot's uncertainty, naiveté, and childlike wonder: "It's kapok!" It is not quite feigned—his diaries are full of such wonder at "the magic of new things"—bananas, for example.

Despite his convictions and desires, Biebl senses in his own actions the violence caused by the white man in the colonies. In his (poetized) account of his first night in Java—one recognizes the main characters of his poems—when a toad appears on his doorsteps, he panics and kicks it away. A Javanese standing nearby cries out unhappily, takes the toad in his hand, "the way one would hold an injured bird," and gently puts it back where it had been before. Biebl writes: "In spite of what had happened, which deeply shamed me, I was unable to avoid doing other stupid things." Later that night, he kills the *toke*—a small, harmless lizard common in Javanese homes—which is hiding behind the frame of a portrait of the Dutch queen. He walks out into the garden to throw out the dead lizard. In the dark he cannot avoid stepping on small animals. "I was afraid to make a single step. Everywhere the soil beneath my feet seemed soft and alive. Until one learns to walk here, one does not know what a banana peel is, what a frog is, or even a snake." Having thrown away the dead lizard, he comes back inside: "My gaze fell on the picture of the Dutch queen, but I did not see her, I saw again the *toke* . . . at the same place where I killed it. As if it were laughing at me: To-ke! To-ke!"[369] (Elsewhere, *toke*, the reader may recall, has the voice of the unhappy girl Viktorka.)

For Biebl, like in much colonial writing, untamed tropical nature is sometimes the mysterious, threatening Other of Western civilization.[370] However,

368 Biebl, *Cesta na Jávu*, 55.

369 Biebl, *Cesta na Jávu*, 56–61.

370 Douglas Kerr, "Ruins in the jungle: Nature and narrative," in *Asian Crossings: Travel Writings on China, Japan, and Southeast Asia*, ed. Steve Clark and Paul Smerhurst (Hong Kong: Hong Kong University Press, 2008), 131–8.

in that "hidden force," and through his own distress and powerlessness, he senses the vitality of nature, the land and the people.

> You must not throw your weight around here too much with your western reason . . . you are the guests of the jungle, which has sufficiently convinced you that even today it has not lost its power over Batavia and other cities and kampongs all over Java; jungle, eternal and truly mysterious, which does not disappear even where tigers have been all shot dead and old forests cleared. No, it becomes only more mysterious and uncanny. Where in the past dammar trees rustled, now the silence of millions reigns. Millions of Javanese, who are silent about their rights. In their stead, other millions raise their voice. Millions of creatures, a giant and invincible army, against which the white *tuan* cannot do anything.[371]

The whole Javanese world, not just people but even animals, trees, and the soil, reproach the "white tuan" (*tuan* is Malay for "sir, master"). They remind him, by remaining stubbornly alive and uncanny for him, that he is the guest or the intruder. Biebl, a white man too, feels perhaps more a stranger than anyone, yet—and in this he differs from many colonial writers—the demise of the white man is a sign of hope and justice. More than that, he hears civilization in the sound of the tropical nature, thus annihilating, with his poetic mirror, the colonial distinction and opposition between civilization and jungle. It is a new and different civilization, a civilization of the millions. As he walks, weak and confused, on the soft, living soil of the garden, he is

> magnetized by the sounds with which the tropical night quivers! What awesome heralding of civilization! Do you hear those beetles? All those insects? Those files, those knives, those chains and augers?[372]

In the sound of this "giant and invincible army," one hears, as well, the heralding of an uprising.

Even before the *Yorck* leaves the Genoa harbor, Biebl descends into the engine rooms.

> I am terrified, like Dante upon entering hell. And I see naked devils, from whom hot oil and sweat pours. I say nothing, because words are nothing. But I intentionally stain my coat with oil, so that I don't have to be so ashamed of my white suit. Someone might

371 Biebl, *Cesta na Jávu*, 61–2.
372 Biebl, *Cesta na Jávu*, 60.

remark, perhaps in the saloon: "Sir, you have a spot on your coat!"—"I know," I will say, and will remember what happens below.[373]

The passage foreshadows images of light and dark skin, of people above and people below, without mentioning race or colonialism. Colonial racism is situated in a larger picture of class difference, just as social actuality is integrally part of poetically known actuality.

Since his student days, Biebl's poems were concerned with social wrongs, the predicament of the working class under capitalism, and conservative bourgeois ideology. His views of the colonial situation were continuous with his existing socio-political worldview. In this, he was like other leftist writers—one may think of, among many others, the Dutch communist, anti-colonial poet Jef Last.[374] "I intentionally stain my coat with oil, so that I don't have to be so ashamed of my white suit." Should one *also* think, in terms of both continuity and difference, of stigma in the Christian sense, the "mark of shame," which is also a sign of allegiance with "the crucified"?

However, it would be reductive to represent Biebl's images of colonialism as merely political messages. Collages of images, impressions, feelings, and sounds, they cannot be distilled from the workings of his poetics, from the totality of actuality. Bohemia is an exotic land; Christmas, a Muslim holiday; Prague café, a Chinese temple; jungle, the future of civilization. Seeming opposites recognize themselves one in the other. Distinctions and oppositions are destabilized and released from the gravitational force of habit or prejudice. These mirrorings are both playful and serious. They reveal silenced relationships. "To poetize [*básniti*]," writes Biebl, "is a desire for *poznání* ["cognition/knowledge"]. The poem is the poet's *poznání*."[375]

"The sea, too, has its comrades and friends. They are sown fields, meadows and clouds. It is billiard cloth, the uniforms of Italian legionaries, and the emerald, which our teacher wore on his tie."[376] Do not these surprising poetic camaraderies and friendships already transgress against "racial purity"?

Java and Bohemia are brought together as conventional limits of thinking and imagination are dynamited, but only in order to catch, in things turned into mirrors, glimpses of hidden truths.

Perhaps that is why Biebl keeps coming back to mirrors, mirrorings, reflections.

373 Biebl, *Cesta na Jávu*, 20.

374 See, for example, Jef Last, *Liedjes op de maat van de rottan: Indische revolutionaire gedichten*, ed. Harry A. Poeze (KITLV: Leiden 1994); and <www.jeflast.nl>.

375 Biebl, *Dílo*, 5:262.

376 Biebl, *Dílo*, 5:189.

> The air and the water pervade one another on the horizon; the air becomes wet and salty, the water breathable and transparent; they are merely two mirrors looking at themselves in each other. To glance into the sea means to look at the sky and vice versa. The Plancius sails with its mast toward the bottom, which pushes aside white clouds, from which dolphins surge out to wander through the sky. Look, an albatross! It is flying below the sea, it flies with its belly upward. And the sun is rising.[377]

The first-class Englishman was "the one up there"; the Arab "devils," or the "naked devils" in "Dante's hell" of the machine room, were below. In this vision of the sea and the sky, opposites pervade one another. What is one and what is the other, what is above and what is below, is upset, disoriented. "On the other side of the world / people walk with their feet above them," he writes from Java about the European "antipodes." This vision, this disorientation that undermines purity and hierarchy—could it be more profoundly un-colonial than explicit anti-colonial statements?

But also: under the surfaces of the mirrors, does not one feel the depth of the sea and the cosmos, the darkness and emptiness below and above? "Deep under me the heavenly abyss glows . . ." The mirroring, is it just a mirage? And the mirror but a surface, like a fragile window pane, concealing horrific depths? Are we drowning, "with eyes heavenwards"? This too, somehow, is part of the traveler's intoxicated, stunned *poznání* of the colonies.

Both before and, more powerfully so, after his journey, Biebl's poetry dreamt of moving across oceans and connecting continents. Biebl writes—dreams? —this about the poet's vocation:

> His fantasy moves with mile-long strides and his associations extend their hands toward each other across oceans. Poet, the promoter of polygamy, the promoter of polyandry, the implacable promoter of free love, unites the most distant and apparently the most unblendable images, forcing them to publicly celebrate weddings even at the cost of absolute misunderstanding, because, in an instinctive mania to relate all things of this world, he had long ago intuited their liaisons.[378]

No wonder that images of "mixed race," including the vision of mestiza-Earth in *New Icarus* (discussed in the next section), should emerge in Biebl's writing—the whole body of his poetic imagination is antagonistic to anything in the nature of racial purity.

The 1931 illustration of *Plancius* by the surrealist artist Jindřich Štyrský intuits the "liaisons" and the "union" of what is "apparently the most un-

377 Biebl, *Plancius*, 8.
378 Biebl, *Dílo*, 5:263.

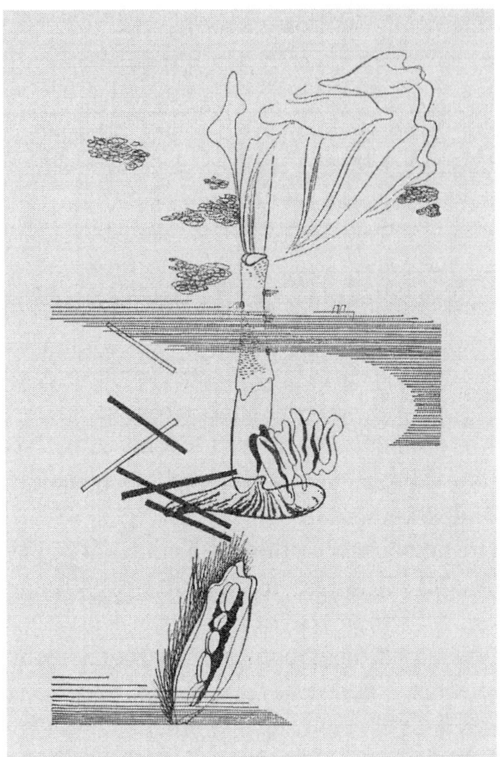

Figure 17. Jindřich Štyrský, illustration in K. Biebl, *Plancius*, 1931.

blendable," catches air and water in the act, and may evoke the vision of mestiza-Earth. The miniscule *Plancius* sails on the horizon (Figure 17).

Biebl (who was often described by his contemporaries as having rather darker skin) narrates how on his journey to Java, he was repeatedly mistaken for a *míšenec*, mestizo. (As English lacks a general non-derogatory term, I will use the Czech words *míšenec* [masculine], *míšenka* [feminine], and the Spanish "mestizo." The Czech words, like "mestizo," relate to a verb meaning "to mix.")

> A Dutchman told me: "Man, are you crazy? He is sunbathing! Damn, don't do that! You know, I don't want to offend you, but you already look like a *míšenec*. Half-black, you understand? Here you have to be careful!"[379]

Without the concept of the mixed race—defined as a disgraceful impurity—there could be no pure race; and to disregard this distinction or to cross the color line is to aim at the heart of racism.

379 Biebl, *Cesta na Jávu*, 47.

Moreover, images of mestizos resonate with the awkward, half-black position of Czechs among Western European colonists: they come from the eastern margin of the imperial West, a white people whose land has been for much of its history in the position of a colony.

> "Can you speak Malay well?" Mr. Jansen assured me of it. "I have lived in Java for fifteen years." "How do you say *thank you* in Malay?" I asked him as if I did not know that I was aiming at his heart. . . . [H]e had to admit he did not know . . . nor did any other of our companions. "Wait," said Mr. Sachse, "we will call Ing.[380] Bergr." . . . Ing. Bergr was not thrown off balance: "I do not know," he said, "I have never needed that word and nor have you, gentleman, I hope. What for? Do we talk to each other in Malay? Never! We speak Malay only with the natives. But if you want to quench your curiosity, ask someone more suitable than me," and he pointed at me over his shoulder, not considering it proper as much as to turn his head. . . . Mr. Jansen was the first to realize that there was a misunderstanding: "You don't know each other, gentlemen?" and he introduced me. I thought he was about to pounce on me but instead he embraced me. "So you are from Czechoslovakia? That's a good one! And how come you are so black? Forgive me, I thought that you were a *míšenec*." And he offered me a cigar.[381]

The whites are the bearers of civilization, where rudeness and discrimination towards the non-white are part of proper behavior. The poet gets into embarrassing, comical situations with his sins against colonial propriety, against a sense of what is up and what is below, against pure Whiteness, against clarity of distinctions.

The Dutch colonists, "proud of [their] refined manners," embarrassed by the momentary confusion of the color line, try to attract the Czech into their circle—"he offered me a cigar." But the poet—who has "an instinctive mania to relate all things of this world"—likes "blood-mixing." About Mr. Jansen, in whose house Biebl stayed for a while in Java (and who, in the text above, mediates between the self-confident Bergr and Biebl), he writes:

> Evil tongues claim about him that he has some black blood and that it makes him unsuitable for the office. I cannot notice anything, only those little brown crescents on his nails, only his way of life, which also causes problems in his office. . . . I was charmed by you and I like your crescents.[382]

Biebl is drawn to transgress colonial conventions, he does not heed the Dutchman's advice to stay out of the sun:

380 Ing. (from French *ingénieur*, "engineer") is an academic title, common in many countries, for graduates in various engineering/technical fields.

381 Biebl, *Plancius*, 22–24.

382 Biebl, *Cesta na Jávu*, 71.

> I am not afraid of the sun for I love it above anything else . . . like the natives, I like to entrust my naked body to it, and I feel a sadistic bliss growing from a thousand of fine needles tattooing my trembling skin.[383]

It is as if he were trying to become a *míšenec*, someone who is able to thank across color lines; or to obliterate the white man that he also was;[384] or at least to defile the whiteness, like when he soiled his white suit with oil down below in the ship's machine room.

For to obliterate the white man in himself, to cross to the other side, is not a simple matter, as the following excerpt further illustrates. In a dream about penetration, "I" (the poet) am at a mosque gate in Port Said, attracted to enter because "I" want to hold a fallen banana blossom which resembles the human heart (the passage was quoted earlier), but an Arab guards the "forbidden entrance." Port Said, at the entry to the Suez Canal, was Biebl's first port of call in the "Orient" and the entrance to "the mouse hole leading to the larder," as he described the Suez Canal.[385]

> [The Arab guard] wanted to hold my arm, but his hand closed in emptiness, as if it were only air that he caught. He was startled and attempted to grasp me with both his arms around my waist; he embraced only himself. I did not feel the slightest pressure when his arms passed through my body. I saw he was trembling in horror. To overcome it, he began to curse and scold. I told him both the Arabic words I had heard from Richard, the steward. He flew into a rage. He took out a long knife and lifted it above my heart. My chest did not put up any resistance. He fell down. And because he had been standing just in front of me, his head passed through my head and his heart through my heart. —I turn. He lies on the floor, dying. Blood is gushing from his chest. He is insistently whispering something, his last wish. He speaks so quietly that I have to put my ear to his mouth. He speaks in Czech. But I don't understand Czech and I ask him in Arabic what he is saying. He looks at me silently. —In the end he lifts his hand heavily, points to a blossom lying under a banana plant, and dies. His arm stays uplifted in the air. — . . . I hear the crunching of sand. Steps are approaching. I recognize in them the steps of a European. . . . They have seen the corpse, and the woman screams out, recognizing who it is: "That is our friend from the ship!" The man begins to pursue me. "Catch him! Catch that Arab!"[386]

---

383 Biebl, *Plancius*, 14.

384 Thow Xin Wei noted that Biebl's word choice here— "sadistic bliss," rather than "masochistic bliss"—suggests a split of his personality "into both torturer and tortured."

385 Biebl, *Cesta na Jávu*, 33.

386 Biebl, *Cesta na Jávu*, 31–3.

The movement of the "I" resembles what happens when one identifies with a stranger—to an extent, one feels like the other. "I" become the Arab: it is a communion, mirroring, becoming almost one, not unlike when Plancius sails with mast toward the bottom, as water and air pervade each other, and indeed not unlike the "marriages" of what at first seems strange to each other.

And yet, even as "I" become an Arab, otherness persists, like the dark abyss that is a mirror. Throughout, "I" remain an objectified Other, ever under attack—a European in the eyes of an Arab at the outset of the excerpt, an Arab in the eyes of Europeans in the end. Even when the dying Czech whispers his last wish and "I," the Arab, lower my ear to his mouth, trying to understand, there are only unintelligible whisper and silent looks.

However great the desire to unite opposites or become one with the other may be, it is far from simple and easy; it may be a matter of life and death—although, in Biebl's poetry, death is also a desirable release.

The action was propelled by the Czech's lack of resistance—not his choice, but something about who he was, or something about the traveler's intoxicating displacement (recall the intoxicated images of Biebl's departure from Prague I discussed in the beginning of the Preamble). "I," the Czech, did not feel any pressure when the Arab "attempted to grasp me with both his arms around my waste; he embraced only himself." The Czech-as-Other malfunctioned as Other. It was this absence of resistance, this insubstantiality, that put the guard off balance, so that he fell through the Czech's mind and heart. The shift of the "I" was disorientingly smooth—not willed, not resisted. "I" do not control or grasp what happens. The words of the air-like, immaterial Czech poet have no effect. All he can do is to lift his arm to point at the blossom that resembles the human heart, only to die with that comically rigid member.

Biebl's passage evokes the dream-like, insubstantial, and sometimes comical (non-)presence of a Czech in the colonial world. Again one could envision Biebl's narratives staged in an avant-garde theater—imagine thickly painted faces, exaggerated gestures and expressions, and over/undersized props; or a film with special effects for the ghost-like Czech poet. Face painted white, he would look like a clown, or a moon-struck Pierot—hardly someone even asking, as "mad Hamlet"[387] did, if he was "born to set things aright." "His fantasy moves with mile-long strides and his associations extend their hands toward each other across oceans." His fantasy might—but the man?

And yet, who can say that there is no truth in that comic erection, in the poet's lonely whisper, in ridiculously immense desires and fantasies, in being out of place (truly a traveler, truly intoxicated by travel, truly unsettled, truly

387 Biebl, *Nový Ikaros*, 12.

Figure 18. František Tichý, illustrations in K. Biebl, *Cesta na Jávu* (Journey to Java), 1958.

uncolonial?), in being of no consequence, in awkwardness and confusion? A mestiza truth, a truth comically in love with her insignificant Other, with disorientation and confusion? A mestiza reality, comically in love with fantasy? The history of race reminds us of the disastrous consequences of equating truth with sober propriety, efficiency, self-confidence, well-functioning management, or the clarity of distinctions and representations.

Another conversation between Biebl's poetry and a visual artist: František Tichý's illustrations of a posthumous edition of Biebl's *Journey to Java* show, in another way, liberating unions of the apparently unblendable, and discover healing magic and mystical cosmic visions in irrational, intoxicating concoctions of children's drawings—I think again of a boy dreaming under the artificial palm. (Figure 18)

Biebl never finished the planned book "Journey to Java," and his travelogue remained a collection of fragments. His poetic reflection on colonialism remained unfinished also in another sense: images and ideas of the tropics would continue to reappear in, or haunt, his later writings. This is also true about *New Icarus*.

NEW ICARUS AND THE MESTIZA MY BEAUTIFUL ARSITI

The book-length poem appeared on the 1st of May 1929, as is prominently stated on its title page—the publication on the Labor Day, like the poet's journey two years earlier, was a poetic performance.

In the poetic flight of *New Icarus*, and in his fall, central poetic and human themes, concerns, memories, and experiences of Biebl's poetry intersect. Images of tropics, seas, and traveling permeate the poem, and one recognizes echoes of Biebl's earlier writing. And yet, the poetry has changed.

New Icarus, from which I have already quoted several times, won the prestigious Prize of Aventinum before it was published, and over the years it has attracted more attention from critics and literary scholars than any other work by Biebl. One theme in these discussions has been the relation of *New Icarus* and Apollinaire's 1912 *Zone*, and the place of Biebl's work in the history of "zone" (*pásmo*) as a Czech poetic genre inspired by Apollinaire's poem.

Zdeněk Pešat emphasized how the reception of *Zone* was conditioned by tendencies of Czech poetry that prefigured Apollinaire's new poetics. The much admired translation of *Zone* by Karel Čapek helped to ease its way in, since Čapek incorporated the latest developments of Czech poetry on the level of language and poetic techniques.[388] One of the first two significant works in the history of *pásmo*, understood as a new genre, was Biebl's 1921 "One Day at Home." Nezval, among others, wrote several important poems in the zone genre in the following years. Scholars, however, have singled out *New Icarus* as the work that went furthest in fulfilling the potential of Apollinaire's inspiration, even as it grew farthest from it.

Czech poets were, in diverse ways, inspired by *Zone*'s polythematic "free flow of poetic consciousness, in which inner and outer reality, lyrical and epical elements, the present and the past, and till then the strictly separated categories of the comic and the tragic, pervade one another."[389] Jan Wiendl describes the differences of *New Icarus* from *Zone*:

> However divergent and unlimited Apollinaire's excursions into the world of memories may appear . . . [his] cluster of perspectives is characterized by an emphatic conver-

388 Zdeněk Pešat, *Dialogy s poezií* (Prague: Československý spisovatel, 1985), 137–54.
389 Pešat, *Dialogy s poezií*, 143.

> gence on the theme of an individual, autobiographically based pilgrimage through space as a key signifying base of the zone's tectonics. . . . [In *New Icarus*] confession is not this cohesive element . . . but it becomes only one of the elements in the composition's much looser thematic structure . . . [Biebl] unveils life's fragmented character. . . . [There] is consistent disruption of monothematic concentricity into smithereens of very loosely cohering, or often entirely incoherent themes or motivistic bunches.[390]

The difference of *New Icarus* from Biebl's own earlier poetry, as well, can be seen in relation to this contrast between Apollinaire and Biebl. It was in 1931, not long after *New Icarus*, that Biebl wrote about "associations extend[ing] their hands toward each other across oceans . . . in an instinctive mania to relate all things of this world, [the poet] had long ago intuited their liaisons." However, especially in *New Icarus*, and more generally in his poetry after his journey, increasingly such poetic flights and a belief in the power of poetry are the other side of a pervasive emptiness and darkness—just as love is juxtaposed to death, flight to fatal fall, paradise to apocalypse. These oppositions are never resolved; they remain in suspense; neither one in a pair prevails. This also applies to the opposition between the desired blending and unity ("extending hands across oceans") on the one hand, and fragmentation and emptiness on the other. Increasingly one senses that the "mania to relate all things of this world" is just that, a mania in the face of a nothingness, a part of which is the darkness and emptiness of the Great War, here poeticized more hauntingly than ever, as the poet's two journeys, one to the war and the other to the tropics, blend and clash. Šalda emphasized that the experience of the War separates Biebl and Mácha; both the World War and the Javanese journey lie between *New Icarus* and the *Zone*.

Africa, China, and America are only fleetingly evoked in Apollinaire's poem by birds from those continents, and Oceania and Guinea through a mention of "your fetishes," but in his travel memories, which form a distinct part of *Zone*, the poet (or the poem's subject) remains in Europe, the farthest and most exotic place for him being Prague, with its ancient buildings and singing natives—only a train ride away from modern Paris. Travel figures in Apollinaire, but its images are much more limited compared to *New Icarus*'s flights to other continents and oceans—not only in geographic coverage (although the expansive geographic space and the freer movement do have poetic significance), not only in that Biebl dedicates long, elaborate passages to images of travel and faraway continents, islands and oceans, and his vision of tropical colonies is complex, but in that in *Zone*, the images are framed con-

390 Jan Wiendl, "Syntézy v poločase rozpadu," in *Dějiny nové moderny* II, ed. Vladimír Papoušek et al. (Prague: Academia, 2014), 336–7.

sistently as memories of the subject's past travels, while in *New Icarus*, this is only one of various poetic and temporary modes of travel, some of which are not firmly anchored in individual experience or in the logic of individual memory. *Zone* always remains a walk through Paris. In the early part of *New Icarus*, a stroll near Biebl's village is briefly evoked, but it is just a moment, not even the initial one, in a polyphonic flow of associations which moves ever elsewhere.

Let a few fragments illustrate the poetic travels of *New Icarus*. The poem begins:

The night comes already in the dark the steamship sailed into the streets
    of Constantinople
over the warm waves of the crimson sea
and as it is midnight a Chinese coolie is awakened by hunger
and as it is morning barefoot Javanese women sing in a palm grove
and as it is a beautiful evening I come to rest at the edge of this quickly yellowing forest
with my head thrown back into the clouds

God give wings to poets
just like to angels to maple seeds
all birds have them
ravens jays even the little rabbit in the bush
fish that glide over the Indian Ocean
and in the autumn leaves so gently descend also without a motor[391]

Names of countries, cities, rivers, seas, animals, Javanese and Malay words for demons and tropical fruits, sensations of movement across continents and oceans, and images from all climatic zones permeate the poem and bring the whole world into it. Already in the poem's first four lines, there are images blending, strangely effortlessly: a steamship, the sea, Constantinople, a Chinese coolie living in hunger, a palm grove, Javanese women . . . and home that is "full of wings."

Poetic imagination learns from, and shapes itself in the image of, flying and floating, which are the movements of dreams and physical travel. Poetry and travelling become one another.

391 Biebl, *Nový Ikaros*, 9–10.

The poet new Icarus lightly floats in space and time
from a plaster statue to the founding of Rome
from the founding of Rome to the history of the first rose
from the first rose to all women on earth
to China India Java
and then back again through Egypt over blue Italian sky
directly to your straight nose
its beauty my love
my love only the air and the sea[392]

In Greek mythology, Icarus could not resist flying freely, ever higher and closer to the sun, only to fall into the sea and die. *New Icarus* is—among other things—an ecstatic flight across times and spaces, across memories and continents, and a fall into nothingness. Reading the poem, too, is like flying, now slowly descending like a gently falling leaf, now soaring upward and forward at an ecstatic speed. There is a change of scale, from humble, intimate songs of Biebl's earlier poetry to a grand polyphonic composition, from gentle evocation to a bold flight of imagination, from a train ride through countryside to a mad aerial circling of the globe.

There are also steamships, sailing boats, sharks and other fish and sea creatures, as well as coconuts floating in the sea. In colloquial Czech, the word for coconut, *kokos*, is used as a playful word for "head." Coconuts, in Biebl's prose texts, are "well-known travelers of tropical seas."[393] In *Plancius*, Biebl writes that in the sea he saw "plenty of wandering coconuts, with hair covering their foreheads, like the heads of drowned men, on whom fate plays strange tricks when seagulls sit on them and burst into cynical laughter."[394] In the following excerpt from *New Icarus*—in an image that is, as is common in Biebl, simultaneously mischievous and deadly serious—the poet's head, too, is like a coconut.

and mad Hamlet the ocean
rolls coconuts all the way to somewhere in the Red Sea
where in vain they wander around the desolate shores of Arabia
I experienced everything
my every step even one so slow madly carries me away somewhere
so many times in one day with a wave of my hand I went around the whole Palestine
even these verses trot in the same speed

392 Biebl, *Nový Ikaros*, 37.
393 Biebl, *Cesta na Jávu*, 36.
394 Biebl, *Cesta na Jávu*, 122.

this poem too will follow the Stations of the Cross
as if it were my fate to follow in the steps of coconuts
as if my head it is so marvelous
how hopeless it is
were the glowing fruit of the tropics
lying with obstreperous laughter in the laps of the most beautiful women
where in vain it wanders around the desolate shores of Arabia[395]

One is reminded of the poet drowning in "With Eyes Heavenward"—but in *New Icarus* one is thrown about by the ocean waves of the long verses, and "my every step even one so slow madly carries me away somewhere," also to other narratives that are as if superimposed on the coconuts/heads floating in the ocean, such as Shakespeare's Hamlet contemplating the dead jester's skull, and the whole story of avenging cruel killing. Later in the poem we recognize "Hamlet the mad ocean," Hamlet the avenger perhaps: "it had to be the ocean that came up with it / to wash away that million of dead from Verdun," from the deadliest battle of the Great War.

The home to which the poet returns in *New Icarus* now seems deserted.

in the house where since morning the arara parrot grumbles
and with her head down wauwau your black monkey from Java dies
while slowly swinging on the chandelier now it's extinguished it shines no more
my poor wauwau

while the last of all white elephants
deep in the burning jungles of Ceylon
raises his bugle all silver
And it is an angel
and he will blow to Last Judgement

It woke a tiger it scared a peacock you dumbfounded monkey
. . . .
The Angel blows
but none of the dead listen
on his alarm not even one soldier turns in his grave
and so many lie there[396]

Home is swallowed in an apocalyptic vision of burning jungles, which begins with the little decorative sculptures of baroque angels that his friends

395 Biebl, *Nový Ikaros*, 12–13.
396 Biebl, *Nový Ikaros*, 14–5.

remember seeing in his childhood home. In what follows, the remainder of Canto I and Canto II, insane images of the Great War and death predominate, punctuated by the refrain of the mad drummer.

A grave calm more terrible than when the war raged
the silence at night in November bombarded only by the beating of your desperate heart
You are a drummer gone suddenly mad who drums into darkness and emptiness
he wants to settle old scores with god who made a fool of him
drums the drummer drums to attack into darkness and emptiness
where all the dead gaze forward forward into darkness and emptiness[397]

At the end of Canto II, images of war overflow into a great deluge. Prague is flooded by the Indian Ocean:

farewell you do not know what it is to escape from shark's teeth
how quickly the ship passes by the wrongly aimed torpedo
and it is a fabulous glass maker
with its sparkling diamond it engraves in the middle of the Indian Ocean
whose blackened water fills me again with its bottomless anxiety
and nowhere even a purple strip of land
not even a piece of rock juts out
onto which you could hold with your eyes at least
that is the flood of the world

You look down at your face distorted by waves like by horrible laughter
you grasp the railing
but in vain
your heart a heavy weight as it tolls it alone pulls you down into the depths
under the water Prague home all your friends
café Slavia is filling with seahorses
waves go to the theater[398]
there [*tam*][399] down there [*tam*] hear the tam-tam
there [*tam*] below sounds again voiceband
there [*tam*] below an octopus writhes in spasms
a lobster drags her on a bloodied cart into madhouse

But it had to be the ocean that came up with it
to wash away that million of dead from Verdun

---

397 Biebl, *Nový Ikaros*, 24, 26.

398 Café Slavia is across the street from the National Theater, next to the river. Slavia was the meeting place of poets and artists, as well as people going to the theater.

399 In Czech, *tam* means "there"—here a wordplay on tam-tam, the African drum.

Everything is over but love
for your favor fish fight in the water
with a thief's lamp
which throws light on your pale face
and one after the other they offer you their round mouths
made up with carmine[400]

The "voiceband," mentioned in the poem, refers to an avant-garde musical group, created and lead by the singer, composer, and poet E.F. Burian, to whom *New Icarus* is dedicated. The voiceband (in English in original) brought together jazz, African music, dance, and "the beauty of Czech speech," also in dance and musical renderings of poems, including some by Biebl. E.F. Burian enthusiastically promoted and wrote about jazz, emphasizing its African roots; he also especially loved Smetana.[401] *Tam dole tam . . . tam-tam . . . dole tam . . . dole tam. . . .*

It is immediately after this catastrophic vision, after the sound of the African tam-tam, which echoes the military drummer's drum drumming into darkness and emptiness, that the focus shifts to tropical islands. Quietly they emerge from the deluge. Canto III begins:

When I saw Ceylon
When I saw Borneo Sumatra Java Celebes
and all the islands down there[402]

In the poem "With Eyes Heavenward" (in the collection *With the Ship*), comparable images of flood and the drowning poet lead to the part of the book that focuses on Java. In hindsight, Biebl's earlier poems and prose texts about his journey appear almost like sketches for *New Icarus*, where everything is painted on a more monumental scale and brought together into one work, only to allow the reader to feel a disturbing fragmentation. In *With the Ship*, the memory of the war is gently evoked in the first part of that book. In *New Icarus*, the juxtaposition is more intense: tropical visions are constantly superimposed on images of war to the sounds of the military drum and the angel's clarion.

Again the tropics "mirror in me" the long-gone childhood home. But now the mirroring become ever more intoxicated, like the decorative figure of an angel from the childhood home turned a white elephant turned the angel of

400 Biebl, *Nový Ikaros*, 39–41.

401 E. F. Burian, *Jazz* (Prague: Aventinum, 1928). See also Andrea Jochmanová, "Voiceband," in *Heslář české avantgardy*, ed. Josef Vojvodík and Jan Wiendl (Prague: Univerzita Karlova, 2011), 403–10.

402 Biebl, *Nový Ikaros*, 45.

apocalypse turned the army drummer turned the tam-tam and voiceband. The poetry dances to the beat of the "drummer gone suddenly mad" and other sounds which become, in the passage below, a "mad orchestra." The waves that used to rock the boy's toy ship swell and, in a storm raging "in the folds of your brain," the violent waters of the great flood again sweep away home and childhood.

Everything is so terribly familiar and again so stunningly strange
I recognize animals which I have never seen before in my life
the toke lizard it always warns you in its sad human voice
those large bugs of all colors like fragrant cosmetic soaps
even the tall damar trees I recognized at once
and the familiar taste of wild fruits duku salak durian
or papaya
mirrors in me memories of this tropical landscape
which is the paradise of black panthers of my boyhood years

just like the surf waves rocked my old Dutch sailing boat
loaded with St. John's-bread and peanuts
and now forgotten and lost under hay and images of saints in the attic
between bottles of soda water with the fizz long gone

But the overpowering sea resounds equally fiercely from malachite depths
from the very bottom of your soul billowed into darkness
like along a twisting path from past ages furious green water rises roaring
threateningly
in the folds of your brain eternally rising up into darkness
like the oldest music in the world
50 000 000 years old
a mad orchestra conducted by god-knows-which of your calcified ancestors
whose prehistoric desire to proceed in the already begun rosary of all life
forces us into vertiginous somersault into eternity[403]

Colonialism appears in the midst of this jungle, clashing again with boyhood fantasies:

I could still find that place where with a single lightning of a long knife
I slew a tiger to the astonishment of the brave Acehnese[404]

403 Biebl, *Nový Ikaros*, 47–8.

404 The Acehnese were the fiercest and most persistent fighters against the Dutch, who appear repeatedly in Biebl's poetry—more on which later.

into the fresh blood they dipped their arrows
so that they would never miss
fifty days and fifty nights the feast lasted when we finished three hundred grilled
buffaloes
. . . .
But why none of the natives recognize me

All of them look like strangers at my white suite and polished shoes
I had to tear off my sleeve and reveal old wounds on my chest
Hegebet mahat mara
I have always fought loyally on your side against white dogs

O sweet vision of my brave childhood
how long ago was it in winter I stood by the window afraid to breathe on these palm leaves
their feverish shadows fall far into my dreams
again I am afraid to breathe that they may not vanish anew
it is enough that the Dutch are breathing deeply on everything[405]

In the early poem "Primeval Forest," the jungle on the frozen window disappeared in the poet's breath, although the Dutch were not yet named. In his travelogue, Biebl stained his white suit with oil on his way to Java so as not to be ashamed of it. In "On Mount Merbabu" (*With the Ship*), too, colonial reality upset childhood dreams. But the clash of dreams and colonialism now penetrates deeper into the subconscious and becomes a feverish nightmare.

Jungles again evoke a childhood home for one who has become a stranger at home. What remains of it is like "soda water with the fizz long gone," or like pits of an exotic fruit; the sweetness is only a memory.

I walked around Prague like in a foreign land
like someone who thinks of home only when he throws away pits from dates
I never liked schools
nor winter
I liked women
in their embrace I sought at least a somewhat milder climate[406]

In the final part of *New Icarus*, the *míšenka* My Beautiful Arsiti appears. The image of the earth or landscape as a woman occurs often in Biebl's poetry. In *New Icarus*, it is foreshadowed in a passage that begins with these verses:

405 Biebl, *Nový Ikaros*, 52–3.
406 Biebl, *Nový Ikaros*, 54.

On women's breasts all Slavs despaired
despaired Russians and Poles
Czechs weep on women's breasts
which remain forever their pilgrimage site like the Říp hill
with a little memorial chapel on the top[407]

Breast-shaped, Říp is the holy hill, the mythical and symbolic center of Bohemia. On the wall of the old inn near the hill's top is a large sign: "What Mecca is to Mohamed, Říp is to a Czech."

Worshiped and loved, the *míšenka* with the Javanese name Arsiti[408] gathers in herself near and distant places. Born of a love that crossed race, in the *míšenka* apparent opposites and differences blend. More than only an image, the *míšenka*-Earth mirrors Biebl's poetry, its movement and its *poznání*. The blending of races, the annihilation of racial "purity," becomes an initial image, a spark setting off a flare-up of associations, which "extend their hands toward each other across oceans," and through which the poet "unites the most distant and apparently the most unblendable images/concepts . . . in an instinctive mania to relate all things of this world." The *míšenka* is the bridge across all races, she is all the lands and the seas, above which the poet New Icarus flies, to whom he makes love, and into whose eternity he falls as the most fundamental opposition, love and death, collapses.

Yet one is compelled to say this also in a different voice: as the poet the new Icarus the moonstruck Pierot sings "how great is love," he tumbles into bottomless nothingness, and along with an ode to *míšenka* Arsiti, again the clarion of the angel of apocalypse sounds. It is the military bugle, the voice-band, the whole "mad orchestra," "with the melancholy echo of black men's songs sung by colonial soldiers." In the multitude of voices and echoes, one hears darkness and irony, too— "how great is love / I throw myself from the rock." It echoes the earlier image of the fish kissing the drowning poet: "everything is over but love / for your favor fish fight in the water . . . and one after the other they offer you their round mouths."

Traced on Arsiti's body, as the routes of ocean liners unite the world, we notice Biebl's steamship journey to Java – "Genoa Port Said Aden Colombo Singapore."

with the melancholy echo of black men's songs sung by colonial soldiers
which daring engineer vaulted the bridges between Africa and Asia?
between China and Europe?

407 Biebl, *Nový Ikaros*, 61.

408 "Arsiti" is on the list "Javanese women's names" in Biebl's travel notebook. Archive of the Museum of Czech Literature, Prague.

between your almost classical profile and at some moments almost African
but very nearly blue yet also somewhat Mongolian eyes

My Beautiful Arsiti within you the steamers of all the five continents cross their paths
on the line Hamburg Genoa Port Said Aden Colombo Singapore
Hong Kong Yokohama San Francisco
and down to South America
from New South Wales you glanced at me
now again in Honolulu
somewhere from Liu-Kiu
under a pirate flag when the wind tousles your hair
from the Gobi Desert you breathed on me

Was it Etna? Was it Krakatoa that exploded when you laughed?
Was it in Java or perhaps in Japan?

And whose are the black hands you hide in the white fingers of the gloves?[409]

. . . .

That is why I loved the *míšenka* whose name is My Beautiful Arsiti
to remember some Swiss lakes
to catch a glimpse from my window of the blue flow of the Amazon
to knock suddenly on the gate of a Tibetan monastery high in the mountains
to immerse myself deep into the half-light of primeval forests
to let all the colors and fragrances of her heart and body
rise within me

As soon as I began to kiss My Beautiful Arsiti
magnificent birds flew here
warpers birds-of-paradise around her head like a halo
even woodpeckers with red caps
from paradise too

And all the birds began to peck at Eve's apple
at that apple of eternity
which never diminishes
at that apple of vanity
which never diminishes

409 Biebl, *Nový Ikaros*, 64–66.

at the apple of love of eternal damnation
which rolls around the whole equator
and falls through all centuries

at the apple on which one sees
the marks of king Solomon's teeth

Oh how many times still
you sweet vanity
I will feel that horrible fall
straight into eternity

The angel blows the trumpet
and at his alarm roses pour from heaven over the whole world
I feel everywhere at home under a roof
like a fish protected by fins
farewell farewell how great is love
I throw myself from the rock
how great is love
farewell farewell

I love change
I sail all the seas[410]

410 Biebl, *Nový Ikaros*, 70–73.

AGAIN SOME MALAY LANDSCAPE

> afterimage /ˈɑːftərˌɪmɪdʒ/ noun 1. a sustained or renewed sensation, esp visual, after the original stimulus has ceased[411]

> I love actuality but also dreaming, and thus I like to move on the border between the two worlds, where actuality overflows into dream and dream into actuality, where beauty is born from a beautiful sight and resonates for a long time behind closed eyes.[412]

Let us not try to separate too sharply actuality from dreaming; or Biebl's writings "about" his Javanese journey from those in which tropical motifs and experiences lurk in the background and only occasionally emerge. Let us think, rather, how one overflows into the other, how a journey "resonates for a long time behind closed eyes"—for years, for decades—and how tropical dreams overflow into ever new reality, ever anew.

In 1931 Biebl married, but he and his wife lived mostly separately; they had no children. In the 1930s, he revisited the Balkans several times, and went on a short trip to Algeria, where he was again impressed by other landscapes as well as the racism under colonialism, but references to these trips are rare in his poetry. He was involved, as a writer rather than a politician, with the activities of the Communist Party, and published strongly-worded statements, reports and open letters about the exploitation of workers and miners in Czechoslovakia.

During this decade, Biebl published only two slim volumes of poetry—very little compared to the five years between his first collection of 1924 and *New Icarus* of 1929, or compared to his peers. He also published in magazines and/or read on radio a number of prose texts, including ones based on his Javanese trip; those that survived (many did not) would later constitute, along with texts published earlier, his posthumous editions of *Journey to Java*. His literary output was small in terms of quantity, but not in terms of its depth and power.

---

411 *Collins Online Dictionary*, https://www.collinsdictionary.com/dictionary/english/afterimage (accessed November 11, 2021).

412 Biebl, *Cesta na Jávu*, 79–80.

From its beginnings, poetism shared certain tendencies with surrealism (Teige had spoken of surrealism already in *Life* in 1922, two years before the movement's official establishment in Paris) and the former gradually metamorphosed into a distinctly Czech version of the latter.[413] Biebl was a founding and active member of the Czechoslovak Surrealist Group (established in 1934 under Nezval's leadership), and his work of the 1930s, including his fragmentary travelogues, was strongly inspired by surrealism. For example, his prose "Na hostině mrtvých" (At the feast of the dead), about a Chinese funeral in Java, was published in the journal *Surrealismus* in 1936.

Instead of the more playful and colorful free associations of poetism, the tropics of Biebl's surrealist poetry emerge in flashes, in fragments, from a deep darkness of the subconscious—pervasively in his 1931 *Nebe peklo ráj* (Heaven hell paradise), less often in the 1939 *Zrcadlo noci* (Mirror of night).

Heaven Hell Paradise opens with such flashes in the poem "Vichřice letí" (The storm flies)—there are glances from a speeding train again, but more darkly intoxicated; more like from a car speeding through jungle at night in a storm, occasionally illuminated by lightening (to evoke another text, "Ing. Baer"):

A painted ceiling
A lion passed by
From the bloody footprints

The storm flies

In the basket a hare
Instead of paper
Instead of all rubbish

André Gide
Congo
And you can never have peace

Instead of love
Paris
Again some Malay landscape

This is not all this is just the beginning[414]

413 On Czech surrealism, see Sayer, *Prague*.
414 Konstantin Biebl, *Nebe peklo ráj* (Prague: Sfinx, 1931), 9.

Tropics flash from the subconscious, now less as a new sight but more as something seen long ago, or like a recurrent dream— "again some Malay landscape." Yet, "this is not all"— and one recalls a poem from *With the Ship*: "It is not the end. We must go farther, we must go deeper, just like every proper drowned man."

Among these dark flashes: André Gide / Congo. The French author travelled there in 1925–1926, a year before Biebl's trip to Java. His journey, an official French "mission," was very different from Biebl's, but his 1927 travelogue *Voyage au Congo* (Journey to Congo), published in 1928 in Czech translation, contains disturbing images of the "terrible savagery" of the colonial commercial enterprise, which would spark a public debate on colonialism in the French parliament. (Presumably because of Gide's later repudiation of Communism, in 1953 these three lines in the poem disappeared in Biebl's posthumous collected works, just as Teige's name did from *New Icarus* in that edition.)[415]

"Džungle" (The jungle), another poem from *Heaven Hell Paradise*, is the most intense return to the tropics from this time, and also one of the most drunken, torn dreams in the book:

I do not know greater vertigo than tropical nature
Freer animals and greater chaos
When the tiger is heard
In the bloody rags of an approaching dawn

What human nests in the treetops in the jungle
Which way following an erased trail
Comes out to hunt when the ferns move
Arrow flies so lightly

Now you lose now you find again the lost trail
How sensitive flora is
In the virgin heart of tropics

And before the sun rises above green jungle
Which is the ballet school of butterflies
Whenever one of the marvelous birds moves on the branch
And begins to call
In the yellow and purple scales of the equatorial zone[416]

---

415 Biebl, *Dílo*, 3:7.
416 Biebl, *Nebe peklo ráj*, 21.

Heaven Hell Paradise, the title of the book, is the name of a children's game, in which fortune is foretold using a kind of origami (in English commonly known as the "fortune teller" and under other names); and childhood fantasies of hunting in the jungle return in this poem. But it also makes me think of Biebl's comments on his first experience of real tropical nature: "To step on the ground in Ceylon means to be stabbed into the heart with the knife, so stunned you are by immense tropical nature." "Look how dreaming takes revenge when it is realized. I am lying next to a wall like a dervish in the rags of reason and in spasms of fantasy, in the darkness attacked from behind by Ceylon's dagger."[417] These are dreams intoxicated with reality, with real vertigo.

The dream and experience of tropical nature are increasingly entangled with imagery of the human psyche as well as humanity as the poem continues:

Stars
Night
Sea oars and other desires

A hundred views offer a stronger drink

A thousand and a thousand music entangles us
In a mysterious jungle full of lianas and adventure

Now you lose now you find again the lost
You will hear the peacock
And crash into a tiger which flees with a gazelle

You aim at the bird of paradise and shoot down a fabulous antelope[418]

Reading this poetry— "a desire for cognition"—is itself like being in a jungle: Now you lose now you find again the lost

The last part of the poem awakens from tropical nature into cold Europe, only to recognize again an inescapable sameness: Europe turns out to be a reality no less dream-like, "shaking with cold," pervaded by dreams of tropics and faraway lands.

Deep in the jungle the bird of paradise screams
Its screams wake up a child from dreams
And in the whole Europe the plague rages

417 Biebl, *Cesta na Jávu*, 53.
418 Biebl, *Nebe peklo ráj*, 22.

When at six in the morning the alarm clock rings to work
And trains crisscross
And a steamship disappears
Far on the sea
In another land
Under other circumstances
With similarly alternating fever and chills[419]

The progression of the poem is reminiscent of Biebl's earlier work (such as "On Mount Merbabu"), yet both dreams and reality have become more feverish and chilling, and the allure of the abysses of human psyche has grown darker.

Whether or not Java or the tropics are explicitly mentioned in a particular poem, reality and dreams are often revealed through visions of the sea and distant lands (including, in the poem below, the Sahara, where Biebl travelled on his trip in Algeria). The poem "Setkání" (Meeting) evokes the immensity of the most fragile, most intimate of moments—the whole world is precariously part of it, both poles and the Sahara, freezing cold and scorching heat, like snowflakes and apple blossoms:

In the world there is no place so bitter and so sad
That two people could not meet each other
Far beyond the seas or even in a desolate landscape
Like the sand of the Sahara
Like the snow around both poles
....
Don't be frightened by my smile or by my crumpled hat
A coolie in Singapore stepped on it
And the wind carried it back again
In a great arch
Taking before you so far its greatest
Global bow[420]

In the poem "Májový den" (May day), a village man dying on a beautiful Spring day is a man drowning in the sea. The playfulness of the past is almost gone. The poetry is raw, colder, sarcastic; on a beautiful day in May—"the time of love," poetized most famously by Mácha in *May*, the most famous of Czech poems—one feels the breath of death.

419 Biebl, *Nebe peklo ráj*, 23.
420 Biebl, *Nebe peklo ráj*, 24–25.

Mercy! Who forces him to make strokes
Those desperate strokes with his arms
Which draw apart night
O death you exert yourself in vain
You will not make a sailor out of that old man
How did the gypsum pipe suit him
It too is lost

I see it fall
Something white in his eyes shines and falls
Five thousand meters into the sea it falls

I see how he breathed out for the last time
And his head descended to the bottom
Of the Pacific Ocean

But how far will the road lead
Of your eyes gazing into dying

Hear the sea garbling the words of those who drowned[421]

In the 1930s, the threat of Nazism was increasingly felt, especially in Central Europe. In 1938–39, Hitler effectively took over Bohemia. At this time, and in the next few years, leading Czech poets, many of whom were previously strongly internationally oriented, wrote some of the most poignant poetry about their homeland. Biebl and his poetry were equally affected by the dark atmosphere, but his image of home at this time is different from most other poets: as in Mácha, his homeland is, more than ever, the whole suffering Earth. This is the first poem from the collection *Mirror of Darkness* published in 1939, when Bohemia became a "protectorate" of Nazi Germany. The title, "Na Lovčenu" (On Lovćen), refers to the chief mountain in Montenegro, after which the country is said to be named (Montenegro, "Black mountain").

Judging from the cymbals thrown
On the pavement of an old military harbor
I think that the sea is launching
Its gigantic concerts

421 Biebl, *Nebe peklo ráj*, 29.

Always to have before one's eyes
Only the greatness and the lamentation of the world
To do what every Montenegrin does
To dwell
As the snow dwells in a ravine

To have the abyss for one's threshold
And eagle's wings
For one's native roof[422]

The sea and its "gigantic concerts" set the tone for "the greatness and the lamentation of the world," but also for the vastness and vertigo of the world that has become one's home. The local and present anxiety expands far beyond the here and now. The invocation of the Montenegrins and their homeland, the "Black Mountain," like the images of the stormy sea, takes us to another time and place: during the First World War Biebl fought in Montenegro; beyond Biebl's personal experience, in 19th century Czech literature the Montenegrins symbolized bravery and resistance. One could think back to home at the end of *New Icarus*, as he falls into the ocean:

I feel everywhere at home under a roof
like a fish protected by fins

Poetic travel in 1939: to be at home only in the greatness and the lamentation of the world. The home and the sea: old dreams written ever more clearly, ever more darkly.

422 Biebl, *Zrcadlo noci*, n.p. Also in Biebl, *Dílo*, 3:71.

THE JUNGLE AROUND US

During the Second World War, Biebl kept a low profile, living mostly in the countryside, away from Prague and from his home. Documents from the Protectorate authorities show that he was watched—they note his commitment to communism, and the fact that his wife is "from a mixed marriage of a Jewish man and an Aryan woman."[423]

The extensive collection of poems *Bez obav* (Fearlessly), published in 1951, just months before Biebl's suicide, contains poems written in the 1940s. Colonial and tropical themes appear in all parts of the book. In one part, "On the Throne of Rice Fields," Java is the main theme.

Some of the tropical poems in *Fearlessly* sound almost as gently and lightly as Biebl's early poems. Other poems have harder edges and sometimes tend toward something like clear messages—during the war called for by the vile circumstances, and later by an uneasy effort at relevance and intelligibility in line with the socialist ideology of art, but perhaps also in tune with his old feelings: "to earth binds us love, wrath, grief, / let us remain on the ground!"

The ten-page poem "Na trůně rýžových polí" (On the throne of rice fields) is dated 1940. In the first part of the poem, "an aeroplane takes off from a palm grove" to throw letters into gardens in Prague—

Samira from the Dutch Indies is writing to you,
two black lilies for breasts,
a beautiful butterfly for the mouth[424]

The poet dreams Java and Bali and evokes their beauty again, lightly and sensually like in his early poetry, yet now, in the very intoxication with beauty, in the mirror of gods, there is a menace and impending doom:

Do not let girls in Bali
Inhale that intoxicating fume
In rituals since childhood

423 National Archive in Prague, especially letter number 1332, dated 21. September 1941, from the authorities in Louny, responding to telephone enquiry from the Ministry of Interior.

424 Konstantin Biebl, *Bez obav* (Prague: Československý spisovatel, 1951), 76–7.

Do not believe that the Indies is only the rippling of temples
In the breeze of narcotic jungles
. . . .
Never walk alone on the dike
Under which you see
Only groves of broken palms
In the mirror of gods where everything
Disappears escapes and flutters[425]

These verses, as they return to ground, set the stage for the final section. (Samira in Arabic means "friend" or "companion.")

Remember, Sarina, that evening
When I began to call you Samira?
. . . .
There are also Europeans like you, Sarina
Who love your islands
And are ashamed of those who wring rubber out of their light
There are also Europeans like you
There are Europeans
Who have shackles on their hands
They think of you and never will, Samira,
Never will, my lyre
Betray you[426]

Recall again the "Indian" of Biebl's early poetry, although now, in 1940, the poet speaks of "Europeans / Who have shackles on their hands," not workers. The continuity with his earlier images of colonialism is obvious, but now, there is a new urgency under the different circumstances. When this poem was written, Bohemia was occupied by Nazi Germany, after it was betrayed by the great European and colonial powers, Britain and France, when they acquiesced to Hitler's annexation of large parts of Czechoslovakia, "a faraway country . . . of whom we know nothing," as British Prime Minister Neville Chamberlain said.[427] The poem is one of the more direct expressions of the nearness of a small nation (dis)located in the middle of Europe to colonized Indonesia. Old ties are stronger than ever—a war again connected the world.

On 27th May, 1942, a commando of the Czechoslovak Foreign Army assassinated the Nazi Protector Reinhard Heydrich. In the following weeks,

425 Biebl, *Bez obav*, 82–3.
426 Biebl, *Bez obav*, 84–85.
427 Sayer, *The Coast of Bohemia*, 5.

the Nazi retaliated by a wave of terror which involved the execution of some 2000 Czechs, including leading intellectuals and writers, such as Vladislav Vančura, the first Chair of Devětsil and one of the country's greatest novelists. It was immediately following these darkest weeks of the war that the Dutch Indies reappeared in Biebl's "Džungle kolem nás" (The jungle around us), dated July 1942. The month and year are written under the poem, almost as if they were part of it. The Gestapo—the German secret police that perpetuated the torture and killings in the Protectorate—is mentioned in the poem, the tropical "frightening flight of silver birds" evoke military planes, the darkness of the jungle is not just there in Sumatra, but all around us. Biebl's tropics and reality again overflow into each other.

In the poem, Biebl evokes again the most notorious and bloodiest colonial conflict in the Dutch Indies, the Aceh War (1873–1914). The image of the "brave Acehnese," which appears already in Biebl's *New Icarus*,[428] is developed in the earlier writings of the Czech physician Pavel Durdík, who lived and worked in the Indies from 1879 until 1883. Part of this time he served as a medical officer with the Dutch colonial army in Aceh. He was sharply critical of colonialism and admired the bravery of the Acehnese and their struggle against the colonial invaders. He compared the fierce Acehnese resistance against the Dutch "intruders" to the "awakening" of the Czechs under the Austrian empire, and posed the brave Acehnese as a model for the meeker Czechs.[429] One is reminded of Mácha and Sládek when Durdík describes in the same breath the beauty of Aceh and the destruction of Acehnese homeland by the colonial army.

Biebl must have been impressed by Durdík's writings. What re-emerges in Biebl is not an exotic figure of the "brave Acehnese," but the parallel between the Czech and Acehnese struggle for freedom—for the right of a small nation to exist in the face of an empire. Even in Durdík, the recognition of a common lot—the same suffering and struggle—already begins to blur certain distinctions and upset distances. He writes of Acehnese "homeland" using vocabulary and imagery associated with descriptions of (Czech) homeland. In Biebl's poetry, space is even more collapsed, as is the distinction between "us" and "them"—at a time of blindness to the humanity of the other. As one reads "The Jungle Around Us," Prague becomes the drowning Sumatra, and it is here, everywhere, that the brave Acehnese fight the invaders. The linden tree, the symbol of the Czech state and, in Czech poetry and music, a quiet and tender image of love for our country, stands in the jungle. The same desperate call to battle is heard in Prague and in Aceh—it matters no more where one is.

---

428 Biebl, *Nový Ikaros*, 52.

429 For more on Durdík's "brave Acehnese," see Mrázek, "Czech Tropics," 179–88.

The Jungle Around Us

Only you jungle you are everywhere
In the frightening flight of silver birds
Above the marshes of drowning Sumatra
Concealed by flames of flamingo wings

On a muddy coast woven into lianas
The life of brave Acehnese is as hard
In the Dutch Indies as for us in Prague
On the fifty-second parallel

II
In ancient blindness
In the roots slowly rotting
Grow in the darkness
Insidious dwarfs

In darkness all around
They blow their poisoned arrows
One of them climbs not far from here
Into the crown of the Czech linden tree

III
How many of us friends will be overgrown
By bushes thickening with death
Do not ask the jungle for mercy
Just as the tall damar tree pleads not

Let us not think how many of us will remain
Let us be like the weaverbirds
Who see the sun rise red
Above the dark jungle whose war will soon end

IV
Let us be brave like the Acehnese in Sumatra
Let him fall who must fall no-one matters
As long as we show to the Gestapo rabble
How the tall damar tree overgrows the jungle

V
Penetrate through bushes future new world
With all your soul and all your body
Struggle through upward like the damar tree
Like the damar tree through the greatest dusk

And rise above the jungle higher and higher

Like the Acehnese over the enemy
In the sign of the damar tree you'll attain victory

July 1942[430]

One might expect that it would be in the name of the linden tree that victory is attained, but it is not. The hope lies rather in the tropical damar tree. The Czech struggle against Nazi Germany becomes a struggle that is not just "ours." It turns out to be the same as one on the other side of the globe. One recalls Biebl's images of "mixed blood" in the texts about his Javanese journey, and especially My Beautiful Arsiti of *New Icarus*, images of the transcendence of race and nation. But more than a call for an idealistic humanism, there is the sense that the same jungle is everywhere.

"Do not believe that the Indies is only the rippling of temples / In the breeze of narcotic jungles": there is no "rippling of temples," not even "narcotic jungles," in the hard, exhortative lines of "The Jungle Around Us." The darkness and emptiness, too, are different, drained and tired by yet another world war, by the horror and poison of it all, but also by the "ancient blindness / in the roots slowly rotting"; or something like the "mud, which reaches up to our shoulders."

430 Biebl, *Bez obav*, 115–9.

SAILORS OF ALL SEAS UNITE!

In the years after the end of the World War Two, the Communist Party came to power and in 1948 consolidated its control. Czechoslovakia was incorporated into the "socialist camp" led by Soviet Union. For some, this was a nightmare; for others, it was a dream coming true—yet one thinks again, and Biebl might have thought, of what he wrote about his first days in the tropics: "Look how dreaming takes revenge when it is realized."

In *Dobrodruh* (Adventurer), a selection of Biebl's poetry published in 2008, the editor, Vladimír Justl, writes in his afterword that

> the postwar [poems] are products of their time [*poplatné době*, literally: paying a toll to their times]; they have a strongly propagandist [*agitační*] character. Today most of them are buried under the wall of forgetting. It is a sad epilogue of a poet, who belongs among the great personalities of Czech interwar avant-garde.[431]

From *Fearlessly*, which has close to eighty poems, only four were selected by Justl for the *Adventurer*. For comparison, sixteen poems—two thirds of the original collection—were selected from *With the Ship*. Justl's comments and selection are typical of current post-communist perceptions.

Many poems in *Fearlessly* advocate communism and search for poetry that would be consistent with it. To understand Biebl's involvement in this project, however, it is not enough to see his poetry *only* as a toll paid to the ruling party that would ensure safe passage. The internationalism of communism in the 1920s was part of the avant-garde's opening to the wide world, and for Biebl, the dream of a future just world was not unlike his dreams of faraway tropical lands. The playfulness and intoxication of poetism, with its parrots and monkeys, were part of this political vision. In a poem first published in the communist paper *Red Right* on Labor Day 1924, the struggle for a better world is imagined as a journey: "Perhaps as a pilgrim, eyes on the horizon shielded by the hand / you'll behold your way . . ."[432] When in 1929, faced by the realities of Stalinism, some poets (including Teige and Seifert) left the Communist Party, Biebl (together with Nezval and others) decided to remain,

---

431 Konstantin Biebl, *Dobrodruh*, ed. Vladimír Justl (Prague: Odeon, 2008), 122.

432 Originally published in *Rudé právo*, 1 May 1924.

but even then the dream of communism, as it began to be realized, also began to take its revenge. For Biebl, this was especially true in the last years of his life, under the communist government. The main artistic movements of the interwar avant-garde—Biebl was their prominent representative—were labelled as degenerate. A number of the poets were viciously attacked and their work condemned, among them Seifert and Halas. Záviš Kalandra was a prominent communist journalist, historian, and critic, who in the 1930s worked closely with Teige, Biebl, and other surrealists. Kalandra was arrested in November 1949 and executed in June 1950. The campaign against Teige was ferocious and the hunted man died of a heart attack on 1st October 1951, six weeks before Biebl's suicide.

Biebl probably never believed that he could be innocent, whether as a white man in the colonies or as a teenage soldier: "Three years, my dove, you were in the war, / And you did not kill anyone?" In a late poem, he advises young poets: "Learn to climb the tallest masts / even if they were erected by pirates."[433] As other great poets, his friends, were silenced and denounced, he (along with Nezval) was alternately lauded as a model communist poet and attacked as a representative of degenerate ideology. In his verses, it is not always clear where the line between self-preservation and conviction lies; or whether such a line always exists. It is clear that before his suicide, he lived in horrific fear.

In *Fearlessly*, Java, and more generally Asia, appear naturally in expressions of anti-capitalist and anti-imperialist sentiments. The tone and style have changed (again), in some verses more than others. There is, for example, "Korejská balada" (Korean ballad), a condemnation of the American aggression in Korea. "Javanka" (as in the case of *míšenka*, the English translation, "Javanese woman," sounds harder and colder than the Czech) was written in 1949, the final year of the Indonesian revolution against the Dutch. The repetitions and the gradual unfolding of the poem loosely evoke the *pantun*, a Malay poetic form adopted by European poets since the nineteenth century. Love and jealousy are common motifs of pantuns. This poem involves a profoundly colonial "love triangle."

The Javanese Woman

The white tuan
Appeared so surprised
When I asked him
In the evening

433 Biebl, *Dílo*, 5:447.

How his white wife
In Amsterdam is doing

I said it
Merely to be polite
I had no other reason
Why should I lie?
I only wanted to know
How many guests she usually has

How many guests she usually has
The grand white lady
Who is her whole life
Alone in Amsterdam

How many guests she usually has
That from Surabaya
The white tuan sends her
So many boxes of tea

So many boxes of tea
So much of cocoa beans
The white tuan sends her
Throughout the year

So many boxes of tea
So many packs of coffee
The white tuan sends her
Every week from Java

So many sacks of sugar
From the trembling cane
On plantations it throws
Long black shadows

So many boxes packs sacks
All to a single woman
Who has daily for her breakfast
One cup of white coffee[434]

434 Biebl, *Bez obav*, 86–7.

The Javanese woman is reminiscent of the one in "Court Report" in *With the Ship That Carries Tea and Coffee* (and the title of this collection resonates with the "boxes, sacks, packs" of "Javanka"), who equally politely and sweetly undermines colonialism— "why is it that all the white orchids / one day will burst into bloom all over Java." One also recalls the final question of "On Mount Merbabu," about golden ducats, the riches of the tropics, falling into the lap - "but never ask / to whose?"

Even the title of the 7-page "V zrcadle oceánu" (In the mirror of the ocean) may make one think: ocean again, mirror again. Initial images: a "heavy American warship," Ku-Klux-Klan, and

The Statue of Liberty in front and without a cape
To see better who will be lynched today in Tennessee
In Chicago or in the colonies

In the dusk of early morning, a black man appears— "I see him in the mirror of the ocean, in the harbor rags of the half-naked surface of water"— descending on a rope on the side of the ship and writing on her hull:

We want peace! Long live Stalin!
Sailors of all seas unite
And in the struggle for peace take courage!

The rest of the poem speaks to "sailors of all countries . . . also you, American sailors":

Tear off the striped prison garb from your flag
And keep only the sky full of stars!
From the American flag tear off slavery
of black men and colonial nations
. . . .
Sailors on the sea unite with workers on the pier
And around the whole world
Create an e q u a t o r of all races and nations

An equator that would pass from the blood-washed shores of Korea
Through Hong Kong Singapore Sydney Cape Town Gibraltar
Bordeaux London Hamburg Leningrad Vladivostok
New York Tokyo to the blood-washed shores of Korea
Sailors of all seas and port workers of all countries
Unite—let the sea everywhere be blue![435]

435 Biebl, *Bez obav*, 246–52.

"Long live Stalin!"—in the twenty-first century, that alone might make one quickly dismiss the poem as merely a piece of sloganeering, and certainly this poetry sometimes verges on that. Yet, "the blood-washed shores of Korea" might also make one think of the horrific 1951 painting *Massacre in Korea* by the Stalin Peace Prize laureate Pablo Picasso, a painting which can't be fully understood as communist propaganda either. Vast seas, star-studded skies, ships and ports, blacks and Asians, and the horrors of war again come together to form an image of the whole world and whole humanity "equated," reminiscent of the ecstatic image—grieving, wrathful, and loving—of the *míšenka* My Beautiful Arsiti and the ocean into which New Icarus falls; it is again a sight of "the greatness and the lamentation of the world." The image of the unity and equality of humanity mirrored in the vast blue ocean is not *only* a product of its times either.

Blood flows blood flows
Through the ages
Your blood
O human
Ever of ancient times[436]

Just before his death in November 1951, Biebl reportedly burned most of his unpublished poems,[437] but a few dozen survived. One could imagine some of them included in *Fearlessly*, while others are markedly different, especially those that reveal his struggle with painful illness and thoughts of death, or express Biebl's despair because of the political situation and attack "my own party, which I love," a suicide of sorts— "they will die by their own poison, like scorpions."

Oceans, ships, Java, travel, and racism appear here, too. In "Elektrické křeslo" (Electric chair), for example:

Dark and feverish West's world lies before you
At night
At whites' negro dance
In the mirror of parquets where blacks have no access

Except through the lower stream of their melancholic songs
Except through the rhythm of their blood which rapidly overflows
Into the entertainments of the white race

---

436 Biebl, *Bez obav*, 235.
437 Nezval, *Z mého života*, 220.

Which amuses itself by hanging blacks
For presumed rape of white girls
Although without a single kiss
Without a single black man's kiss
In the sounds of saxophone black blood
Crosses over into their veins

And it is a world without poetry
If it had imagination
It would lynch its own shadows[438]

The poem is a renewed reflection on the "ancient blindness" to the human potential to overflow one into the other through love, dance and music. One thinks again of the poet as a "half-caste" and the hopeful dream of *míšenka* Arsiti; of bridges between continents built "with the melancholy echo of black songs sung by colonial soldiers," or the voiceband and the 1920s avant-garde's love of jazz and African music and dance. The poem bemoans the lack of poetry. The poet, we recall, is "an alchemist, and each thing that he takes into his hand, he changes into gold," because he believes "that in the essence of all things, in the veins of all images and behind the curtain of all phenomena, pure gold quivers, the golden stream of poetry." In Biebl's poetry, still, the "overflowing of blood"—blending of races, of people—is part of revealing "the golden stream of poetry" behind the curtain of appearances.

438 Biebl, *Dílo*, 5:436.

YOUR LONGEST AND MOST ADVENTUROUS JOURNEY

Among his unpublished late poems, glimpses of the "ill century,"[439] and the sharp pain of pancreatitis that Biebl suffered since 1949, one motif appears repeatedly and with a new urgency: the final departure. Visions of tropical seas and islands—childhood dreams and reminiscences of travel, specters from the past—now constitute a poetics of approaching death.

In childhood they gave you all you wanted
Brehm's Life of Animals
and a little island Bali on your bed

Both hands skinny and pale laid on the atlas:
Africa, India, Java, cholera . . . and now pancreas!
And then grave silence for a moment
before it deflated—ready to sail away—
like a balloon without wings:
for your longest and most adventurous journey
already prepared belly![440]

The long poem "Durga" remembers and dreams of Java and the wrathful goddess, with a "rosary of human skulls," at the Javanese Prambanan temple. Images of drowning are not new in Biebl's poetry, but now life seems to be in a remote past. The ship on which the poet sailed to Java sank (the *Plancius* was indeed sunk in World War Two), "my friend Paviro" was killed in anti-colonial revolution (we met him in the 1929 text "Javanese Demons"), and the previously happy monkeys have become annoying.

The Plancius sank but that does not matter
In the distance floating a luxurious white door frame shines
On which you can lie and sleep so well
When you faint and the ocean carries you away

---

439 Biebl, *Dílo*, 5:422.
440 Biebl, *Dílo*, 5:380.

Become accustomed to sharks and jellyfish
To waves that arrange pillows under your head
On a black bed from which you can better survey all the sweet horror
Which chases you pushes you somewhere to Java

Above the jungle the moon rose and hesitated a while
Whether to hang its swing between craters or into lianas
If only the cheeky monkeys would come to their senses
He would like to swing in dark jungle all alone

Where's my friend Paviro? Why hasn't he come? Perhaps he fell
The wind said quietly from the hill over a Chinese graveyard in Semarang
In front of Rose Park from silent barricades
He welcomed with his bow seven enemy tanks[441]

We meet Paviro again in "Smrti" (For Death), where the encounter between the poet and Death takes place again on the Indian Ocean, "the flood of the world" in *New Icarus*. The final verses of "For Death," "the immense love of the world," recall yet again "how great is love" in the final lines of *New Icarus*. Love and poetry are thrown with contempt into Death's face.

I feel how green Death enters the skeleton
after first symptoms of Asian cholera
with the broad smile of the first helmsman,
to signal departure she tolls the ship bell.
. . . .
Indian Ocean, I loved you so,
can you help me somehow
into my shoes worn thin by the world,
before the Titanic sinks and waves and sharks open their jaws?

In Java the uprising died away,
Paviro, Suran and Riso are dead;
who will hear my call in vain,
Death, sink with me, you ship rat!

Before you begin your feast, Death, use the sea water to add salt
to the poet's meat, which has a sweetish taste like roses,
when you pick all the meat from the skeleton, you ship rat,

441 Biebl, *Dílo*, 5:382.

you will sail through the night, you will sail through rose morning,
on water silver-colored like mercury
on a ship on which I will be the captain,

when we sail together through the Indian Ocean,
I'll be in front and you—a boat in tow,
bound by a long steel rope
like one of my shining strings

to the ship of our demise
in the waves of my singing steamship.

The ocean will be my grave,
its surface silver like mercury,
the ocean will be my song,
my swollen chest—immense love for the world.[442]

Paviro, Suran and Riso, dead in faraway Java, are doubly remote. The poet is alone, as if home were an inhospitable island. People from beyond the seas are closer to him—such as Liat in Java:

To die in a distant foreign land, how cruel!
But Liat, if only she knew, would feel compassion with me.
I saw once how she set aside a fish bone
on the edge of a little Chinese plate with her gentle hand.[443]

The "longest and most adventurous journey" feels to be, in some poems, a much anticipated escape from pain—

don't be sorry for the sick one
he loved so much lands strange and distant[444]

—and a way to be again with the loved ones, the dead:

Cradle knell cradle knell
My journey is long!
Far to nirvana
. . . .

442 Biebl, *Dílo*, 5:372–3.
443 Biebl, *Dílo*, 5:371.
444 Biebl, *Dílo*, 5:367.

But we father we will go together
Like stardust
We will journey from pole to pole
My father long buried[445]

In 1948, Biebl's young relative, a military pilot, died in an airplane accident. Biebl wrote a poem, the first part of which was engraved on the pilot's grave, where three years later Biebl himself would be laid to rest, after he, too, fell to his death. These are the final lines of the poem, not inscribed on the grave:

I search your maps in vain
So many journeys awaited us
You fly over the sea or the Alps
In fog wanders your plane[446]

Biebl jumped from the window of his Prague apartment on the night of 11th November 1951 and died the following morning.

445 Biebl, *Dílo*, 5:364.
446 Biebl, *Dílo*, 5:366.

AGAIN AND AGAIN MAN IS PROVING THAT HE HAS NO WINGS

Various texts written on the occasion of Biebl's death were published in newspapers and read at his funeral; later, many of them were collected in a memorial volume. Images of Java and the poet's travels appeared in many of them—in yet another light, in yet another sense.

Nezval, one of Biebl's closest literary friends, who a few years earlier compared Biebl's childhood to sunflower roots, read a poem at the funeral. Here is an excerpt:

Life is magnificent and hard
you jumped from the masts of barks
over meridians and parallels,
from towers, a hopscotching child.

....
we will say that you left for Java,
so that we do not mourn so much,
that you lead a great expedition

to the lands where you sailed with that ship,
which carried coffee, tea,
where people will also gain their freedom,
and celebrate the First of May,

the day of love, the day of labor,
in a world where there'll be no hunger,
or that you fell asleep in your garden,
and that after work you want to slumber.[447]

Nezval's poem was the first public disclosure, albeit veiled, that Biebl committed suicide. As the poet, a hopscotching child, jumps from masts and towers, over meridians and parallels—the whole world shrinks into a pattern

447 Vítězslav Nezval, "Rozloučení s Konstantinem Bieblem," *Za Konstantinem Bieblem*, 15–17.

on the ground drawn in a child's hand, his life's journey becomes a game, and the shadow of the poet's suicide blends incredibly with a light, sweet memory of childhood. The poet's departure to Java is juxtaposed to peaceful napping in his garden: two consoling images, yet images of death nonetheless. Even as it is marked by the fearful times, Nezval's poem gently reflects Biebl's life and poetry.

This cannot be said about many other poems and texts in memory of Biebl. Mentioning the poet's voyage appears to have been almost an obligation. In many cases, Java is paradoxically evoked in patriotic, behind-the-baking-oven home-sweet-home statements that violently simplify and negate the depth, joy and pain of Biebl's poetic cognition of *země*—homeland, soil, the Earth. Karel Šiktanc wrote in his poem:

And you were recollecting your poems from Java
Where in the most ardent verses you think of Bohemia[448]

In Josef Rybák's text, Java is represented equally reductively: "Toward [Slavětín] your memories flew even from faraway, tropical Java, and here you always returned from your travels and adventurous poetic expeditions."[449] In Jindřich Hiller's poem, too, oceans and the Equator appear to have existed for Biebl only to return to home-sweet-home. The word *dospěls* has the double meaning of "you arrived" and "you matured," implying surreptitiously that the travels of the "simple boy" were childish, while love of home was mature.

Over stormy waves—
Comrade, a simple boy—
Along the Equator you arrived/matured
To magnificent Prague[450]

Both Taufer and Vilém Závada cited the last poem from *With the Ship*. According to Taufer, in his eulogy, it shows that Biebl "overcame" "barren experimentation" and a "romantic desire for the exotic."[451] Závada, a notable poet and a member of Devětsil in the interwar period who became strongly engaged with socialism by the time of Biebl's death, wrote that Biebl "departs for travels of searching and experimentation which had to end in a blind alley" and that the journey "revived his love for home."[452] (The logical deduction

448 Karel Šiktanc, "Konstantinu Bieblovi," *Za Konstantinem Bieblem*, 45.
449 Josef Rybák, "Slavětín 19. XI," *Za Konstantinem Bieblem*, 48.
450 Jindřich Hiller, "Za básníkem," *Za Konstantinem Bieblem*, 51.
451 Jiří Taufer, "Zemřel Konstantin Biebl - zemřel český básník," *Za Konstantinem Bieblem*, 10.
452 Vilém Závada, "Básník Konstantin Biebl," *Za Konstantinem Bieblem*, 30–31.

that home is a dead end is unintended, although it would complicate "sweet home" in a way that would be closer to Biebl's poetry.)

Tropical Java has become a cliché whose emptiness conceals or caricatures Biebl's own complex poetic cognition. Yet in another sense, the references to Biebl's journey are not empty—much worse. The journey comes to represent the poet's past sins and deviation from the right path. The seriousness of this offense, and the viciousness of the half-veiled references to "barren experimentation," need to be understood in the context of current debates about socialist art and attacks on the interwar avant-garde.

The review of *Fearlessly* in *Tvorba*, by the socialist poet Michal Sedloň, gives one a fuller sense of the new meaning of the Javanese journey around the time of Biebl's death.[453] It followed months of silence in the press about the book, exacerbating Biebl's fears about the verdict on *Fearlessly*, apparently due to editors' fear to publish the first evaluation. Sedloň made a point of discussing at length the poet's past association with poetism and surrealism, two "foreign degenerate movements." Part of this text was published just below an article aggressively condemning (in the words of the article's title) "Teigovština—trockistická agentura v naší kultuře" (Teigish [-ish as in English or Spanish]—Trotskyist agenda in our culture).[454] Teige, attacked and hunted as the cultural enemy of socialism and the Soviet Union, had died less than a month earlier. It was general knowledge that Biebl was among the leading personalities of poetism and surrealism, that he was personally and artistically close to Teige, and that he never denounced him. In Sedloň's review, Teige's influence on Biebl is repeatedly mentioned. Biebl believed the juxtaposition of the review of his book with the article attacking Teige, as well as the formatting in which the two texts fitted together like two pieces of a puzzle, represented a veiled threat. What a darkly ironic specter of Teige's typographic designs for Biebl's books!

In the review, the word *cesta* (way, path, journey) figures prominently. The text is titled "Cesta Konstantina Biebla k bojovnému humanismu" (The way/journey [*cesta*] of Konstantin Biebl to combative humanism). Sedloň praises Biebl's early, proletarian poetry—such as his first book, *Way/Journey [Cesta] to the People*. Then, he represents the development of the avant-garde as the choice between the right *cesta*, exemplified by Biebl's friend Wolker, and the wrong *cesta*, epitomized by Teige. The "larger part of Biebl's generation let

453 Michal Sedloň, "Cesta Konstantina Biebla k bojovnému humanismu," *Tvorba* 20, no. 43 (25 Oct 1951), 1034–6. For a discussion and evidence relating to Biebl's death, see *Bojím se jít domů, že uvidím kožené kabáty na schodech: zápisky Vítězslava Nezvala a jiné dokumenty k smrti Konstantina Biebla*, ed. David Voda and Michal Blahynka (Olomouc: Burian a Tichák, 2011).

454 Mojmír Grygar, "Teigovština—trockistická agentura v naší kultuře," Part 2, Tvorba 20, no. 43 (25 Oct 1951), 1036–8.

itself be dragged to the way of cosmopolitanism, a way foreign to [them], and [dragged to the way] of enemy poetry" because they were not

> sufficiently ideologically armed to resist the attacks of foreign degenerate movements, propagated and spread . . . by the deft cosmopolite Teige. . . . Wobbling is manifested also in the case of Biebl who . . . let himself be misled by the liquidatory aesthetic theories of K. Teige into the waters of poetism [here follows an attack on Teige].

Cosmopolitanism was construed as the opposite of both national art as well as international socialist art, and its condemnation was commonplace in the socialist critique of "degenerate" art. While the arch-enemy was the capitalist West, there was a general mistrust of anything broadly foreign and cosmopolitan, especially whatever was not clearly allied with Soviet socialism. Despite claims of a certain kind of internationalism and global solidarity, one senses a paradoxical fear of gradations, fluid borders, crossing of boundaries.

In Sedloň's review of *Fearlessly*, Biebl's way/journey to Java, and his book *With the Ship*, are the main examples of the poet's past offenses, of how he was "seduced by false 'mentors' on the way/journey of poetism." According to Sedloň, "poetism manifests itself . . . in exotic elements, which Biebl collected on his way/journey to Java, allowing himself to be carried away mainly by sensual impressions and noncommittal dreaming." He speaks about Biebl's "dreamy, indifferent stance toward social reality, to actual life, which is replaced by lyrical, poetist image." These ready-made accusations do not so much show Biebl's work as aberrant in any unique way, but as part of larger movements already known as "degenerate" and as the ways of the "enemy."

The speakers at Biebl's funeral would have read the review, and they were all familiar with its underlying ideology—after all, the review merely applied currently dominant socialist criticism to Biebl's work, in predictable ways. The equation of the "wrong" way/journey and the Javanese journey was not unique to Sedloň. Závada, for example, makes it explicit in his obituary:

> Sometime in the thirties [sic!] the poet undertook a long journey/way [*cesta*] to Java and this journey/way [*cesta*] roughly corresponds with his journey/way [*cesta*] away from social art to art released from reality, away from man and his struggle for concrete improvement of conditions on this earth.[455]

The repeated references to Biebl's Javanese journey at his funeral—whether veiled in praises of home and "magnificent Prague," or made more

455 *Lidové noviny*, 16. 11. 1951.

explicit in evaluations such as "barren experimentation"—were ways to (re)assert the writers' allegiance to the party line and their condemnation of "enemy poetry," of the "foreign" and the "cosmopolitan," with the aim, in part at least, to protect themselves against the kind of attacks to which Biebl and others were subjected—at the cost of perpetuating the same violent discourse that had likely lead to Biebl's death. At Biebl's death, his Javanese journey, and the poetry in which "his associations extend their hands toward each other across oceans," have become symbols of everything from which people needed to disassociate themselves, regardless of what they actually believed.

In the middle of World War Two, an earlier time when he might also have been contemplating suicide, Biebl wrote about his father in a letter to his mother: "He took onto himself the suffering of individuals and of the whole world. His voluntary departure was not a weakness, but a refusal of what he saw around him."[456] After the poet's own suicide, his brother-in-law Bohuslav Brouk—who in the 1930s had been a member of the Surrealist Group—wrote in a letter about the poet: "he was not a bad man, and when the party was forcing him to do things that would be in disagreement with his conscience, he chose suicide."[457] Perhaps the weakness and fear of the soft-spoken "Pierot lunaire . . . somewhat unsure on this wildly spinning planet," the "little citizen" among "Martians," gave him the power for the ultimate refusal of what he saw around him.

In 1921, Biebl wrote to his friend Wolker, as he was leaving for Prague: "Write something pleasant to that great city, because I will be probably very sad when I reach there, a frightened villager, taking half an hour to evade the tram."[458] "I walked around Prague like in a foreign land," he wrote in *New Icarus.* After he returned home from Java, he wrote of the "mud, which reaches up to our shoulders" in his village, where one "moves with difficulty, perhaps like a fish pickled in aspic"; and how "a man is not at home among his own." In 1947, he wrote to Nezval from Slavětín that the year "began badly for me . . . One day I will tell you what the village is capable of."[459] Seven years after Biebl's death, his mother wrote to her friend about the "horrible circumstances" in the village, "envy and hate, of which we, too, are victims. When K. [Konstantin] was here, he would comment how terrible the air was in the

456 Letter from Konstantin Biebl to Hermína Bieblová dated 1. November, 1943. Archive of the Museum of Czech Literature.

457 Quoted in Voda and Blahynka, *Bojím se jít domů*, 116.

458 Jiří Wolker and Konstantin Biebl, *Listy dvou básníků* (Československý spisovatel, 1953), 25.

459 Letter from Konstantin Biebl to Vítězslav Nezval, dated 5 Jan 1947. Vítězslav Nezval, archive of the Museum of Czech Literature.

village."[460] His last poems, such as "Žaluji" ("I accuse"; published neither in *Fearlessly* not in his collected works), speak with pain about homeland:

O the destiny of talent in Czech lands
so many blows
into the body arrows penetrate
like into biblical Sebastian.[461]

But then, already in *With the Ship*, he felt the anxiety/narrowness (*úzkost*) of home:

I would like to ask you, sparrows,
whether you also feel anxious
when suddenly at night you dream about a malicious boy
throwing stones at you

Biebl never travelled lightly, and he was never easily at home. But at the end of his life, the air became impossible to breathe. Biebl's own poetic images of Java and his journey—his openness to the "magnificent and hard" (Nezval) vastness of the world—represented that which was utterly incompatible with the ideological terror and the atmosphere of 1951; threateningly incompatible also because it expressed a dream that was pervaded by the spirit of an earlier communism, not stifled by the poisonous air of the current political, cultural and personal attacks. Nezval probably meant what he said about Biebl in his memoirs, that Biebl "wrote his revolutionary poems from the depth of his inner purity."[462] And so did the young communist writer Milan Kundera in a poem published on the first anniversary of Biebl's death, where the image of distant lands and a flight to "unimagined regions," appears again; a poem about "enemies of life and poetry . . . who want to change socialism into an inhospitable desert":

But you know, Konstantin: they knew communism, only as it was mirrored
in the frog pond of their own heads.
When someone saw more in communism,
they dressed him in a pervert's robe.

460 Hermína Bieblová, letter to K. Janda dated 10. 3. 1958. Archive of the Museum of Czech Literature.
461 Konstantin Biebl, *Dobrodruh*, ed. Vladimír Justl (Prague: Odeon, 2008), 115.
462 Nezval, *Z mého života*, 219.

Yet you knew that in communism there are keys,
With which thousand-year old cages can be opened.

And that from those cages free human spirits
Will fly to unimagined regions.

About those regions let the poet write,
you, Konstantin, called,
so that humans can breathe the fragrance of that realm,
before he dies ——[463]

In the 1930s, in one of his "degenerate" poems, Biebl wrote:

Lightning would be the tree of eternity
In the abysses of fleetingly glimpsed universes
Where poets hurl themselves where painters go
Thirsty hunters of those fractions of seconds
Full of wings and light[464]

The poet's death seems to have been foreshadowed so many times in his poetry—in images of dark abysses, sinking ships, drowning, suicidal jumps from towers, or the fall of Icarus, whose wings disintegrated as he flew to near the sun. If the poet's journey to Java was a performance, his suicide appears almost like the final poetic act. Yet, the last fall was different in the utter, final absence of wings and light. František Hrubín:[465]

What a Night
After the death of Konstantin Biebl

What a night,
comrade night,
and nowhere a friend!

What daring despair:
thousands on thousands,

---

463 Milan Kundera, "Vy jste, Konstantine, nikdy neuvěřil," *Literární noviny*, 15 Nov 1952.
464 Biebl, *Zrcadlo noci*, n.p. Also in Biebl, *Dílo*, 3:78.
465 Hrubín (1910–1971) was an important poet somewhat younger than Biebl. His 1948 *Hirošima* (Hiroshima) is a long, powerful poem in the Czech "zone" tradition, akin to *New Icarus* also in its earth-wide reach and in equating, in a particular sense (also like in "Jungle Around Us"), Asia and Central Europe.

again and again
man is proving that he has no wings.
To whom?
What a night,
comrade night!

What anxiety [*úzkost*]
that emptiness curbed by a window frame
appears as infinite freedom . . .

What a night![466]

466 "Jaká to noc." František Hrubín, *Můj zpěv* (Prague: Odeon, 1980). Originally published in 1956. My translation is problematic in many ways, including: "comrade" in the second and tenth lines is female in Czech (*soudružka*), following but also emphasizing the feminine grammatical gender of *noc* (night); "man" in the seventh line mistranslates *člověk*, which refers to any gender, so "human" rather than "man."

PART TWO
A HUNDRED ROSE PETALS, ON THEM NO WORDS

the poet's time has come
when like a rose smells he would want
a hundred rose petals
on them no words

SILENCES

"A forgotten poem is a silenced truth," I quoted my father's words at the beginning of the first part. "The dead speak only when we remember them," wrote Biebl. Yet, at the poet's funeral, and probably since the beginning of speech, words also served to silence truth. In texts by and about Biebl, and in what we know of his life and work, diverse manners of silence, silencing, and wordless moments disclose themselves; absences of words that, like and unlike words, can conceal and reveal, repress and shelter, bind and set free.

It is, in part, the silence of the poet's death that I want to face, to prolong, in this part of the book, like when I stood on the wild grass before his modest grave in Slavětín. Yet this silence evokes for me the silences thought and felt by the poet in his work and life, and the various ways in which he, a poet, at times wandered or glanced, not only away from home, but also away from words. Some of these wordless moments exude the air of death, others resemble a stroll in a magnificent fragrant park, many do both, like that village graveyard in May. Travelling itself was one of such journeys beyond words, as were Biebl's photographs and incursions into the visual realm. Moreover, travelling was for Biebl's generation associated with modern visuality, epitomized by photography and cinema. I hope I will not equate the different moments and manners of not speaking, in life and in death, but I would like to gather them and let them mirror one another, or not.

The Czech word *ticho* rather easily translates into English as "silence." Another word, *mlčení*, is more difficult to translate. The verb *mlčet* means "not to speak," and *mlčení* means not just silence, but usually intentional, active not-speaking, such as when one keeps a secret, or when one keeps silent despite a pressure to speak, or out of fear. The emphases and feelings of *ticho* and *mlčení* differ, although *ticho* may encompass the more specific meaning of *mlčení*.

In Biebl's images of the colonies, the Javanese are often silent—sometimes it is *ticho*, more often, or perhaps always latent within it, *mlčení*. Earlier, I translated *mlčení milionů* as "the silence of the millions." In Czech, Biebl's phrase evokes a restrained force, which has the power of millions, in this active not-speaking in the face of injustice. It is, moreover, not a neutral silence, but silence *about* something, a silence with an object. "Where in the past dammar trees rustled, now the silence [*mlčení*] of millions reigns. Millions of Javanese, who are silent [*mlčí*] about their right."

In Biebl's early poetry, listening to the silenced—the dead soldiers of the Great War, Biebl's beggars, or poor workers—prefigured the poet's later attitude to the colonized people. Remembering this here helps us more richly understand the silence of the millions that Biebl heard in the colonies, and how he perceived it in relation to his past experiences.

In 1923, Biebl wrote in a letter to his lover:

> This morning General Foch rode down the street. People were saying that he was alone in his car, but I saw his dead regiments walking behind him. Flowers were thrown in his path. Perhaps so that people would not be able to hear the fallen ones, as they silently walked behind him over the flowers.[467]

For Biebl, the dead, too—and especially those who died prematurely or unjustly—are silently but insistently present, asking to be remembered and heard. This, and his images of life after death and reincarnation (as in the poem "Amin"), illuminate what Biebl writes about colonial houses in Batavia, just before speaking of the "silence of millions":

> The Indies house is the home of the dead, a stopover to nirvana, the limbo of bats, the purgatory of frogs and other souls, who move around here in a rather casual manner, as if at home, ignoring the Dutch, ignoring you, because we all are here lodgers in after-life, voluntarily and temporarily suffered.[468]

Like tropical nature—"which does not disappear where trees are cleared and tigers are shot"[469]—the dead and the silenced living do not go away, but constitute a defiant force silently awaiting justice, awaiting hearing. Like tropical nature, or like the Czech linden tree in "Vojenská" (Soldier's song):

> Under the canteen's window I stood
> linden trees bloomed and the gramophone played.
> From the black disk
> like from grave's darkness
> the voice of dead Caruso trembled.

---

467 Letter to Jára Mikešová dated 14. 5. 1923. Archive of the Museum of Czech Literature.
468 Biebl, *Cesta*, 61.
469 Biebl, *Cesta*, 61.

In the voice, defiance,
defiance and pain,
and something from the tree's crown, broken by God's lightning,
something of human will remained.

In that voice there was belief, belief and dream,
that one day, brothers, when our day comes,
and we will be no more,
from earth we will raise our hands, our voice.

Our voice![470]

It is the poet's task to listen for the silence and the silenced: for Biebl, we recall, to write poetry is "a desire for cognition [*poznání*]"—a desire for truth and justice, or a defiant dream born out of that desperate desire.

The following unfinished text on Batavia shows how through sound and silence—and whiteness and darkness—colonialism is manifested.

I walked through the European quarter. . . . Although I have not met a single white man in the black stream of natives—because in the tropics white people walk on foot only exceptionally—you cannot doubt for a single moment the domination by the white race, which manifests itself here, aside from the luxurious villas from where occasionally women's laughter sounds, by a battle between a Wagner's opera with a Beethoven's sonata, which cross their arms across the asphalt street. The shy gait of the natives, who walk and keep silent [*mlčí*], creates an impression of a city that does not exist, except in a dream disturbed by the piano brawl, which suddenly ceases at the last villa where the European quarter ends. When under the supervision of that blue and steel discipline [the manuscript ends here][471]

Sound manifests the European presence in their villas and their absence on the streets. Biebl hears it against the silence of the "natives," which has its own, suppressed presence—strong enough to create the impression that the Dutch quarter "does not exist," that it is only a dream. In another brief unpublished text, Biebl mentions

the Plancius, a modern ship kept anxiously clean by a cadre of native servants. They walk by inaudibly and almost unnoticeably. Anonymous order, taking place behind your back, is the result of stiff discipline.[472]

---

470 Biebl, *Dílo*, 5:105.
471 Biebl, *Dílo*, 5:242.
472 Biebl, *Dílo*, 5:243.

At the core of this scene is, not the colonizer's voices, but the silence, the action of not-speaking, "taking place behind your back"—concealed there by the "anxiously clean" colonial discipline (can one not think of Marx?). Biebl's images are "close" to colonial tropes—one thinks, for example, of Louis Couperus's famous 1900 novel *De Stille Kracht*— "The silent power/force" (in English translation published as *The Hidden Force*)—yet Biebl perceives the silence as if from different position, with different sym- and antipathies.

In the text *Plancius*, we encounter the silent servants, "*djongos*." In a scene that would easily translate into a silent movie, Biebl tries in vain to evade their perfect service and thus his position "in the same boat" with the colonizers.

> The djongos annoys me especially with his excessive attention. See that? How he follows my lit cigarette with his eyes! I pretended not to see it and when he least expected it, I shook off the ash, which, instead of falling on the floor as I had anticipated, dropped into an ashtray which he was able to hold out at the last instant, I don't know by what magic. Shamed by my failure, I tossed away the unfinished cigarette. The djongos, having licked his finger, put it out. With a quick movement, so that he would not be able to assist me, I turned my back on him, moving my chair. This victory has so satisfied me that I remained calm even when he moved to sit in front of me again.[473]

However, for the Dutch passengers, at least as Biebl depicts them, the service on the ship is the fetishistic showcase of a smoothly functioning system built on "blue and steel discipline."

> I am slowly beginning to understand why, not long ago, Mr. Sachse was so upset on the board of the German ship *Yorck* whenever the steward did not bring a requested tea:
>
> "That could not happen on a Dutch ship! There everything happens as if of its own will! Do you know what it is, djongos? You don't know, you can't know it! No one who hasn't been to Java can know it." . . . "Djong . . . !" Mr. Jansen wants a glass of sherry. Already it is here. Slowly I am beginning to comprehend, a single word, half a word, you can swallow the other half, yet immediately the whole wish is fulfilled. "Djong . . . !" Mr. Makelaars wants a fish. Already it is here. It is like [in the fairy tale] "Little table, spread thyself!" "Djong," that is a roasted chicken, crabs, syllabub, pineapples and all the Indies comforts. Slowly I am beginning to comprehend.[474]

"Djongos" exemplifies speech that is exceedingly effective. The carrying out of an order by the servant is one with the master's utterance of the word, which becomes like a magic formula in a fairy tale: the servants and their la-

473 Biebl, *Plancius*, 19–20.
474 Biebl, *Plancius*, 16–17.

bor disappear, are silenced as the magic words perform the tasks. This is also why "thank you" is unnecessary and unthinkable, as Biebl's text brings out. The word "djongos," in its perfect performative effectiveness, like the absence of "thank you," reveals colonialism smoothly at work, or as Biebl says, "all the Indies comforts." This is the other side of the silence of the natives.

The "silence of millions" gives a feeling of restrained power that, like silenced truth, will eventually be released. Here again Biebl's imagery approaches that of Couperus, yet while for the Dutch author the "silent power" forebodes a tragic end, for Biebl it is a source of hope. At the end of *Plancius*, Mr. Bergr tells Biebl about the perfect workings of the colonial system and how the Javanese are "so nice and so gentle."

> Mr. Bergr would have revealed his whole colonial heart to me, were it not for a sudden radio transmission from Batavia, a bulletin as odd as it was incomprehensible, which sent tremors through the ship . . . "There is an uprising in Java." . . . Mrs. Sachse was the first to scream. "My pearls!"[475]

A pandemonium ensues, in which a knife appears in a servant's hand, and "Ing. Berger saw how on plantations an uprising was ripening." The smooth surface of the colonial language is stirred, the illusion is broken, and the power of the "silence of the millions" is released—by a message "as odd as it was incomprehensible" to those living the illusion.

The socializing, the polite conversations praising the virtues of colonialism, and the smoothly functioning language on the Dutch ship, set against the backdrop of the *mlčení* of servants, are reminiscent of scenes in Biebl's early poetry, such as in the 1924 poem "Oni" (They), published in a satirical magazine:

> They call themselves: democratic society,
> the top hats speak to the whole nation,
> how topsy-turvy their virtue appears,
> let the old woman who cleans the toilets speak.
> . . . .
> O, speak to us, woman, after this gentleman,
> flush his speech down the toilet
> and open for us the gate of paradise
> perhaps with the key to the toilet.[476]

At the beginning of *Plancius*, Biebl describes how, at night, he listened to the Dutch passengers speaking, as their language "became more beauti-

475 Biebl, *Plancius*, 26.
476 Biebl, *Dílo*, 5:139–40.

ful and more sad with aromatic tributaries of Malay and Javanese words . . . words which I did not understand, for hours letting myself be thrilled by their music, so mournful. BURUBUDUR. Is not each 'U' a niche for one Buddha statue?"[477] (On the Javanese Borobudur temple, there are hundreds of Buddha statues in ∩-shaped niches.) The music, fragrance and form of incomprehensible words contrast with the effective language of colonialism encountered later in the text. Words that function like a well-oiled machine, words that get things done, are in *Plancius* connected with oppression and colonialism, while fragrant and musical words, which evoke rather than having unambiguous, definite meanings, manifest a different, less violent way of being in the colonial situation, a refusal—or inability—to participate in the colonial set up. When the poet hears speech as music and as fragrance, he lets it overflow into realms beyond words.

In *Plancius*, the poet listens to these words in "triple darkness"—at night, with closed eyes covered by his hand. Silence and darkness have much in common. In another, unpublished text, he describes how the Plancius landed in Batavia's harbor. It was still dark: "The Dutch were giving orders to their servants, as if they were speaking into darkness; darkness stirred and carried their travelling rugs and lacquered suitcases."[478] Again, it is as if the servants did not exist, and as if the orders were magically executed by darkness. But—somewhat like in his account of Batavia in which silence was an insistent reality and the sound of piano and opera music a dream-like intrusion—he perceives darkness as an overwhelming, wholesome presence in which the loud whiteness "illuminating" the faces of the Europeans is alien:

> I was not quite sure whether the darkness, which veiled everything, did not hide a deeper meaning: perhaps so that the dissonance would be brought out between the European faces and this mysterious land forming a single indivisible night of dark fragrances, black trees, people and distances.[479]

This darkness is not an exotic unknown; rather, Biebl's attention to darkness is an attempt at respecting it and a refusal to manage it. The text continues:

> From my pocket, I took a bottle of cognac. Don't worry, no pirate scene! Just a sip! Only one polite toast to the people and gods of this land, as a sign that I have come neither to fell their trees nor to wring rubber out of them![480]

477 Biebl, *Plancius*, 7.
478 Biebl, *Cesta na Jávu*, 53.
479 Biebl, *Cesta na Jávu*, 54.
480 Biebl, *Cesta na Jávu*, 54.

Biebl sides with silence and darkness, in part out of solidarity with the silenced and the recognition of the violence of speaking—poetry is (re)cognition of truth—but also, possibly, because words fail. In an excerpt that I quoted earlier, in which Biebl descends to the ship's machine room and sees the workers there in inhuman conditions, he writes: "I say nothing, because words are nothing." He stains his coat with oil, so that he doesn't have "to be so ashamed of [his] white suit" and so that he would "remember what happens below." There is shame and guilt, and a promise that he will remember—that he will not be deaf to their silence. One recalls the sense of guilt from his early poetry and especially the silence of the war dead:

> The dead speak,
> only when you remember them . . .
> Even if another was shooting
> our deeds are in those wounds.

Or:

> With uncertain eyes, holding our breath,
> we stand silent [*mlčky*] like murderers.

In a 1932 text protesting the exploitation of coal miners in northern Bohemia, there is the powerful silence of the exploited miners, the silence that comes from respect and guilt, and the speeches of politicians resembling the socializing on the *Plancius*.

> I saw them coming, the forty thousand emaciated men and women, united by poverty. . . . A crowd that just kept silent [*mlčí*]. So clear was their truth that there was no need for words. There was no need to convince anyone. I think that none of those who are on the side of the coal barons would be able to stammer out a single word in front of this multitude. It is easy to talk in the parliament, it is too easy to write in the editorial offices of some *Nation*.[481]

Biebl neither travelled nor wrote easily. Frequently one senses a desire to go beyond words, or to remain silent. At the beginning of a section of his 1931 book *Heaven Hell Paradise*, there is this motto (again I realize the violence of the work of translation, and the attraction of silence), verses that were originally part of an unpublished poem about Java:

---

481 Biebl, *Dílo*, 5:277.

the poet's time has come
when like a rose smells he would want
a hundred rose petals
on them no words[482]

482 Biebl, *Nebe peklo ráj*, 41. The verses were originally part of the unpublished "Předzpěv" (Prelude) for the poem "Slametan." Archive of the Museum of Czech Literature.

SOUNDS, SMELLS, TASTES

As I was working on this essay and reading Biebl's poetry, there were times when I would copy a poem and all I could comment was, paraphrasing the poet: "Writes like a rose smells." (Or, at other times: "With a brick over the head.") In a poem in the same collection, Biebl writes: "Speak like a rose opening toward the morning."[483]

It is, in the first place, through his writing that Biebl went beyond words and spoke like a rose smells. But the metaphor can be taken somewhat more literally to lead us to reflect on smells and fragrances—and more generally, physiological sensations—in Biebl's poetry. As we read it, it is interesting to keep in mind—but keeping the volume low—ideas articulated by Teige, the theorist: "a poetry for the five senses" which would be "based on a sensual, physiological alphabet"; it includes "a poetry for the sense of smell [*poesie pro čich*] . . . a symphony of fragrances." Teige speaks of the smells of "blood, dust, perfumes, flowers, animal smells and smells of petrol, oil, medicine and drugs," and he notes about the "speech of fragrances" that "master gardeners knew its alphabet and its emotive responses, just like the liturgies of various religions did. So: to poetize with fragrances as directly, as it is possible to poetize with color and sound."[484]

In this and other cases, Biebl's poetry should not be reduced into a product of Teige's theories. Teige and Biebl—and theory and poetry—are engaged in a conversation, even as they speak in different voices and have some fundamental differences.

Teige speaks of a "symphony of fragrances." Biebl describes "the music of fragrances." Some of his most intensely fragrant poems and prose accounts are about the tropics. It was in Java, Biebl writes, that he first realized "what the music of fragrances is." Since the nineteenth century, intense, strange, heavy, intoxicating fragrance figure in descriptions of tropical nature by Czech authors (and no doubt others). For instance, the popular author and traveler Jan Havlasa writes in his novel *Propast rozkoše* (The abyss of bliss), set in Malayan jungles and published in 1929, just two years after Biebl's journey:

483 Biebl, *Nebe peklo ráj*, 11.

484 Teige, "Manifest poetismu," 334. See also Esther Levinger, "Czech Avant-Garde Art: Poetry for the Five Senses," *The Art Bulletin* 81, no. 3 (Sep., 1999): 513–32.

> Various perfumes of the vegetation, earth, even water asserted themselves most strongly then. Dancing and then again crawling, rushing forward and then again transfixed, that jumble of fragrances and stenches evoked for me images of a great congregation of phantoms. Indeed, that theory of Heralt is not just a fantasy: the world as fragrance.[485]

I remember how, when as a teenager I first came to Southeast Asia, I stepped out from the air-conditioned space of Singapore airport into the tropical night—it was past midnight—and my first impression, strong and unforgettable, was the warm humid night air filled with a blend of intense fragrances that were new to me, and some of which seemed to belong to an overheated shop with perfumed soaps rather than to evening air. While to an extent the intense fragrance of tropical nature was part of Czech images of the tropics, perhaps Biebl did indeed realize for the first on his journey time what the "music of fragrances" was.

Upon arrival to Java, he encountered "a single indivisible night of dark fragrances, black trees, people and distances." Here, he is in the mountains in Central Java:

> I inhale deeply the night air of Java. The villa of Mr. Jansen is a crossroads of fragrances. They flow in through the window and sail out through the door. They walk in through the door and float away through the windows. There are rivers of fragrances, which have their established riverbeds in the darkness. Sometimes they dry up, at other times they overflow their shores. Such as when on the plantations people shake down nutmeg. That is why sometimes in Java, breathing feels like being force-fed with coffee, oranges and all kinds of fruits.
>
> Warm wind coming from the island pours into my mouth a mixture of all the fragrances and smells, forming a kind of thick porridge, in which the sweetish power of bananas makes one lightly dizzy; this is interrupted by the filth of Javanese canals, immediately again carried away by the fragrance of drying tea. First the first time I realize what the music of fragrances is.[486]

Back in Bohemia, he wrote to a publisher: "I approach the writing of the book . . . with the aim to capture the air of Java rather than her firm land, the fragrance of flowers rather than her botanics." When Java is evoked through fragrance at night, is not there something of the *mlčení* of the poet who hesitates to say too much, who knows the violence caused by words? Is it that he prefers to create an image of Java that is as volatile and immaterial

485 Jan Havlasa, *Propast rozkoše* (Prague: Ústřední nakladatelství a knihkupectví učitelstva československého, 1929), 315.

486 Biebl, *Cesta na Jávu*, 71–72.

as fragrance, to tread lightly on his own childhood dreams and to respect what remains largely unknown to him and what does not belong to him, "to capture the air of Java rather than her firm land"? To breathe in, rather than to breathe out like when one speaks?[487] And rather than to breathe on:

> Again I am afraid to breathe that they may not vanish anew
> it is enough that the Dutch are breathing deeply on everything.

Havlasa was a very different writer and traveler than Biebl, but a juxtaposition is thought-provoking nonetheless. A character reflects in Havlasa's *The Abyss of Bliss*, in the jungles of Malaya:

> Our truths are simultaneously lies. Our truth and our beauty are three-dimensional and with every consciousness and mastering of any fourth dimension, they fall. *The world as an image . . . The world as a fragrance.* The [latter] is just a variation of the first definition. If our sense of smell were more sensitive, our image of the world would probably change.[488]

Is part of the effort to represent the world through fragrances—to capture "the fragrance of flowers rather than [Java's] botanics"—also an attempt to use words differently, in such a way that our image of the world changes, becoming more gentle and less assertive? An effort to breathe less deeply?

The long poem with the Javanese title "Slametan" was published about a year after Biebl's return from Java in *ReD*, a periodical founded and edited by Teige. The long poem is pervaded by diverse smells and fragrances—flowers, tar soap, cigarette smoke, smell of bullet casing, wooden furniture, fruit trees, turpentine. . . . Each part of "Slametan" grows from one smell or a combination of smells, and each evokes a multitude of associations. This poem, too, suggests that poetry itself has something of the nature of fragrance:

> Who quickly opens a bottle of ether
> might catch a glimpse of the poet
> as he wafts away
>
> He chases his chimera

Across time and space, the ephemerality of smell evokes beauty and love, death and eternity.

---

487 Thanks to Thow Xin Wei, whose comment inspired this sentence.
488 Havlasa, *Propast rozkoše*, 312.

And therefore every woman washes herself for the night
with black soap made of tar
so that she would smell like that royal mummy
with a thousand-year old fragrance of hair and cinnamon nails

And:

Jasmine that is the parting of Hector and Andromache
Jasmine love beyond the grave
that volatile fragrance of eternity
of a billion hearts rotting in dust[489]

The title of the poem in *ReD*, "Slametan," is not directly translated or explained—it is only if one knows the meaning of the word that one can grasp its connection to the subtitle of the poem, "a celebration in ten cantos." One may remember the beginning of *Plancius*, where the poet listens to the music of "aromatic tributaries of Malay and Javanese words" in the Dutch language. Untranslated and unexplained Malay and Javanese words appear in many of Biebl's poems, perhaps often for the same reason, to make words into music and fragrance. Jiří Holý, in a study of Biebl's Javanese poems, writes that these foreign words give a sense of "mysterious magic."[490] Yet, the words are used meaningfully by Biebl if the reader understands, like Biebl did, their Malay or Javanese meanings. Thus their use also suggests the impossibility of fully translating Biebl's experience into Czech, and bridging the gap between him and his readers who have not shared his experience. (Seifert: "What can one write about what one does not know?")

That does not mean that the words are not also musical, fragrant, or magical for Biebl and his readers: poetry brings into communion the meaning and the music of words, speaking and not speaking, understanding and not, rather than insisting on distinct borders. In 1921, Biebl attended an event in Prague where, as he describes in a letter to a friend,

> Rabindranath Tagore recited his poems in the original. . . . Even though you understand nothing, you feel the gentle rhythm of his pieces, as if you were listening to music, which, too, speaks and does not speak. Indeed, we understood every word of his verses, even though we do not know Bengali. How poor are those Czech translations.[491]

---

489 Konstantin Biebl, "Slametan: slavnost o deseti zpěvech," *ReD* 1 (1927–28), 218–20.

490 Jiří Holý, "Chór moravských učitelů v javánské džungli: Bieblova exotická sbírka S lodí jež dováží čaj a kávu," *Literární Archív* 39 (2007), 240.

491 Biebl's letter published in Slabý, *Potkávání*, 51.

In some cases, Biebl clearly intended to use words without a conventional semantic meaning. For example, in "Děti" (Children), a poem from *Heaven Hell Paradise*, a poet's words, children's counting rhymes and playful gibberish, magic incantations, and tropical dreams are brought together (the magic of children's games in the poem resonates with the "heaven hell paradise," in the book's title; as mentioned earlier, it is the name of a children's game, the "fortune teller"):

The poet mumbles invented sentences
unaware that he toys with hell's powers
marvelous amulets he always carries
the ships on which he sails through rough nights

Burumum byhájo am čahody gůna
veháty lája ó koloriny
from the clouds an orange moon swung up
casting down coconuts fans and other timid shadows

On the village green children play in front of the vicarage
and one of them counts eeny meeny miny moe
one to paradise will go
deep in green jungle beyond the sea a peacock flies[492]

Czech Radio published a CD of archival recordings of famous Czech poets reciting their own verses. Biebl is represented by two recordings—one is a poem, while the other is more difficult to label: a chant of unintelligible words, indistinctly resembling the Muslim call to prayer or the chanting of a Javanese shadow theater puppeteer. This may not be Biebl's "typical" mode of expression, but, along with other clues, it does suggest something about his attitude to words. There are times when he wants to write "like a rose smells . . . with no words," he listens to the music and fragrance of words, he chants a "text" with no referential meaning, he treats words as evocative sounds, he respects and desires silence, yet he is also unwilling or unable to live without words and their magic. The result is that, while ever returning to the realm of words, he travels beyond it and summons sounds and smells to enter his poetry, invoking words' oldest power to be what they are not.

Slametan is a Javanese word which refers to a variety of ritual celebrations, usually involving a communal meal with a symbolic combination of ingredients, offerings (often jasmine flowers), prayers, ceremonial speeches,

492 Biebl, *Nebe peklo ráj*, 43–44.

and, for larger scale events, a performance. Biebl's use of the word *slametan* for the title suggests that the poem has something of its nature. The whole poem is characterized by the sensuousness and spirituality of a ritual celebration—"the volatile fragrance of eternity"—and in the last section of the first canto, the fragrance of flower and fruits rises to "the feet of the Virgin Mary" (who, mystical and intimate like My Beautiful Arsiti, metamorphoses into a beautiful girl, reincarnated into a rose), just like how in a *slametan* the fragrance of flowers and incense is offered to spirits, or—as Biebl observed—in a Chinese funeral "the dead feast together with the living by breathing in the fragrance of the food that has been prepared for them."[493]

All ripe pears toll the bell
and the honeyed fragrance of fruits blends with the honeyed fragrance of flowers
and all fragrance raises to heaven
to the feet of Virgin Mary.
. . . .
In every rose you sleep
my little Mary

My beautiful girl[494]

Slametan is veiled in a kind of silence: it is evoked through an untranslated word that for most readers will be unintelligible, although, as the scents of flowers and fruits blend with the fragrance of an unknown word, something of the nature of a *slametan* is revealed, not by translation or explanation, but poetic enactment.

Aside from the implication that this particular poem is like a *slametan*, this "celebration in ten cantos" implies the possibility that poetry generally is, or can be, a *slametan*-like, multi-sensory, spiritual celebration; that poetry is not simply words, but an event or an action—such as a journey—possibly not even involving words.

In Java, Biebl first realized "what the music of fragrances is." It is in his poems evoking Java that he travels especially often to the world of aromas, tastes, and music. The verses in which the poet desires to speak like a rose smells— "a hundred rose petals / on them no words"—which he used as a motto to a part of *Heaven Hell Paradise*, were originally part of a never-published "prelude" (*předzpěv*, lit. fore-song) in the unfinished "Slametan." Its stanzas begin: "It was necessary for me to climb these volcanoes . . . It was necessary for me to see the palms . . ." The "Prelude to the Poem Slametan" ends:

493 Biebl, *Dílo*, 5:202. "He is right," comments Thow Xin Wei.
494 Biebl, "Slametan," 219–20.

To sing oh to sing
like pure water sings[495]

I have suggested that Biebl's journey to Java was a poetic act, which resonated with current Devětsil ideas of poetry as the "art of living and living it up" (Teige). Travelling as poetizing and the exploration of different poetic modes (senses, media) are two facets of a single movement. Writes Teige:

> Having renounced the dictionary of concepts, we have appropriated the dictionary of actuality. We have pointed to the possibility of poems without words . . . to poetize with color, shape, light, movement, sound, smell, energy.[496]

> Poetry today is not deposited in books, it is possible to make poetry with color, light, sound, movement, to make poetry with life.[497]

Another kind of poetry for the senses mentioned by Teige is the "poetry for the sense of taste," which involves food, drinks, as well as narcotics. "The pleasure from a good dinner is not less noble and less aesthetic than any other"; and "the poetry for taste, culinary art (about which Apollinaire wrote in 'Poète assassiné'), aside from its gustative values, should affect the whole concert of senses through forms, colors, variations of fragrances."[498]

There is a curious unpublished text by Biebl titled "Makanam Djawa" (sic), or "Javanese food" in Malay (*makanam* should be *makanan*, "food," from *makan*, "to eat"). The text, a brief description of a festive dinner at a Javanese court, opens, like the event itself, with a sound reminiscent of flowers: "With a stroke on the gong the festive dinner begins. Makan Djawa. Bronze sound swings the darkness, spreads in concentric circles and fades away like the light of wilting sunflowers."[499] (Does this "sunflower" recall the floral decoration, sometimes gilded, on some Javanese gong stands?) Follows a long column of words, a list of Javanese dishes: *sambel hati* (liver chili sauce), *sambel ketimun* (cucumber chili sauce), and so on. Out of the twenty kinds of dishes, only three are translated. The list is followed by an account of the fruits which were brought at the end of the dinner, again dominated by untranslated Malay and Javanese names, in Czech spelling—the details of the fruits' taste are a mystery, and one gets rather a sense of the variety of fruits and sensations:

495 Konstantin Biebl, "Předzpěv k básni Slametan." Archive of the Museum of Czech Literature.
496 Teige, "Manifest poetismu," 332.
497 Teige, "Manifest poetismu," 336.
498 Teige, "Manifest poetismu," 335.
499 Biebl, *Dílo*, 5:240.

First I reached for *mango*, because it dazzled me with its golden skin and strong fragrance; I cut the *mangostán*, with flesh as refreshing as ice cream; I will never forget the *rambutan*, but I don't understand how anyone could like the *duku* or the *džambu*. I am not sure yet what to think of the *papaja*, but I know for sure that the boys from our high school would fight till blood over the *džuwit*.[500]

The typed text reads almost like an entry in a traveler's diary. Yet it is also another instance of poetry infused with tastes, scents, sounds, the music and fragrance of words, and the impressions of an event experienced on a journey. At the end of the text, the exploration of the tastes and fragrances of tropical fruit is interrupted when a telephone rings: it is *pan Jetel* ("Mr. Clover," the Dutch official who interrogates Biebl in "Night in Wonosobo," discussed in Part One). He is requesting further interview.

Many names—Javanese, Malay, and Czech—of tropical fruits, spices and food appear in Biebl's poetry, especially poems that evoke his journey. In *With the Ship that Carries Tea and Coffee*—aside from the tea and coffee prominent in the title— "Orient" is first evoked in the poem of that title with spices: "I always envied cooks / anise, nutmeg, vanilla." The first poem in the section on Java begins: "First I raise my hands to reach fruits . . ." In that section alone, there appear coconuts, sugar cane, "manga [sic; *mangga*, mango], pisang [banana], mangistan [mangosteen] that tastes like grapes" (in the same poem where bread, gingerbread, and milk grow on trees), nutmeg, rambutan, "lombok [chilli pepper] and salt," as well as fragrant pineapples. The last verses of the whole book are: "At home strawberries grow /At home there is cold drinking water."

In his diaries, there are lists of Javanese and Malay words for fruits, vegetables, and dishes, often with translations or descriptions. They appear alongside descriptions of the *slametan* and a Chinese funeral.

When one reads Biebl's annotated lists of dishes, fruits, and spices, or the recipe for *sambal asem* (tamarind chilli sauce)— "into cut chilies, two spoons of onion, a piece of *asam* [tamarind], a bit of salt"—one can't help suspecting that Biebl liked cooking, making wordless poetry with tastes and smells. In a brief letter to Biebl (probably sent from abroad), Nezval writes of homeland, in the form of a poem:

the heart weeps in a fountain's drizzle.
I must return to St. Vitus![501]

500 Biebl, *Dílo*, 5:241.
501 The Prague cathedral.

O my forests! O mushrooms! --
Our Chinese dishes!"[502]

In his memoirs, Nezval writes about Biebl:

In his studio, he managed to create a charming ambience [*ovzduší*, from *vzduch*, "air"]. Mementos from Java, a gramophone, here and there a painting, and a kitchenette, in which he was able to charm into being interesting dishes—that was the stage of his poetic plays.[503]

502 Letter published in Slabý, *Potkávání*, 82.
503 Nezval, *Z mého života*, 219.

TYPOGRAPHY—OPTIC CONFIGURATIONS

Teige was not only the leading theoretical voice of the interwar avant-garde, but also a practicing artist. As a graphic designer and illustrator, he collaborated with Biebl on several books: *With the Ship*, the second edition of *Break*, and *Heaven Hell Paradise*. Let us look at them as a starting point for an exploration of visuality in Biebl's work and its links with travel.

Although Teige wrote about the "poetry for the five senses," he often privileged the sight as the dominant sense of modern sensibility. He wrote extensively on the history of painting, photography, cinema, and architecture. As an artist, he worked especially with typography and photomontage. He was interested in the growing emphasis on the visual in modern poetry, which he connected to "contemporary civilization":

> The fact that contemporary civilization, from among the five senses, cultivates seeing the most (in part its refinement and increased flexibility is due to photography and film) has directed poetry on the path of progressive opticization (*zoptičtění*).[504]

Teige saw his own work in typography and book design as a culmination of developments in poetry:

> Apollinaire subordinates words to *optic configurations*. . . . The word in these poems . . . is an optic sign, a typographic word, with a series of semiotic associations, like the word of a signboard or a poster. . . . Optical, poster-like composition will require a new form for books of poems, organically unifying image and text.[505]

When in 1927 Teige created his first design for Biebl, he already had behind him several years of experience as a designer of seminal works of Czech avant-garde poetry. In Nezval's 1924 *Pantomime*, Teige used strikingly contrasting fonts. The last poem-image in the book looks like a death notice, with a thick black frame, an image of crucifix and a feather on the top, phrases in a variety of fonts arranged non-linearly on the page. In some cases, the semantic meaning of a phrase is expressed also typographically, such as the rais-

504 Teige, "Manifest poetismu," 325.
505 Teige, "Manifest poetismu," 323.

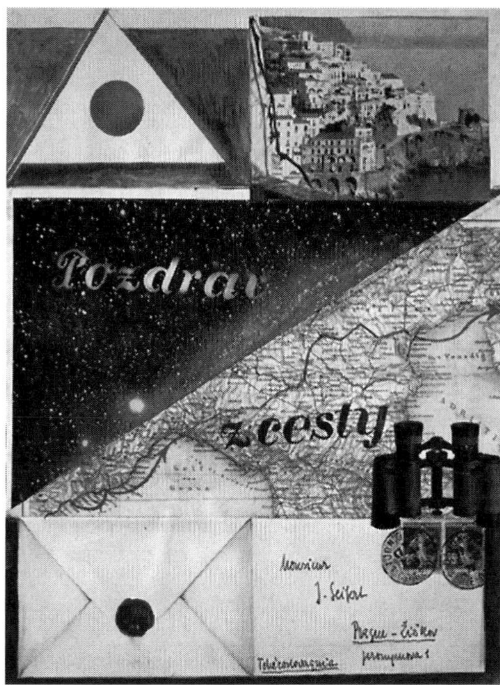

Figure 19. Karel Teige, *Greetings from the Trip*, 1923. Prague City Gallery.

ing and descending line formed by the words "birds fly away."[506] This poem foreshadows an even bolder typographical approach, which Teige developed in Jaroslav Seifert's 1925 *On the Waves of TSF*. Words are foregrounded by contrasting fonts. Some poems give the impression of banners or signboards. Some incorporate images—such as a map of the Caribbean in the poem "Objevy" (Discoveries).

Already in Teige's examples of the "opticization" in French poetry, one may notice that "opticization" is connected to travel—Apollinaire's "Ocean-Letter," Cendrars's "La prose du Transsibérien et de la Petite Jehanne de France" (Prose of the Trans-Siberian and of Little Jehanne of France) or Jean Cocteau's "Le Cap de Bonne-Espérance" (The Cape of Good Hope). The early typographical/illustration designs by Teige—and by other Czech avant-garde artists at this time—are saturated with images evoking travel, distant places, ships, harbors, and the tropics, echoing the preponderance of these motifs in Devětsil imagery generally, in all media. Photographs, postcards, maps, and simple, colorful drawings of black men, sailors, palms, and parrots are central to the artists' visions of travel and distant lands. Yet, in the visual and verbal poetry preceding Biebl journey, there is little of the physical and

506 Nezval, *Pantomima*, 137.

mental experience of travel that one finds in Biebl's poetry—vertigo, fatigue, seasickness, the saltiness of the sea, the fragrance of flowers, or the taste of strange fruits.

Related to Teige's book designs were visual images that he called "picture poems." Reproduced repeatedly in various publications, they became emblematic of modernist visual poetics. The best known of these were all about travel. "Pozdrav z cesty" (Greetings from the trip), for example, combines a map of southern France, Italy, and the Mediterranean Sea, binoculars, a postcard showing a sea-side town,[507] a ship's sign flag, a letter addressed to J. Seifert in Prague with a Côte d'Or stamp, and the words "Greetings from the Trip" (Figure 19). Teige's picture poem "Odjezd na Kytheru" (Departure for Cythera) borrows its title from a 1717 "fête galante" painting, swarming with Amors and amorous couples, by Jean-Antoine Watteau, "L'embarquement pour Cythère"; Cythera being the island where Venus was born, according to Greek mythology. Teige's modern version features, among other images, a steamship and a sailboat, and the words "Au Revoir," "Bon Vent," and "America—American Line." Teige published this picture poem also under the title—or description?—"touristic poem,"[508] a designation that applies to the other picture poems as well.

Other Czech artists produced similar picture poems. One of the best known was Jindřich Štyrský's "Souvenir": again a map of the Mediterranean, three images of sailboats of different kinds, a palm, a starfish, a *poisson lune* ("moon fish," labeled in French [English: sunfish]), and a photograph of five young women in swimming suits on a beach, with one of them circled (Figure 20). Štyrský also illustrated Biebl's *Plancius* (Figure 17).

The cover to Nezval's *Pantomime*, designed by Štyrský, resembles these picture poems. The collage includes a map of Asia, an astronomical map, the planet Earth (again with Asia foregrounded), coconut palms, a large sailing boat, a metal ornament in the shape of flowers, a lace, and a fainting Harlequin (the last two motifs, as well as "sea, sun and poetry," are mentioned in the book's last poem). Among the images illustrating the book are Štyrský's artworks, as well as "African sculpture," "Indian miniature," "light advertisements of a cinema in New York," and a photograph of the famous circus clowns, the brothers Fratellini.

Such was the visual culture in which Teige had been actively involved for several years when he approached Biebl's book *With the Ship*. While this design was continuous with the earlier work in terms of its underlying ideas about the integration of the visual and the verbal, and the association be-

507 Teige refers to the picture as postcard in his text "Obrazy," in *Avantgarda známá a neznámá*, ed. Štepán Vlašín et al. (Prague: Svoboda, 1971), 1:542.

508 *Host* II (1924–25), 93.

Figure 20. Jindřich Štyrský, *Souvenir*, 1924. National Gallery, Prague.

tween visual poetry and travel, it is at the same time quite distinct, in part as a result of the development of his style, but also, I think, because of the nature of Biebl's poetry and its own visual style.

How poetry was musical and visual for Biebl can be already sensed from a letter that he wrote to his friend in 1921, several years before he published his first book: "A poem must have a rhythm. . . . the poet lays down words one after the next like a music composer, not following any template, but according to feeling. You can cultivate feeling just like musical hearing. . . . A poem has a free rhythm when it reads well. You do not trip and it flows nicely like water. The more inconspicuously words flee under your eyes, the better the rhythm."[509]

Biebl's strong feelings about the visual appearance of poetry can be also glimpsed from a letter he wrote to the artist František Muzika, the designer of *New Icarus*, with its long verses, for the publishing house Aventinum directed by Dr. Štorch. Biebl's tone is unusually forceful.

> At no cost may the verses be broken. . . . The most important thing about the whole poem is its rhythm, which is broad, a current that may not be arbitrarily interrupted; every break is a floodgate and the aim of the poem is to flow and not to collect water for a mill. I have a feeling that Dr. Štorch wants to squeeze *New Icarus* into the Aventinum format, which in my judgement is entirely impossible, there is no font in the world

509 Letter published in Slabý, *Potkávání*, 52.

> from which healthy lines for *New Icarus* could be born in this format. . . . Aside from breaking, which I will not allow (in no case!) I would like, as in the case with my other books, the lines not to be cramped together, to have air both in breadth and in height. The lines should be as far from each other as the lines of this letter, they should not be pressed together, that spoils the verses. . . . I hope you would not lend yourself to break verses, even if Dr. Štorch were to request it despite my protests.[510]

Browsing through the various drafts and finished manuscripts of Biebl's poems, I was impressed by his attention to appearance. Part of composing a poem was a search for the right visual design, from indentures, blank lines and larger white spaces within the poem, to the poem's position on the page. As Biebl's letter suggests, the visual design is indivisible from the temporality of reading, a kind of musicality. Each poem has its own visual rhythm and dynamics, each flows differently, yet all finished poems were typed with meticulous care, and the designs are generally neat and uncrowded, with plenty of air for each line and each poem.

Biebl began to regularly use the typewriter, it seems, almost immediately after his return from Java—as he was working on his Javanese poems and prose. Some two months after his return, in a letter describing how he felt back at home after his trip ("like a fish pickled in aspic"), he wrote: "I am also clapping on the typewriter, butIamwritingeverythingtogether, before one begins to remember to separate each word."[511] A surrealist historian might feel (as I do) that his Javanese poetry and the typewriter form an "unusual friendship." Already around this time, it was not just the final versions of poems he typed out: much of the process of fashioning a poem into the final version consisted in retyping, with revisions in wording as well as in design.

A passage in Nezval's memoirs helps us imagine what the typewriter meant for the poets of Biebl's generation. Nezval describes how he began to use the typewriter in October 1927—only five months after Biebl—when writing his long poem *Edison*.

> I happened to get hold of a prospect for the typewriter Corona, and I desired it so much I could not sleep. . . . We ordered it and after a few days it arrived like a shining angel, to bedazzle me day and night with its magic. . . . Once, on a Sunday at the end of October 1927, I was seized by a strange restlessness. . . . [U]nwittingly I sat down at the piano and I began to improvise. I searched for long and heavy chords in the deep register, which would reflect the state of my spirit, but I didn't play for long. I walked to the room where I usually worked. My typewriter began to glow—the lightbulb above it gave it all its magic. Slowly I typed out the first verse of Edison. The same evening, I

510 Correspondence of František Muzika in the archive of the National Gallery, Prague.

511 Letter published in Slabý, *Potkávání*, 246.

> finished the first canto. I am really convinced that my shining Corona deserves credit for my poem, inspired by the inventor of the lightbulb. . . . The straight flow of my lines, carried forward by an eleven or twelve-syllable trochee, that regularity present in the avenues of great modern cities, had something mysterious and machine-like at the same time. Three to eight syllable trochees could be a folk song, but the rhythm that I caressed out from the waves of deep notes on the piano opened for me like an unknown world and opened for me unknown worlds. Finally I could "write" like when I played piano.[512]

One must think here of the music of "my beautiful typewriter" in the poems of Blaise Cendrars:

> My beautiful typewriter which sounds at the end of every line and
> which is as quick as jazz
> My beautiful typewriter which prevents me from dreaming to the portside
> or the starboard
> And which makes me follow an idea until the end
> My idea[513]

The poem is found in the 1924 collection *Feuilles de route* (Roadmaps), in the section of the book titled "Formose" ("Formosa" [today Taiwan]), according to the name of the ship on which Cendrars sailed to Brazil. The poem was presumably written on board of the *Formose*. Amaranth Borsuk has explored how in Cendrars's work, "the typewriter seems to supplant the train in Cendrars's world of metaphors."[514] On the *Formose*, Cendrars' typewriter is entangled with a steamship.

In *Life*, the 1922 key Devětsil publication, a large photograph of a typewriter illustrates the article "Made in America" (title is in English in original) by the editor of *Life*, the architect Jaromír Krejcar (Figure 21). It is an ode to functionalist, constructivist "new beauty" from "a world without aesthetic traditions," "the fatherland of the machine."[515] The main section of the text, which the photo of the typewriter illustrates, is titled *Stroj*, "the machine." The Czech for typewriter is *psací stroj*, "writing machine" (similar to French *machine à écrire*) or commonly just *stroj*, "machine." This is a key word in the imagery of the modern artists, and the "(writing) machine" is here privi-

512 Nezval, *Z mého života*, 154–5.

513 Blaise Cendrars, *Poésies complètes* (Paris: Denoël, 2005), 188.

514 Amaranth Borsuk, "'Ma belle machine à écrire': Poet and Typewriter in the Work of Blaise Cendrars," *Writing Technologies* 2, no. 1 (2008).

515 Krejcar, "Made in America," *Život: sborník nové krásy*, ed. J. Krejcar (Prague: Umělecká beseda, 1922), 191 and 193.

Figure 21. "Oliver." Photo of a typewriter in *Život* (Life), 1922.

leged as the first visual example of the machine. Krejcar writes in the section "Stroj" (Machine):

> Having changed the system of work, [the machine] also changed its product. . . . Two worlds, the past and the modern age, are sharply divided by the moment when the machine brought out its first product, on whose form it indelibly imprinted its character, that is, when it showed itself as a more perfect, precise creator of form than mere hand manufacture.[516]

In *Life*, the picture of the (writing) machine is followed, overleaf, by a picture of a steamship (Figure 22) and a railway snowplow, with the caption:

> Steamship of the "Standard" type and railway snowplow, these are two masterpieces of American technique. Cleanliness of form, beauty flowing from proportions, precise functionality—these are characteristics that should be the unconditional model for architecture.[517]

The "(writing) machine"—alongside steamships, trains, cars —was a part of a constellation of images relating to technology, modernity, and new beauty. Nezval's comparison of the straight lines of poetry produced by the machine to the avenues of "great modern cities" follows this paradigm. I can't help mentioning that on the back cover of the 1926–1927 train schedule—cur-

516 Krejcar, "Made in America," 193.
517 Krejcar, "Made in America," 196.

Figure 22. "The deck of the steamship Standard." New York, 1918. Published in both *Život* (Life) and *Revoluční sborník Devětsil* (Revolutionary collection Devětsil), 1922.

rent at the time of Biebl's journey to Java—there is a whole-page advertisement for a typewriter, with an image similar to that found in *Life*, although this one is "portable" and shown inside an open briefcase.[518] It was not just in the artists' imagination that the writing machine was juxtaposed with a means of transport.

It is not surprising that poets would feel the transformative power of the machine closest to their craft. One can only imagine what the typewriter meant for Biebl, but looking at the meticulously typed pages of his poetry, one senses that the qualities that Krejcar and others admired about the steamship or the typewriter, which the architect took as a model for modern buildings— "cleanliness of form, beauty flowing from proportions, precise functionality"—are "indelibly imprinted" on the pages of Biebl's poetry. It is a kind of clarity that belongs to the (writing) machine. Cendrars writes in one of his steamship poems: "My Remington [typewriter] is beautiful . . . my writing is precise and clear [*nette et claire*]."[519] It is tempting to conclude this way: Biebl's verses aspire to the new beauty of the steamship.

In an essay on typography published in the same year that he worked on the design of *With the Ship*, Teige emphasized "understanding the spirit

518 *Jízdní řád.*

519 Cendrars, *Poésies complètes*, 186.

of each font and using them according to the nature of the text."[520] In the case of the earlier *Pantomime* or *On the Waves of TSF*, unconventional typography loudly calls attention to itself. This is not the case with his designs for Biebl's books. In his writing on typography from this time, Teige admires the "clear form and architectural beauty" of "classic" fonts, dislikes the "eccentric, illogical, fantastic willfulness of decorative mania," and has faith in the "laws of optics [from which] we can learn about book formats and their standardization, about the layout of the page and the proportions of text in relation to the margins, about the balance of black and white, the mutual influence of colors and their complementary and spatial effects."[521] This sounds like science: more the functional new beauty of the machine—typewriter, steamship—than the merry, playful side of poetism. Jan Rous writes of a "move toward balanced forms culminat[ing] in Teige's typography and illustrations for Biebl's verse volume."[522] This culmination was also a moment when Teige's style was especially in tune with that of Biebl, and when he was able to create typography "according to the nature of the text."

"Unprinted surfaces, too, have a strong aesthetic value,"[523] emphasized Teige. In some poems in *With the Ship*, the title is on the top of the page, divided by blank space—sometimes as much as half a page—from the text of the poem, in the lower part of the page. In some cases, such as in "On Mount Merbabu," where the effect is especially pronounced, this balanced composition resonates with the meaning of the poem. If I were writing in Czech, I could say that the title, <u>*Na hoře*</u> *Merbabu*, is <u>*nahoře*</u>, "above" ("on-the-mountain"). The first line of the poem, "In the ferns . . ." is deep below the top, as if on the slopes, where the loud colors of Biebl's jungle contrast with the white silence of distance, toward the mountain top.[524]

The last poem of the book, "Antipodes," includes large unprinted surfaces. For example, there is a conspicuous space on the bottom of the second page, just under the lines "Deep under me the heavenly abyss glows / I walk like Christ Southern Cross on my shoulders." The empty space mirrors the silence "deep under me" where the "heavenly abyss glows." The poem continues on the following page—in Czech, one could say *na druhé straně*, which can mean "on the second page" or "on the other side"—with the words: "*Na druhé straně světa jsou Čechy*," "On the other side of the world is Bohemia." As one's sight moves across the blank space and then to the other page/side, one moves from Java to the other side of the world.

520 Karel Teige, "Moderní typo," *Typografia* 34 (1927): 196.

521 Teige, "Moderní typo," 190, 191, and 194.

522 Jan Rous, "The New Typography," in Rostislav Švachá, *ed.*, *Devětsil: Czech Avant-Garde Art, Architecture and Design of the 1920s and 30s* (Oxford: Museum of Modern Art, 1990), 59.

523 Teige, "Moderní typo," 193; emphasis in original.

524 Biebl, *S lodí*, 50.

On the last page, the appearance of the poem changes. This part consists of single and double lines, separated by visual breaks. The last line of the poem, "At home there is cold drinking water," is set off from the previous lines by a larger white space. The lower half of the page is blank, silent. Visually, the last page suits the increasingly plain, pure, and quiet images evoked by the verses, as the poem trails off into silence.

Perhaps it snows
or the cherry trees bloom

At home strawberries grow

At home there is cold drinking water[525]

The images that Teige designed for Biebl's books have been cited as landmarks of Czech avant-garde art in theoretical publications on the subject (Teige himself featured one of the images on the cover of an issue of the *ReD* magazine that he edited). They combine lines, circles, and various geometric shapes, blocks of color, a few letters and words, as well as other signs. Teige did not refer to these images as illustrations, but typographies. The books credit him for "typographical montage," as if to highlight his aim to "organically unify image and text." Commenting on his "typophotos" for Nezval's poem "Abeceda" (Alphabet), Teige writes: "I tried to create a 'typophoto' of a purely abstract and poetic nature, setting into graphic poetry what Nezval set into verbal poetry in his verse, both being poems evoking the magic signs of the alphabet."[526] According to Teige, the title page—"a visual transcript of the book's literary content"[527]—and the cover are organically part of the book design, both functioning as "posters" for the book.

Aside from the book cover and the title page, *With the Ship* contains four full-page images in a unified style and color scheme: black and pink on white background. In the first of these (Figure 23), the word "Java" appears twice, in different fonts (one of them imitates neat handwriting, perhaps evoking the address on a letter). The line of three O's in this image evokes cabin windows on a steamer, the central vertical rectangle resembles the ship's chimney, the

525 Biebl, *S lodí*, 64.
526 Teige, "Moderní typo," 198.
527 Teige, "Moderní typo," 197.

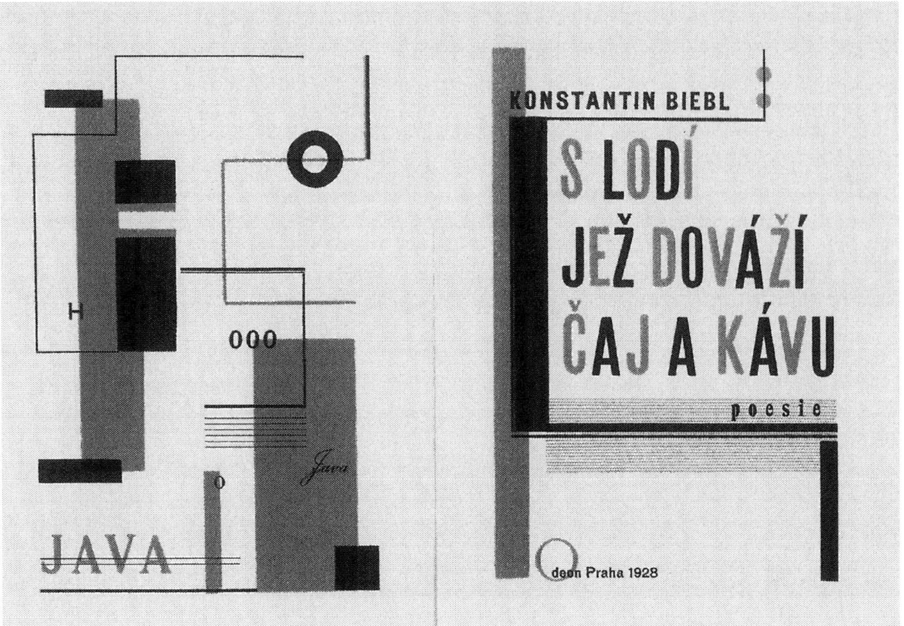

Figure 23. Karel Teige, title spread "typography" in K. Biebl, *S lodí jež dováží čaj a kávu* (With the ship that imports tea and coffee), 1928.

thick black circle looks like a life saver, and the horizontal parallel lines, the surface of the sea. This page faces, balances, but also forms a whole with, the title page, which is executed in a similar style and color scheme. It is dominated by the title in large capital letters of alternating black and pink—creating a jazzy and perhaps somewhat clownish polyrhythm—as well as the name of the author and the publishing company Odeon, in which the capital O becomes a large pink life saver, mirroring the black circles and **o**'s on the other page.

Teige moves in the intertidal zone between shapes and words, working with both as poetic signals that evoke more or less precise associations. In his theoretical writings, he shows an interest in the international maritime flag signal system, or, in Czech, *vlajková řeč*, "flag speech," as an inspiration for visual poetry—another intersection of the routes of modern poetry and modern ships, like and in *With the Ship*.

While the image we have just looked at functions as the visual title for the whole book, each of the three remaining full-page images is placed at the beginning of one of the book's three sections, functioning as "a visual transcript" or a "poster" for each section. Let us look at the image placed at the head of the second section, "With the Ship that Carries Tea and Coffee," in which the poems concern the voyage to Java (Figure 24). The "typography" (as Teige refers to such images) distinctly represents a ship, through a combina-

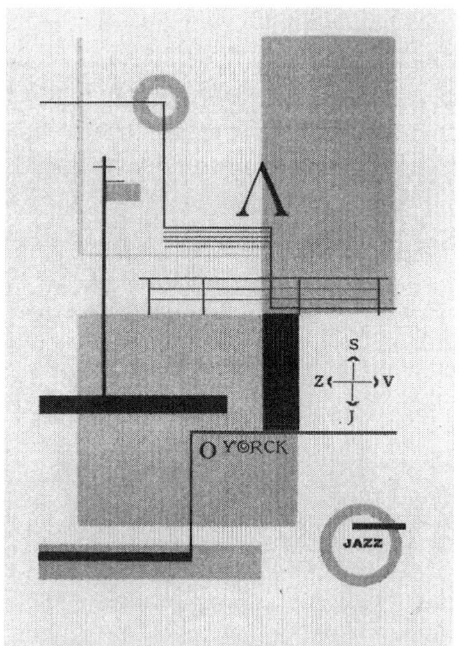

Figure 24. Karel Teige, "typography" in K. Biebl, *S lodí jež dováží čaj a kávu*, 1928.

tion of geometric visual signs and words. The name of the ship on which Biebl sailed, the *Yorck*, appears prominently, as does a compass, with the letters S, V, J, Z (Czech equivalent of English N, E, S, W) at each compass point. The word "jazz," in modern lettering and in a pink circle, is a key word in avant-garde's imagery, and one might think of the poem "Yorck" in that section: "At night they drink! / Till the morning they dance!" In the geometric patterns one sees the railing on ship's deck, a flag on a high mast, and parts of a steamer's silhouette. These elements are like ideograms, traffic signs, or maritime flags; they are midway between pictures and writing.

Like other artists of his generation, Teige often used the ship as an example of modern beauty. A photograph of a modern steamship appears as the first illustration to Teige's major 1922 programmatic text, "Umění dnes a zítra" (Art today and tomorrow). In the caption to the photograph, Teige comments:

> Beautiful, like a modern painting. Naked construction, purity of form, harmonious composition, the highest discipline and precise mathematical order, given by functionality, in short all the virtues of an art work. . . . measured by life experience, it is more important than the most beautiful painting.[528]

528 Teige, "Umění dnes a zítra," *Revoluční sborník Devětsil*, 188.

Teige's 1927 typographical ship shows his admiration for modern beauty, which is most often connected to modern means of transport; as well as for "naked construction, purity of form, harmonious composition, the highest discipline and precise mathematic order," which he also sees in letters of the alphabet and brings out in his typographies. While this enthusiasm for beautiful technology was shared by some, it is not a prominent feature of Biebl's imagery. At their most divergent, when Teige lectures on technology, science and functionalism, the *Pierot lunaire* speaks softly of fragrances, dreams, and death—although Biebl does juxtapose flying fish to airplanes; the sounds of jungle to "files . . . knives . . . chains and augers"; and poetry to film. In the book *With the Ship*, the different sensibilities, Biebl's and Teige's ships, are brought together, in a way, it is my impression, that both artists enjoyed: Teige's style does not merely bring Biebl's poetry into the visual realm, but he introduces something different and beautifully unexpected into it, like in that chance meeting of a sewing machine and an umbrella on an operating table.[529] In turn, the kind of dreamy, child-like imagination of Biebl's poetry leaks into Teige's techno-aesthetics. The loosely constructivist geometry appears more toy-like than ever, like a building kit.

At the beginning of the last section, titled "Antipodes," the dominant image is a large black sphere with an arrow pointing down. Inside the pink arrowhead, there is a small N—for North, I assume, no longer in Czech (S for Sever) but gone "international" (*noord, Norden*)—now we are in a world that is upside down, appropriately to the section's title, as well as the content of the titular poem.

I walk as if on the ceiling
With my head below

Deep under me the heavenly abyss glows
I walk like Christ Southern Cross on my shoulders

Diverging from the geometric, constructivist style of the typographies, there are little black and pink stars scattered across the image, including a conspicuously placed constellation outlining a cross—an intersection of geometric and lyric poetry. (This, however, is not how the Southern Cross appears in the southern hemisphere—perhaps more the constellation as fantasized from Bohemia, under an artificial palm)

Let us look selectively at the visual aspect of some of Biebl's other books. The title page of his first single-authored collection, the *Věrný hlas* (Faith-

529 As in the key phrase of French Surrealist aesthetics.

ful voice), features a small, decorative engraving by Cyril Bouda, who would go on to become an artist well-known especially for his book illustrations. Inspired by the poem "Butterfly" translated earlier (where the image is reproduced; Figure 12, page 99), the drawing shows a butterfly of an *art deco* ancestry flying over sea waves depicted in the style of Japanese woodblock prints. There is a bouquet of grasses and flowers floating on the sea. The picture has the tender simplicity of the verses, and it mirrors Biebl's poetic dreaming and metaphors, through which one is transported from a village meadow to faraway seas. The book's miniature format, although not designed specifically for the collection, feels appropriate for the soft tone of the poems.

Beginning in 1925, Biebl's books were illustrated by leading avant-garde artists. That year, Josef Čapek contributed the cover for *The Thief from Baghdad*, and, the following year, designed *With Golden Chains*. I have already discussed his image of waves and a steamship—yet another ship—that functions as the title image of the "Waves" section (Figure 13). Čapek's images are very different from Teige's visual imagination, resembling more folk art and children's drawings.

Another prominent artist, František Muzika, designed and illustrated *New Icarus*. The large, horizontal format makes enough space for the long lines of the poem's verses. The title page is white, except for the bluish letters of the title forming a descending diagonal, echoing Icarus's flight and fall; the poet's name is in a corner in smaller type. The arrangement of the verses on pages subtly respects and interacts with the verbal poetry, sometimes breaking stanzas so as to bring out movements in the flow of imagination. The first page of the poem in this large-format book is almost entirely blank, except for the first four lines of the first stanza, which begin at the corner of this white silence. In these four lines, the poet travels the whole world—a steamship in Constantinople and Javanese women, sea and palms. The stanza continues on the next page, yet, with the turning of the page, the reader returns from distant lands to Bohemia, from flashes of fantasy to a moment of rest in simple actuality. A similar arrangement of text, at the beginning of the third canto, evokes different associations. The first three lines, in the lower right corner of an otherwise blank, silent double page, appear like an archipelago in the southeast corner of a map of Eurasia. The lines read:

When I first saw Ceylon
When I first caught sight of Borneo Sumatra Celebes
And all those islands down there[530]

530 Biebl, *Nový Ikaros*, 45.

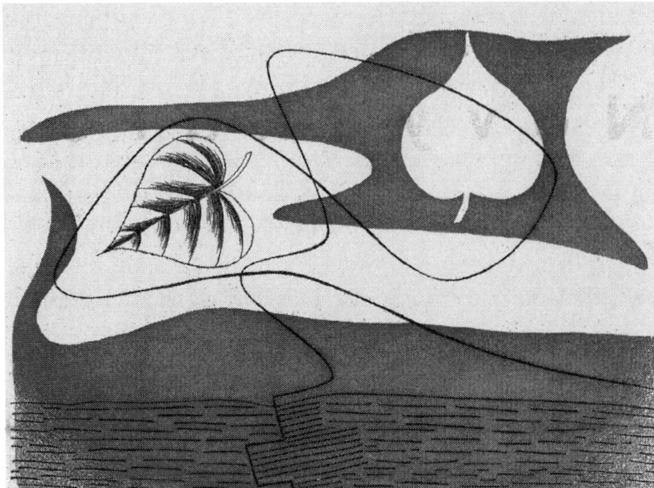

Figure 25. František Muzika, illustration in K. Biebl, *Nový Ikaros* (New Icarus), 1929.

One may be reminded of how the school map sparked a flight of imagination in Biebl's text "The Sea," discussed earlier; as well as the many maps in "image poems" of the time.

New Icarus is illustrated with one image, placed opposite the title page (Figure 25). It admirably visualizes the poem's themes and poetic motion. The leaf of the linden tree, the symbol of Bohemia, of homeland, is cut off, cut out, yet at the same time liberated, having thereby become more material and real, like an image that comes alive, like a realized dream, like a journey. It flies freely like Icarus yet like him it is destined to fall into the ocean which is also a graveyard and *země*. Now my sight is drawn back: the winding line begins from *země* and the upward flight can be felt as a release from death, from the cross, from the earth, from homeland—mirroring the release of the cut out linden leaf. Now, somewhat disoriented and dazed, I see the two leaf shapes, the embodied fullness of one and the open emptiness of the other, mirroring each other, fatally attracted. As in the poem, opposites merge even as they remain unresolved. In the image is the poet's journey across the ocean, across the world, open and full of wings, as well as humanity's graveyard. Muzika's image, like those rose petals with no words on them, grows from Biebl's poetry and propels it into non-verbal realms, only to give back to words something from that other world.

PHOTOGRAPHS, CINEMA, AND THE MAGAZINE *HOME AND THE WORLD*

In his discussion of *New Icarus*, Šalda admires Biebl's "captivating cinematographic method."[531] Biebl's poetry is indeed exceptionally visual, and at some moments his verses and prose feel almost like a scenario for a film.

Upon his return from Java, he wrote in a letter to the publisher and Mácha scholar Karel Janský about his plans for a long poem titled *Vajang*. *Wayang* (in today's spelling; *wajang* in the Dutch spelling in Biebl's time, sometimes also used by Biebl) refers to various forms of Javanese theater, but mainly to shadow puppetry, a highly revered and sophisticated art in Java, in which flat, colored and perforated puppets—the poet brought a few home—are placed or moved on a large white, translucent screen. It is a kind of storytelling, with moving pictures, which richly blends visual and verbal poetry and music in a multimedia, multi-sensory celebration.[532] Biebl wrote in the letter that the planned poem *Vajang*, "in several cantos, will perhaps require several pictures, which will not be a decoration, but a necessity, a kind of continuation [of the poem] in the text."[533] While the poem was never written, or has not survived, we can take the cue to look at Biebl's published photographs as a "continuation" of his poetry. Biebl's idea of *Vajang* also suggests a poetic resonance between *wayang*, as part of his Javanese experience, and poetic uses of photography.

Many photographs from his journey were published in the illustrated weekly *Domov a svět* (Home and the world) between March 1927 and May 1928. He took and developed most of them (as he writes), but also included some that he collected (such as postcards). The photographs are typically ignored by scholars and editors.[534] And yet, they afford us a chance to see how images of Biebl's trip, and more generally his verbal and visual poetry, grew form and into the culture of the 1920s and its visual imagination. In these photographs, the poet ventured on a journey beyond words, quietly bringing something of

531 Quoted in Rudolf Mrázek, "Jávánské motivy," 239.

532 Jan Mrázek, *Phenomenology of a Puppet Theatre: Contemplations on the Art of Javanese Wayang Kulit* (Leiden: KITLV Press, 2005).

533 Letter published in Slabý, *Potkávání*, 247.

534 Many of the original prints of these published photos are among Biebl's photographs from Java in the archive of the Museum of Czech Literature, Prague. A recent exception to the dearth of interest in the photographs was Michala Tomanová's exhibition of Biebl's photographs at the Czech embassy in Jakarta in 2014.

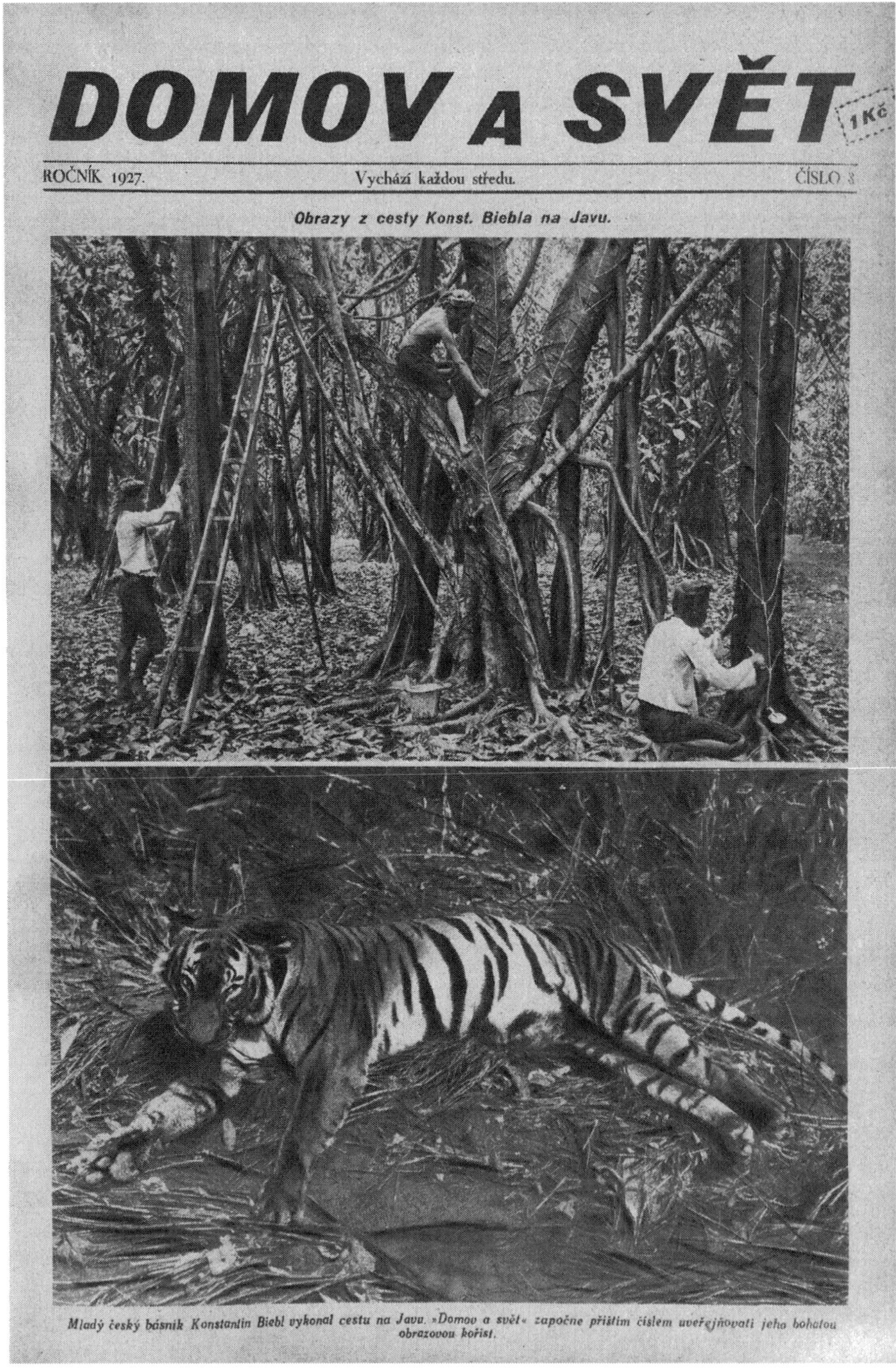

DOMOV A SVĚT

1 Kč

ROČNÍK 1927. Vychází každou středu. ČÍSLO 8

Obrazy z cesty Konst. Biebla na Javu.

Mladý český básník Konstantin Biebl vykonal cestu na Javu. »Domov a svět« započne příštím číslem uveřejňovati jeho bohatou obrazovou kořist.

Figure 26. "Pictures from Konst. Biebl's journey to Java." Cover of *Domov a svět* (Home and the world), vol. 1, no. 8, announcing the publication of Biebl's photos in upcoming issues of the magazine, 1927.

his poetry into another sensory and social realm, and discovering unusual friendships between modern poetry and photography, between their technics and their magic.

The first two photos from Biebl's trip appeared on the cover of the magazine on 16th March 1927, only a few weeks after his return (Figure 26). The caption above reads: "Pictures from the journey of Konst. Biebl to Java"; and below: "Young Czech poet Konstantin Biebl carried out a journey to Java. In the next issue, 'Home and the World' will commence to publish his rich visual prey."[535] One of the pictures on the cover shows a resting tiger looking at the reader, who may connect it with the final words of the caption ("visual prey") —whether one thinks of the tiger as a hunter's prey, or about the tiger's prey. The other picture shows men cutting the bark of rubber trees to harvest the sap.[536] In Biebl's texts, the "wringing" of rubber would become a recurring image (and rubber plantations would figure in other critical writings, most famously in Madelon Szekely-Lulofs's 1931 novel *Rubber*). In the prose piece "Přistání" (Landing), he toasts "the people and gods of this country as a proof that I have come neither to fell trees nor to wring rubber out of them!"[537] Much later, during the Second World War, he would write in a poem:

> There are also Europeans like you, Sarina
> Who love your islands
> And are ashamed of those who wring rubber out of their light[538]

The tiger captured on the photograph might call to mind the circus tigers in Biebl's earlier poetry— "Tigers with indelible shadows / of iron bars—stay with us!" In the persistent vitality of tropical nature, Biebl would feel a repressed resistance—the "silence of the millions"—against the colonial civilization of rubber-wringing, plantations, and cities: "jungle, eternal and truly mysterious, which does not disappear where all tigers are shot dead and primeval forests are cleared."[539] The phrase "the royal tiger is dying" is repeated like a refrain in "On Mount Merbabu," a poem in *With the Ship*, which is about, so to speak, the wringing of wealth from fertile Java. A tiger also appears in a letter that Biebl wrote to Karel Nový, the editor of *Home and the World*, on the 3rd of November 1926, when he was on the ship heading to Java. The poet promises photographs from his trip, laughing at both at himself and colonial imagery:

---

535 *Domov a svět* 1, no. 8 (1927), cover.

536 The original print, in the archive of the Museum of Czech Literature, has the word "rubber tree" [*gumovník*] written on the back side.

537 Biebl, *Cesta na Jávu*, 54.

538 Biebl, *Bez obav*, 84.

539 Biebl, *Cesta na Jávu*, 61.

> Perhaps I will also do some animal hunting. The hunter's blood, which flows in my veins, will not let me rest. Every Englishman who comes to the Indies wants to shoot a tiger and be photographed on its carcass. I don't know where they find all those tigers. Or do they perhaps have there a single stuffed tiger, and on its hide before the camera the hunter's foot can assume its position for a few shillings? We will see![540]

In one issue of the magazine, on the page titled "Singapore," Biebl included just such a picture, with the caption "Tiger hunter"[541]—most readers would not realize that the "Englishman" wearing a tropical helmet is actually Sultan Ibrahim of Johor.

Biebl looked at photographs both as images that spark imagination and with a playful suspicion, amplifying their unexpected associations and semantic slippages, and following the interplay sparked by the juxtaposition of images and words, as well as between images—for example, between the tiger and the rubber plantation, growing where the jungle was cleared.

His "Názorné vyučování moderní vnímavosti" (An object lesson in modern perceptivity) encourages us to look in this way. It is a series of annotated photographs published in several instalments in a literary magazine. About a photo of a stack of large concrete pipes at a construction site, with one of them protruding like the barrel of a cannon, Biebl notes that "these concrete pipes must awaken within you a horrifying image of war." About a picture of a man sitting at his office desk with a pen in his lifted hand, he writes:

> May the official at the American consulate, with a random lifting of his *pero* ["pen; feather"], which then appears to stand in his hair, awaken in you a suspicion that somewhere in a corner of his soul there remains a fear that people in his office would discover that behind his black hair and eagle's nose, the great-grandson of an Indian is hiding.[542]

"Random" details and resemblances "awaken" images and associations "within you," as well as suspicions that the images betray what is hidden or unconscious.

The obsessively recurring images of coconuts are a case in point. Already in 1924, before he travelled to the tropics, Biebl wrote in a poem: "In the crowns of the coconut trees / the heads of children weep."[543] Coconuts, as the heads of dead men or as the poet's own head, haunt the poet's prose texts

---

540 Konstantin Biebl's letter to Karel Nový, 3 Nov 1926. Archive of the Museum of Czech Literature, Prague.

541 Konstantin Biebl, "Singapore," *Domov a svět* 1, no. 11 (1927): 13.

542 Biebl, *Dílo*, 5:273.

543 Biebl, *Dílo*, 5:136.

Klíčící kokosy v botanické zahradě.
Najednou se vymotáte z
uliček a octnete se v úplném

Figure 27. "Germinating coconuts in the botanical garden." K. Biebl's photo in *Home and the World* 1, no. 11 (1927).

about his journey as well as *New Icarus*. In *Home and the World*, among Biebl's photos from Ceylon, there is a striking image of a grotesquely large mound of coconuts, rather resembling human heads or skulls. Below it, there is a picture of coconuts on a palm (Figure 33).[544] In the next installment, about Singapore, a large photograph shows dozens of coconuts on the ground. The caption reads: "Germinating coconuts in the botanical garden."[545] (Figure 27) There are more coconuts and coconut trees in later issues.

I mentioned that the Czech word for coconut, *kokos*, is often playfully used to mean "head," and Biebl's repeatedly brings out this double meaning in his poetry. If in these photos coconuts (*kokosy*) evoke human heads (*kokosy*), visual resemblances and verbal language may be reinforcing each other. But rather than being unequivocal symbols, the coconuts haunt with uncontrolled associations. The "germinating coconuts" look so much like decapitated heads, yet new life grows from them. Coconut palms appear in Biebl's photographic and poetic representations of lush tropical nature. Such conflicting sensations are felt from a passage on the "Ceylon" page of *Home and the World*, which describes the poet's first impressions of the tropics:

> You do not see Ceylon before you see her trees. Already the first strip of land, when it appears, is deeply green with innumerable coconut palms. To step on the ground in Ceylon means to be stabbed into the heart with a knife, so stunned you are by immense tropical nature.[546]

544 Biebl, "Ceylon," 3.
545 Biebl, "Singapore," 13.
546 Biebl, "Ceylon," 3.

Figure 28. Photo of a house on Biebl's photo page "Arrival in Java" in *Home and the World* 1, no. 13 (1927).

Among the first photographs from Java published in *Home and the World*, placed under the photo of a coconut tree, is an image of the ruins of an old brick house (Figure 28). Plants with giant leaves grow inside and roots of trees penetrate the walls. Here, too, one senses life and death with equal intensity. Biebl must have been struck by the contrast between this skull of a house and inhabited colonial houses, which were as a rule brilliantly clean and white. It may have been this silent, ruined house that inspired the poet to write that "the Indies house is the home of the dead, a stopover to nirvana, the limbo of bats, the purgatory of frogs and other souls, who move around here in a rather casual manner, like at home, ignoring the Dutch, ignoring you, because here we all are lodgers in after-life, voluntarily and temporarily suffered." He goes on to speak about the jungle, which "has not lost its power over Batavia," and which "does not disappear where all tigers are shot dead and primeval forests are cleared." One senses a similar sentiment in a later issue of *Home and the World*, where, among photographs showing the fertility of Java, there is a picture of a snake, which is also mentioned in the accompanying text: "But everywhere in the fields danger lurks: a giant poisonous snake fights with man and his culture, protecting the primeval wildness of nature."[547]

Photography captures life. It is involved with life and death. Photographed, the "house of the dead" and the skull-like coconuts are doubly dead, doubly silent; the tiger, doubly shot, first by a hunter, then by a photographer. And yet, like when a glance of actuality triggers poetic dreaming, photographs can awaken perception, allowing the dead to come to life and the silent to be heard. Letting the dead reappear is another power of the photograph.

In Biebl's later scenario for the "filmic poem" *Black Tower*, the village boy Jan, a dreamer and a fool, who "actually is the poet,"[548] gazes at a graveyard and notices a girl between the trees. He follows her, but she disappears behind a grave. When Jan looks at the gravestone, he finds himself "face to face with an old photograph of the girl who had disappeared."[549] He also finds a shard of colored glass. He looks through it. "*Color shot*": The grave and the gravestone disappear, and he sees the girl, alive and merry, in the midst of

> a garden celebration, where all the dead, who lay in this vanished graveyard, now are happy; some drink at tables, dead children are playing, and lovers are hugging and kissing. Jan is distinctly recognizing the faces of the dead—indeed they are the revived photographs from crosses and gravestones. He puts down the colored glass and the celebration sinks into an empty graveyard.[550]

Photographs are here associated with death, yet they enable the poet-dreamer Jan, with the help of a magical lens—so much like a camera, but also recalling the tropical nature on a window in winter—to bring, momentarily, the dead to life, all in the medium of film. Should one also think of Biebl's interest in *wayang*, which is said in some Javanese sources to represent ancestors?[551] When Biebl took pictures of the house of the dead destroyed by the vigorous life of nature, or germinating coconuts resembling decapitated heads, it is not just in what the photos represent, but in the *medium* of photography itself—almost a shamanistic medium—that life, death, revival, and the hearing and seeing of silence are at stake.

Among the photos from Singapore, there is one that recalls the account of the Englishman throwing coins to workers in boats near Perim (see the section "Half-black, you understand?"). The accompanying text reads:

547 Konstantin Biebl, "Z cesty K. Biebla na Jávu. Nejkrásnější podívanou . . .," *Domov a svět* 1, no. 25 (1927): 7.
548 Biebl, *Dílo*, 5:287.
549 Biebl, *Dílo*, 5:301.
550 Biebl, *Dílo*, 5:301.
551 Mrázek, *Phenomenology of a Puppet Theatre*, 70–71.

> About natives who live in utter poverty, one could write long and infinitely sad chapters. When a ship enters the harbor, in a moment it is surrounded by a crowd of tiny boats, resembling our hand puppets, from which the natives throw themselves into the sea to catch small coins which are thrown from the deck by amused first class passengers.[552]

In other photographs one sees a Javanese nanny—a *babu*—carrying a plump white baby, Chinese graves, rice fields (here already described as "the mirrors of rice fields," an expression that would recur in Biebl's texts, and the title of a section on the Indies in his final collection of poems published a quarter century later), volcanoes, a "Javanese spirit" called *momo*—all words and images that would grow and manifest their powers in his texts.

But it is not just a constellation of motifs that the photographs share with poetry. If Biebl was said to employ a "captivating cinematographic method" in his poems, he also works with photos like with words. The tiger, the poisonous snake, the coconuts, or the crumbling house are for him poetic metonyms, metaphors, and haunting glimpses. Verbal and photographic poetry are "continuations" of each other, to invoke *Vajang* again.

Each photo in *Home and the World* is a part of a larger picture, or something like a cinematic montage. In every issue with his photos, one full page is reserved for them. Alongside a variety of rectangular formats, there are also cut out figures and buildings. Often these are superimposed on the borders between other photos. They invade their space and conceal the borders between them. The result is a montage, a new entity, in which images interpenetrate, overlap, contrast or blend. In most but not all cases, there is a brief accompanying text, and some photographs have captions.

In their collage-like arrangements and focus on travel, these pages are reminiscent of the "picture poems" produced earlier by artists like Teige and Štyrský. Avant-garde ideas about photography resonate with Biebl's work. There was an interest in plain, anonymous photographs and conventional postcards—the kind used in the picture poems. Teige saw in them a possibility to bring together the "tragically estranged worlds" of professional art and amateur creativity. The technological possibilities of photography were appealing both because images could be cheaply multiplied, disseminated and made accessible to everyone, such as in magazines like *Home and the World*, and because photography made possible the representation of exotic places, actual yet fantastic. Photography was one of the modern technolo-

552 Konstantin Biebl, "Singapore," 13.

gies that were central to avant-garde imagination, like ocean liners, trains, and aeroplanes—which frequently appeared on avant-garde photos. And it was in reference to photographs that Teige spoke of "surrealism" in 1922 in *Life.*

Each page of Biebl's photographs is rather like a sequence in a (silent) film. It is a combination of shots—from panoramic views to close ups—connected by a more or less narrowly defined topic. Some shots are separated as if by "cuts," while others blend into each other through more gradual transitions.

Biebl's photo pages are akin to film also in that the representation of distant lands and travel was at this time one of the most often mentioned attractions of cinema. In one issue of *Home and the World,* partly on a page facing Biebl's photos, there is an article titled "Film a jeho výroba" (Film and its production). It was probably obvious to the magazine's readers how this topic is central to the main theme of the magazine, travel and "the world" (represented in great part by photographs). The introductory paragraph makes these connections explicit.

> Cinematography, today an industry of immense significance, thanks its existence to a whole series of inventions, beginning with photography . . . [T]oday we face things that border on magic. In the warmth of the cinema, effortlessly we ride through wild lands, we descend into deep canyons, climb mountains, fly in an airplane—transport ourselves into distant past—among brontosaurs and ichthyosaurs—and so on.[553]

Film was one of the modern modes of transport. It was the only intercontinental one that most people could afford—and part of film's appeal was the dream-experience of riding in aeroplanes and on steamships.

In manifestos and theoretical texts, film was the model for all modern art. Teige wrote in his 1922 manifesto "Art Today and Tomorrow":

> Cinema is a true encyclopedia of new art, a universal show and a universal lesson. Let us rejoice and be merry in the cinema: it is the Bethlehem from which the salvation for modern art arrives. From cinema, which is the only folk / people's [*lidovým*] art today.[554]

> With its motifs—Far West characters, the street, the prairie, the tropics, American dancing rooms and bars, harbors, thousands of realities of the world, a sense for healthy courage and adventure . . .—and with its origin in the optical invention of chronophotography and mechanical and chemical production, it is the model and

553 "Film a jeho výroba," *Domov a svět* 2, no. 7 (1928): 3.
554 Teige, "Umění dnes a zítra," 191.

> prophetic vision for all new art, which unconditionally must contain all its elements and conditions.[555]

For modern artists, too, travel to distant lands was a major attraction of cinema. In "O proletářském divadle" (On proletarian theater), published in the same collective volume, the prominent avant-garde theater director and theorist Jindřich Honzl wrote:

> Cinema is the celebration of what is: instead of the mystery of myths it has the stunning actuality of all continents and all the seas, it connects the most intoxicating exoticism of tropical forests with the most thingly actuality of the plainest of little backyards. In these new actualities it is able to find new forms and relationships.[556]

Two years later, in a lecture, Teige spoke of "the poetry of cinema" again:

> It is the poetry of the travel diary, the Eiffel Tower, the Baedeker [travel guide], the poster, the postcard, the map . . ., the song of the modern sirens of the Red Star Line [ocean liner company], the touristic poetry of long hotel and ship corridors with enigmatic and numbered doors of rooms and cabins. Globetrotting and frivolity, clowning and adventure equipped with all comfort.[557]

Teige began this lecture by pointing out cinema's origin in the "newness" of the world, epitomized by travel. One may recall Biebl's prose text "Express to Paris," which, I have suggested, reveals the method of his poetic travelogues. Teige:

> The realizations of contemporary art are nothing but the results of a contemporary new sensibility and mentality, directly bound up with the newness of the world. . . . Landscape, which we cut through at the hundred-kilometer speed of an express train or car, has lost for us its descriptive and static values; our senses suck in a summary and synthetic impression. We stand behind the windows of an express train, and at the speed of the steam engine—in relation to our person, immobile and standing firmly with legs astride, hands in pockets, pipe between the teeth, and with an immense, voracious desire in our hearts—the space of the landscape, a seemingly-turning plate of the Earth, rushes by rapidly backward, winding itself up into a ball of swiftly experienced past.[558]

---

555 Teige, "Umění dnes a zítra," 193.

556 Jindřich Honzl, "O proletářském divadle," *Revoluční sborník Devětsil*, 92.

557 Karel Teige, "Estetika filmu a kinografie," in *Avantgarda známá a neznámá*, ed. Štepán Vlašín et al. (Prague: Svoboda, 1971), 1:546.

558 Teige, "Estetika filmu a kinografie," 544.

Silent film evoked the dreams of distant lands also in another way. In Nezval's words, "film is the mother tongue without home country, the Sanskrit of new humanity. . . . equally well understandable to the Papuans and the French."[559]

Biebl signaled his affection for cinema when in 1925, he titled one of his collection of poems after the 1924 movie *The Thief of Baghdad*, one of the grandest American films of the silent era. It is a classic fairy-tale love story, in which an outcast, a thief, a trickster, is the hero. It exudes the dreamy exoticism of *Arabian Nights*, on which the story is based, yet the otherness, luxury and mystique of the Orient is represented with light irony and humor. The fanciful sets representing Baghdad add to the sense that this is visual poetry and not real life. Aside from the extravagantly exotic Baghdad and its inhabitants, its main characters include princes and their retinues from India, Persia and Mongolia. The thief transforms himself into the Prince of the Isles and the Seas. He and others travel to faraway lands, across and into the depths of the sea, and enter magical realms guarded by dragons. There are flights on a magic carpet and a winged horse. These fantastic travels and fairy worlds were the magic of film to which Biebl paid homage.

The Czech artists who so admired film never produced one in the 1920s and 1930s. While it was easy to travel to distant lands "in the warmth of a cinema," creating an actual movie turned out as much a fantasy as sailing on an ocean liner. A number of brief film scenarios were published, but they were never realized, and the scripts became the "finished" works (rather like Biebl's later *Black Tower*), further proclaiming the almost fetishistic fascination with film.

This is true also about the "touristic" (Teige's designation) picture poems, which have much in common with Biebl's photo pages. In Czech, a word commonly used for cinema is *biograf*, "life-writing" or "life-image." Teige called film a "living photograph"[560]—one can almost see him looking at a photograph and fantasizing about a film. In his book on the cinema, there is a reproduction of one of his picture poems—a collage of photographs of a harbor and boats—with the subtitle "a moment of a lyrical movie." Below the picture, there is a brief scenario describing the progression of shots in an (unrealized) film, of which the reproduced picture poem is imagined to be a moment.[561] The touristic picture poems imagine film, without actually becoming them—they are dreams that have accepted un-fulfillment as their fate, not unlike the unrealized tourism of poets dreaming of steamships and

559 Nezval, "Film," in *Avantgarda známá a neznámá*, ed. Štepán Vlašín et al. (Prague: Svoboda, 1971), 2:163–64.

560 Teige, "Estetika filmu a kinografie," 548.

561 Teige, *Film* (Prague: Nakladatelství Václava Petra, 1925), 125.

Figure 29. Photo on Biebl's photo page "Arrival in Java" in *Home and the World*, vol. 1, no. 13, 1927.

giraffes in the tropical warmth of Prague cafés; or the dreams of people looking at the photographs of ocean liners and distant lands in magazines.

Avant-garde publications and magazines like *Home and the World* were part of the same culture, and the themes and desires of one continually overflow into the other. Still, Biebl's photos appeared, not in the midst of manifestos, theoretical articles, and the latest poetry and prose, but in a weekly "meant for the broadest [spectrum of] social classes,"[562] covering everything from current events to leisure and latest fashion. They follow (or fit in rather well) the style of the magazine where they were published. However, that is something that is less a deviation from the ambitions of the Czech avant-garde, but rather a step toward the realization of its dreams—poetry with the powers and broad appeal of cinema; an "art of living and living it up."

Let us look at a few examples of how Biebl's photos work like a filmic montage. A semiotic or poetic punch is dealt, not merely by individual photographs, but by their combination.

On the page "Příjezd na Jávu" (Arrival in Java), there is a photograph of a Javanese *kampung*, with a basket maker in front of a simple bamboo house (Figure 29).[563] To his side, a barber is shaving a customer's head. The overall

562 [Karel Nový], "Úvodem," *Domov a svět* 1, no. 1 (1927): 1.
563 Konstantin Biebl, "Příjezd na Jávu," *Domov a svět* 1, no. 13 (1927): 9.

DOMOV A SVĚT 5

Z CESTY K. BIEBLA NA JÁVU.

Jávský šofér.

Čínští bohové.

Všechen obchod na Jávě mají v rukou Číňané. Žádný žid nemůže s nimi konkurovati. V obchodě jsou bez srdce, naprosto bezohlední, ale když překročíte práh jejich domu, tak najdete něco, co se může zváti opravdu rodinným životem. Mnoho generací žije pohromadě a celé rody udržují vřelé přátelské styky. Každý rod má svůj zvláštní chrám, zvaný tenkleng, kde na oltáři jsou postaveny malé pamětní destičky se jmény zemřelých. Konají se tu slavnosti na památku mrtvých, je tu pro ně prostřeno, neboť zemřelí hodují s živými a sice tak, že vdechují vůni z jídel jim připravených.

Jávští duchové.

Ulice ve Wonosobo.

Čínský hrob.

Hrob čínského majora Oei Tiong Homa.

Duch Momo.

Na cestě z Wonosobo.

Jávští duchové.

Děti z jávské vesnice.

Mladé Číňanky ze společnosti.

Asfaltová silnice do hor.

Jávští duchové.

Figure 30. Biebl's photo page in *Home and the World*, vol. 1, no. 19, 1927.

impression is that of ordinary Javanese men at work. Just below this photograph there is a cutout image of a Javanese woman holding a very white, very well-fed baby. (Should one think of the Javanese *babu* taking care of white children in *Plancius*?) The upper part of this image—the *babu*'s head and torso, and most of the baby's body—is superimposed on the photograph of the working Javanese men above, the white baby invading the borders and space of the other photograph, and appearing out of place in those surrounding. It may or may not be a coincidence that the basket maker's right hand, which holds a tool, appears on the baby's head (half-covered, the tool looks rather like a knife in this montage, but the original archive print shows something like a wooden block); and that the words "Konstantin Biebl" and the title, "Arrival in Java," appear just next to the white baby. (Recall Biebl writing about his first day in Java: "Indeed I should have such a nanny, a black babu, which would lead me from animal to animal, from flower to flower . . .")[564]

Let us look at one whole page more closely (Figure 30).[565] A brief text focuses on the Chinese in Java. My eye is first drawn to the upper right corner, a loud image of "Chinese gods" in a temple. I see the picture balanced along the diagonal by the photo in the lower left corner, "Young Chinese women socializing." The intense depiction of wrathful male deities makes an evocative counterpart to the smiling, elegant, modern women—like palm leaves on a frozen window.

"Chinese gods," above right, is immediately next to "Javanese chauffeur," above left. The accompanying text begins: "All trade in Java is in the hands of the Chinese." Both pictures display Chinese affluence, yet I sense a tension between the polished dark surface of a modern machine and the baroque expressions of the religious effigies. The caption leads me to notice the Javanese man, a chauffeur, a servant—and I see luxury and power from the point of view of the servant ("and into the lap / golden ducats rain // But never ask / to whose?").

I look below "Chinese gods," at "Chinese grave." The connection between the two seems clear, yet when my eyes move down from the wrathful-looking gods, the plain grave below feels like a moment of sudden silence after leaving a crowded and noisy place. The text in-between the two photographs helps to link them, and, in the silence of the photographs and the graves, it evokes the sounds and smells of a celebration.

> Every clan has its own temple, called the tengkleng, where small memorial tablets with the names of the dead stand on the altar. Here celebrations take place in memory of the deceased; the table is set for them, because the dead feast with those who are alive, by inhaling the smell of the dishes that are prepared for them.

---

564 Biebl, *Cesta na Jávu*, 55.

565 Konstantin Biebl, "Z cesty K. Biebla na Jávu. Všechen obchod . . ." *Domov a svět* 1, no. 19 (1927): 5.

I recall a similar accord of clamor and silence in Biebl's text about Chinese funeral, "At the Feast of the Dead":

> Very touching is the shape of Chinese coffin, as it descends into the grave to the sound of tinkling glasses. At both its ends the coffin transitions into the shape of a womb. Raise your glasses, let us toast! From the womb of the night, the human emerged and into night's womb he returns. Raise your glasses, let us toast! But also the tombstone has the shape of a womb! Raise your glasses, let us toast! But also the sandy path around the grave multiplies this mysterium! Raise your glasses, let us toast! But also the plot of grass, which surrounds everything. Raise your glasses, let us toast! But even the graveyard wall turns into that mysterious shape. Raise your glasses, let us toast! But even the grove behind the wall is planted—raise your glasses, let us toast![566]

As I look at the photo page, I am haunted by the multiple wombs and their silence in the midst of a loud celebration; life as the lining of death; plurality and all oppositions contained and united in the womb-grave (Mácha: "into her womb again earth will embrace me"; but Biebl's "our graveyard is not large . . . in a few graves there are many dead" resonates as well, with a strangeness, like palms on a frozen window again). I sense an unusual friendship, a liaison, between the photo page and the graveyard. Raise your glasses, let us toast!

To the left of the "Chinese grave" is an image that extends the theme in an unexpected direction: "the grave of the Chinese major Oei Tiong Homa" shows an effigy of a lion, on whose pedestal a smiling, plump Caucasian baby stands, held by a Javanese servant. Three contrasting expressions and attitudes, three different worlds, dissonantly co-exist. Supported by a Javanese servant in formal attire, the European baby in a white dress and a hat, having a touristic jolly good time, is irreverently or ignorantly stepping on the grave of a respected Chinese man, marked by a stylized effigy of a mythological lion. I think of how Biebl bitingly wrote about Javanese servants taking care of white children in *Plancius*. I think of the other lions and tigers in his poetry ("Circus Konrado has fifty blond lions, / more the fragrance of blood than the fragrance of honey—you, belittled and humiliated ones / with eyes like oases without water—stay with us!"), and even, as if in a distance, other Czech lions, such as those "like tamed power, like fainted anger" at the graves of the Czech kings in Mácha's poem, or those in Neruda ("like lions captured in a cage . . . we are bound to Earth"). This photo is at the center of the page, at the intersection of its two diagonals. The image is a cut-out superimposed

566 Biebl, *Cesta na Jávu*, 71.

on other photographs—making it stand out and appear, so to speak, on another level.

I turn to four other cut-outs, four effigies, all with the same caption, "Javanese spirits." Two of them, at the left and right margins, flank the centrally located image with the white baby. All four appear to be released not just from their photographic frame, but also from the grid of horizontal and vertical borders of the rectangular photographs—as if they were floating above. (All four were cut out from a single postcard representing Balinese statues, a copy of which is in Biebl's collection in the archive.[567] As a note on the back of the postcard shows, Biebl knew that they were Balinese, but, I surmise, he called them "Javanese spirits" because it was they that were needed for this composition).

The Javanese spirits lead my eyes to the lower part of the page. Here, aside from the Chinese ladies, there are photos of peaceful, mountainous rural landscape. Biebl knew that mountains are sacred places for the Javanese and the abodes of Javanese spirits—I see "them" here, floating around the page. Among these photos—sharply contrasting in mood with the Chinese graves and other grave sentiments—there laugh and frolic "Children from a Javanese village." In the lower right corner, there is the "Asphalt road into the mountains," which links for me with the image of the car diagonally across ("Chinese chauffeur"). The "Asphalt road into the mountains" reminds me of Biebl's later text, "Ing. Baer," which, it seems to me, makes me understand much about how Biebl saw and worked with photographs—just like with poetic images.

> We ride . . . where? One cannot finish that thought on this modern highway, lost in the jungle. . . . We ride into the mysteries of disturbing details, visionary clearings, which only the lightning can accomplish, the teacher of philosophers and poets. It shows the jungle in a forceful and unusual light. It shows only a part and you must imagine the rest.[568]

My reading of the page of photographs has nothing inevitable about it, and one could travel across the page in thousand other ways, letting one's sight and mind be pushed to and fro by the images. Where do the images lead us? "One cannot finish that thought on this modern highway, lost in the jungle." I have not gone far enough in revealing all the personal, half- and sub-conscious associations the photographs evoke for me, and in laying out my thoughts, I have misrepresented the play of unarticulated associations and eye movements. But I have made that excursion to suggest the possibility

567 Museum of Czech Literature, Prague.

568 Biebl, *Cesta na Jávu*, 76–77.

Figure 31. "Typical landscape with a resting elephant." Photomontage by K. Biebl published in *Home and the World*, vol. 1, no. 14, 1927.

of a certain general style of looking at the photographs, which I believe is close to, or a "continuation" of, the style of Biebl's seeing and the ways of his poetry.

One of Biebl's photographs is titled "Typical landscape with a resting elephant" (Figure 31).[569] The massive elephant takes up the lower third of the picture. In the background, we see a mountainous landscape. When I first saw the photo, I noted down that it looks almost as if a cut-out elephant were superimposed on the landscape. As I looked more carefully, I became increasingly suspicious, and began to feel that the photo was designed to make me suspect something. When I checked the archive collection of Biebl's photos, I did find the landscape—but without the elephant. The aim of this image does not seem to be to mislead the viewer, and if so, then only in play. One of its aims may be to alert the viewer that this is play and poetry, and to urge him and her to join in the game of hide and seek with multiple images, and to "ride into the mysteries of disturbing details, visionary clearings, which only the lightning can accomplish, the teacher of philosophers and poets."

---

569 Biebl, "Semarang," 7.

Figure 32. "Volcanoes in Java," the upper part of Biebl's photo page in *Home and the World*, vol. 2, no. 7, 1928.

Not entirely unlike on postcards, verbal language is part of the photographic montage in *Home and World*. Captions and brief texts become part of the play of images, affect what the reader-viewer sees in the photographs, and make people see even the invisible.

Biebl's brief accompanying texts tend to run parallel to the images and only occasionally intersect with them, letting the reader make connections. On the page "Sopky na Jávě" (Volcanoes in Java), the writer appears to parrot tourist information, with the feeling of a poetist theater play, especially when one looks at the Chinese painting of a grumpy-looking god floating above the volcano's crater (Figure 32). Perhaps the poet is warning the reader not to take him too seriously:

> The Bromo volcano has a circular crater, two hundred meters deep, from whose bottom hot mud gushes and flames flare. Through this crater, the souls of the Javanese pass before they stand before god. This god is morose. When he is not erupting in anger, he grumpily hums and this bad mood is oppressive for the whole land. The natives, to appease his wrath, perform pilgrimages to the mountain slopes every year and there they give offerings to him under the naked sky. These celebrations . . . are also performed on the little Krakatoa island. Evidently, these days even gods don't care much about the prayers of the faithful.[570]

570 Biebl, "Sopky na Jávě," *Domov a svět* 2, no 7 (1928): 5.

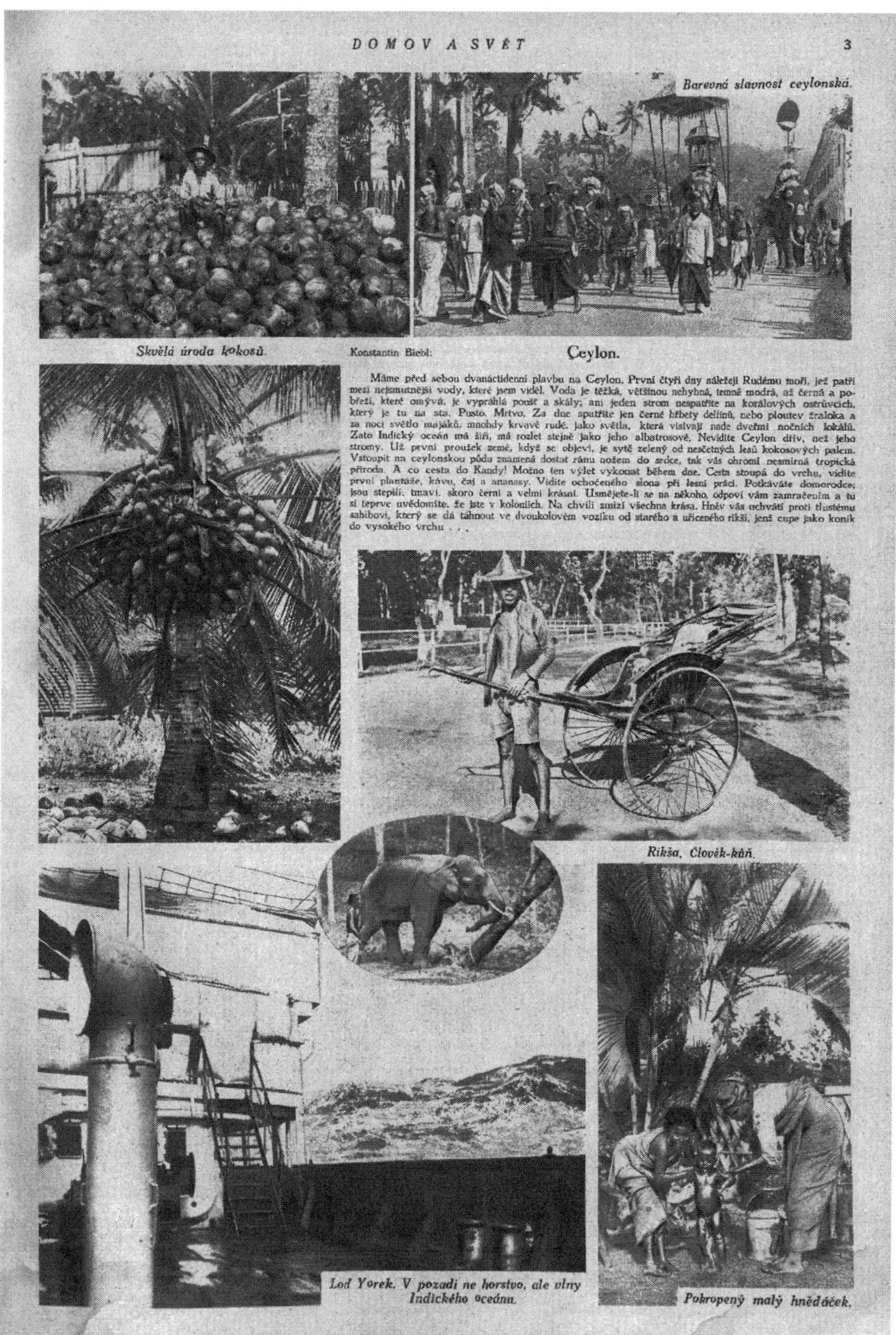

DOMOV A SVĚT 3

Barevná slavnost ceylonská.

Skvělá úroda kokosů.

Konstantin Biebl:

Ceylon.

Máme před sebou dvanáctidenní plavbu na Ceylon. První čtyři dny náležejí Rudému moři, jež patří mezi nejsmutnější vody, které jsem viděl. Voda je těžká, většinou nehybná, temně modrá, až černá a pobřeží, které omývá, je vyprahlá poušť a skály; ani jeden strom nespatříte na korálových ostrůvcích, který je tu na sta. Pusto. Mrtvo. Za dne spatříte jen černé hřbety delfínů, nebo ploutev žraloka a za noci světlo majáků, mnohdy krvavě rudé, jako světla, která visívají nade dveřmi nočních lokálů. Zato Indický oceán má šíři, má rozlet stejně jako jeho albatrosové. Nevidíte Ceylon dřív, než jeho stromy. Už první proužek země, když se objeví, je sytě zelený od nesčetných lesů kokosových palem. Vstoupit na ceylonskou půdu znamená dostat ránu nožem do srdce, tak vás ohromí nesmírná tropická příroda. A co cesta do Kandy! Možno ten výlet vykonat během dne. Cesta stoupá do vrchu, vidíte první plantáže, kávu, čaj a ananasy. Vidíte ochočeného slona při lesní práci. Potkáváte domorodce; jsou štíhlí, tmaví, skoro černí a velmi krásní. Usmějete-li se na někoho, odpoví vám zamračením a tu si teprve uvědomíte, že jste v koloniích. Na chvíli zmizí všechna krása. Hněv vás uchvátí proti tlustému sahibovi, který se dá táhnout ve dvoukolovém vozíku od starého a uřiceného rikši, jenž cupe jako koník do vysokého vrchu . . .

Rikša, Člověk-kůň.

Loď Yorek. V pozadí ne horstvo, ale vlny Indického oceánu.

Pokropený malý hnědáček.

Figure 33. "Ceylon," Biebl's photo page in *Home and the World*, vol. 1, no. 10, 1927.

Some texts are like film scenarios—brief glimpses, separated more often by "cuts" than gradual transitions. Like in some of his poems, great distances are covered effortlessly in the space of a few short lines. One such text begins (Figure 33): "Ahead of us we have a twelve-day voyage to Ceylon." The next four lines evoke the Red Sea, with "the lanterns of the lighthouses, often blood-red, like the lights that hang over the doors of night bars"; by the sixth line we are sailing across the Indian Ocean; in the seventh line we see Ceylon; and on the eighth line we set foot on the island. The remaining six lines describe Ceylon and British colonialism, including a daytrip to the mountain town Kandy. Despite the great speed, we move lightly, propelled by poetic "close ups" and metaphors.[571]

The first three texts, which describe sections of the journey before his arrival in Java, are longer than the later ones. When I read Biebl's text about Singapore, where I now live, I feel as if I am going for a walk with the poet, who tells me, almost like a hypnotist, where to look, and makes me see through his eyes:

> When you walk into the city, you don't know whether you are in China or in India. . . . The Chinese street is overcrowded, yet silent enough; as you move to the outskirts, the number of opium dens increases; you would not dare to enter. In the evening, in the half-light, the dirt, which is at home here, disappears, and the city is transformed into a theater set with large Chinese signs. . . . Suddenly you disentangle yourself from the little Chinese street and you stand in an entirely modern luxurious European city. Huge hotels and cafés. . . . The whites in colonies are all rich, they desire only luxury. About the natives who live in utter poverty, one could write long and infinitely sad chapters.[572]

Biebl's texts about Java are mostly shorter, increasingly fragmentary, merely pointing things out, more prosaic than ever:

> You find here the belief in the transmigration of the soul, sacred trees, you find here everything that you also find in British India. Java is a mountainous and volcanic land. The vegetation changes quickly with the changing height above the sea level. In Semarang I saw white birds of paradise—they have just settled in front of the hotel.[573]

As if he were tired of writing; as if he and his texts were distracted by photographs; as if the poet were torn between speaking and letting me wander among the silent photographs and listen to their conversations; as if he

571 Biebl, "Ceylon," 3.
572 Biebl, "Singapore," 13.
573 Biebl, "Semarang," 7.

wanted to stop writing and let the photographs point, to let them bridge dreams and reality. In some of the later installments, there is no text or no captions—only the poet's silence.

Biebl's photo pages are not autonomous art objects. In the magazine, they appear among many other photographs and texts. They blend in. Variations of the motifs of his photos—and his poetry—are found throughout the issues of the magazine. I will explore these in some detail, in the hope to see how Biebl's images of the tropics, ships, and oceans were part of contemporary visual culture, and how his poetic imagination was part of modern Czech intercourse between home and the world.

The first issue of *Home and the World* appeared on 25th February 1927, only seven weeks before Biebl's first photographs were published there. The magazine's title was likely inspired by Rabindranath Tagore's novel with the same title, published in Czech translation in 1920. The brief introduction in the first issue was most likely written by the magazine's editor, the writer Karel Nový.

> With all our powers we conquer the world. Means of transport devour distances, and wires proclaim today what happened in America, Hong Kong, Tokyo, or Cape Town yesterday. With each day our horizon expands, the world is becoming close at hand, our life multiplies itself at a stunning speed. The tasks of a magazine have increased hundredfold: with words and pictures to capture all that urgently affects our present, that interests, charms and enriches.[574]

With these initial sentences, we are drawn into a Czech fantasy of "conquering the world" with modern means of transport and "wires"; a dream of overcoming distances, broad horizons, stunning speed, and the sudden nearness of other continents. One senses a similar enthusiasm for modernity, technology, and travel, and perhaps the same anxiety about remaining at home, that one finds in Teige and some other avant-garde writers. The magazine is an instrument of the modernity it celebrates: it aims "with words and pictures to capture" the world. Pictures here turn out to be almost exclusively photographs, one of the celebrated modern technologies. Nový goes on to say that "we will bring images of daily life and significant phenomena and moments from all continents and all fields," and that the "modern pictorial and also literary" weekly is "meant for the broadest [spectrum of] social classes."

574 [Nový], "Úvodem," 1.

The "Introduction" itself is part of a larger visual-textual complex, which furthers Nový's message. Let me highlight just a few components of this "montage" in the first issue.[575] On page three, there is an article "O meziplanetárním cestování" (About interplanetary travelling):

> When half a century ago Jules Verne dreamed . . . no one in the world thought that the dream of this French novelist would become an actual technical project. Yet today people seriously talk about these ideas, which are no longer discussed by writers of utopias, but by astronomers, physicists and engineers. . . . The element of fantasy, which until recently dressed the question of cosmic travels in the misty colors of a beautiful dream, vanished, and in its place a distinct skeleton of a somber technical idea appeared.

The article describes how the "innocent" rocket commonly used in fireworks is the "archetype of one of those gigantic interplanetary argosies that will hurl themselves one day into the bottomless ocean of the universe." Utopian dreams of classic novels and adventures in the age of discovery (evoked by *koráb*, "argosy") are superimposed, like in photomontage, on a "somber technical idea" of future space travel. Jules Verne, who fantasized in one breath tropical and technological adventures, was also chosen by Teige, Seifert, and others as their model for modern poetry. On the border between dream and actuality, like in a film or child's imagination, a common firework rocket dissolves into a modern spaceship, which dissolves into an ancient gigantic argosy, while night sky and "bottomless ocean" merge into a single image. The text explodes the limits of travel and imagination and gives a cosmic dimension to both, so that other images and accounts of travel in the magazine, including those of Biebl, are juxtaposed to what is more fantastic than the most utopian novels and dreams: "the somber technical idea" and "actual technical project" of interplanetary travel.

On the next page, page four, there is the first installment of a translation of H. G. Wells' 1909 serialized novel, *Ann Veronica*, in which modernity shatters limits through a feminist rebellion against social conventions. In the climatic penultimate chapter of the novel, "In the Mountains," the heroine travels with her lover, a married man, away from home (Britain) and into the world, to the Alps, where tourism and free love blissfully unite.

By turning the page we are suddenly transported to different mountains (Figure 34). Page five features photographs of fantastic snowscapes, snow formations, cottages buried under snow, and trees in heavy snow garments—an otherworldly world in which snow is the only element. It is titled "Pohádka

575 The quotations in the paragraphs that follow, about the first issue of the periodical, are from *Domov a svět* 1, no. 1 (1927). Page numbers are in the text.

Pohádka krkonošská.

Naše hory se oděly panenským hávem. Jsme to v horách nebo kde? Neocitli jsme se snad v pohádce? Skoro! Člověku se zdá, že je dítětem a že se dívá na zázraky. A přece je to skutečný svět a jeho krása — strýček prosinec a leden nám ji vykouzlil pro potěšení očí a srdce. Pohleďme na strom! Pohleďme na chaty! Nejbujnější fantasie lidská by si nevymyslila lepšího oděvu. A jak se to dýchá v tomto vzduchu! A pitoresknost

mužských zimních je dokonalá. Ach, lyžařské nohy dostávají nemoc, t. zv. stehánia. Vzhůru na hory! Dotknouti se vrcholů, dosáhnouti míst nikým nedotčených, dobývati severních točen a potom s nich řítit dolů do údolí, litnout jako blesk, necítiti pod sebou sníh, zemi — letět a letět!

Krkonošská pohádka září — každý den jiná, ale stejně krásná a kouzelná, jako dětské snění. Vzhůru na hory!

Figure 34. "The Fairy Tale of Krkonoše," a photo page in the first issue of *Home and the World*, vol. 1, no. 1, 1927.

krkonošská" (The fairy tale of Krkonoše; Krkonoše is the highest mountain range in Bohemia). As with interplanetary travel, the accompanying texts move between fantasy and reality, finding one in the other:

> Are we in the mountains or where? Or do we perhaps find ourselves in a fairy tale? Almost! One feels that one is a child watching miracles. And yet it is the actual world and its beauty. . . . Up to the mountains!

Here in the humid heat of Singapore, the photos make me miss home. But this fantasy and this tourism are not simply domestic or earthbound. The text continues:

> To touch the peaks, to reach places never before touched by anyone, to conquer the "North Pole" and then whiz down into the valley, to fly like lightning, not to feel the snow, the earth underneath—to fly and fly!

The first of many such thematic photo pages in the magazine, this arctic fairy tale introduced the distinct format in which Biebl's tropical images would start appearing a few weeks later, in late winter.

The first issue begins to give us a sense of the kind of montage of images and texts where—as Raymond Williams wrote about television "flow"—"the elements of speed, variety and miscellaneity can be seen as organizing,"[576] but where certain motifs and desires recur, and loose, fragile, but insistent connections are formed across various texts and images.

The format of photo pages, introduced by the snowy landscape, occurs in almost every issue of the magazine, which makes Biebl's pages blend easily into the larger stream of imagery. However, they are unique in that they form a series across many issues, whereas other photo pages are either not serialized, or a topic stretches over only two or at most three issues.

In the eighth issue, on whose cover Biebl's "visual prey" was first advertised with the photos of a tiger and rubber trees, there is a photo page titled "Pekin" (Peking/Beijing). A caption informs us that the photos are by "Mr. Fraňek from Písek [a picturesque town in Bohemia], who has lived in China for a long time."[577]

In the next issue (no. 11), there are two photo pages from the European tour of the Singing Association of Prague Teachers. They pose in front of well-known sights in Paris, Reims, London, Brighton, Gdansk, Bucharest, Gothenburg ("teachers in front of the house where Bedřich Smetana lived"),

576 Raymond Williams, *Television: Technology and Cultural Form* (Hanover and London: University Press of New England, 1974), 99.

577 *Domov a svět* 1, no. 8 (1927): 11.

and Stockholm ("a view of a harbor with airplanes"). The pages are titled "FROM WANDERINGS ACROSS EUROPE,"[578] which chimes with "WANDERINGS ACROSS THE WORLD" in the middle of Biebl's photos of Singapore in the same issue. Also in the midst of Biebl's pictures from Singapore, there is an announcement: "The next issue of *Home and the World* will carry original snapshots by the Czech traveler Viktor Mussik." Thus, within the body of the Semarang photo page, as one element of its montage, the announcement points beyond it, leading the reader to see Biebl's photo page(s) as part of the larger montage that is the magazine.

In issue No. 12, the photo page "From the journey of Viktor Mussik across the Himalayas" is similar to Biebl's contributions, except for the superlatives: "The world's highest mountain range," "The most sacred temple in Sikkim," ". . . giant prayer mill."

In the following issue (no. 13), which includes Biebl's "Arrival in Java," there begins a three-part series of photo pages titled "From Mr. President's journey . . ." The latter two installments appear in no. 14—alongside Biebl's "Semarang"—and no. 15.[579] Although President Masaryk's visit to Palestine as an outspoken supporter of the creation of the Jewish state was of historical importance, the series is presented not primarily as an official visit, but the journey of a traveler in search of recreation and knowledge.

> Every year, Mr. President Masaryk travels out to the world, to refresh himself, to catch some sun, of which there is so little here in the North, and to breathe the air which moves so swiftly on the world's crossroads.[580]

> It is a journey of a scholar, who looks at excavations, be it in Egypt, Palestine, or Greece. His interest in archaeology is well known. And that he also carefully observes living people and their conditions, in short, that he observes the countries and lands through which he travels with the eye of a sociologist, can be taken for granted. [581]

Some of the pictures, such as a town street or a palm grove, could easily appear on Biebl's photo pages. A related photo page in issue no. 14 is titled "Struggle with Palestinian desert" and shows the settlements of Czechoslovak Jews and their hard life.[582]

In addition to many such photo pages that feature foreign lands, there are also those showing the homeland, including "The Fairy Tale of Krkonoše"

---

578 *Domov a svět* 1, no. 11 (1927): 8–9.
579 *Domov a svět* 1, no. 13 (1927): 3; no. 14 (1927): 15; no. 15 (1927): 3.
580 *Domov a svět* 1, no. 14 (1927): 15.
581 *Domov a svět* 1, no. 15 (1927): 3.
582 *Domov a svět* 1, no. 14 (1927): 3.

mentioned earlier. No. 17 is an issue dedicated to the boy scouts. Several photo pages show their activities in Czech forests and near rivers. Some show American Indian teepees, totems, and "chiefs": just as Czech winter mountains are dreamed into the North Pole, so Czech scouts dream themselves into "Indians." In the same issue, a photo page reports on the travels of the poet Karel Toman and the painter Jan Slavíček. It shows Slavíček's paintings of ships, harbors, and seaside towns in southern France, accompanied by Toman's verses—about home:

> I return under your faithful roof,
> a child again, O Home . . .[583]

One is never quite sure where one is and where one wants to be; except, perhaps, as Biebl writes, "on the border between the two worlds, where reality overflows into dream and dream into actuality"—which could be taken as a definition of the photograph. In ways that are akin to his poetry, in the magazine the dreams and realities of Singapore, Java, Marseille, Krkonoše, Czech "Indians," Czechoslovak Jews in Palestinian desert, interplanetary travel, palms, and snow all overflow one into the other.

This is true also about other images and texts, beyond the photo pages. An article in *Home and the World*, by the poet and Biebl's friend Jan Alda, suggests that

> our substitute/compensation (*náhrada*) for these exotic delights [of a holiday by the sea] are our rivers, streams and fishponds, festooned with willows and alder trees. With a bit of imagination, we can conjure a beach and palms even on the grassy slope by a village fishpond. . . . Swallows, airplanes of our sea, greet the sea for us![584]

In issue no. 13, there are these various images of the sea, palms and tropical islands: Biebl's photo page "Arrival in Java" with two photographs of beaches and tropical sea with palms and fishermen; a palm grove in the Holy Land on the Masaryk photo pages; Somerset Maugham's story "The Pacific Ocean"; and a report on flora in Sumatra, "The Paradise of Flowers." The cover of that issue is as unexpected as a metaphor in modern poetry (Figure 35). The full-page photo shows a small bathroom. A naked toddler (I must think of the white baby, next to Biebl's name, in "Arrival in Java") stands in a simple sheet-metal bathtub and observes the water that she is pouring from a metal watering can. The caption reads, "Children's spring play in Prague bathroom." Perhaps this, a small sunless interior space of a Prague flat, is (to borrow

583 *Domov a svět* 1, no. 17 (1927): 3.
584 Jan Alda, "Na pláži - v slunci, vodě a písku," *Domov a svět* 2, no. 29 (1928): 9.

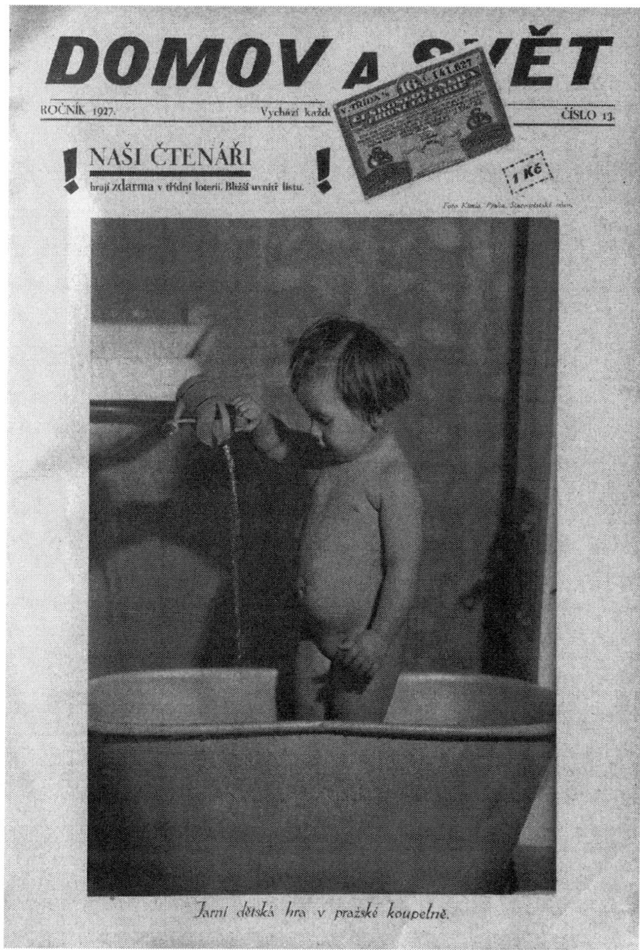

Figure 35. "Children's spring play in a Prague bathroom," the cover of an issue of *Home and the World*, vol. 1, no. 13, 1927. Biebl's photo page "Arrival in Java" appears in the same issue.

the title of the first part in *With the Ship*) the ultimate "enchanted spring" of the dreams of vast seas—equally so in the magazine "meant for the broadest [spectrum of] social classes" and in avant-garde poetry of the time.

Biebl's images of the ocean liner *Yorck* and his other photos of vessels and harbors appear alongside the argosies in the metaphors of the "interplanetary travel" as well as numerous photographs of modern ships. On a photo page of emphatically modern ships and ship engines, titled "Perfect machine—the ruler of the seas" (Figure 36), a brief text situates the pictures:

> Modern technology shortens distances to the greatest measure. The ruler of the seas is a machine, the ruler of the air is a machine. The machine, a perfect robot of human intelligence. Look, what a beautiful picture it forms! . . . Modern technology is modern poetry. Its shine, perfect planes and perfect, functional circles and lines are an unsen-

DOMOV A SVĚT 13

Dokonalý stroj — vládce moří.

Moderní technika zkracuje vzdálenosti světa na nejmenší míru. Vládcem moří je stroj, vládcem vzduchu je stroj. Stroj, dokonalý robot lidského důmyslu. Hle, jaký tvoří krásný obraz! První foto je ze strojovny moderního člunu — rozváděcí stěna a kontrolní stanice, pod ním motory a generátory, zřídla energie. Nahoře vpravo obrovský parník »Leviathan« v newyorském přístavě — posléze hlava lodi, kolo kormidelníkovo. — Moderní technika je moderní poesie: její lesk, dokonalé plochy a dokonalé účelné kruhy a linie jsou nesentimentální písní ke chvále člověka, jeho mozku, rukou, vůle a odvahy, jež všechno přemáhá.

Figure 36. "Perfect machine—the ruler of the seas." A photo page in *Home and the World*, vol. 1, no. 7, 1927.

timental song in praise of man, his brain, hands, will and courage, which overcome everything.[585]

Recall Teige's caption for a photograph of a ship in his text "Art Today and Tomorrow" quoted above (Figure 22)—the ship is "beautiful, like a modern painting," its "naked construction" has "all the virtues of an art work." Both in revolutionary avant-garde publications and magazines like *Home and the World*, the technology of modern ships was modern poetry.

Standing out among the images of modern ships in the magazine is the ocean-going vessel sailing under the Czechoslovak flag and manned by a

585 *Domov a svět* 1, no. 7 (1927): 13.

Czechoslovak crew, the *Legie* ("the legions"), seen in numerous photos—a floating island home in the middle of the world's oceans.

An ocean liner, with the caption "Luxurious fast-speed ship the *Empress* of France," is juxtaposed to a photo of the Taj Mahal. Titled "Social Journeys," it is an advertisement by the Canadian Pacific Railway Company for a tour of the world, including Ceylon, Sumatra, and Java. The text starts:

> Today the realization [*uskutečnění*] of an extensive travel plan is connected with thousands of obstacles and difficulties, constant hassle and disappointment, so that often the beauties and delights of travel do not outweigh all these inconveniences. All inconveniences entirely disappear when someone else takes care of the preparations for the trip for you, of the research and the realization [*uskutečnění*] of the whole travel plan.[586]

The promised separation of the "beauties and delights" of travel from its "obstacles and difficulties, constant hassle and disappointment" calls to mind cinema and travel photography. Yet the advertisement goes a step further. It promises "realization"—*uskutečnění*, from *skutečnost*, "reality, actuality." Like the article on interplanetary travel, like Biebl's poetic travels, it breaks the dike between dreams and actuality, stimulating fantasy (even for those who cannot afford to travel) by a vision of turning it into actuality.

Other advertisements navigate between dream and actuality in other ways. The last double page of one issue, for example, features advertisements for several kinds of tea and tea margarine (Figure 37).[587] Long before the 1920s, tea was a part of Czech fantasies about the Orient and about the English. In 1873, after describing the hard work of poor Chinese coolies he met in America, Josef Václav Sládek thinks of tea:

> Perhaps this image will greatly surprise those who imagined this Asian as a mandarin or a wealthy man emanating prosperity, whom we commonly see on the boxes of strawberry leaves boiled and processed God knows how many times, which are sent to us from England as genuine Chinese tea.[588]

In *Home and the World*, the tea advertisements are juxtaposed to a text about tea, which invites the reader to an intoxicated fantasy of home:

> When frost draws flowers on the windows of our homes and freezing wind frolics in the streets, it is the right time for a cup of tea. It brings us greetings from lands flooded

586 *Domov a svět* 1, no. 25 (1927): 11.
587 *Domov a svět* 2, no. 4 (1928): 14–15.
588 Sládek, *Americké obrázky* 1:205–06.

Figure 37. A page dedicated to the discussion and advertisement of tea, in *Home and the World*, vol. 2, no. 4, 1928.

with sun, light and the fragrances of the gardens and palaces of the Far East. . . . At that moment we find ourselves in the empire on which the sun never sets and a smile of lively joy settles on our lips.[589]

In these vaguely imperial hallucinations, which also feature hazy fantasies of gentle Japanese and slim British women—evidently the Czechs desire them all—this text promises, this time not the actuality of a voyage, but the experience of home—like the travel "in the warmth of the cinema" that "borders on magic," or like looking at photos in a magazine at home. At home, courtesy of the ship that carries tea and coffee, we can have an actual physical sensation—the fragrance, the taste—of distant lands. Like in Biebl's poetry,

589 *Domov a svět* 2, no. 4 (1928): 14.

actuality sparks imagination (with the helpful guidance of the magazine) and we "find ourselves" in distant, sun-flooded, fragrant gardens.

The rapid overcoming of distance is also evoked by a Lipton advertisement: "Direct from the tea garden to the teapot," it claims in English. It shows an Indian man with a tray of tea leaves standing on the seashore, with a sailing ship visible in the background. Other advertisements on the double-page offer a Leica camera, highlighting its small size, ideal for travel; and fur coats—for the readers of this winter issue no doubt as desirable as hot tea.

On 5th May, 1928, the last of Biebl's photo pages appeared.[590] Among Biebl's photos, there is one of a ship, with five white men posing in white suits. The accompanying text, which concludes the series of photo pages, and which apparently was not composed by Biebl but by Nový (it speaks of the poet in the third person), describes the "world of heavy labor and white people's chase after mammon" in the colonies, and refers to the photo of the ship as "the ship that imports tea and coffee."

This reference, in the middle of Biebl's pictures, to a book of his avant-garde poetry (published a few months earlier), is just one more cue to see the close affinity, continuity and overflowing between his verbal poetry and his photographs, and between his work and the wider culture of the 1920s Czechoslovakia. The pictures exist together in unlikely juxtapositions and interpenetrations of views as if from a speeding train, a bold film montage of snow and tropical sun, home and the world, dreams and actuality, fur coats and tea gardens, space shuttles and ancient argosies, "Indians" and cherry trees, Java and the North Pole, the peaks of the Alps and ocean waves, all interconnected by ships, planes, cinema, photographs, and modern poetry. In all this, we still recognize Biebl; in this loud world, we still hear his silences. The poet moves, less with the burning enthusiasm of Teige, instead searching more quietly, hesitatingly, a dazed "little citizen," travelling farther and deeper than most, at one moment absorbed in daydreams of travelers, tiger hunters, and travel magazines, at another moment smiling as we stare in awe at a non-existent "elephant resting in Javanese landscape," at yet another moment asking us to pause and gaze at a mound of coconuts that look like human heads, a crumbling colonial house, or a white baby trampling on a grave and attended by a silent, unspeaking Javanese servant.

590 *Domov a svět* 2, no. 18 (1928): 7.

PICTURE POSTCARDS

Biebl's photo pages resemble multiview postcards, which typically represent a place, region, or perhaps a ship through multiple shots (such as Slavětín and the *Yorck* in Figures 4 and 38, respectively). In other ways as well, the pictures of faraway places in *Home and the World*, as they trace and evoke a particular traveler's journey for people at home, are akin to postcards.

In describing a picture of a town that is part of his picture poem "Greetings from the Trip" (Figure 19), Teige does not speak of the picture's subject (town), but rather of "a postcard." He introduces the work as "a touristic poem, a reflection of travel lyricism," where the postcard is one of the "typical photogenic elements," "hints which should suffice to evoke impressions of an illustrativeness unreachable by words." Rather than merely showing a town, the postcard evokes travel—similarly to the ship's flag, a photo of a starry sky, a travel map, binoculars, and a letter that are all part of the "tour-

Figure 38. A postcard featuring the *Yorck*, the ship on which K. Biebl sailed from Genoa to Singapore, 1907.

istic poem."[591] Moreover, each "picture poem" (Figures 19 and 20) resemble multiview postcards.

Czech modern poets had a thing for postcards. In the year that Biebl travelled to Java, Nezval's collection *Básně na pohlednice* (Poems on postcards) appeared.[592] A year earlier, František Halas, another prominent poet, published an essay titled "Pohlednice" (Postcards). "Through [the postcard's] silent contrast, even on the tumultuous intersections of a metropolis it evokes an image of the snowy Alps . . ." A collection of postcards is "miniature waxworks [*panoptikum*] of all the beauties of the world . . . all for a few cents." He calls for modern, mass-produced postcards, "above all, photomontage picture poems."[593]

Browsing through the correspondence of Biebl and other modern poets and artists, one notices that they enjoyed sending postcards to each other. The sense of fun can be sensed from a "magnificent postcard" that in 1923 Teige and Honzl sent from northern Bohemia to Seifert in Prague (Figure 39). The picture shows an old-fashioned courting scene in the theater-like setting of an atelier, with roses in foreground and a romantic representation of an Arcadian landscape in the background. Teige and Honzl wrote "Da²=dada" between the man and the woman; DISK● ("disc," the name of the Devětsil periodical founded that year by Teige and Seifert) in upper right corner; ZDE ("HERE") below the man's hand so that now the man appears to point at the marble bench, and one is made to wonder about his intentions; and JAZZ on a romantic pavilion in the landscape, turning it into a jazz venue. They amended the woman by adding a moustache and a pipe, and drew a plane in the sky above—with a cloud of smoke behind it, it seems. Under the cloying verses originally on the postcards— "Little rose, why are you wilting? / And you, our love / whether you will not slacken"—they drew an elephant, among the trees next to the pavilion. Clearly, sending a postcard can be a seriously Dadaist, poetist fun.

I have already mentioned the postcards that Biebl sent home during the Great War, including some showing palms and veiled Muslim women, who would keep reappearing in his poetry (Figure 7). In later years, Biebl travelled to the same places, remembering the war, and sending more postcard home. One of them, sent to Nezval in 1932, shows an old cemetery of Sephardic Jews in Sarajevo. Biebl wrote:

---

591 Teige, "Obrazy," 542.

592 Nezval, *Básně na pohlednice* (Prague: Aventinum, 1926). When another artist of the generation, Adolf Hoffmeister, travelled much later to China, he titled his travel book *Postcards from China*. In the preface, he writes about the sadness of "all that there is not and cannot be," in the postcard-like book. *Pohlednice z Číny* (Prague: Československý spisovatel, 1954), 8.

593 František Halas, "Pohlednice," *Pásmo* 1, no. 7–8 (January 1925): 11–12.

Figure 39. A postcard sent in 1923 by Karel Teige and Jindřich Honzl to Jaroslav Seifert. Archive of the Museum of Czech Literature, Prague.

23/VI 1932
Greetings from Sarajevo.
Graveyards are everywhere
the most beautiful.
Yours,
Kosťa Biebl

One thinks of Nezval's book of short poems *Nápisy na hroby* (Inscriptions on graves), published alongside his *Poems on Postcards*—the two cycles were originally conceived as two parts of a single work, at a time when Nezval was "seduced by the objectness of life and things."[594] There are many graves and graveyards in Biebl's poetry; as well as letters, which are often associated with death, as in "Smrt v dopise" (Death in the letter):

A letter arrives
from a faraway foreign land unawares;
when the hand tears the envelope,
one does not know yet

594 Nezval, *Z mého života*, 152–53.

that someone dear is passing away
in the white letter.[595]

A letter, like a photograph, like a grave, embodies a person's absence—making her hauntingly but physically present, even in not being here. From "Japonský dřevoryt" (Japanese woodblock print):

there is too much of you in the white letter.

I couldn't crumple it in my hand,
I would feel
that under its wings I press a dove,
which dies breathlessly.[596]

A few postcards have survived from Biebl's Javanese journey. The texts are brief. As in Teige's "Greetings from the Trip," the postcards above all evoke travel. Evoke, but also embody, in the way of archaeological finds—the photographs are the material traces of distant lands, now present here as if despite time and space; they were held in the hand and inscribed on the other side of the world with thoughts of home; and they themselves travelled across the seas, on ships and trains, to bring home their greeting. As remembrances of home and friends at home, they are like Biebl's metaphors that stretch hands across oceans.

From Port Said, Biebl wrote to Josef Hora on a postcard with an image of a lighthouse, with a few ships visible in the harbor. To these elements of poetism, the minimal text adds "African soil." This is more than a childhood dream of Africa—jungles, deserts, lions, antelopes, elephants. The conjured earthy physicality of "soil" is like the materiality of the postcard, an actual object that actually came from Africa, and that one holds in hand—even as a poetist playfulness persists. In its brevity, the message stirs the silence just enough to spark imagination.

4/11. 26
Dear Hora,
Greetings from African soil.
Yours,
Kosťa Biebl

595 Biebl, *Věrný hlas*, 21.
596 Biebl, *Věrný hlas*, 22.

Figure 40. A postcard sent by K. Biebl to Josef Hora, 1926.

One wonders if this is one of the postcards from Port Said mentioned in Biebl's travelogue. "I bought so many postcards that whole Prague does not have as many inhabitants."[597]

In Singapore, Biebl wrote a message on a postcard with a photo of elephants with mahouts:

> 26/XI. 26
> Christmas greetings from Singapore.
> The journey was at times hard, but we are good. Last week is ahead of us. Regards to all friends. Yours, Kosťa Biebl

The Christmas greetings is dated 26. November. It happens across a fracture in time, introduced by travel. The text is all travel, a quick glimpse of it: the present position, past journey, and future plans. The postcard is a trace of travel in another way as well: it was written in Singapore, but most likely bought in Ceylon, and, according to the postal stamp, sent from Semarang in Java— "via Genoa," the address specifies—to Prague.

597 Biebl, *Cesta na Jávu*, 27.

Hora received another postcard from Biebl, this time showing (in the words of the postcard's caption), "A Javanese food seller—Djocja [i.e., Yogyakarta]" (Figure 40). The photographer might have conceived of the "Javanese food seller" as a touristic/ethnographic curiosity, but one could also see in it ordinary working people, like in some of Biebl's photos in *Home and the World*. His message on the postcard foregrounds this perception, and makes the photo evoke much more. He was in Java at the time of major communist anti-colonial revolts, and, according to his accounts at least, he was under surveillance and repeatedly interrogated by the colonial authorities. Biebl wrote on the postcard:

3/XII. 26
Greetings from the tropics
  From Kosťa Biebl
There is unrest —

The first line sounds like "Greetings from African soil," but the last three words, written in smaller, hushed letters, create a different silent contrast—an ominous hint of social unrest, followed by a long dash, *pomlčka, mlčení*. It is an uneasy silence, as if the poet was afraid to say more. After the poetic lighthouse and exotic Africa of his previous postcards, it is also something like a return to reality, a return to the ground. But recall also Nezval's *Dispatch on Wheels*, a burlesque framed as a message, a news of revolution, sent from the colonies.

To Nezval, Biebl sent a postcard a few days later. The photograph showed Javanese women in sarongs bathing in a river and washing laundry. He wrote:

    6/XII. 26
  Slávku,[598]
  Good-bye, we will
talk a lot.
  Greeting you
    Your Kosťa Biebl

The message starts with *na shledanou* (lit., "till we meet again"), the equivalent of the English "good-bye," as if the writer wanted to end the message at the point it begins. With the "we will talk a lot," it extends the silence, for there is too much to say.

598 Informal form of Nezval's first name.

On his return voyage, he wrote a postcard with just one phrase: "Greetings from India as an apology for long silence [*mlčení*], Yours, Kosťa Biebl."[599]

A postcard is a mute yet overflowing sign and physical trace of the writer's absence, his travels, the poetic performance of sending, and the distance the object itself has crossed. Aside from the technologies of writing and photography, which are forms of space and time travel, there is the added magic of the postal service, whose "functional poetry"[600] is that of ship and train schedules. Biebl's postcards, too, are a "continuation" of his poetry, as he said about illustrations of his planned *Vajang*.

599 Text of postcard from 10. January 1927 published in Slabý, *Potkávání*, 63.
600 Halas, "Pohlednice," 11.

SNAPSHOTS AND REFLECTIONS: POETRY | TRAVEL | PHOTOGRAPHY | DEATH

What we have of Biebl's poetry, and what we know about his journey, are only fragments. One of them is the text "Ing. Baer," unpublished in the poet's lifetime. I would like the fragment to introduce what may not quite be a conclusion, but a final series of snapshots, my final reflections on the mirror of his poetry and his silence, as it continues to reflect after death.

Ing. Baer

Until my death I will be grateful to the old Dutch lady that introduced me to Ing. Baer. I was with a small company at the wedding of a Javanese princess and in the evening we sat in the local club. I will never forget that slovenly manner with which he liked to enter into people's consciousness. He burst in unexpectedly, boastfully proud of the red mud on his planter's shoes; and, can you believe it, he intentionally did not close the door so that people could see—the rain and the night! So that he would show what he soaked up and where he came from! He spoke somewhat lazily and was wringing his sleeves at the same time; from them the water of tall damar trees was falling.

"Sir, what a ride that was!" and with that he uttered his whole life.

His plantation was almost three hundred kilometers away. He had some business in Wonosobo, so he took a trip to Solo!

"Will you come with me?" he said unexpectedly.

"Where to?"

"Why, . . ." and he spat on the parquet floor, so as not to finish a thought unnecessarily. He did not understand certain distinctions. Such as between the porch of his planter's hut and this Dutch society. He would come to the city only to stop by; he offended many, to some he was the object of ridicule, others were fascinated by him—if for nothing else, because of the red mud on his planter's shoes.

In any case, everything occurred as a matter of course, according to yet little understood laws of inner necessity, concealed by the noise of unforeseen circumstances, which we claim to be the fruits of good luck, but which may be the bitter fruit of coherent and dramatic movements directed by a whole headquarters of forces whose black hands move the secret levers of human courage; and perhaps, I do not hesitate to say, they took charge of driving our little Fiat, which plunged forward into the furious night—despite an extreme lethargy of the ignition, wet from the rain—after a lengthy hesitation agreeing to join its rusty fate with ours, which it apparently did not hold in high esteem.

I don't like unnecessary thunder, but I do love a voice which no one can silence! I love the storm, this high-voltage[601] pathetic symphony, when trees lick electricity like the sheep lick the salt they need! We drive on an asphalt road into the mountains. It's raining! It stopped. It's raining! With each curve, lined with the certain death of deep precipices, always a new storm. O night, who sparkle on my forehead! Lightning slides down into green abysses, crosses its arms with a waterfall and engraves a deep furrow on the forehead of an old memory. It also throws light on the intonation of words that I once misunderstood, uttered under other circumstances by a woman who has already died; and we drive over smooth asphalt over torn leaves, the chalices of flowers, and other sewage of life. In the glow of the headlights we pass lengthening arabesques of escaping snakes, among whom some, the stronger and bigger ones, assume the fighting pose of titans and perish in an unequal battle, dying with the poison of hate on their tongues, dying like the brains of calmly sprawled frogs, bluntly crushed like gravel on the road by the ever rising car; and we drive . . . where? One cannot finish that thought on this modern highway, lost in the jungle, where finally the sense of superlatives, so often misused by poets, manifests itself to you, on the slopes of an active volcano, swelling with the horror of its terrible yeast, which grows and grows until it becomes the most beautiful poem—but only for those who are at least twenty miles away; and we drive in living rain, in that scarlet rain of flying ants, crawling out of the mouths and eye sockets of terrible trees, trees-beggars; and we drive in living rain, in that scarlet rain of flying ants, falling from the sleeves of curious trees-widows, walking unstoppably to the graveyard; and we drive in living rain, in that scarlet rain of flying ants, wiped off powerlessly in desperation from faces stricken with leprosy; and we drive over millions owlet moths[602] and mayflies, on the snow of their only just extinguished life, which forms into dangerous snowdrifts, where suddenly the wheels, strangely grinding, go into a skid in sticky minced meat, sad and silky; and we ride into the mysteries of disturbing details, visionary clearings, which only the lightning can accomplish, the teacher of philosophers and poets. It shows the jungle in a forceful and unusual light. It shows only a part and you must imagine the whole, ever veiled in darkness. Again it slides into the bushes, illuminates darknesses never seen, and remains hanging on my retina! I see it at night, I see it during the day! I see it always even after years, that golden liana, as it abseils down.[603]

Bright electric lighting, asphalt roads, interiors increasingly isolated from the outside world, a particular kind of order and cleanliness, and "certain distinctions" were the anxious obsessions of late colonialism.[604] Baer

601 *Napětí* - voltage, tension, suspense.
602 *Můra*: owlet moth; nightmare.
603 Biebl, *Cesta na Jávu*, 75–77.
604 Rudolf Mrázek, *Engineers of Happy Land: Technology and Nationalism in a Colony* (Princeton: Princeton University Press, 2002).

speaks in fragments, does not "understand certain distinctions," brings mud on his shoes into the club, and opens the door to the darkness outside. As the car rushes "on this modern highway, lost in the jungle," poetizing and traveling become one. And what of "certain distinctions"?

We see Java through disturbing details caught from the window of a speeding car, revealed by lightning that illuminates fractions of the world and of the subconscious as the wall between inside and outside crumbles; details haunting like photographs, like inscriptions on graves, like this fragment of Biebl's work for me now. This poetry is entangled with death. Again the search for poetic cognition struggles with any kind of colonialism, its own above all, as it cuts through distinctions, reveals fragments that defy coherent narratives, and shows the inescapable violence inherent in any speaking and seeing, even the poet's, as he sits in the planter's car that allows him to see the world only as it crushes, on the smooth asphalt of a colonial highway, millions of living beings—where even the power of nature's "most beautiful poem" results in destruction and death.

The poet's personal symbols return like the visions and signs of dreams: "the giant poisonous snake" from his photograph; the poet's nightmarish sense that in Java with his every steps he destroys life, by "stupid actions" (as when he kicks away a frog) or unintentionally, inescapably (the "soil beneath my feet seemed everywhere soft and alive . . . one does not know what is a banana peel, what is a frog, or even a snake"); the persistent "silence of millions" that he hears in the primeval forest, even where it has been cleared; one recalls the Javanese man, who holds and feeds a frog, "and no-one in the world can swear / that it is not his dead child."

On the back side of one of the two typescript versions of "Ing. Baer," Biebl wrote a poem in pencil, titled "Světoběžníci" (Globetrotters). I translate a fragment:

Had I not interrupted my journey
from Lisbon to Moscow
I would not have met you in Paris
at quite an unusual hour
You walked along the Seine
I sent you a long letter from Montevideo
in return for your brief note from Genoa
Remember me when you will be in the jungles of Sumamangli[605]
just like I did that time when I was there without you
and like this time when you will not be with me

605 A place in Java.

when you see Merapi[606]
and those palm groves behind the pasangrahan[607]
at Borobudur
I will probably travel to Japan
We could arrange a meeting in Singapore
It is on the way for both of us
when we are on our way back to Europe
How beautiful it would be if we sailed together across the Indian Ocean
I love to stand behind the chimney at night when an albatross
shines like a mirage above the bridge
and flies and flies over the prairies of lead waters
with superhuman loyalty
If you won't be God-knows-where
You always raved about Sumatra
Bali is not far either
and I have never been to the Philippines
and I also don't know if my letter arrives on time[608]

The poem, whose world is smooth like asphalt, contrasts with "Ing. Baer" like day and night. And yet, the two texts are like the two surfaces of the paper on which they are written. The bright emptiness of the poem is the other side of the "darknesses never seen" of the prose. Both texts illuminate fragments of the same world, seen through the unsettled eyes of emphatically modern travelers, who move and dream at disorienting speeds and see—like in Biebl's poetry—through fragmentary, fleeting glimpses, as if from the windows of a speeding car or train, where they find themselves by what appears to be coincidence; or as if intoxicated by photographs or postcards from a journey.

In Biebl's poetics, I sense fragile, loose, but insistent connections between a number of movements, desires or realms (imagine them scattered like the photos on Biebl's photo page, in no regular pattern, juxtaposed, and sometimes overlapping): poetry, travel, photography, and death. Four mirrors reflecting each other. Sometimes the mirrors of travel and photography reflect poetry; at another time they are visions of death; at another time poetry takes the form of photography or travel; and behind it all, a search in the darkness for glimpses and mirrorings of what is hidden or buried, silent or silenced.

606 A sacred volcano in Central Java.
607 *Pasanggrahan:* guesthouse (Javanese).
608 Biebl, *Dílo*, 5:352–53.

Two poems juxtaposed in the collection *Mirror of Night* usher us into this dark hall of mirrors, in the air of the 1930s. The first poem has the same title as the book. This is Part One:

Sometimes at night
But also during the day
Fleeting views open for you

Look the train of things is gaining speed
And from its windows it throws colors

The sight of your psyche doesn't last longer
Than the white explosion of magnesium

It radiates through itself

A Mohammedan woman without a veil
Again disappeared unrecognized
In time that is shorter
Than any reminiscence in a dream

Lightning would be the tree of eternity
In the abysses of fleetingly glimpsed universes
Where poets hurl themselves where painters go
Thirsty hunters of those fractions of seconds
Full of wings and light[609]

In Czech, the same word, *blesk*, denotes both lightning and the camera's flash. Magnesium, which produces brilliant light when ignited, was used in photographic flashes. One recognizes the "Mohammedan woman without a veil," the flash of veiling-unveiling, from the poet's travel writing, postcards, and photographs.

Poetry is "the desire for cognition." Lightning is "the teacher of philosophers and poets." In the "Mirror of Night," the poet hurls himself into dark abysses as he thirsts to know "fleetingly glimpsed universes." The brevity of those glimpses is like, but exceeds, the mystery of dreams— "shorter than any reminiscence in a dream." Yet they are brief on a cosmic scale, exceeding the limits of human perception and consciousness—in those universes, "lightning would be the tree of eternity." To evoke these worlds, to evoke

609 Biebl, *Zrcadlo noci*, n.p. Also in Biebl, *Dílo*, 3:78.

poetic desire and cognition, the poet turns again to glimpses of travel and photography—a speeding train, photographic flash, a Mohammedan woman—as well as lightning, such as the one he saw from a car in Javanese jungle, "ever veiled in darkness."

If Part One of "Mirror of Night" can be read as an image of poetic desire and cognition, in Part Two there is a fear of poetic vision, of what appears in the "night for which one lacks developer" (*vývojka* means specifically "photographic developer"). "Who would have enough courage," the part starts. Freud joins the Mohammedan woman in Part V, which ends:

There is no guarantee what will come to light
And what will still remain
Behind the wall that is *our continuous attention*[610]

One might think here of Walter Benjamin's point about photography that

> it is another nature which speaks to the camera rather than to the eye: "other" above all in the sense that a space informed by human consciousness gives way to a space informed by the unconscious. . . . we have no idea at all what happens during that fraction of a second when a person actually takes a step.[611]

Biebl's poem ends:

Black lilies walk hand in hand
Before all abysses close themselves

Reflections of death, glimpsed in "Mirror of Night," in the darkness of abysses where "poets hurl themselves," come to the fore in the collection's next poem, titled "Když voní arnika" (The fragrance of arnica; or, more literally, When arnica exudes fragrance). In Part One, we inhale the fragrance and freshness of flowers and feel nature's eternal procreation. Only in Parts Two and Three do we realize that on this spring day we are in a graveyard. I recall that photograph of germinating coconuts that look like human skulls. Here I translate Part Two of the poem. (According to the myth of Pyramus and Thisbe, the gods made mulberries blood-red in memory of the lovers deaths.)

---

610 Biebl, *Zrcadlo noci*, n.p. Also in Biebl, *Dílo*, 3:80.

611 Walter Benjamin, "Little History of Photography," *Selected Writings*, ed. Michael W. Jennings (Cambridge: Belknap, 1999), 2:510.

A dead woman looks from the mulberries
You guess nearly nothing
Only from the force of the air
And flashes of those earrings

Like in a hall of mirrors
Without a smile and wordlessly
You meet each other endlessly
In the magic glow of black marble stones[612]

A dead woman concealed in the darkness of the mirror of night; the desire to meet the silent dead again; one may recall—if only to escape this poem—the scene in his film scenario, where the dead in the photographs on graves come alive when the poet looks at them through a glass and the graveyard is for that moment transformed into a magnificent garden full of people celebrating life.

In Part Three of the poem, we find ourselves in a maze of grave stones, although we are at the same place as in Part One, the place of nature's *poesis*, the fragrant arnica and roses. Poesis and death mirror each other; the desire for poetic cognition and the desire for the dead mirror each other. "Unusual friendships:" opposites recognizing themselves in each other. The desire to strike fire, life, from the gravestones mirrors the poet's desire to catch "those fractions of seconds / full of wings and light" in the darkness "where poets hurl themselves." The darkness of poetry mirrors the darkness, the ultimate unknown, of death: it is in the graveyard that "the coolness of night falls / of that mystery that betrays the metaphor."

In the maze of stones the coolness of night falls
Of that mystery that betrays a metaphor
How to spark the weeping
Of the living from dead stones[613]

Over the tears of female saints with crumpled halos
Rain has wiped verses' golden letters away
And it's wiped away everything even shyness from dead faces
As it rains on crosses and on names

---

612 Biebl, *Zrcadlo noci*, n.p. Also in Biebl, *Dílo*, 3:82.

613 I feel particularly unhappy with the translation of these two lines. A more literal translation might be: "How to strike [*vykřesat*, to strike fire from stones by hitting them against each other] the weeping of living human creatures from dead blocks."

What has become of the faith of the artless scholar
Away with women's beauty there lies the poet's grave
There color flows down from the painter's brush
That which is concealed in the background stands out the most[614]

I can neither translate nor explain this poem well—and increasingly I sense the violent brightness and loudness of my constant explaining, "the wall that is *our continuous attention*"—yet the sensation it gives me is plain and familiar like the countryside near Biebl's village. I think of Biebl's family grave, modern and plain, which does not stand out among other similar graves, and lacks the charm of a few older graves in the village graveyard, some of which are adorned with weathered statues of angels and saints. There are no photographs on the grave. Instead, on the vertical gravestone of black polished marble, as I stand silently before it, I see my reflection, invasive, seemingly out of place, behind the names of Biebl and his family members and a fragment of Biebl's poem, engraved in the black mirror. He wrote it in memory of his relative, a pilot who fell to his death three years before him. On the white horizontal gravestone below, there is a large black cross.

Over a church tower an airplane flies
And casts a shadow like a black cross
On the grave in which a young pilot lies
On the grave in which you dear Péťa dream

About distances that opened themselves
About heights in which you know how to fly
Daring hero of night flights
Will you overcome our grief?

Poems and graves are curious friends. As I stand before one, a grave or a poem, or both at once as with Biebl's grave, for a moment at least I like to keep silent, to listen and not to think, and let *them* reflect—not out of respect, grief, or sentimentality, but because of my desire to sense, "almost not guess," what is concealed and revealed in the fragmentary reflections of poems and graves and "behind the wall that is *our continuous attention*," in the abysses where poets hurl themselves, those daring heroes of night flights.

———

614 Biebl, *Zrcadlo noci*, n.p. Also in Biebl, *Dílo*, 3:83.

Both the grave and the poem—all his writing—are fragmentary remains, the shards of a mirror, the briefest flashes of light, that reveal and conceal, veil and unveil, the poet's absence, his silence—so that "that which is concealed in the background stands out the most."

Before his death, Biebl burned much of his unpublished poetry; no doubt he discarded much more over his lifetime. Some "harmful" writings and possessions disappeared when agents of the Ministry of Interior searched his flat immediately after his death. Much of his remaining papers, notebooks, and letters, used or reported by the few scholars who wrote about Biebl over the past decades, have been lost, disappeared, or were stolen from archival and other collections, as scholars and archivists know. "Yes, Biebl is popular," said one archivist.

When Biebl's friends and acquaintances talked about him, frequently they mentioned that he was an excellent storyteller, regretting that most of his stories, and his way of telling them, are lost forever. Zdeněk K. Slabý, the editor of Biebl's collected writings, recalled:

> He told stories about his travels and we were carried to lands about which we had previously read about only in his *Plancius*, and we saw with his eyes. Perhaps that is why we perceived with so much feeling the fragrance and color of those countries, perhaps that is why we saw before us with such lifelikeness their inhabitants. Biebl, the poet and the storyteller . . . How could you know where one is interwoven with the other, where the poet ends and where begins a captivating word-painter of natural beauties of the colonies and their struggle against the imperialists?[615]

Even in Biebl's poetry and prose, one often senses reminiscences of children's adventure novels and old travel accounts, and hears a storyteller's voice. The prose text "O tropických nocích" (About tropical nights) begins: "Perhaps another time, if you would like, I will tell you something about Java during the day."[616] Wolker wrote a short story "following word for word"—according to Kalista—a narrative from the Great War that Biebl told his friends in a Prague café, and Kalista writes that his story "A Man and Three Elephants," too, was Biebl's "dream of a journey," that Kalista "captured" in writing.[617] And yet, these echoes and shadows of the narrator's voice are no consolation, no substitution for listening to Biebl.

Karel Konrad wrote several pages about Biebl's impromptu storytelling in cafés.

615 Z. K. Slabý, "Konstantin Biebl a mladí," *Za Konstantinem Bieblem*, 41–42.

616 Biebl, *Cesta na Jávu*, 52.

617 "V prvním únorovém týdnu . . .," 1961. Zdeněk Kalista, Museum of Czech Literature.

His lyrical gayness, which was conditioned by his powerful and restless fantasy and his tendency to invent remarkable tales and elevate them with further fabrications (behind which however there was always something nearly real or observed from reality), had a seductive grace: you were smiling perhaps not only at the tale itself, but at the manner and quality with which it was presented, when the waggery and clownery acquired a psychological depth of folk wisdom and when psychology wore poetic clown's bells.... These were moments of magical entertainment.[618]

The well-known actor Eduard Kohout, admired for his recitation of Biebl's poetry, recalled:

Recently he returned from Java and it was as if his spirit was still there. He was telling us stories about it in his Slavětín house, where leeks grew on the flat roof, and all around the cones of Middle Mountains were heaping up in a fantastic manner. His memories sounded like Oriental music, he was reciting rather than speaking. He gave me a Javanese puppet and this poem.[619]

Marie Pujmanová, another writer of Biebl's generation, wrote in her obituary:

You were always so shy, and yet you told me more in one hour than close relatives had in years. Life experiences were folded in you like in a fan painted with magically beautiful and horrible scenes, and looking at it one was astonished.[620]

Many times, Biebl's storytelling was heard on radio. Only fragments of his notes, drafts, and recordings are preserved.[621]

In so many ways, Biebl's life and work is present for us through "the mysteries of disturbing details," fleeting views from a train's window, a few silent photographs. The lightning "shows the jungle in a forceful and unusual light. It shows only a part and you must imagine the rest, ever veiled in darkness."

"Rain has wiped verses' golden letters away"—can one not mourn the loss? And yet, is not this darkness, this silence, precisely what Biebl's poetry (un)veils through its brief flashes of light? In *Mirror of Night*, immediately after "The Fragrance of Arnica" and its image of the poet's grave and verses

618 Karel Konrád, "O Konstantinu Bieblovi," 72–3.

619 Eduard Kohout, *Divadlo aneb snář* (Prague: Odeon 1975), 136.

620 Marie Pujmanová, "Drahý Kosťo," *Za Konstantinem Bieblem*, 19.

621 For instance, the text "Where we would like to be," from which I quoted previously, is the only surviving fragment (transcribed from a recording) from four travel narratives presented by the poet on the radio; the text "Night in Wonosobo," similarly, is a fragment from the original "Three nights in Wonosobo." See notes by Slabý, in Biebl, *Dílo*, 5:455.

erased by rain, Biebl placed his poem "Památce Karla Hynka Máchy" (To the memory of Karel Hynek Mácha). It begins:

In the abundance of His robe
Above us inexhaustible night

You will feel the pressure of transformation entering
The force that fills those who sleep
In that rich silence[622]

That, too, one feels, even as "rain wiped verses' golden letters away."

It seems that Biebl never mourned his lost notebook from his journey to Java:

> if it is not the poet's task to present a precise list of all rivers that he crossed . . . he would rather approach the writing of a book, provided he wants to do that, much later, at a time when he is lucky enough not to be able to find the notebook that he lost somewhere on the ship on his way back, when he cannot remember anymore the names of . . . I approach the writing of the book . . . with the aim to capture the air of Java rather than her firm land, the fragrance of flowers rather than her botanics.[623]

Biebl's uncle and mentor, the poet Arnošt Ráž, died of tuberculosis. Biebl's two eulogies, inspired by a profound admiration, are as much eulogies to silence, to poetry that does not insist on immortality. "As if I saw the row of eyes raised in surprise: Ráž? But we have never heard of him!"[624] And yet, Biebl writes, in his eyes Ráž was equal to the most famous Czech poets. After publishing his first two books of poems, Ráž stopped publishing.

> He wrote only for himself on scraps of paper, on old envelopes, in pencil, in handwriting intentionally undecipherable, so that no one could read after him. After his death, we (with Zdeněk Kalista) found many such poems, where not even one in ten words could be deciphered. He read many poems to his closest friends and then he usually burned them.[625]

Biebl admired both his uncle's poetry and his silence—if the two are separate at all. It is—and it is not—the silence of untranslated Javanese words in Biebl's Czech poems, of photographs on graves, of snapshots in *Home and the*

622 Biebl, *Zrcadlo noci*, n.p. Also in Biebl, *Dílo*, 3:84.
623 Biebl, *Dílo*, 5:250–51.
624 Biebl, *Dílo*, 5:172.
625 Biebl, *Dílo*, 5:176.

World, of the film running outside the windows of a speeding car, of his very particular incarnation of the generation's desire "to make poetry with life"; the "silence of the millions" and the silence of the dead; and also the silence of the poet's journey away from home, away from words.

Yet the poet never travelled easily, and he never quite left poetry, never quite stopped writing poems, "the poet's cognition"—perhaps in part because he knew that, after all, as my father wrote, a "forgotten poem is silenced truth." Unveiling silence with words, thirsting for lightning that "could illuminate darknesses never seen" as much as for the fragrance of arnica, the poet stood between words and silence, between life and death, beauty and decay, reality and dream, fragrance of flowers and thoughts of death in a graveyard, home and the world, ever on the border—like an electric spark between two poles, between opposites, between unusual friends recognizing themselves in each other.

"It is for our sake that we care for the paths he made for us by his steps." Even if, especially if, the paths lead to that precipice where, with truthfulness both abyssal and strangely gratifying, in that "inexhaustible night," words end and silence begins. A century before Biebl, Mácha journeyed on the dusty roads of Europe to reach the outer edge of language, the soil and home of poetry, and became a wayfarer in/on his *země*, in his estrangement finding *země* more beautiful and desirable than ever. The wandering Gypsy in Mácha's tale half-speaks, on the border between language and silence, homeless at home, more truthfully at home than ever:

> 'Alone, alone then?—nothing again?—away?—unknown—no home?—' and other strange words floated one by one from his half-open mouth.[626]

Outside my office, and often inside, I hear the eager, smooth asphalt talk of:

hypotheses
literature review
research questions
so what's your argument
deliverables and realistic timelines
ranking of journals publishers universities
theoretical and methodological contributions

---

626 Mácha, *Prosa*, 31.

"Benchmarkingexcercisesimpactindexescitationcounts," I hear floating from my half-open mouth. Never are the thoughts of tropics as warming as on a winter day. I see the world from vehicles that crush everything in their way. In the midst of old and new colonialisms, I think of Biebl. "It is for our sake that we care for the paths . . ." Nowhere is a walk over fresh snow as refreshing as here in tropical Singapore.

It is not a coincidence that these words are written near the end of winter
since a certain time you love everything that disappears without a trace
with your cane you like to write in the snow
verses that will disappear in April or May
in a meadow
or in a café between billiard tables
while the sun smiles
and drives its melancholy mill
spring summer autumn winter
you write poems
like the sun you work with gold
the snow melts
you smile
more
or less[627]

627 Biebl, *Dílo*, 5:124.

AUTHOR'S NOTE ON TRANSLATIONS AND SOURCES

All translations in this book are mine, unless otherwise noted.

In the case of Czech periodicals, I have chosen to take some liberty with stylistic conventions. At the first mention, the original Czech title is followed by its English translation, as usual, but when a title is used subsequently, I use the English translation of the title in italics rather than the original Czech, for better comprehensibility and in order to allow the titles' meaning better resonate in the English text.

Konstantin Biebl commonly revised his texts, often more than once. Many were published in different versions in periodicals and books or read on radio, some were published only posthumously, a few were never published. As far as possible, I have examined various editions of Biebl's published work as well as unpublished archival materials.

Between 1951 and 1954, Biebl's collected works (*Dílo*) were published in five volumes. The first volume was edited by the poet just before his death, while the remaining four volumes were edited by Z. K. Slabý. While generally useful, all five volumes differ from earlier editions and/or manuscript versions in typographical design, there are no illustrations, and there are omissions and deviations, in some cases reflecting political sensitivities. Nonetheless, for the sake of convenience (as *Dílo* is relatively easily accessible), I refer often particularly to Volume Five, which contains unpublished poems and texts, as well as those scattered in various periodicals but not published in previous book collections. Still, even in some of these cases, as when I discuss texts that originally accompanied photographs, or because of textual deviations or omissions in *Dílo*, I refer to earlier publications or archival manuscripts. When referring to Biebl's texts that were published in his earlier books, I refer to these publications rather than *Dílo*. I refer to other manuscript and periodical versions when appropriate, such as when I compare different versions. In the case of his poems published in the collection *Zrcadlo noci*, which has no page numbers, I refer to the book but also include a reference to the relevant volume and page of *Dílo*.

A number of Biebl's prose texts related to his Javanese trip, published in periodicals, read on radio, or unpublished, did not appear in *Dílo*, but were posthumously collected and published separately, in 1958 and 2001, in both cases under the title *Cesta na Jávu* (Journey to Java). I use the 2001 edition.

BIBLIOGRAPHY

Alda, Jan. "Na pláži—v slunci, vodě a písku" [On the beach—in the sun, water and sand]. *Domov a svět* 2, no. 29 (1928): 9.

Alexanderson, Kris. *Subversive Seas: Anticolonial Networks Across the Twentieth-century Dutch Empire*. Cambridge: Cambridge University Press, 2019.

Benjamin, Walter. "Little History of Photography." In *Selected Writings*, vol 2, edited by Michael W. Jennings, 507–30. Cambridge: Belknap, 1999.

Biebl, Konstantin. *Bez obav* [Fearlessly]. Prague: Československý spisovatel, 1951.

Biebl, Konstantin. "Cejlon" [Ceylon]. *Domov a svět* 1, no. 10 (1927): 3.

Biebl, Konstantin. *Cesta na Jávu* [Journey to Java]. Edited by Jakub Sedláček. Prague: Labyrint, 2001.

Biebl, Konstantin. *Dílo* [Works]. 5 vols. Vol. 5, edited by Z. K. Slabý. Prague: Československý spisovatel, 1951–1954.

Biebl, Konstantin. *Dobrodruh* [Adventurer]. Edited by Vladimír Justl. Prague: Odeon, 2008.

Biebl, Konstantin. "Hrob K. H. Máchy" [The grave of K. H. Mácha]. In *Ani labuť ani lůna: sborník k stému výročí smrti Karla Hynka Máchy*, edited by Vítězslav Nezval, 9. Prague: Otto Jirsák, 1936.

Biebl, Konstantin. *Modré stíny* [Blue shadows]. Královské Vinohrady: Kamill Resler, 1926.

Biebl, Konstantin. *Nebe peklo ráj* [Heaven hell paradise]. Prague: Sfinx, 1931.

Biebl, Konstantin. *Nový Ikaros* [New Icarus]. Prague: Aventinum, 1929.

Biebl, Konstantin. *Plancius*. Prague: Sfinx, 1931.

Biebl, Konstantin. "Příjezd na Jávu," *Domov a svět* 1, no. 13 (1927): 9.

Biebl, Konstantin. "Semarang." *Domov a svět* 1, no. 14 (1927): 7.

Biebl, Konstantin. "Singapore." *Domov a svět* 1, no. 11 (1927): 13.

Biebl, Konstantin. "Slametan: slavnost o deseti zpěvech" [Slametan: celebration in ten cantos]. *ReD* 1 (1927–28): 218–20.

Biebl, Konstantin. *S lodí jež dováží čaj a kávu* [With the ship that carries tea and coffee]. 2nd edition. Prague: Odeon, 1928.

Biebl, Konstantin. "Sopky na Jávě" [Volcanoes in Java]. *Domov a svět* 2, no. 7 (1928): 5.

Biebl, Konstantin. *Věrný hlas* [Faithful voice]. Prague: Hyperion. 1924.

Biebl, Konstantin. "Z cesty K. Biebla na Jávu. Všechen obchod..." [From K. Biebl's journey to Java. All trade...]. *Domov a svět* 1, no. 19 (1927): 5.

Biebl, Konstantin. "Z cesty K. Biebla na Javu. Nejkrásnější podívanou..." [From K. Biebl's journey to Java. The most beautiful sight...]. *Domov a svět* 1, no. 25 (1927): 7.

Biebl, Konstantin. *Zlatými řetězy* [With golden chains]. Prague: Čin, 1926.

Biebl, Konstantin. *Zlom* [Break]. Prague: Hyperion, 1925.

Biebl, Konstantin. *Zrcadlo noci* [Mirror of the night]. Prague: F. J. Müller, 1939.

Bieblová, Hermína. *Můj syn Konstantin Biebl* [My son Konstantin Biebl]. Prague: Československý spisovatel, 1955.

Boháč, Jaroslav. "Vzpomínka na Jávu" [A reminiscence of Java]. In *Cestami odboje*, edited by Adolf Zeman, 5: 345–8. Prague: Pokrok, 1929.

Boháč, Jaroslav. *V tropické Asii. Cesty legionáře po Singapore, Borneu a Ceylonu* [In tropical Asia: the travels of a legionary in Singapore, Borneo and Ceylon]. Prague: Památník Odboje, [1922].

Borsuk, Amaranth. "'Ma belle machine à écrire': Poet and Typewriter in the Work of Blaise Cendrars," *Writing Technologies* 2, no. 1 (2008). <https://www.ntu.ac.uk/writing_technologies/back_issues/Vol.%202.1/Borsuk/index.html>.

Bracewell, Wendy, ed. *Orientations: An Anthology of East European Travel Writing, ca. 1550–2000*. Budapest and New York: Central European University Press, 2009.

Bracewell, Wendy. "Travels through the Slav World." In *Under Eastern Eyes: A Comparative Introduction to East European Travel Writing on Europe*, edited by Wendy Bracewell and Alex Drace-Francis, 147–94. Budapest and New York: Central European University Press, 2008.

Brouwer, Joel. "The Early Poetry of Jaroslav Seifert by Dana Loewy." Book review. *Harvard Review* 14 (Spring, 1998): 114–116.

Burian, E. F. *Jazz*. Aventinum: Prague, 1928.

Carr, Helen. "Modernism and Travel (1880–1940)." In Peter Hulme and Tim Youngs, *The Cambridge Companion to Travel Writing*, 70–1. Cambridge: Cambridge University Press, 2002,.

Cendrars, Blaise. *Poésies complètes* [Complete poems]. Paris: Denoël, 2005.

Daneš, J. V. and Karel Domin, *Dvojím rájem* [Through double paradise]. 2nd edition. Prague: J. Otto, 1925.

Dluhosch, Eric, and Rostislav Švácha. *Karel Teige: L'Enfant Terrible of the Czech Modernist Avant-Garde*. Cambridge: MIT Press, 1999.

Ederer, Antonin. "Máchův zájem o Orient" [Mácha's interest in the Orient]. *Nový Orient* 1, no. 6 (1945–46): 18–9.

Eliášová, B. M. *Rok na jižní polokouli: Jáva, Australie, Afrika* [A year in the southern hemisphere: Java, Australia, Africa]. Prague: Českomoravské podniky tiskařské a vydavatelské, 1928.

"Film a jeho výroba" [Film and its production]. *Domov a svět* 2, no. 7 (1928): 3–4.

Forbes, Meghan. "In the Middle of It All: Prague, Brno, and the Avant-Garde Networks of Interwar Europe." PhD Diss., University of Michigan, 2016.

Frankl, Pavel. "Básnický projev Konstantina Biebla" [Poetic expression of Konstantin Biebl]. *Host* 2 (1924–25): 146–9.

Fussel, Paul. *Abroad: British Literary Travelling Between the Wars*. Oxford: Oxford University Press, 1980.

Grygar, Mojmír. "Teigovština—trockistická agentura v naší kultuře" [Teigeism—Troczkist agenda in our culture], Part 2. Tvorba 20, no. 43 (25 Oct 1951): 1036–8.

Halas, František. "Pohlednice" [Postcards]. *Pásmo*, vol. 1, no. 7–8 (January 1925): 11–12.

Hašek, Jaroslav. *Osudy dobrého vojáka Švejka* [The Fates of the Good Soldier Švejk]. Prague: Cesty, 2000.

Hašek, Jaroslav. *The Good Soldier Švejk*. Translated by Cecil Parrott. London: Penguin, 2005.

Havlasa, Jan. *Propast rozkoše* [Abyss of bliss]. Prague: Ústřední nakladatelství a knihkupectví učitelstva československého, 1929.

Healey, Kimberley. *The Modernist Traveler: French Detours, 1900–1930*. Lincoln and London: University of Nebraska Press, 2003.

Hiller, Jindřich. "Za básníkem" [For a poet]. In *Za Konstantinem Bieblem: vzpomínky a projevy jeho přátel*, 51–2. Prague: Československý spisovatel, 1952.

Hilmar Farid and Razif. "*Batjaan liar* in the Dutch East Indies: A colonial antipode." *Postcolonial Studies* 11, no. 3 (2008): 277–292.

Hoffmeister, Adolf. *Pohlednice z Číny* [Postcards from China]. Prague: Československý spisovatel, 1954.

Holý, Jiří. "Chór moravských učitelů v javánské džungli: Bieblova exotická sbírka S lodí jež dováží čaj a kávu" [Choir of Moravian teachers in Javanese jungle: Biebl's exotic collection With the ship that carries tea and coffee]. *Literární Archív* 39 (2007): 235–71.

Honzl, Jindřich. "O proletářském divadle" [On proletarian theater]. In *Revoluční sborník Devětsil*, edited by Jaroslav Seifert and Karel Teige, 87–98. Prague: Večernice, 1922.

Hora, Josef. "Mladí z Devětsilu" [The young from Devětsil]. In *Avantgarda známá a neznámá*, vol. 1, edited by Štěpán Vlašín et al., 425–30. Prague: Svoboda, 1971.

Hrubín, František. *Můj zpěv* [My song]. Prague: Odeon, 1980.
Ireland, Sophie. "Paris-Prague: regards surréalistes croisés; Naissance poétique d'une ville" [Paris-Prague: exchanged surrealist glances; poetic birth of a city]. PhD Diss., L'Université Paris Ouest Nanterre La Défense, 2016.
Janský, Karel. *Karel Hynek Mácha: život uchvatitele krásy* [Karel Hynek Mácha: the life of a usurper of beauty]. Prague: Melantrich, 1953.
Jízdní řád železniční, paroplavební a automobilový republiky Československé: 1926–27 [Rail, steamboat and automobile schedule]. Prague: Čedok [1926].
Jochmanová, Andrea. "Voiceband." In *Heslář české avantgardy*, edited by Josef Vojvodík and Jan Wiendl, 403–10. Prague: Filozofická fakulta Univerzity Karlovy, 2011.
Kalista, Zdeněk. *Tváře ve stínu* [Faces in the shade]. České Budějovice: Růže, 1969.
Kerr, Douglas. "Ruins in the jungle: nature and narrative." In *Asian Crossings: Travel Writings on China, Japan, and Southeast Asia*, edited by Steve Clark and Paul Smerhurst, 131–38. Hong Kong: Hong Kong University Press. 2008.
Kohout, Eduard. *Divadlo aneb snář* [Theater, or dream book]. Prague: Odeon 1975.
Konrád, Karel. *Epištoly a vavříny* [Epistles and laurels]. Prague: Československý spisovatel, 1954.
Konrád, Karel. "O Konstantinu Bieblovi" [On Konstantin Biebl]. In *Za Konstantinem Bieblem: vzpomínky a projevy jeho přátel*, 60–88. Československý spisovatel: Prague, 1952.
Konrád, Karel. *Rozchod!* [Dismiss!]. Prague: Sfinx, 1934.
Kozák, Martin. *Zeměpis pro školy obecné* [Geography from public schools]. Prague: Unie, 1904.
Krejcar, [Jaroslav]. "Made in America." *Život: sborník nové krásy*, 189–200. Prague: Umělecká beseda, 1922.
Krejcar, J., ed. *Život: sborník nové krásy* [Life: collection of new beauty]. Prague: Umělecká beseda, 1922.
Kundera, Milan. "Vy jste, Konstantine, nikdy neuvěřil" [You, Konstantin, have never believed]. *Literární noviny*, 15 Nov 1952.
Last, Jef. *Liedjes op de maat van de rottan: Indische revolutionaire gedichten* [Songs to the measure of the rottan: Indies revolutionary poems]. Edited by Harry A. Poeze. Leiden: KITLV, 1994.
Levinger, Esther. "Czech Avant-Garde Art: Poetry for the Five Senses." *The Art Bulletin* 81, no. 3 (Sep., 1999): 513–32.
Linkov, Z. "Bieblova cesta na Jávu" [Biebl's journey to Java]. *Kultura* 9 (1958).
Mácha, Karel Hynek. *Máj* [May]. Prague: Academia, 2003.
Mácha, Karel Hynek. *Prosa* [Prose]. Prague: Fr. Strnad, 1940.
Macura, Vladimír. *Znamení rodu: České národní obrození jako kulturní typ* [The sign of clan: Czech national rebirth as a cultural type]. 2nd ed. Prague: H & H, 1995.
Marek, Jiří. *Země pod rovníkem* [The land below the Equator]. Prague: Mladá fronta,1956.
McNab, Robert. *Ghost Ships: A Surrealist Love Triangle*. New Haven and London: Yale University Press, 2004.
Mrázek, Jan. "Czechs on Ships: Liners, Containers and the Sea." *Journal of Tourism History* 13, no. 2 (August 2021): 111–37.
Mrázek, Jan. "Czech Tropics," *Archipel* 86 (2013): 155–90.
Mrázek, Jan. *Phenomenology of a Puppet Theatre: Contemplations on the Art of Javanese Wayang Kulit*. Leiden: KITLV Press, 2005.
Mrázek, Jan. "Primeval Forest, Homeland, Catastrophe: Travels in Malaya and 'Modern Ethnology' with Pavel Šebesta / Paul Schebesta," 2 Parts, *Anthropos* 116 (2021), no. 1: 29–54; no. 2: 345–65.
Mrázek, Jan. "Returns to the wide world: errant Bohemian images of race and colonialism." *Studies in Travel Writing* 21, no. 2 (2017): 135–155.
Mrázek, Rudolf. *Engineers of Happy Land: Technology and Nationalism in a Colony*. Princeton: Princeton University Press, 2002.
Mrázek, Rudolf. "Jávánské motivy v životě a díle Konstantina Biebla" [Javanese motifs in the life and work of Konstantin Biebl]. *Nový Orient* 34, no. 6 (1979): 175–80; no. 7: 209–13; no. 8: 238–42.

Nejedlý, Otakar. *Malířovy vzpomínky z Ceylonu a Indie* [A painter's reminiscences from Ceylon and India]. Prague: Fr. Borový, 1923.

Neruda, Jan. *Básně* [Poems], vol. 2. Prague: Státní nakladatelství krásné literatury, hudby a umění, 1954.

Nezval, Vítězslav, ed. *Ani labuť ani lůna: sborník k stému výročí smrti Karla Hynka Máchy* [Neither swan nor moon: a collection on the occasion of the hundredth anniversary of the death of Karel Hynek Mácha]. Prague: Otto Jirsák, 1936.

Nezval, Vítězslav. *Básně na pohlednice* [Poems for postcards]. Prague: Aventinum, 1926.

Nezval, Vítězslav. *Dílo* [Works], vol. 1. Prague: Československý spisovatel, 1950.

Nezval, Vítězslav. "Drahý příteli" [Dear friend]. In Konstantin Biebl, *Dílo*, vol 5, edited by Z. K. Slabý, 5–9. Prague: Československý spisovatel, 1954.

Nezval, Vítězslav. "Film." In *Avantgarda známá a neznámá*, vol. 2, edited by Štěpán Vlašín et al., 163–7. Prague: Svoboda, 1972.

Nezval, Vítězslav. "Kapka inkoustu" [A drop of ink]. *ReD* 1 (1927–28): 307–14.

Nezval, Vítězslav. *Moderní básnické směry* [Modern poetic movements]. Prague: Dědictví Komenského, 1937.

Nezval, Vítězslav. *Pantomima* [Pantomime]. Prague: Ústřední nakladatelství, 1924.

Nezval, Vítězslav. "Rozloučení s Konstantinem Bieblem" [Farewell to Konstantin Biebl]. In *Za Konstantinem Bieblem: vzpomínky a projevy jeho přátel*, 15–18. Československý spisovatel: Prague, 1952.

Nezval, Vítězslav. *Z mého života* [From my life]. Prague: Československý spisovatel, 1959.

[Nový, Karel]. "Úvodem" [By way of introduction]. *Domov a svět* 1, no. 1 (1927): 1.

Oplt, Miroslav. *Indonesia dalam kesusasteraan Tjeko* [Indonesia in Czech literature]. Jogjakarta: Universitas Gadjah Mada, 1957.

Oplt, Miroslav. *Hledání Indonesie* [In search of Indonesia]. Prague: Panorama, 1989.

Pešat, Zdeněk. *Dialogy s poezií* [Dialogues with poetry]. Československý spisovatel: Prague, 1985.

Píša, A. M. "Básník na Javě" [The poet in Java]. *Host* 7 (1927): 199–206.

Polák, Josef. *Americká cesta Josefa Václava Sládka* [American journey of Josef Václav Sládek]. Prague: Státní pedagogické nakladatelství, 1966.

Přikryl, Jaroslav. *Putování po Cejlonu a v nejjižnější Indii* [Wandering across Ceylon and the southernmost India]. Prague: Al. Srdce, 1934.

Pujmanová, Marie. "Drahý Kosťo" [Dear Kosťa]. In *Za Konstantinem Bieblem: vzpomínky a projevy jeho přátel*, 19–21. Prague: Československý spisovatel, 1952.

Roth, Joseph. *Report from a Parisian Paradise: Essays from France, 1925–1929*. Translated by Michael Hofmann. New York and London: Norton, 2005.

Rous, Jan. "The New Typography." In *Devětsil: Czech Avant-Garde Art, Architecture and Design of the 1920s and 30s*, edited by Rostislav Švachá [sic], 58–61. Oxford: Museum of Modern Art, 1990.

Rutte, Miroslav. *Batavie* [Batavia]. Prague: Kvasnička a Hampl, 1924.

Rutte, Miroslav. *Doba a hlasy* [Times and voices]. Turnov: Müller, 1929.

Rutte, Miroslav. "Jak jsem se stal spisovatelem a co z toho povstalo" [How I became a writer and what came about from it]. *Rozpravy Aventina* 1, no. 3 (1925): 28–9.

Rybák, Josef. "Slavětín 19.XI." In *Za Konstantinem Bieblem: vzpomínky a projevy jeho přátel*, 47–50. Prague: Československý spisovatel, 1952.

Šalda. F. X. *O poezii* [About poetry]. Prague: Klub přátel poezie, 1970.

Sayer, Derek. *The Coast of Bohemia: A Czech History*. Princeton: Princeton University Press, 1998.

Sayer, Derek. *Prague, Capital of the Twentieth Century: A Surrealist History*. Princeton: Princeton University Press, 2013.

Schulz, K. "Jazz nad mořem" [Jazz above the sea]. In *Život: sborník nové krásy*, edited by J. Krejcar, 35–8. Prague: Umělecká beseda, 1922.

Schulz, Karel. *Sever Jih Západ Východ* [North South West East]. Prague: Vortel, 1923.

Schulz, [Karel]. "Sever Západ Východ Jih" [North West East South]. In *Život: sborník nové krásy*, edited by J. Krejcar, 65–73. Prague: Umělecká beseda, 1922.

Sedloň, Michal. "Cesta Konstantina Biebla k bojovnému humanismu" [The journey of Konstantin Biebl toward combative humanism]. *Tvorba* 20, no. 43 (25 Oct 1951): 1034–6.

Seifert, Jaroslav. *Dílo Jaroslava Seiferta* [Works of Jaroslav Seifert], vol. 2, edited by Filip Tomáš. Prague: Akropolis, 2002.

Seifert, Jaroslav. *The Early Poetry of Jaroslav Seifert*. Translated by Dana Loewy. Evanston: Northwestern University Press, 1997.

Seifert, Jaroslav. *Na vlnách TSF* [On the waves of TSF]. Prague: V. Petr, 1924.

Seifert, Jaroslav. "Paříž" [Paris]. In *Revoluční sborník Devětsil*, edited by J. Seifert and K. Teige, 168–71. Prague: Večernice, 1922.

Seifert, [Jaroslav]. "Všecky krásy světa" [All the beauties of the world]. *Život: sborník nové krásy*, edited by J. Krejcar, 5–6. Prague: Umělecká beseda, 1922.

Seifert, Jaroslav. *Všecky krásy světa* [All the beauties of the world]. Prague: Československý spisovatel, 1982.

Seifert, Jaroslav. *Samá láska* [All love]. Prague: Večernice, 1923.

Seifert, Jaroslav. "A Tribute to Vladimír Holan." *Index on Censorship* 4 (1985): 4–7.

Seifert, J. and K. Teige, ed. *Revoluční sborník Devětsil* [Revolutionary collection Devětsil]. Prague: Večernice, 1922.

Šejbl, Jan. *Archibald Václav Novák: hříšná exotika*. Prague: Národní museum, 2020.

Šiktanc, Karel. "Konstantinu Bieblovi" [To Konstantin Biebl]. In *Za Konstantinem Bieblem: vzpomínky a projevy jeho přátel*, 45–46. Prague: Československý spisovatel, 1952.

Slabý, Z. K. "Konstantin Biebl a mladí" [Konstantin Biebl and the young]. In *Za Konstantinem Bieblem: vzpomínky a projevy jeho přátel*, 41–4. Prague: Československý spisovatel, 1952.

Slabý, Zdeněk K. *Potkávání setkávání: listování v osudech* [Encountering meeting: leaving in fates]. Prague: Volvox Globator, 2015.

Sládek, Jos. Václav. *Americké obrázky a jiná prosa* [American pictures and other prose]. 2 vols., edited by Ferdinand Strejček. Prague: J. Otto [1914?].

Sládek, J. V. *Na hrobech indiánských* [On Indian graves]. Prague: Československý spisovatel, 1951.

Švachá [*sic*], Rostislav. *Devětsil: Czech Avant-Garde Art, Architecture and Design of the 1920s and 30s*. Oxford: Museum of Modern Art, 1990.

Taufer, Jiří. "Zemřel Konstantin Biebl—zemřel český básník" [Died Konstantin Biebl—died a Czech poet]. In *Za Konstantinem Bieblem: vzpomínky a projevy jeho přátel*, 89–94. Československý spisovatel: Prague, 1952.

Teige, Karel. "Estetika filmu a kinografie" [Aesthetics of film and cinematography], vol. 1. In *Avantgarda známá a neznámá*, edited by Štěpán Vlašín et al., 544–53. Prague: Svoboda, 1971.

Teige, Karel. *Film*. Prague: Nakladatelství Václava Petra, 1925.

Teige, [Karel]. "Foto Kino Film" [Photo Cinema Film]. *Život: sborník nové krásy*, edited by J. Krejcar, 153–68. Prague: Umělecká beseda, 1922.

Teige, Karel. "Manifest poetismu" [Manifest of poetism]. *ReD* 1 (1927–28): 317–36.

Teige, Karel. "Moderní typo" [Modern typo]. *Typografia* 34 (1927): 189–98.

[Teige, Karel], "Nové umění proletářské" [New proletarian art]. In *Revoluční sborník Devětsil*, edited by J. Seifert and K. Teige, 5–18. Prague: Večernice, 1922.

Teige, Karel. "Obrazy" [Images]. In *Avantgarda známá a neznámá*, vol. 1, edited by Štěpán Vlašín et al., 539–43. Prague: Svoboda, 1971.

Teige, Karel. "Obrazy a předobrazy" [Images and fore-images/models]. In *Avantgarda známá a neznámá*, vol. 1, edited by Štěpán Vlašín et al., 97–104. Prague: Svoboda, 1971.

Teige, Karel. "Poetismus." In *Avantgarda známá a neznámá*, vol. 1, edited by Štěpán Vlašín et al., 554–61. Prague: Svoboda, 1971.

Teige, Karel. "Umění dnes a zítra" [Art today and tomorrow]. In *Revoluční sborník Devětsil*, edited by J. Seifert and K. Teige, 187–202. Prague: Večernice, 1922.

Todorova, Maria. *Imagining the Balkans*. Oxford: Oxford University Press, 2009.

Voda, David and Michal Blahynka, ed. *Bojím se jít domů, že uvidím kožené kabáty na schodech: zápisky Vítězslava Nezvala a jiné dokumenty k smrti Konstantina Biebla* [I am afraid to go home because I might see leather coats on the stairs: notes of Vítězslav Nezval and other documents concerning the death of Konstantin Biebl]. Olomouc: Burian a Tichák, 2011.

Weiskopf, F. C. "100 Procent." In *Avantgarda známá a neznámá*, vol. 1, edited by Štepán Vlašín et al., 78–82. Prague: Svoboda, 1971.

Wiendl, Jan. "Syntézy v poločase rozpadu" [Synthesis in the half-time of collapse]. In *Dějiny nové moderny: česká literatura v letech 1924–1934*, vol. 2, edited by Vladimír Papoušek et al., 322–86. Prague: Academia, 2014.

Williams, Raymond. *Television: Technology and Cultural Form*. Hanover and London: University Press of New England, 1974.

Wolker, Jiří and Konstantin Biebl. *Listy dvou básníků* [Letters of two poets]. Československý spisovatel, 1953.

Závada, Vilém. "Básník Konstantin Biebl" [Poet Konstantin Biebl]. In *Za Konstantinem Bieblem: vzpomínky a projevy jeho přátel*, 26–35. Československý spisovatel: Prague, 1952.

Zeman, Adolf. *Československá Odyssea* [Czechoslovak Odyssey]. Prague: J. Otto, 1920.

Zeman, Adolf, ed. *Cestami odboje* [On the roads of resistance]. 5 vols. Prague: Pokrok, 1926–1929.

INDEX